ISBN 978-1-331-89841-2
PIBN 10251379

1 MONTH OF
FREE
READING

at

www.ForgottenBooks.com

By purchasing this book you are eligible for one month membership to ForgottenBooks.com, giving you unlimited access to our entire collection of over 1,000,000 titles via our web site and mobile apps.

To claim your free month visit:

www.forgottenbooks.com/free251379

English
Français
Deutsche
Italiano
Español
Português

www.forgottenbooks.com

Mythology Photography **Fiction**
Fishing Christianity **Art** Cooking
Essays Buddhism Freemasonry
Medicine **Biology** Music **Ancient**
Egypt Evolution Carpentry Physics
Dance Geology **Mathematics** Fitness
Shakespeare **Folklore** Yoga Marketing
Confidence Immortality Biographies
Poetry **Psychology** Witchcraft
Electronics Chemistry History **Law**
Accounting **Philosophy** Anthropology
Alchemy Drama Quantum Mechanics
Atheism Sexual Health **Ancient History**
Entrepreneurship Languages Sport
Paleontology Needlework Islam
Metaphysics Investment Archaeology
Parenting Statistics Criminology
Motivational

GENOA

HOW THE REPUBLIC ROSE AND FELL

BY

J. THEODORE BENT, B.A. Oxon.

AUTHOR OF

"A FREAK OF FREEDOM ; OR, THE REPUBLIC OF S. MARINO"

" How now, Tubal, what news from Genoa ? "
SHAKESPEARE, *Merchant of Venice*

WITH EIGHTEEN ILLUSTRATIONS

LONDON

C. KEGAN PAUL & CO., 1, PATERNOSTER SQUARE

1881

PREFACE.

THE history of a powerful naval and commercial common-wealth, which indeed occupied but a small speck of Europe but which through its colonies and research spread an influence over the then known world, must be regarded by the Anglo-Saxon race with especial interest, as forming one of the steps in that ladder of progress by which we have succeeded in attaining such a pitch of commercial prosperity.

Beneath us on this ladder are the Dutch, Hanseatic, Portuguese, Venetian, and Genoese steps, each and all assisting us out of that maze of barbarism which was incident on the fall of the Roman Empire.

The Italian Republics were the first to succeed in substantially gathering together the threads of commerce which had been known to the old world of Phœnician, Greek, and Roman merchants, and when this firm foothold had once been re-established, the upward progress was greatly simplified.

Pisa and Amalfi were amongst the first to assist in this direction, but Pisa and Amalfi fell powerless before more than mere local prosperity had been attained.

In these pages we shall see that it was Genoa who was first in the ranks of commerce and discovery in the Black Sea, in the Mediterranean, and outside the pillars of Hercules. She was closely pressed by Venice, indeed, all eager to stand in rivalry with her on the same footing; but Genoa for well nigh a hundred years was greatly superior in strength and resources to the Queen of the Adriatic, and when Venice did hold the position of leader in the mercantile world her position was distinctly that of Genoa's successor.

In the counting-houses of Genoa were worked out many of the early problems of finance. Her Bank of St. George ushered in many new monetary systems, essential to the carrying on of an extensive commerce. Her population was a hard-working shrewd race of mariners. In short, Genoa was the Manchester and Liverpool of the Middle Ages combined in one.

I have endeavoured in the following pages faithfully to work out the career of this Republic from rise to fall, deriving my information from such authors as had taken manuscripts in the various archives as the basis of their works, and, thanks to the kind assistance of friends in Genoa, I was enabled to consult manuscripts myself in archives not generally open to foreigners.

I am greatly indebted to H.B.M.'s consul in Genoa, M. Yeats Brown, Esq., and to the Contessa C. di Langosco (*née* Gresley), for their valuable assistance in aiding my research.

J. THEODORE BENT.

43, *Great Cumberland Place, W.*
    May, 1880.

CONTENTS.

―――•◦•―――

CHAPTER I.

GENOA IN THE OLDEN TIME.

PAGE

Petrarch's description of old Genoa—Extent of Genoese commerce—Glance at
the palace of Vialata—The old narrow streets and domestic architecture
—Genoese ladies and their love of processions—The "*Cassacie*," and
their procession—The "*casse*," the pilgrims, penitents, and cross-bearers
—Origin of the Cassacie, and their suppression—The Doge: his costume,
and ceremonies connected with him—His Christmas gift from the Val
di Bisagno—Genoa's foreign guests—Charles V. entertained by Andrea
D'Oria—Dark side of Genoa : her factions, and her stones of infamy—
The Jews in Genoa—Hebrew refugees from Spain, and their reception
—How the Jews got immunities—Case of child surreptitiously baptized
—Plague of pigs—The Lerinensians and their customs—Genoa's lament
over her bygone glory   1

CHAPTER II.

GENOA AT THE CRUSADES.

Position held by the Italian Republics at the Crusades—Ligurian sharp
practice and robbery, instances thereof—First Crusade—Godfrey de
Bouillon leaves Genoa—Guglielmo Embriaco—Caffaro the annalist—
Return of the Genoese—Their robbery at Myrrha—John the Baptist's
bones brought home, and duly honoured by succeeding generations—
Matteo Civitale and Innocent VIII.—Second Crusade—Embriaco and
the Genoese at the siege of Jerusalem—Their inventions and prowess—
Torre degli Embriaci—Genoese decide to build their cathedral—Siege
of Cæsarea—Riches divided—Embriaco gets the "*sacro catino.*"—
Curious history of this relic, its pretensions, and the deception thereof
—Siege of Ptolemais—Dastardly conduct of Genoese—Commercial
position established by Genoa—Third Crusade—Richard of England
and Philip II. of France at Genoa, and their treaty with Genoese—
Richard adopts standard of St. George ; writes for reinforcements to
Genoa from Accon—Englishmen in Genoa at that time—The "*Commenda*" of St. John, and its history—William Acton—Pope Urban VI.

PAGE

—Fourth Crusade, and the infantile contingent—Siege of Damietta, and
the part Genoa took at it—Excitement at home—End of the Holy
Wars, and their effect on Genoa—St. Louis' Crusade, and decline of
crusading spirit—Some Genoese troubadours : Folchetto, Cicala, and
others   .   .   .   .   ,   ,   **23**

CHAPTER III.

GENOA AT HOME UNTIL HER FIRST DOGE.

Diverse opinions as to origin of the name Genoa—Norman and Saracen
invaders—Hastings, and his capture of Luna—Dante on Luna—The
Saracen scourge, and first attempts to resist it—The old castle and cathedral—The Bishops, sole depositaries of Roman civilization—S. Siro,
and legends connected with him—Wealth of the bishops, and their
government, their palace, the Cintraco—The companies, the consuls,
and the growth of the Commune—General assemblies—First act of
emancipated commune, building of the Cathedral—Description of the
same, and of the Church at Porto Venere—Second act of the Commune,
nobles obliged to swear fealty, and their enrolment as citizens—Quarrels
of the Castelli and Avvocati—Greatness of the Consulate—The Podestà :
his election, and how restrained—The first Podestà—Revolts along the
Riviera—Introduction of Guelph and Ghibelline factions—Guglielmo
Boccanegra the first Captain—His success, and subsequent deposition—
The four chief families of Genoa—Origin of the Spinola, and Grimaldi
Lords of Monaco—Captains of the Spinola and D'Oria families, and
their power—The abbot of the people—Genoa gives away her liberty
to Henry of Luxemburg—The contract—His visit to Genoa, and death
—Popular feeling aroused—Election of the first Doge, Simone Bocca-
negra—His rule and his power—His death and his tomb—Dante in
Liguria, and what he learnt there **44**

CHAPTER IV.

GENOA AND HER PISAN RIVAL.

Pisa in her glory—Origin of the rivalry between the Griffin and the Fox—
Benedict VIII.'s grant—Corsica prefers Genoa—First Lateran council—
Calixtus II. decides against Pisa—Anger of Pisan Archbishop Roger
—Discomfiture of Pisa—Peace brought about by Innocent II. and St.
Bernard—Second Pisan war—Frederic Barbarossa, and his dealings
with Genoa—Building of new city walls—Barrisone, a judge of Sardinia,
embroils Genoa and Pisa in war—Lucca and Florence assist Genoa—
Peace for Third Crusade, at which Genoa gains much—Frederic II. and
Pisa against Innocent IV. and Genoa—Pope visits Genoa: his reception
in his native town ; his victories, and his death—Desperate state of Pisa
after the Emperor's death—Preparations for the last struggle with Genoa
—Evil omen at the blessing of the fleet—Morosini and his silver arrows

PAGE

—Genoese armament—Battle of Meloria ; defeat of Pisans—Number of prisoners taken to Genoa—Dismay of Pisa—Desultory warfare for some years, and final overthrow of the port of Pisa by Conrad D'Oria in 1290, and chains taken to Genoa—Final restoration of these—Monument to celebrate this capture—Dante on this victory—Wretched future for Pisa   66

CHAPTER V.

GENOESE COMMERCE IN THE MEDITERRANEAN.

Position of Italian republics in the commercial world—Result of the Crusades—Treaties with Baldwin, Raimond of Toulouse, and Guy de Lusignan form basis of Genoese commerce in Palestine—Result of Venetian and Genoese quarrel at Acre—The Genoese at Antioch and Laodicæa—Their dealings with the Sultan of Egypt—Treaties of 1177 and 1290—Genoese at Tunis and Tripoli—Philip D'Oria's treachery— Later dealings with Tripolines—Coral fisheries on Island of Tabarca— The Lomellini and their wealth—Tabarca eagerly sought for as a haven —Other ports of Northern Africa—Ceuta, and the origin of "*Mahones*" —How early expeditions were organized—Genoa and mediæval Spain— Crusades against the Moors—Taking of Almeria, and booty therefrom— Importance of this Spanish intercourse—Tortosa and Lisbon—Treaties of commerce with Moorish and Christian kings in Spain—Genoese and Catalonians—Marauding spirit of the latter—Their adventures under Roger de Flor, finally defeated by Genoese near Constantinople in 1302— Genoa and Southern France, Marseilles, etc.—The fairs of Champagne, and their political significance—Genoa in the Northern seas—Petrarch's comments on her extended commerce   88

CHAPTER VI.

GENOESE COMMERCE IN THE BLACK SEA.

Three roads eastwards—Importance of Black Sea route—Genoese dealings with the Byzantine Empire—Emmanuel Comnenus—Overthrow of the Latin dynasty by Genoese, and treaty of Ninfeo in 1261 with Michael Paleologus—Islands in Greek Archipelago given to Genoese families— Pera and Galata, at Constantinople, given to them, and their consequent monopoly of Black Sea trade—Colonies in the Crimea—Caffa, when founded, its position, power, and government—The Tatars—Instance of the power of a citizen of Caffa—Remains of Genoese Caffa—The Gazzaria in the Black Sea—Crim—Soldaia—Balaclava—Inkermann— War with Tatars—Kertch—Various commodities of Black Sea commerce—The slave trade—Inland towns whereat Genoa traded—Onroad of the Turks—Genoese lethargy and troubles at home—A few ships sent to protect Constantinople—Unaccountable conduct of Genoese at Galata—Fall of Constantinople—Mahomed II. destroys walls of Galata

PAGE

—Reminiscences of Black Sea commerce in Genoa—Crimean colonies
handed over to the Bank of St. George—Fall of Caffa and all the Black
Sea colonies—Italian language in Levant—Chios under Genoese rule
—The Zaccharia—Simone Vignoso seizes it—His probity—The Giustiniani in Chios—Their government and army—Their kindness to
escaped slaves—Jealousy of the Turks—Seizure of the island—Fate of
the Giustiniani—The martyr boys   108

CHAPTER VII.

THE GENOESE IN CYPRUS AND IN ENGLAND.

Earliest Genoese commercial treaties with Cyprus—Genoese galleys convey
the Lusignans from Acre to Cyprus—Genoese activity in the island—
Their robberies and disputes—Venetians league with Cypriots against
Genoa—Peter I. of Lusignan—Expedition to Setalia—Peter II.'s coronation, and tragedy thereat—Rage at Genoa—Armament and final conquest of the island by Genoese—Horrors of the war—James de Lusignan
succeeds to kingdom of Cyprus in prison at Genoa—Birth of his son
Janus—Both are tools in the hands of Genoa—Grasping policy of Genoa
and her Bank—Fate of King Janus—Genoa loses power in the island,
which falls into Venetian hands—Early dealings with England—Correspondence with the Plantagenets—Curious document relative to the
alleged death of Edward II. in Italy: the writer and his family identified
—Chaucer's visit to Genoa on an embassy from Edward III.—Probability
that he met Petrarch there, and learnt the tale of the patient Grisaldis—
Dante, Byron, Shelley, on the Genoese coast—Genoese archers: their
organization ; their appearance on the field of Crecy; their slaughter
there—Intercourse with England extended—Genoese consul in London
—The Pallavicini in England—Sir Horatio and his cunning—Their
marriages with the Cromwells—Oliver Cromwell's attachment to Genoa   129

R   CHAPTER VIII.

GENOA AND HER VENETIAN RIVAL.

Petrarch's forebodings unattended to—The affair of Candia—Intensity and
continuity of rivalry for three centuries—Defeat of the Genoese at Malvasia—Simone Grillo elected over Genoese fleet—His victory at Durazzo—
Oberto D'Oria's early renown and influence—The Venetians are jealous
at Genoese success in Black Sea—James of Varagine—Oberto D'Oria's
challenge unaccepted—Venice lays waste the Black Sea colonies—
Lamba D'Oria sent to retaliate—Genoese victory at Curzola—Touching
death of Lamba D'Oria's son—Old Dandolo's end—Lamba D'Oria's
honours—Peace restored—Occupation of Chios causes next dispute—
Greek emperor and King of Aragon join Venice—Terrible battle in the
Bosphorus—Hollow victory for Genoa—Petrarch's account of this
battle—Venetians' defeat—Antonio Grimaldi at Alghero— Pagano

PAGE

D'Oria appointed to the command—Victory over Venetians at Sapienza
—Genoa's factions stand in her way—Position of the two republics
before their final struggle—Tenedos forms a point of dispute—Miserable
dissensions at Constantinople complicate matters—Carlo Zeno and his
document—Pola captured by Luciano D'Oria—On his death Pietro
D'Oria sent from Genoa—Capture of Chioggia by Genoese—Dismay in
Venice—Embassy of Genoese prisoners fails to soften D'Oria's heart—
Insolent message—Preparations for last struggle—Vettor Pisani and
Carlo Zeno together save Venetians from abandoning their town—
D'Oria in his turn besieged in Chioggia—Venice gets allies—Genoese
taken prisoners to the Piazza S. Marco—All traces of Genoese driven
from the Adriatic—Peace restored, and the rivalry virtually at an end . 154

CHAPTER IX.

GENOA AT HOME TILL THE DAYS OF ANDREA D'ORIA.

Principal features of this period—Dogeship of Antoniotto Adorno—Lordship of Charles VI. of France—Tyranny of the Marshal Boucicault—
Lordship of the Marquis of Monferrato—The Adorni and Fregosi—
Terrible civil discord—Distress in Genoa—Tommaso Campo Fregoso's
dogeship—His success in ruling Genoa—Fate of Luca Pinelli—The lord-
ship of the Visconti of Milan—Genoa fights Milanese battles—Victory of
Ponza—Capture by Genoese of the King of Aragon—Milanese diplo-
macy—Overthrow of Milanese influence—Lordship of Charles VII. of
France—Archbishop Paolo Fregoso—The Sforza Lordship—Charles
VIII. of France affects Genoa but little—Pisan supplicants for aid—
How received—Louis XII. of France—His lordship in Genoa—His
visit to Genoa—Differences with the French—The *Bianchi* and the
Neri—Arrogance of nobles—The *capetti*, and reign of terror—Paolo, a
dyer of Novi, elected doge—His salutary measures—Louis XII. invades
Genoa—Rebels abandon their doge—Louis' triumphal entry and harsh
treatment—Paolo da Novi's end—Ottaviano Fregoso's temperate rule
—Charles V. helps Adorni and Fieschi—Horrible siege, and wretched
state of Genoa under an Adorno dogeship—Genoa allotted to Francis I,
after treaty of Madrid—Andrea D'Oria 178

CHAPTER X.

GENOESE VOYAGES AND DISCOVERIES.

Marco Polo as a prisoner in Genoa incites desire for travel—Benedetto Zaccharia and his exploits—Missionaries and their tales—Luca Tarigo at
the Caspian Sea—Genoese shipbuilding—The *S. Niccolò* and *Gran
Paradiso* described, also smaller trading vessels—The Vivaldi expedition along the African coast—Supposed discovery of the Canaries—
Grounds for this claim—The Madeira—Antonio Uso di Mare's voyage
—His *itinerario*, and its value in nautical archæology—The Genoese

PAGE

family of Pessagno as admirals in Portugal for a century pave the way
for Vasco di Gama's discovery of the Cape of Good Hope—Antonio
di Noli discovers Cape Verde Islands—Christopher Columbus considered from a purely Genoese point of view—His birth and parentage
—How his Genoese nationality affected his after career—How it was
Genoa did not discover America—How Columbus assisted to ruin
Genoa—John Cabot came from Savona and settled in Bristol—Travels
of Adorno, S. Stefano, Interiano, and Camilli—Genoese assist in discovering Molucca Islands—Paolo Centurione employed as Russian
discoverer—The Genoese East Indian Company, and their dealings with
Cromwell—Close of Genoa's maritime career 199

CHAPTER XI.

THE BANK OF ST. GEORGE.

Machiavelli's opinion of it—Curious phenomenon of a republic within a republic—Its origin in loans for crusading, and other purposes—The
Mahones—First regular debt incurred by the government in 1148—
System then inaugurated for security to shareholders—The loans
increase in number—Regulations drawn up—" The consuls of the debt "—
Instances of loans—The "Compere of St. George"—New commission
of 1339—Further steps towards consolidation—Position of the Bank as
an independent republic—Difficulties in Genoa—Francesco Vivaldi and
his donation—His speech, and first ideas of accumulating interest—
Various benefactors—Reorganization in 1407, and the Bank now
thoroughly consolidated—The new constitution given to it—A floating
debt in 1456—Some debts made irredeemable, and some taxes handed
over to the Bank in perpetuity—Cession of colonies to the Bank—Their
mismanagement of them—Old system of auctions for raising the loans
not abandoned till 1675, and title of the Bank of St. George then regu-
larly adopted—The "*monti*" or public pawn loans—Difficulties of the
Bank during the last two centuries of its existence—The Austrian
demands—Close of the Bank at the time of the French Revolution—
Vain attempts to reopen it—Origin of the name St. George—The
palace of the Bank as it now stands—The foundation—The statues to
benefactors therein—The large council hall, and reminiscences of the
old system to be found—The archives—The fresco by Tavarone—The
Porto Franco—Its former importance—The porters' guild—Niccolò
Paganini 220

CHAPTER XII.

HOW ANDREA D'ORIA CAME TO RULE IN GENOA.

Sketch of the D'Oria family : Its origin, and its heroes, its palaces, and its
church—Character of Andrea D'Oria—His importance in the politics of
the age—His birth, and early life and adventures—Assumes command in

PAGE

Corsica—His cruelty—Boarding of a French ship—His only wound—
Four galleys given to him—His conduct at Monaco—His value to the
French cause—His conduct after the battle of Pavia—His dealings with
Pope Clement VII.—His fickleness—Andrea D'Oria marries—Battle of
Capri—He leaves the service of France—His conduct in so doing discussed—His treaty with the Emperor Charles V.—Benefits gained thereby
for himself and Genoa—His love of art—His palace at Fassuolo—Division
of Andrea's thirty-years' rule in Genoa—French nearly capture him, and
burn his palace—Charles V.'s first visit to Genoa—What Andrea D'Oria
gains thereout—He is made a Prince—War against the Turks—Barbarossa conquered at Corone—Charles V.'s second visit to Genoa—Prince
Andrea's interview with the French King—The Corsair Dragut, and
Prince Andrea's dealings with him—Prince Andrea, at the age of eighty,
conducts an expedition to Algiers—Its failure 242

CHAPTER XIII.

THE FIESCHI CONSPIRACY.

Importance of this conspiracy—The Fieschi family—Their origin—The Counts
of Lavagna—How they came to Genoa—Their policy—Sinibaldo Fieschi,
and his extravagance—His widow, and son, Gian Luigi, at Montobbio—
The lessons young Fieschi there received—Gian Luigi Fieschi repairs
to Genoa—His good looks, and popularity—His enmity with Gianettino
D'Oria—Some of the accomplices in the conspiracy—Paul III., and the
Duke of Piacenza—Verrina—Sacco and Calcagno—Verrina's plans—
Failure of the first schemes—Final plan decided upon—Spanish ambas-
sador not believed by Prince Andrea—Four galleys with armed men on
board arrive for the Fieschi—Excuse given to the D'Oria for this arrival—
Armed men assemble in the palace of Vialata—The old tutor Panza and
Leonora Fieschi—Extent of D'Orian power exemplified—Gian Luigi and
his rival—Nobles invited to Fieschi banquet—He harangues them—Two
only refuse to join—Gian Luigi parts with his wife—Fate of Leonora
Fieschi—Evil omens on starting—Success of the conspirators at first—
Gian Luigi on the D'Orian galleys—His tragic death—Gianettino D'Oria
slain—Prince Andrea escapes—Tumult in the city—The senate take
heart—Girolamo Fieschi assumes the leadership of the conspirators ; but
has to come to terms—Return of Prince D'Oria—His conduct—Denies
Gian Luigi burial, and wreaks his vengeance on the family—Confiscates
their property, and blows up their palace—Girolamo besieged at Montobbio—Garrison gives way—Fate of the rebels—Result of Prince
D'Oria's triumph—Sentence passed on the Fieschi—Fate of Ottobuono
Fieschi—Bonfadio, the historian : his annals, and culture—How treated
by the Genoese—His execution 265

CHAPTER XIV.

ANDREA D'ORIA'S LATTER DAYS, AND THE OUTCOME OF HIS POLICY.

PAGE

Prince Andrea's longevity—The difficulties about his path—Charles V. anxious to build a fortress in Genoa—Jealousy of the other D'Oria—Giulio Cybo's conspiracy—The Cybo family—Giulio's character—His part in the Fieschi plot—His plans for assassinating Prince D'Oria discovered—His execution —Adamo Centurione sent to Spain—The Centurione family—Prince D'Oria's reforms—The "*Garibetto*"—The purport of it—Prince Philip of Spain visits Genoa—Spanish display—Story of peasant—Philip's presents —He wishes to lodge in the Palazzo Pubblico, but not allowed—His visit not a success—Quarrels between Spaniards and Genoese—Philip enters the town but once—His letter to his father—Prince Andrea pursues the Corsair Dragut, and nearly captures him—Prince Andrea's disaster at Naples—His last naval exploit—At eighty-four he goes to quell the Corsican insurrection—His cruelty—Giovandrea D'Oria elected to Andrea's honours—Prince Andrea beautifies the Church of S. Matteo— His heir's defeat—Anxiety about him—Prince Andrea's death—His funeral—The D'Orian burial-places—The monastery of S. Fruttuoso— The weirdness of the place—The D'Orian tombs—The legend—The Benedictine monks, and their power there—How it became a D'Orian monopoly—Prince Andrea restores it—Name of D'Oria no longer cele- brated—Prince Giovandrea's feebleness—The Portici—Three dema- gogues—Spanish aid sought to reinstate Prince D'Oria—His influence lost—Reforms of 1576—Statues to the D'Oria—Absence of statues in Genoa—Uneventful period—Building of palaces—The Duke of Savoy has plans on Genoa—Quarrel about Zuccarello—Prince Giovandrea D'Oria's death—His dog—Vacchero's conspiracy—His origin and early career—His object—His accomplices—Rodino betrays him—His death —Carbone's account of Vacchero—Stone of infamy put up to him   .   289

CHAPTER XV.

THE GENOESE IN CORSICA.

PART I.—Corsican heroes—Their vindictive spirit—Early Genoese and Pisan disputes there—The della Rocca family—Il Giudice, the Pisan adherent, a typical Corsican hero—His end—The Communistic Sect—Arrigo della Rocca, and his rebellion—The "*azionisti,*" and grasping policy of the Lomellini—D'Istria carries on the rebellion—French influence first felt— Siege of Bonifazio—Bravery of Magrone—End of D'Istria—Numerous claimants for power in the island—The Bank of St. George—Rinuccio della Rocca's revolt—Niccolò and Andrea D'Oria succeed in stamping out rebellion— Policy of the Bank—Sampiero di Bastelica—His early days—Why he hated Genoa—French assistance— Andrea D'Oria again successful—Peace of Câteau Cambresis—Desperation of Sampiero—How he treats his wife—Courts of Europe look askance at him—His bravery in Corsica—Cruelty of the Genoese—The first Napoleon—Small assistance from France—Death of Sampiero—Idea of total 'extirpation of Corsicans

PAGE

—Greek colonists—Rebellious condition of Corsica for the succeeding
century and a half—Climax of open war in 1729—Harshness of the
governor Pinelli—Ceccaldi and Giafferi—Austrian contingent—Constitution of 1735—British assistance—Desperate condition of the island—Two
celebrated men—*Résumé* of Genoese career in Corsica.

PART II.—Extraordinary arrival of Baron Theodor von Neuhoff in Corsica
—His early career and eccentricities—His dealings with Alberoni—Ripperda and Law—His Irish wife—How he formed the idea of making
himself King of Corsica—His first acts on his election—How Genoa
treated him—His successes—His promised succour never comes—The
"*indifferenti*"—His address to his subjects—He repairs to Amsterdam
—How the Dutch receive him—Corsicans still struggle on—French now
assist Genoese; but at length withdraw—Genoese in difficulties—King
Theodore reappears on the scenes—French again join them, and the king
retires to England—Put into prison—Horace Walpole's account of him—
His death, his tombstone, and his son—Corsicans at their last gasp—
Pasquale Paoli—His education, his character, his legislation—Hatred of
Genoese—Refuses their terms—Sale of Corsica to France—Paoli holds
out—Defeated at Porto Nuovo in 1769—What we gather from Genoese
archives of his life in England and France—Returns to Corsica—His
cruelty to Genoese prisoners—George III. King of Corsica—Corsica
finally becomes French—Count Guiseppe Gorani's eccentricities   .   315

CHAPTER XVI.

THE BEGINNING OF THE END.

Genoa chooses the Madonna for her Queen—Ceremony of election—The Emperor's unwillingness to admit of the regal state overcome—The doge's
coronation—Disputes between Church and State—The conspiracies of
Balbi and Raggio—Their fate—Great pestilence of 1656-57—The
senator Raggio—Charles Emmanuel of Savoy and della Torre make
an attempt on Genoa—Failure of this—End of della Torre—Louis XIV's
schemes on Genoa—His insults—His ambition aroused—His embassy, and
terms sent to Genoa—The bombardment, terror of the inhabitants, ruin
of the palaces, and final submission to Louis' will—The terms—The
doge goes to Versailles—His reception there—Genoa recoups her fortunes—Instances of wealth in Genoa at this time—The Albergo dei
Poveri—The Carignano church and bridge—Manufactures of paper and
velvet—Austrian invasion in 1746—Misfortune to General Braun's corps
in the Polcevera—General Botta-Adorno's demands—He enters Genoa
and becomes more exorbitant—Indignation of populace—Inertness of
senators—Payment of two instalments—First stone cast by Balila at the
Austrians—Rush of people to arms—Conduct of the senate—The Austrians driven out with great slaughter—Bravery of populace—Carlone's
speech to the doge and council—Senate and people are at variance after
expulsion of Austrians—Destruction of former averted by Lomellini—
French General Boufflers protects Genoese from Austrians—His death—
Duc de Richelieu—Rewards given to Balila—Genoa much weakened
by the Austrian invasion   348

CHAPTER XVII.

ART AND ARTISTS IN LIGURIA.

PAGE

Characteristics of Ligurian art—Disadvantages which prevented the Ligurian from becoming a leading school—The family monopolies—The unappreciative citizens—What is left of early Genoese art—Ludovico Brea the founder of the school—Specimens of his work—Fazolo and his family—Ottaviano da Semino and his character—Revival of art at the time of Andrea D'Oria—Pierino del Vaga and Montorsoli in Genoa—Luca Cambiaso—His youth—His style and earlier efforts—His mean appearance—His unsuccessful suit—Paints at Rome and at the Escurial—His death—His Last Supper—Lazaro Tavarone and his prolific brush—The Castello family—Bernardo Castello a friend of Tasso's—Gian Battista Castello, the miniature-painter—Ludovico Calvi, the mariner-artist—Decay of Raphaelesque school—Cappellino's eccentricities—Bernardo Strozzi, "the Genoese priest"—His productions—His adventurous career—His death at Venice—The Vandyke and Rubens revival in Genoa—Vandyke's works in Genoa—The Castiglione family—Il Grechetto, the second Rembrandt—The De' Ferrari and Piola families—A Genoese artistic coterie—Carlone—The *chef d'œuvre* of Liguria and Pellegro Piola—The Piola family-house, and its family relics—How Pellegro came to paint the picture in the goldsmiths' street—His tragic fate—Domenico Piola, and others of this family—Sculpture in Genoa—Antonio della Porta—How foreign sculptors were summoned—Parodi—The brothers Schiaffino—Engineering skill of Genoese—The aqueduct, the arcades, the first pier, and building of the Bank of St. George—Black and white marble edifices—The Renaissance in Genoa—The palaces—Montorsoli and Alessi—Combination of styles in Genoa—Modern Genoese art . . . 372

CHAPTER XVIII.

THE END.

Rumours of the French Revolution reach Genoa—Attempted neutrality—H. B. M's. consul, Mr. Drake, and his demands—The affair of the Modesta—Drake leaves Genoa—French army under Bonaparte approaches—Faypoult—Nelson at Genoa—Terms with the Directoire—Revolutionists—Morando Vitaliani and Filippo D'Oria—Weakness of senate—Increase of Revolution—Democracy predominant—Faypoult assists them—Senate in desperation—The "Genoese priests," and the counter-revolution—Battle rages in Genoa—D'Oria's death—The poor Turk—Napoleon becomes imperious—His schemes of reform established—The revolutionists triumphant—Burning of the "Book of Gold" etc.—Wild scenes and speeches of demagogues—Religious element—The apostles of democracy—Opposition to the new order of things—The peasants from the neighbouring valleys—Bonaparte in Liguria—His reception—Genoa drawn into the international struggles—Siege of Genoa by the allies—Inci-

PAGE

dent at Casteluccio—Terrible privations of the besieged, and heartrending
scenes of famine and pestilence within the walls—Massena's determination to hold out, but eventually capitulates on 4th of June, 1800—
Reception of the English—Regency appointed—French after Marengo
again enter Genoa—The Cisalpine Republic—New constitution—Union
with France determined upon—The last doge does homage to Napoleon,
and is made prefect of the Genoese department—Napoleon visits Genoa—
Stops in Andrea D'Oria's palace—Oath of allegiance in Cathedral—
Temporary prosperity—English fleet before Genoa in 1814—No wish
for a blockade—French driven out—Vice-Admiral Pellew, the commissary
of marines—Admiral Bentinck received with every mark of joy—Talk of
restoring old régime—Discussion about it at the Congress of Vienna—
Projects for her future—Finally added to Savoy as a duchy ; and she
enters upon a new existence 391

APPENDIX.

I. Roman Liguria 415

II. On Genoese Coins 417

LIST OF ILLUSTRATIONS.

	PAGE
FAÇADE OF THE CATHEDRAL ... ... *Frontispiece.*	
GATEWAY IN THE PIAZZA DI S. MATTEO	6
MONUMENT TO WILLIAM ACTON ON THE WALLS OF THE CHURCH OF THE KNIGHTS HOSPITALLERS IN GENOA	,35
GENOESE CHURCH AND PISAN TOWER, PORTO VENERE	53
LERICI	80
SLAB COMMEMORATING CAPTURE OF PORT OF PISA	86
S. CHIARA, NEAR GENOA	104
PORTOFINO PROMONTORY, FROM THE PRISON OF FRANCIS I. IN CERVARA MONASTERY	145
FAÇADE OF S. MATTEO	162
ANTONIO GRIMALDI'S TOMB	166
CHURCH TOWER OF S. STEFANO	208
CHURCH IN PORTOFINO	235
HARBOUR OF PORTOFINO	251
FROM PONTE CARIGNANO, GENOA	267
ANDREA D'ORIA'S PALACE IN THE PIAZZA DI S. MATTEO	303
CHIEF DOOR OF THE CATHEDRAL	350
DETAILS OF ARCHITECTURE IN THE CLOISTER OF S. ANDREA ..	373
FRESCO BY PIERINO DEL VAGA IN THE D'ORIA PALACE REPRESENTING THE TRIUMPH OF SCIPIO ... ... *To face*	408

LIST OF PRINCIPAL AUTHORITIES MADE USE OF IN THIS WORK.

Canale, Nuova storia de Genova, 4 vols.
———— La congiura di Gian Luigi Fieschi.
———— Vita e viaggi di Christoforo Colombo.
———— Storia della Crimea.
———— Storia della casa di Savoia.
Cuneo, Storia del banco di San Giorgio.
Casoni, Gli annali di Genova.
Varese, Storia di Genova.
Belgrano, Vita privata dei Genovesi.
Spotorno, Storia Litteraria della Liguria.
———— Elogi dei Liguri illustri.
Celesia, Petrarca in Liguria.
———— Dante in Liguria.
Muratori for Earlier Annalists.
Accinelli, Compendio delle Storie di Genova.
Carbone, Compendio.
Giustiniani, Annali.
Guerazzi, Vita d' Andrea D'Oria.
———— Pasquale Paolo.
Alizeri, Guida di Genova.
Martini, La Repubblica di Genova (1814).
Cassarini, Guida di Genova.
Sismondi, Italian Republics.
Bonfadio, Storia di Genova.
Soprani and Ratti, Vite dei pittori Liguri.
Desimone, Esempi Storici.
Ramusio Raccolta dei viaggi.

Atti della Società Ligustica per la Storia patria.

Giornale Ligustico.

" Caffaro" Newspaper.

Mas-Litrie, Histoire de Chypre.

Storia di Genova negli anni 1745–6–7.

Vincens, Histoire de Gênes.

Bréguigny, Histoire des Revolutions de Gênes.

Revue des deux Mondes.

Noble's House of Cromwell.

Seymour's Travels in the Crimea.

Horace Walpole's works.

Gregorovius, Wanderings in Corsica.

Von Altenkirchen, Schiller's Verschwörung des Fieskos.

Ersch und Grüber's Encyclopedia.

Documents in Genoese Archives.

Where not obtained from the above sources authorities are placed as footnotes.

GENOA; HOW THE REPUBLIC ROSE AND FELL.

CHAPTER I.

GENOA IN THE OLDEN TIME.

"Gennes 'superbe,' très fiere et orgueilleuse,
Porte ce nom comme presumptueuse,
De toutes autres ainsi que le prenom,
Se dit estre en biens la plus heureuse,
La plus forte et la plus vertueuse,
Qu'on trouve point en nulle région."
Chronique de Gênes, sixteenth century.

EARLY in the fourteenth century a ship sailed past the city of Genoa on her way to France; on board was an elderly merchant accompanied by two young boys. The elderly merchant was Francesco Petrarca, the father of the gifted poet; and of the two boys, one was the future disciple of the muses, and the other was his bosom friend and college companion, Guido Scettem, for many years an honoured archbishop of Genoa.

Full fifty years after this event Petrarch, then old and crowned with laurels, writing to his friends in Genoa, thus describes these boyish memories, reproaches Genoa for her endless wars and factions, and therewith introduces us to a glowing picture of the Ligurian capital in her palmiest days. "Dost thou remember," he wrote, "that time when the

Genoese were the happiest people upon earth, their country appeared a celestial residence even as the Elysian fields are painted? From the side of the sea, what an aspect it pre- sented! Towers which seemed to threaten the firmament, hills covered with olives and oranges. Marble palaces perched on the summit of the rocks, with delicious retreats beneath them, where art conquered nature, and at the sight of which the very sailors checked the splashing of their oars, all intent to regard. Whilst the traveller who approached by land with amazement beheld men and women right royally adorned, and luxuries abundant in mountain and in wood unknown else- where in royal courts. As the foot touched the threshold of the city it seemed as if it had reached the temple of happiness, of which it was said, as of Rome of old, ' This is the city of the kings.' "

Under the banner of the red cross, and the emblem of St. George, countless galleys left this port of Genoa day by day to bring back from far distant lands the wealth of India, China, and the East. No port or harbour of the then known world was unvisited by them ; from Moorish Spain, from England, Flanders, and the far north they brought back cargoes of mer- chandize, which they had got in exchange for the silks and spices of the East. In a word, these mediæval Italian re- publics, Genoa, Pisa, and Venice, re-wove the web of inter- national intercourse which barbaric hordes had broken. Again might Italy have ruled the world, had not the constant rivalry between her commercial cities stood in her way.

Of the towers mentioned by Petrarch but few are seen to- day. Of the marble palaces of the poet's days the squalid remains of many may be visited even now. But if we would contemplate a Genoese palace in all its magnificence we must wander in spirit to far distant days.

Let us then enter a Genoese palace which once stood on the summit of Carignano, approached through lovely terraces and hanging gardens, rich with oranges and lemons, and playing fountains. Glorious is the view over distant mountains and deep blue sea, from the one limit of the republic's territories even to the other, from Nice to the Gulf of Spezia, the whole length of that glorious "*Cornice*" is here spread out before the view, a rich and gilded "frame," for the blue waters of the Mediterranean, in which Genoa regards her blushing beauty as in a mirror, and is at once its chief corner-stone and its pride.

The palace of Vialata was its name. Early in the sixteenth century Sinibaldo Fieschi was its lord, a man of untold wealth, a descendant of the noble family of Lavagna, whose ancestors had held high offices in Genoa during her greatest prosperity. Two popes, seventy-two cardinals, and full three hundred mitred heads had gone forth from this family. Kings had been allied to them by marriage, and kings had here been their guests. When staying here, Louis XII. of France had been greatly struck with its magnificence. "More fitted for a monarch," he said it was; and probably far more luxurious than any palace of his own.

It was built of marble, in courses of black and white, for the Fieschi family was one of the honoured four[1] who alone shared with the municipality the right of thus adorning the exterior of their dwellings. Large towers flanked it on either side, battlemented and adorned with statues in niches. A courtyard, covered with bas-reliefs by skilful workmen, led to a vestibule, the ceiling of which was brilliant with a fresco representing Jove hurling down the giants from Olympus. In the centre was a furnace for melting silver and coining money, a privilege which the Fieschi had enjoyed from the year 1249, by imperial grant.[2] Each room was a fresco study in itself, and from here the artists of this glorious age took copies for their work. A halcyon's nest floating on the bosom of a peaceful sea illustrated the tranquillity then enjoyed by this

---

[1] They were the Fieschi, Doria, Spinola, and Grimaldi.
[2] Canale, "Conjuira dei Fieschi."

family. Sinibaldo's loves and aspirations were depicted on the walls by the best artists ; in short this palace was the sanctuary of learned men : hither repaired the poet, the artist, and the sculptor, and were always welcomed at the Fieschi's hospitable board. Hard by, a little black and white marble church, of perfect Lombardo-Gothic design, was the temple of the family, built by a cardinal of this house, and named by him S. Maria in Vialata, after his diocese in Rome.

From Vialata numerous subterranean passages lead down to the sea and without the walls, for the Fieschi's bark did not always float on such peaceful waters, and though this palace had extraordinary immunities from the pursuit of justice, such as only churches elsewhere enjoyed, nevertheless the Fieschi often found it expedient to retire to their mountain fastness of Montobbio, where they had a stronghold which combined with defence all the delicacies and luxuries of art.   The end of all this grandeur is typical of Genoa herself. Sinibaldo's son conspired against Prince Andrea D'Oria,[1] and his palace on Carignano was levelled with the ground, and a stone inscription was put up to testify to his infamy. What now is Montobbio save a bed of thistles and briars ? Where now is Vialata, of which not one stone is seen, save a desecrated church, shorn of its tower, its objects of art scattered, and handed over to a timber merchant as a warehouse for his stores ?

In the dusky narrow streets of Genoa lines of marble palaces speak of her bygone glory. Here, amidst dim squalor and decay, where on a starlight night but one or two of the twinkling orbs can be descried between the overhanging eaves, is the cradle of Genoa's greatness. He who would see Genoa aright must dive into these narrow bypaths. There it was that the rich merchants coined and lavished their earlier gains. It was not till Genoa was in her decadence that foreign artists were summoned to beautify and widen some of her streets

---

[1] *Vide* ch. xiii.

with the hoarded capital for which she had no other outlet; her colonies had gone from her, her commerce was rapidly going, and in the hands of an aristocratic government at home her end was slowly though steadily approaching. An English traveller in the seventeeth century[1] describes these narrow streets thus,—"Genoa looked in my eye like a proud young lady in a straight-bodied, flowered gown, which makes her look tall indeed and fine, but hinders her from being at her ease and taking breath freely!"

These old and fast disappearing palaces form a perfect study of Genoese domestic architecture; there are the gateways, befitting entrances to the frescoed halls within, each with its carved lintel in the black slate-marble of Lavagna, perchance representing St. George in his mythical contest with the dragon, or perhaps a triumphal car drawn by festive bacchanals; others, again, more modest, have only a festoon of grape leaves over their door, whilst others indulge in coats of arms and monograms, and have thin cords of marble as door-posts. The vestibules are generally profusely decorated with rows of pillars and frescoed roofs, whilst elegant marble staircases, perhaps with lions or griffins resting at the base of sculptured bannisters, lead to the upper stories, and in not a few cases are the walls ornamented with a rich "*dado*" of Savona tiles.

All these things may be seen in a disjointed fashion to-day. Some bits here and there give us an idea of what the whole once was. But all is bathed in squalor and misery; and if perchance you detect some exquisite architectural gem, it is because the plaster which hid it has fallen off, and Italian laziness has not found time to replace the curtain of cement. As another distinctive feature of these old buildings, we see the marked division between the first and second stories by a row of little gothic arches, which when, as formerly, carried out in their entirety, must have given an air of relief to the

[1] Lassel's Voyage in Italy.

streets to which the straight stalwart edifices of modern days are strangers. Curious devices of the Agnus Dei, and coats of arms, are thrown at haphazard against the walls, whilst

GATEWAY IN THE PIAZZA DI S. MATTEO.

outside each palace of the richer merchants we can still see the "*loggie*," or raised platforms, where the family used to walk to and fro during stated hours of the day, and transact their business with their clients. From one of these which still remains in the Piazza S. Matteo, Andrea D'Oria harangued his countrymen when he seized the government in 1528.[1]

But it was not on their palaces alone that the Genoese lavished their gold; none loved so dearly as they did a gay street life. To garland their houses with flowers and to witness from open windows amidst festoons and streaming banners, the numerous processions, religious or municipal, was the height of a Genoese lady's ambition, in fact, almost her sole dissipation. Those unfortunate Genoese ladies, indeed, have been much maligned by the biting proverb describing Genoa as possessing "a sea without fish, mountains without wood, men without a conscience, and women without honour." But Boccacio has stood up for them bravely in the second day of his Decameron. Boccacio, who was only too thankful for a handle wherewith to introduce some scandal, represents some Italian merchants in Paris, who over supper discuss the virtue of their wives. Bernabo Lomellini, from Genoa, alone scorns to believe that his absent consort is any_thing but faithful, loving and true. Let us hope that Lomellini's confidence was not misplaced, and that all Genoese matrons were like his, so that to their innocent amusement of watching a procession we may accompany them without being compromised.

We must again waft ourselves back a couple of centuries if we would witness a procession in all its glory, before the companies of the "cassacie" had degenerated into a mere vulgar display of some political feeling, and before the lavish flow of unstinted wealth had ceased to pour into the coffers of the twenty-one confraternities, who vied with one another in displaying a profusion of all that was rich in velvets, brocades and gilded apparel.

On a bright morning of the 3rd of May let us take up our position in one of those decorated balconies which surround

---

[1] *Vide* ch. xii.

the cathedral's little square. On this day, in anticipation of
the "Cassacie" procession, Genoa is stirred to her basis, and
the inhabitants are prepared to enjoy a right merry festival
with their friends, who have come from far, all eager to behold
this annual profusion of wealth displayed in their streets.
A hundred thousand spectators formed what was considered
an average concourse, and twenty thousand actors figured in
the procession, which took ten hours in its tour through the
city.

On a dais erected at the cathedral door sit the chancellor
and vice-chancellor of the ceremony, whose duty it is from
early dawn to settle all disputes for precedence between the
twenty-one brotherhoods, who are to figure in the scene.
Here they sit the livelong day, giving orders and directions
about the conservance of the peace, and though the least
ornamental part of the ceremony, their office is by no means
a sinecure.   Each confraternity has its patron saint, each
confraternity has its oratory, and the programme of their
proceedings has been posted about the city walls some days
before, and on the morning of this day each brotherhood has
assembled at its oratory to adorn itself for the coming panto-
mime.   Excitement is now at its highest stretch.   What
novelty will be produced for them this year ? is the eager
question from the balconies ; and as the bells begin to ring
and a distant hum is heard, fair necks sparkling with diamonds
peer forth to catch the first glimpse of the moving show.

At length, heralds with brazen trumpets and crimson hose
announce the advent of the coming host. Each of the twenty-
one confraternities is divided into separate bodies, varying in
number according to their wealth, and each body has its
uniform, and a mighty crucifix (the figure on which is life
size), generally made of tortoise-shell, and with silver fittings,
and large silver flowers at the ends. After each " Cassacia " is
carried their "*cassa*," which represents some mystery or some
miracle of their saintly protector, in which each figure is

life-size, and sometimes ten to twelve figures in each. Full forty men in gay liveries labour under the burden of this colossal " machine," as it is called, all surrounded with flaming tapers and flowing banners. These figures are all the work and arrangement of some eminent artist, and are truly grotesque in their results. For here we see St. John the Baptist, the headsman, Herod, and his court, each and all of them dressed in sumptuous golden robes ; whilst the confraternity of St. James follows with its patron saint, represented on horseback with his lance directed against a troop of Turks : his aspect is benign, his stirrups are of silver, his accoutrements are of crimson velvet embroidered with gold, and at his side is fastened a richly inlaid pair of pistols. More humble confraternities content themselves with the figures of hermits and anchorites. All these *"casse"* are carried by the porters of the custom-house, whose monopoly it is, and as they approach the cathedral steps, a sudden mighty rush is made, and pell-mell they enter the sacred edifice, there to take up their appointed stations.

Thirty children dressed as pilgrims pave the way for each confraternity, chanting hymns in the Genoese dialect. Each child has his pilgrim's staff, and his black dress adorned with gold and silver ; likewise his gourd and hat, and loaves of bread are tied round his girdle. Many other youthful performers are got up as Roman soldiers, in armour magnificently resplendent, and with wings of cardboard which sweep the ground.

Each religious order has likewise its accompanying band of penitents, whose robes are of silver and brocaded gold, their capes are of crimson, blue, or violet velvet with wide embroidery, and their staves are each surmounted by a figure of their Protector, full fifteen inches high, of massive silver. The penitents of St. Francis, for instance, have a robe of the order's colour, and a thick cord around their waists, with knots as large as ostrich eggs, naked feet, and a crown of thorns upon

their heads ; whilst in their hands they carry a death's head
and cross bones procured for the occasion from a neighbouring
cemetery.

But of all the actors in this scene, the cross-bearers are
considered of most account. As much as twenty pounds would
sometimes be paid to a confraternity for the honour of carrying one of those massive crucifixes; the skill consisted in
turning the cross adroitly from side to side, and by a spring
to mount the steps at the cathedral door with one bound—
the heavier the cross the greater the honour attached to the
bearer. In this acrobatic feat the noble young men of
Genoa vied with one another ; they wore sandals on their feet,
like capuchins, but with gay silver buckles attached to prove
that they were the reverse of poor priests. Sometimes in one
procession as many as one hundred and fifty crosses would
be carried, each with a band of minstrels playing chosen airs
in its train.

But what of these " Cassacie " ? What gave origin to such
a pompous display of religious mockery ? In 1256, when
Italy was devastated by wars, pestilences, and famines, certain
companies called the " flagellants " appeared to appease the
wrath of Heaven by publicly scourging themselves and
parading the streets almost naked, and with blood gushing
from self-inflicted wounds. When this revival reached Genoa,
it was espoused by the order of S. Lazzaro, a company whose
vocation it was to visit the leprous patients, and strange sights
indeed did they enact in Genoa. Men and women rushed
madly about the streets until the pavement was bespattered
with their gore, and many sank down to die under the weakness incident on the loss of blood and the consequences of a
feverish excitement. And these very men were the originators of this pompous scene we have just witnessed. As time
went on the penitential fanatics found it necessary to adopt
some garb ; they chose a long, flowing, blue robe, and hid
their heads in hoods with holes for their eyes. This is still to

be seen in the streets of Genoa as the livery of the "Miseri-
cordia" brethren, who are at the beck and call of the inhabitants to remove them to the hospital and alleviate their
sufferings, and whose hooded visage and stealthy step causes
the stranger a cold shudder of some unknown dread. But
the advocates of penitence did not long continue their scourging, their nakedness, and their works of piety. If a few
remained faithful to the origin of their establishment and took
diligently to tending the sick and other Samaritan works, by
far the greater number preferred to continue the idea of the
flagellants under the disguise of a burlesque. Thus were
numerous companies, "Cassacie," as they were called in Genoa,
founded ; and each company thought fit to build itself an
oratory, with which the town is still filled. In 1410, there
were no less than thirteen of these. They held their meetings
year by year, and soon ended in rivalry and display of wealth
such as we have seen. In 1622, from a book in which the
rules were laid down for those who went to dine with the
confraternity of S. Lazzaro, we learn that there were then
no less than twenty-one of these orders, and thus they remained till this century, when they made themselves so
objectionable as secret societies for political purposes, and
their processions gave rise to such disturbances, that they were
suppressed by order of the Sardinian Government.

The poor old biennial Doge, too, from his prison in the
Ducal palace, was often the object of much panoply and display.
For the prudent lawgivers of Genoa saw fit to act as jailors to
their supreme magistrate, and for the privilege of appearing
once or twice in his royal robes and ermine mantle the old
man had to pay the penalty of two years' imprisonment, with
hard labour to boot. But when an occasion required his
presence in the outer world, he made the best amends he
could for his seclusion ; he robed himself in purple velvet ; he
had pages to carry his rounded hat, with a sort of curved
proboscis at the top, as may be seen in old pictures ; he had

another page to carry a parasol if necessary and the sun was
hot.   All the nobility walked respectfully behind him in file,
each with a gay attendant lacquey ; but if it chanced to rain,
the old gentleman and his noble friends were carried in sedan-
chairs, and their magnificence was greatly curtailed.

Some of the ceremonies by which the Doge was victimized
were highly ridiculous ; how they dressed him on the day of
his coronation, like the royal puppet that he was, to receive
the homage of Genoa's fair dames ; and at a banquet held on
the evening of this day, all the newly-married ladies sat on his
right, and thus did he bid a tender farewell to the outer world
and the allurements of the fair.   Henceforth for his two years
of office he was forced to live a life of monastic severity.
Twice only in the year was he allowed the pleasure of contemplating himself in his royal crown and ermine mantle ;
twice only could he feel himself every inch a king—once on
the anniversary of the foundation of the statutes,[1] by Andrea
D'Oria, and once on the day of Genoa's patron saint, the brave
St. George.   In our poet Gray's time (1739) the Doge was "a
very tall, lean, stately old figure, called Constantino Balbi, and
the senate seem to have been made upon the same model."
The ducal ceremonies struck Mr. Pepys, too, as very quaint,
who tells us in his diary, that after two years of great state
and panoply, "a messenger is sent to him, who stands at the
bottom of the stairs and he at the top, and says, 'Your most
illustrious serenity is expired, and you can retire home,' and
then claps on his hat ; and the old Doge, having by custom
sent his goods home before, walks away, it may be with but
one man at his heels, and the new one is brought immediately
in his room in the greatest state in the world."

On the eve of the Nativity the Doge and his attendant
nobles went through another curious ceremony.   The neighbouring peasantry of the Val di Bisagno had from time immemorial been a right loyal people to their Genoese masters,

[1] *Vide* ch. xii.

and on Christmas-eve these country folks elected their new "abbot" or governor for the ensuing year. By the banks of their river the people assembled ; two fine-sized stones were placed close to one another, and the retiring abbot in toga and beretta stood on one, whilst the newly-appointed functionary occupied the other, receiving from his predecessor the standard of St. George, and some sage advice which was administered to him. This ceremony concluded, these loyal peasantry proceeded in a body, with their magistrate, to pay their respects to the Doge in Genoa, and take him their annual present. It was a handsome trunk of a tree, covered with branches, and decked with such flowers as the season afforded, after the fashion of a modern Christmas-tree. This they put in a cart drawn by two or more oxen, and, attended by the magistrate, a notary, a senator, and a large concourse of people, it was conducted in triumph to Genoa. On reaching the ducal palace they deposited their gift in the courtyard. The Abbot of Bisagno went to inform the Doge of it. "Well found, Messer Doge," says he ; and "Welcome, Messer Abbot," replies the Doge ; and after mutual wishes for a merry Christmas, the abbot exchanges a bouquet of flowers for the more substantial gift of bank-notes worth a hundred francs, and returns with his followers to his home.

The ceremony of accepting this strange Christmas-box, presented him by his loyal subjects, was enacted by the Doge at the dead of night, as follows. Before retiring to rest the Doge and members of the council stole quietly down the steps of the ducal palace with lighted torches in their hands. His ducal eminence then proceeded to set fire to the tree, which blazed right merrily, and into the flames they cast a vase of good wine, some comfits, and some sugar. Weird must have been the sight of these venerable lawgivers of Genoa standing round the flaming tree with their long flowing robes and lighted torches. None of Macbeth's witches round their steaming cauldron could have presented a more awe-inspiring appearance. This curious ceremony was abolished by the later Doges as entailing too much expense; and the bouquet of flowers, accompanied by protestations of fidelity, was accepted in its stead.

The very existence of this Doge in Genoa was solely due to the love men by nature have for royal display, and the craving they feel for a head on which they may place a crown. He was entirely without power ; he signed obediently everything the council made him, and was brought out on holidays and festivals as the pet plaything of Genoa, which the prudent senators would not allow too often in her hands for fear of her becoming weary of the same. After his two years of office he retired without ceremony into private life, and another puppet was elected in his stead.

Genoa was not unfrequently the hostess of foreign potentates, and this afforded her inhabitants an opportunity for a more extended parade of their wealth. The Emperor Charles V. twice paid a visit to the Ligurian capital, and on the last occasion was sumptuously entertained by his trusted admiral Prince Andrea D'Oria, who, from the frequency with which he received crowned heads under his roof, won for himself the *sobriquet* of the " royal innkeeper."

Let us glance at the noble palace of Fassuolo, where Prince D'Oria had just perfected his most princely residence ; and the freshness of the first bloom of those wondrous frescoes by Pierino del Vaga, the pupil of Raphael, had not yet worn off, on which he had lavished all the excellence of a talent which rivalled his master's in colouring and boldness of design. Montorsoli, the pupil of Michel Angelo, was its architect; and so lovely was this palace, with its hanging gardens and terraces down to the water's edge, that the Emperor on landing stood speechless to admire. In accordance with the etiquette of the day, Prince D'Oria laid everything at the feet of his imperial guest. Contrary to his wont on such occasions, Charles received the proffered gift, instead of graciously refusing. Whether this was to Andrea's liking we are not told, but at length the emperor relieved him from all anxiety by adding that Prince D'Oria should keep all these wonderful things in trust for whomsoever of the emperor's household freak or fortune might lead to visit Genoa.

As a delicate surprise for the emperor, Andrea D'Oria prepared a gorgeous entertainment in an arbour erected at the end of a corridor leading to the sea. Carpets and tapestries from Flanders concealed the walls and floors, and whilst the emperor was held in close conversation, this magnificent bower glided gently into the middle of the harbour, for it was none other than one of D'Oria's galleys which had been anchored so as seemingly to form part of the corridor. The imperial surprise had hardly subsided before heavily laden tables were spread on all sides, groaning under the rarest viands brought by Genoese ships from all quarters of the globe. The attendants were all dressed as sea-gods, and to the strains of soft music the guests quaffed the choicest vintage, and glided slowly across the waves.

Each course was served on massive silver dishes, and as each was removed, the remnants of the feast, silver dishes and all, were cast into the sea. Such profusion and waste at first sight savours much of prodigality; but Andrea D'Oria was no such fool. Though lavish in the extreme and dearly loving pomp, he likewise was loath to waste his wealth when by a little ingenuity he could avoid it. So accordingly he had nets spread under the galleys to catch the dishes as they fell; and when the emperor had departed, they were fished up again for future use. Perhaps he learnt this plan from the rival republic of Venice, where report says that the doge, in his annual visitations to wed the Adriatic with a golden ring, was equally careful to recover the property bestowed on his watery bride.

Thus Genoa and her princes entertained their royal guests, thus did she glory in her name of "the superb," and right well

did she deserve it. For though her population was essentially
mercantile, a population on whom the proud courtiers of Germany and Spain looked down with supreme contempt, yet
they had that amongst them which could make many a
monarch tremble ; and their purse-strings weighed far heavier
in the scale of European politics than many a royal diadem.

But it is not all glittering gold and splendour which marks
the career of the Ligurian republic ; under the cloak of riches
lurked many a festering sore. No city in the course of centuries affords us more instances of bloody factions and civil
wars. We have but to walk through the city to-day and read
on the walls the stories told by those stones of infamy to
learn how internal troubles tore out her very life's blood.
Thus, posted up to everlasting shame, were all her unsuccessful revolutionists ; and if one of them chanced to meet with
punishment at home or die in exile a stone was put up to his
memory by his more fortunate rivals, execrating his very
name, and imputing to him all the most heinous crimes of
which man is capable. Whereas if a man died honoured and
respected amongst his fellow citizens, his name was, on the
contrary, posted up on the church where he was buried, so that
posterity might be mindful of his merits. It is a curious and
interesting study in Genoese life that succeeding ages should
thus inscribe their history on stone. On the façade of the
church of S. Matteo, for example, is written a perfect volume
in stone, relating the deeds and glories of the D'Oria family.
On the church of S. Stefano we can study the history of the
Pessagni better than in any book, bearing always in mind that
the fortunate obtained an inscription erring on the side of the
laudatory, whilst those put up to the unsuccessful revolutionists
erred extravagantly in the other direction.

It is an interesting feature in Genoese story to trace the
fortunes of the Jews in this haughty republic ; the refinement
of cruelty with which these unfortunate wanderers were visited
savours more of ultra-barbarism than of the civilization to

which Genoa had attained. It was indeed a persecution, which they suffered elsewhere as here ; but it strikes us more forcibly when coming from a population essentially commercial, and largely indebted to this money-making race, and from a people moreover who scrupled not on the score of religion to enter into advantageous treaties with Pagan or Mahommedan, to the detriment frequently of other Christian people. But the Genoese were great crusaders, and shared, with other nations interested in the Holy Wars, the hatred of the unfortunate Hebrew.

In the earlier days of Genoa's prosperity it is true that large immunities could be bought by opulent Jews, and by those whom the Republic found absolutely necessary for her commerce, and beyond paying for a light to be kept burning before the high altar of S. Lorenzo, certain richer Jews had only to complain of periodical drains on their purses ; whilst Jews of the lower class, itinerant hucksters and so forth, were only allowed to remain three days within the precincts of the city unless they were rich enough to purchase an extension of privilege.

After Ferdinand and Isabella drove the Jews from Spain, with cruelties almost unheard of and a barbarity worse even than death, we have a vivid account handed down to us by a Genoese annalist,[1] of a remnant who found their way by sea to Genoa. Down by the quay a spot was allotted to these miserable wanderers, where, huddled together in the cold and without food or shelter, they perished like flies before the wintry blast. Suckling children and their mothers lay stiff and bleaching on the rocks, whilst husbands and fathers with sunken eyes and emaciated faces, wandered about in their narrow precincts like ghosts. There was something unearthly in the appearance of those miserable beings who haunted this spot during the greater part of an unusually severe winter, whilst ships were being constructed to convey them they

---

[1] Bartolomeo Senarega.

scarce knew where. The captains of these ships were indeed harsh and heavy task-masters, who for gold had undertaken to remove them from Spain ; and if the supply of gold fell short, they simply threw their cargo of human flesh into the waves, or if they suspected that they were concealing treasures about their persons, they murdered them and cast away their bodies.

As the winter rolled on most of the Jews fell a sacrifice to their misery, and the shore was strewn with their bodies ; and when the summer heats began to appear a terrible plague broke out which counted its victims in Genoa by thousands, a just retribution indeed for their treatment of the nomad Hebrews. About this time one Fra Bernardino da Feltri in his wanderings paid a visit to Genoa. He was one of the most ardent persecutors of and preachers against the Jews in Italy, and the result was not favourable to the pining wretches on Genoa's quay. He maintained that it was wrong to admit them within the walls, that it was even wrong to give them food ; but when worn out with hunger, men should be sent amongst them with bread in one hand and a cross in the other, and that they should only receive the sustenance they craved for at the price of a recantation of their faith. Thus many of those who had abandoned their homes, and withstood the hardships of the winter, were unable to resist the subtle refinement of torture which the Genoese practised on them.

About the beginning of the sixteenth century some few Jews of the humbler class became permanently resident in Genoa, but they were subjected to the supervision of a special officer, and were compelled to wear a piece of yellow cloth as a badge on their breasts under pain of a heavy penalty. So much annoyance was experienced by the Jews at thus being held up to public scorn, that those who went about on business appealed to the Government and were allowed to remove it.

Their cause, however, was a desperate one. They were liable at any moment to be hunted out of house and home, and sent forth into the world as beggars. In 1660, and not till then, was a sort of "ghetto" allotted to them in Genoa, into which they were locked from one at night until daybreak. They were obliged to go and hear mass in Lent in the church of the "Vigne," and so rabid was the populace against them on these occasions that the Government was obliged to keep soldiers on guard to protect them as they came out of church, and lucky was the Jew who escaped to his home in safety without a bruise from brick or tile.

In 1675, so great was their distress, that every one of them determined to depart from this inhospitable city; but the Government, recognizing the loss that they would be to the community at large, to prevent their departure allotted them an oratory close to their quarters, to which they could be driven to mass at less risk of persecution, and for which privilege they paid no little sum, and thus they were induced to remain. This harshness of the Genoese to the Jews prevented many from settling in their city, and those who did formed a wretched care-worn colony.

In 1752, a Christian servant-girl in the family of one Moses Foa, a Jew, was under the impression that if she got an infidel baptized, her own soul would undoubtedly be saved. Accordingly she took one of her master's babies to be baptized into the bosom of the Roman Church, and when the child was four years of age, she betook herself to the archbishop, and told him what she had done. Forthwith the prelate pronounced the child a Christian, and proceeded to take the infant from its parents, and bring it up according to Roman Catholic ritual. A public reception into the church was announced, and everything that was galling to Jewish superstition was to be performed. So enraged was the father, so furious the Jewish colony at this, that the Government had to take up the question; for the Genoese senators were not always on the best of terms with the archbishop, and were perhaps glad of an opportunity for overruling his decision.   Certain it is that any benefits the Jews ever obtained in Genoa came from the secular authorities, and were keenly opposed by the clergy. On this occasion the Government ordered the child to be restored to its parents, and considered it necessary to issue a circular declaring it to be an error, and a popular fallacy that those who surreptitiously baptized an infidel would thereby secure themselves a place in Paradise.

From this time the Jewish cause grew better, but it was not · until the more enlightened influence of the Sardinian Government was felt in Genoa that the Jews could live peacefully, enjoy substantial immunities in the city, and send forth from amongst them a Gambetta to rule in France.

However terrible the persecutions were against this stricken race, and however severe they found the yoke of their oppressors, Genoa at the best of times could not have been a pleasant residence for Hebrews.   For the city in the olden time, and even until quite a recent date, was subject to a scourge of pigs.   Dating from 1184, the followers of St. Anthony built themselves a house in Genoa, where they offered a home and lodging for itinerant monks and priests.   To-day a portion of this ecclesiastical hostelry is still seen, with its portal of black marble, and a carved St. Anthony over the lintel, with the customary beggar on one side, and the pig pulling his garments on the other.   Later on this hospice fell into the hands of the Lerinensian monks, a curious body, who warmly espoused the cause of animals out of compliment to St. Anthony, whom they too claimed as their founder.   Their first care was to secure for themselves the traditional privilege awarded to the followers of St. Anthony, of keeping far more pigs than they had sties for.   So the surplus pigs they sent as scavengers and general nuisances throughout the city. Though numerous, there was at first some limit put by law to these, but as time went on the legitimate number was transgressed, and Genoa presented the appearance of one vast sty.

For the sanitary condition of a dirty mediæval city, this must have been highly beneficial. Natural scavengers for their offal would be an inestimable blessing even at the present day in those narrow alleys where there is still a surfeit of dirt. However, the inhabitants objected to have their streets thus infested, and when in 1751 a terrified pig in its wild career about the town, had the misfortune to upset a senator the fate of its comrades was sealed. An edict was passed against these animals,[1] as obscene and a public nuisance ; he that could catch might slay and eat, and the monks were restricted to the contents of their sties.

A curious custom, however, was kept up by this porcine confraternity until 1798, by which they had the privilege of presenting a pig every Christmas, adorned with laurels and other ornaments, to four pious ladies of the D'Oria family, who in return were supposed to present the brotherhood with a handsome sum of money towards their Christmas dinner.

In the neighbourhood of Genoa, the peasantry still hold fast to customs instituted either by these Lerinensian monks or their predecessor St. Anthony. It is usual for the " contadino " to take his donkey, his mule, or his sheep dog once a year to be blessed before the shrine of St. Anthony, perhaps hoping thereby to atone in some measure for the many hard blows these domestic animals are accustomed to receive from their Italian masters.

Of mediæval cities Genoa was amongst the grandest, of mediæval republics she was about the most powerful. In her career she humbled Pisa, in her day she well nigh set foot in St. Mark's at Venice.[2] Kings were her vassals, kings were her prisoners.[3] She was the pioneer in the paths of commerce for the Dutch and for the English. Her internal

---

[1] Accinelli.   [2] *Vide* ch. vii.   [3] *Vide* chs. v. and ix.

and external wars were long before they could eradicate her inherent vitality.   After each revolution she awoke again with renewed vigour, and it was not till her own citizen, Christopher Columbus, had discovered for other powers new sources of wealth and commerce, and not until her own discoveries had paved the way to the Cape of Good Hope,[1] that her decadence set in.

A native poet[2] early in the sixteenth century utters a wild lament for her departed glory.   Into the mouth of Genoa he puts a story of her former grandeur.   In high flowing tones he describes her victories over Venice, Pisa and the Turks.   But unfortunately for the poet's veracity, in one or two cases he draws with too long a bow.   He relates a victory over the Emperor Conrad III. which never happened, and on the following stanza we must also cast the shadow of doubt.

> " I once was Genoa, at whose very name
>   Quaked Turkish Sultan in his home ;
>   Chance bore me once to Albion's shores,
>   With five-and-twenty galleys laid I siege
>   To London with such right good cheer
>   That of its walls I soon became possessed ;
>   Then at my will I held the town for six short hours,
>   Till wearied of its worthlessness I cast it from me."

Yet this poem, written as it was in the bombastic strain of conscious weakness, shows to us clearly that the glory had departed from Genoa.   Henceforth she lived on the credit of the past ; her princes had hoarded wealth in the national bank during more prosperous days, and until this was exhausted by the drain of civil wars, and aspirants from across the Alps, Genoa proudly held her own as a free and flourishing republic, though the title of " mistress of the seas " had passed into the hands of others.

[1] *Vide* ch. x.   [2] Gio Paolo Baglione.

CHAPTER II.

GENOA AT THE CRUSADES.

THE part played by the Italian republics in the Holy Wars is interesting from many points of view. On the crusades they built all that was great in mediæval commerce, and out of them they were the only Christians who contrived to gain any advantage, and in accepting their humble position of "carriers" one cannot fail to be struck by their astuteness, which not unfrequently might be termed sharp practice, as compared with the bombast and chivalry of the princes who hired them. On the one hand, each potentate and lordly prince who went to Palestine, if he returned home at all did so empty-handed, and with but few of his followers; on the other hand, the Genoese, Venetians, and Pisans rushed backwards and forwards to the Holy Land, filling their empty return vessels with Eastern wealth, and making those who sought a passage home pay trebly dear.

As an instance of Ligurian sharp practice let us quote the following story. A Genoese captain was about to leave some Christian refugees to perish on the burning sands of Africa of exposure and starvation because they had not the wherewithal to pay their passage. The infidel rulers of Alexandria, moved to pity by this barbarous conduct, forthwith offered to pay the passage in full, and only stipulated that this cargo of Christian flesh should not be deposited before reaching Christian soil. In short, this story is typical of the part played by the

Genoese throughout—sordid and mercenary in the extreme. The princes treated them with high-handed insolence as inferiors, but the Genoese retaliated very much in the style of the Venetian Shylock, and drained their employers to the last drop of blood.

No annalist ever alludes to any Genoese as noble, save and except Guglielmo Embriaco, the only Genoese captain who in any degree caught the fever of chivalry, and about whose deeds and prowess hangs the halo of romance. Moreover, the Genoese but seldom fought in battle ; they took the troops to their destination, filled their galleys with the riches which the others squandered, and hied them to their Ligurian storehouse, and woe to any prey that they might come across on their way home.   Christian and infidel booty was to them alike.

The character of international robbers, which the Genoese earned for themselves in these youthful days of their commerce and their fame, is amply testified even to this day.   Be it said, to their credit, that a handsome share of stolen booty was given to their churches, as a means by which to propitiate Heaven, for lodged in the cathedral are the stolen remains of St. John the Baptist, and countless relics they carried off from Eastern monasteries.   Here, too, are Moorish pillars, a Byzantine Christ, and numerous images which could never have issued from Genoese workshops.   In like manner they stole twelve lovely marble pillars from the temple of Judas Maccabeus, in Cæsarea, which unfortunately sank in the waves on their voyage to Italy.   Furthermore, the Bank of St. George was built of stones which had been brought from a monastery near Constantinople,[1] and from the ruined Luna they carried off marble pillars which still adorn the naves of S. Maria in Castello, and S. Maria della Vigne.

Let us now proceed to look in detail at the part played by Genoa in these wars.   The curtain of the crusades is drawn up upon the quay of Genoa, when Godfrey de Bouillon and

---

[1] *Vide* ch. xi.

the Count of Flanders embarked, amidst a busy scene in the
harbour, on board the ship *Pomella*,[1] of Genoese build.
Roused by the preaching of a fanatic in their cathedral of
S. Siro, the Genoese were induced to man twelve galleys in
behalf of Christendom, in 1097, to accompany Godfrey to the
Holy Land, by no means a *terra incognita* to them in those
days. Thirty-five years before, Ingulf, the secretary of William
the Conqueror, tells us how he found a Genoese ship at Joppa,
which took him home to Europe ; and the fact of their being
at once chosen to transport the Christian troops shows that
the sailors of Liguria had long ago attained a position of
renown.

Guglielmo Embriaco was the commander of this Genoese
force, "the hammer-headed," as he was playfully called, from
his habit of butting with headlong fury against his foes. A
doughty warrior and skilful engineer was Embriaco, the pride
of his country and the terror of the infidel. Tasso sings of
him as "the Ligurian leader amongst the most industrious
engineers in mechanic lore, a man without his peer.[2]" With
him went his two sons, both to attain great renown across the
seas.

Caffaro the annalist went too, and to him we are indebted
for a graphic account of the Genoese in their crusade. Caffaro
was a good servant of his country, both at home and abroad,
with the sword and with the pen. He was present at the
taking of Cæsarea and of Jerusalem. At home he was six
times consul, and was employed in many delicate missions of
trust by his country. At seventy-three he led the expeditions
against Minorca and Almeria ;[3] but above all his memory is of
lasting fame from the observant annals that he wrote, savour-
ing at times too much of religious zeal, but on the whole his
facts are well substantiated by contemporary writers.

On arriving in the Holy Land, Embriaco· set off with a

---

[1] Caffaro annalista.   [2] "Gerusalemme liberata," cant. 18.

[3] *Vide* ch. v.

chosen few to assist at the siege of Antioch, where his engineering skill was hailed with thankfulness by the besieging
army, and wrought wonders for their cause. His less warlike
countrymen, however, were all left in charge of the ships.
Whether scared by rumours of a defeat, or imbued with a
wish for plunder we cannot say, at all events they soon settled
to sail off home, and leave the rest to their fate. Cowardly as
this was, perhaps still more so is the story of their theft on
their way.

Afraid to return home empty-handed, they put into the
port of Myrrha, where a small handful of monks guarded the
remains of what they professed to be St. Nicholas, a saint of
special favour to sailors. To those dry bones the Ligurian
mariners took a fancy, and accordingly demanded them from
the monks, who, terrified and in dire despair, confessed that
these bones were no less a prize than those of St. John the
Baptist, and for fear of Turkish marauders they had locked
the secret in their breasts. Be this as it may, the numerous
miracles set down to these ashes have quieted any suspicion
that may have lurked in the Genoese minds that their prize
was not genuine.

For fear of losing all their treasure in one disaster they
divided amongst the ships the poor Baptist's bones ; but the
sea was so furious at the want of confidence reposed in it, that
until all the remains had been gathered together on one ship,
the angry waves would not be still.

Great was the joy of the inhabitants at their return ; for
they just had heard of the fall of Antioch, and of Embriaco's
safety. And the remains of the Baptist were received with
befitting respect, and deposited in the church of S. Sepolchro,
near the quay ; and succeeding ages have vied with one
another in doing honour to his mouldering bones. Often
during the fury of a storm has the unfortunate saint been
conveyed with all the panoply of a Roman Catholic procession in hopes that he would still the fury of the waves.

Once, when civil faction was to be decided by the mortal combat of a dozen Genoese on the piazza S. Silvestro, before an assembled multitude, the pious Archbishop Ugo had the remains suddenly placed before the rows of combatants, and so great was the religious awe thus infused that the quarrel was adjusted. Numerous potentates have knelt before his shrine—Frederic Barbarossa, Charles V. of Spain, and Louis XII. of France ; also popes and cardinals not a few.

To do justice to so great a possession, the Genoese have lavished all the grandeur of the renaissance art. From Florence was summoned a master of the style, Matteo Civitale in 1490, after whose design the chapel in the cathedral of S. Lorenzo, in which the Baptist's bones now repose, was made a perfect labyrinth of art. Statues of biblical worthies adorn the sides, excellent in expression and drapery, and to its inmost recesses every detail is carefully carried out. In a silver shrine are preserved the relics of the saint, and behind the high altar is shown an old Roman sarcophagus in which the crusaders brought them to Genoa.

The Genoese pontiff, Innocent VIII., of the house of Cybo, took a special interest in these saintly relics. He published a bull, still to be read on the wall close by, which forbids all women to enter this chapel, save only on one day in the year, as a verdict on the sex to which Herodias' daughter belonged. By a gracious concession he afterwards permitted all the daughters of the Sauli family to be married therein, by reason of their excessive piety and handsome donations. He likewise presented to the cathedral reliquary a brass plate on which is embossed a trunkless head of the Baptist, and which superstition tells us is the veritable charger on which Herodias' daughter presented the head to her mother. With the theft of these relics, and with the fall of Antioch, closed the first episode in the crusades. Guglielmo Embriaco returned to Genoa, and there collected together a fleet and men with which to continue his conquests in the Holy Land.

Incited by their success at Antioch, the Christians pushed eagerly on to Jerusalem; but their progress was slow under the walls of this coveted city. They talked of abandoning the siege, and of retreating towards the coast, when it was rumoured that Guglielmo Embriaco was on his road to join them with reinforcements. And this time, through the force of circumstances, the Genoese were obliged to abandon their ships and march inland, much against their will; for from the towers of Joppa a mighty squadron was descried bearing down upon their fleet under the banner of the crescent; hence the Ligurians were compelled to run their ships aground and set fire to them, having first extracted all the iron and useful fittings; so that when the Infidels arrived they found nothing but burning hulks, and a goodly shower of arrows to greet them.

Numerous are the romantic tales strung together by Caffaro and others about the·siege of Jerusalem. How Guglielmo Embriaco wrought a wonderful machine or tower made of wood, and covered outside with leather. This was then put on wheels with a battering ram beneath, and the top so constructed that it could bend down on hinges, to form a bridge by which the invaders could reach the walls.

In the hazy dawn of the morning of the attack, the Genoese beheld their patron saint, St. George, galloping down the Mount of Olives to their assistance; with one loud shout they greeted this omen and prepared eagerly for the onset. Over the pontoon passed Godfrey de Bouillon and his brother Eustace, amidst the whistling of arrows and the yells of victory. In vain did the infidel poise bars of iron on the walls to prevent its resting there, in vain did they shower burning tar upon it. The success of the tower was complete, and Guglielmo Embriaco covered his own and his country's name with honour. For Baldwin recognized that without the Genoese assistance the Holy Sepulchre would never have been taken, and to honour his allies he caused to be put up over the entrance to the tomb—" By the powerful aid of the Genoese."

A favourite subject for the pencil of Genoese artists was this tower made by Guglielmo. On the ceiling of the Palazzo Adorno we still see a richly coloured fresco by Lazzaro Tavarone,[1] depicting the besieging army and the wooden tower rising from their midst. And in Genoa the Embriaco family were exalted above their fellows insomuch as they were allowed to retain their family tower when all others were lowered by order of the commune. Almost solitary amongst the private towers of which Genoa was once full now stands the "Torre degli Embriaci" with its Cyclopean stone-work and overhanging battlements, and beneath it a stone relating the prowess of the family as the reason why they were allowed to retain the same.

Delighted at the news of this victory the Genoese held great council together, how best they could commemorate the event. They bethought them that their cathedral of S. Siro was outside the walls, that it was subject to piratical raids, and hence was conceived the plan of building the noble edifice which is still Genoa's cathedral, and has been the recipient of many noble gifts and many a tithe and first-fruits of victory.[2]

In 1101 another Genoese armament found its way across the seas to Palestine, and according to his wont, Guglielmo Embriaco marched inland with his small band of trusted followers, leaving his more mercenary fellow countrymen to return with their ships and cargo. Caffaro, the annalist, was of the party, and again he treats us to a graphic account of the wonders that they saw, such as the Sacred Light which lit up the Holy Sepulchre on Easter Eve. One is surprised at his credulity, so astute is he in his general remarks about the war, and a politician of no mean calibre.

They were warmly welcomed by Baldwin the king, and after a tour in the Holy Land, and a satisfactory dip in the waters of the Jordan, the Genoese joined the king's forces in

[1] *Vide* ch. xvii. [2] *Vide* ch. viii.

the siege of Tyre.   After the fall of this city, Guglielmo and
his followers, consisting of Pisans, Venetians, and a few Genoese
went to the famous siege of Cæsarea, eager for fresh honours
and for fresh booty in this wealthy city.

Deeds of valour were again the order of the day; Embriaco
was seen locked in deadly embrace with a Saracen on the
walls, until the Genoese, like their leader, made their foes
give way, and Cæsàrea fell into their hands—Cæsarea, rich in
all the wealth of those Eastern climes, rich in jewels, rich in
gold, and glorious attire ; and this was all to be divided
amongst a handful of Italian Republicans.   As elsewhere an
eye to commerce was uppermost in the Genoese mind ; here
they established a central mart for their slave trade, and even
managed to secure many of the inhabitants for their nefarious
traffic.

It has been proudly asserted that the Genoese demanded
as their sole share of the booty, a wonderful vessel known as the
" sacro catino."   But Caffaro has freed his countrymen from
such imputed folly by stating that this was separately allotted
to Guglielmo Embriaco, as his share of the profits, whilst
his fellow countrymen carried home an equal share of booty
with Venice and with Pisa.

Embriaco on his return presented this much prized relic
to his cathedral.   As a relic it is equalled by none in the bold
assertions of its value.   It was said to be an emerald of the
purest water ; it was said to have been the dish on which
Christ eat the last supper ; it was said to have been given to
Solomon by the Queen of Sheba; whilst others asserted that it
was the vial in which Nicodemus preserved some of Christ's
blood, no other than the Holy Grail.   Is it that the Genoese
are more perfect than that perfect man Sir Galahad, who saw
it, but died from the sight ?   Well might Tennyson have put
into the mouth of Guglielmo Embriaco, when he accepted this
talisman of mystic fame as his portion of the booty, " I
trust we are green in heaven's eyes."

Very cunning were the canons of the cathedral with their gift. Twelve knights, called "Clavigeri," were appointed as its special guard, each being responsible during one month of the year for the safety of the tabernacle in which it was contained. No mortal hand should touch it "with gold, stones, coral, or any other substance," was their wise decision ; and hence for the centuries which elapsed between then and the French revolution, the vulgar belief was maintained that it was a sparkling emerald, and of priceless value. Petrarch saw it and was charmed. "But we did not depart without first having seen the basin of emerald, a priceless and wondrous vase ; they say that it was used by the Saviour in the last supper: be this so or not, it is in itself a right glorious relic."[1]

But alas for the prying curiosity of Napoleon, and his love for the goods of others, the Sacro Catino was broken on its way to the French capital, and was discovered to be but an ancient piece of Venetian glass. To-day it may be seen in the Cathedral of Genoa, on the payment of five francs, as it was kindly returned by the French ; it is mended with strips of gold, but its talisman is gone, and it is chiefly remarkable for having wrought such a deception for so many centuries.

Lord John Russell, writing to Thomas Moore, gives us a neat little parody on this myth of emerald—

> " In Genoa 'tis said that a jewel of yore,
>   Clear, large, and resplendent, ennobled the shrine
> Where the faithful in multitudes flock'd to adore,
>   And the emerald was pure, and the saint was divine,
>
> " But the priest who attended the altar was base,
>   And the faithful, who worshipp'd, besotted and blind;
> He put a green glass in the emerald's place,
>   And the multitude still in mute worship inclin'd."

After their various successes in Palestine, Genoese avarice was by no means abated, and is again brought prominently before us at the ensuing siege of Ptolemais ; for when Baldwin

---

[1] Petrarch's " Itinerario."

granted the inhabitants permission to leave the town with their goods and their families, the Genoese were highly displeased at such leniency; and as the citizens passed by they fell upon them with the sword, robbed them of their chattels, and sent them away empty-handed. This breach of trust on the part of the Ligurians passed unpunished, nay even they were rewarded for their dishonesty. Baldwin was not strong enough to quarrel with his republican allies, so they got quarters allotted to them in the city in addition to the booty they had stolen for themselves.

The Italian republics were not long in reaping the benefits of their assistance given to the cause by acting as transporters for the Christians. Out of a long list of immunities in every town they moulded for themselves a network of commerce which spread from China to England, the nucleus of which lay in Palestine. When Baldwin, in 1105, gave the Genoese a street in Jerusalem and in Joppa, a third part of Tyre and Cæsarea and of St. Jean d'Acre, and a third part of all the dues in the maritime entrances to his realm, their success was secured; the development of it was only a matter of time. Henceforth the maritime republics fought for their purses, not for their creed. Baldwin and the princes of Europe fought for their creed, without regard to their purses, and such enthusiasm naturally did not long prevail.

The disasters which fell thick on the Christian kingdom of Jerusalem, the fall of their capital, and almost all their positions in the Holy Land, aroused at length the ardour of Europe; and the so-called Third Crusade was preached, in which Genoa's character of "carrier" is brought even still more prominently before our view. Amongst the brave deeds of Richard Cœur de Lion, and Philip II. of France, very little allusion is made to our modest Ligurians. Yet from the treaties made by these monarchs with the republic we really find that their co-operation in the undertaking was as essential to these princes as tools to a carpenter.

Not only at this time were they busying themselves in their commercial intercourse with Christian people, not only were they satisfied with turning many an extortionate penny in transporting to Europe the flying Christians from Jerusalem and elsewhere, but also they were carrying on a brisk trade with the infidels themselves in spite of all the remonstrances which fanatical Europe heaped on their heads. And hence, when in 1189 the Crusade was preached for the recovery of St. Jean d'Acre, France and England had to offer enormous concessions to the Genoese to obtain their co-operation in the undertaking.

Genoese merchants were busily engaged at the courts of France and England in 1190, when Hugh, Duke of Burgundy, granted them liberal mercantile concessions in his towns of Chalons and Dijon. And two days after this treaty the same duke negotiated one on behalf of his royal master, Philip II., by which the king agreed to pay 5850 silver marks for the transport of 650 soldiers, 1300 squires, and 1300 horses, together with their arms and trappings, food for eight months, and wine only for four months from the day of their departure from Genoa; and as a further inducement to secure Ligurian aid he promised them every concession they demanded for their commerce in every town he might take, and in every country over which the flag of the lilies was seen to float. Thus the French monarch swore, and thus did Philip II. and Richard Cœur de Lion repair to Genoa to embark on the eighty ships which Genoa had prepared for the undertaking, of which Simone Vento and Marinocle Rodano, both of Genoa, were elected admirals.[1]

Over the galleys floated their banner of the red cross and the flag of St. George ; and for his ensign the English king chose the device of St. George, out of compliment to Genoa ;[2] thus did he bring home as an emblem for his

[1] Giustiniani, " Annali di Genova."
[2] Accinelli, " Compendio della Storia di Genova."

successors the standard of St. George, which has now become inseparably connected with Old England. Nowhere was this mythical saint more honoured than by the Genoese. Their great commercial bank was called after him.[1] They went to victory under the cry of his name; and it is to Genoa we owe not only the patron of our isle, but also the knowledge of the ocean paths through which we have steered to all quarters of the globe.

From the French monarch's above-mentioned treaty with Genoa, we may reasonably argue that King Richard made a like one, without which the shrewd republicans would not have transported his host to Palestine; furthermore, after his quarrel with his French ally, and when he was left alone in the Holy Land to prosecute the war, it was to Genoa the lion-hearted applied for succour. From Accon he wrote to the republic with his own hand, supplicating for further aid, and addressed his epistle to "the archbishop, podestà, consuls, and council, and other good men of Genoa."[2] He laid before them his plans for confounding the infidels in Egypt, Babylon, and Alexandria, and asserted that every pact he had made with them had been carried out to the letter. By way of a postscript he added that of all he conquered he would give the Genoese a third, even if he only got half of what he asked. But the Genoese did not respond to Richard's eager request, and of the unfortunate conclusion of this crusade every Englishman is aware. However, of the existence of quite an English colony in Genoa at this time not so much is known; but, thanks to late discoveries made in the city archives, we are able to trace the residence of several of our countrymen in the Ligurian capital at the time of this crusade.

The old church of the Knights Hospitallers at Genoa still exists, with its Gothic windows, Lombard tower, and rounded apse. This was originally the old church of S. Sepolchro,

[1] *Vide* ch. xi.
[2] Canale, "Storia di Genova."

close to the water's edge, where the Knights of the Holy Sepulchre founded an hospice, and in the adjoining *"commenda"* gave any pilgrims bound for the Holy Land a night's lodging and a meal prior to their departure on Genoese ships to fulfil their vows. Still may be seen the dark, dank cells in which they slept, and the whole place, even in this nineteenth century, is teeming with memories of the Holy Wars.

Receding into the wall in the old Lombard tower is a

MONUMENT TO WILLIAM ACTON ON THE WALLS OF THE CHURCH OF THE KNIGHTS
HOSPITALLERS, IN GENOA.

singular old monument, still in excellent preservation, and the inscription round it is to this effect:

> † Of Master William Acton I am here the home,
> For whom let whosoever passes by a pater say.
> † In 1180, in the time of William, it was begun. [1]

Curious it is to find an English name thus figuring in Genoa at this time, and moreover in so honoured a position as to fix the date of the foundation of this old hostelry. Besides this, in an old register of the foundation of this building dated the 30th September, 1198, we read the following: " I, William,

[1] *Vide* " Giornale Ligustico," Anno I, Fascicolo xii.

commendator of the Hospital of St. John, admit to having received from you, Master John of England, doctor, thirty-seven pounds in deposit, which deposit Master John made, fearing the judgment of God, in the journey of the most blessed St. Thomas of Canterbury, in which he set out, and if he did not return to Genoa, he bequeaths the said thirty-seven pounds to the said hospital." Is this the same William or not, who after the fashion of the times had built himself a tomb with an appropriate inscription before his death ? At all events, from these meagre facts we can glean enough to prove how close was the connection between Genoa and England in those days, and probably this old hostelry was as well stocked with British tourists in the twelfth century, as are the palatial hotels of this the restless nineteenth.

This old church and annexed hostelry, founded or not by a compatriot of ours, has gone through strange vicissitudes in its long history. Hither came Pope Urban V., in 1367, with eight cardinals, on his way from Avignon to Rome ; and here Pope Urban VI., in 1385, enacted his bloody tragedy as follows :—

When Europe was divided by the schism in the papacy, Genoa espoused the cause of this relentless Pontiff,[1] and sent a fleet to liberate him in Nocera, where he was besieged by Charles of Naples. Out of this Genoa hoped to gain much, but as it turned out, she gained only an unpleasant notoriety for being the scene of one of the most tragic events of that tragic age. The Pope got six unfortunate cardinals into his power, who had espoused the cause of his rival ; so he chose to drag them in chains with him to Genoa. He tortured them on the rack, and he consigned them to a dungeon underneath the rooms where he was sumptuously entertained in this very hostelry. At length, unable to extort by torture any secrets from them, he determined to dispose of them as best he could. Report says he tied them all up in sacks and threw them into the

[1] *Vide* ch. ix.

sea. At all events, he so enraged the worthy Genoese that he was obliged to flee, leaving behind him a name accursed by all. Of the six cardinals, one alone escaped this fate, and he was Adam, Bishop of Hertford, saved, they say, by the intervention of the English king. Slabs put up in the oratory of St. Hugh, beneath the church, still attest to the visit of the two Urbans.

On this spot the companies of the Cassacie were first located. Here the Knights Hospitallers fixed their abode. Here the pious St. Hugh lived and died, and numerous tablets, now nearly all dispersed by the congregating of houses and shops thickly around it, told of noble guests and noble sufferers whose woes had been alleviated by this kindly confraternity.

Still this relic of the Crusades is a highly picturesque object down near the port, with coloured shops and gay merchandize contrasting oddly with the grim old walls, where hundreds of pilgrims and countless devotees slept their last night before embarking on an expedition from which but a small portion of them returned; and when the age of pilgrimages had passed away, here many a sufferer was relieved by the pious Knights Hospitallers.

But very little crusading spirit was left in Genoa, when they refused Cœur de Lion's offer. They even looked on with uninterested silence at the whole of the Fourth Crusade, when the avarice of the Venetians wrecked its whole course by directing it against an old Byzantine emperor who stood in the way of their commerce. In short, in Europe the spirit was dying out, and Genoa had too much to do at home, with her warehouses and her commerce, to care much about knight-errantry, and the quixotic exertions of the later crusaders.

In August of the year 1212, the inhabitants of Genoa were witnesses of one of the most eccentric episodes in the whole history of the wars between the Crescent and the Cross. One day as they looked from their city walls they beheld clouds of dust arising, as if from a mighty host proceeding against their town. The gates were forthwith closed ; all eagerly awaited to learn what brought this unexpected armament to Genoa. Great was their surprise when a band of seven thousand children, headed by a lad of thirteen years of age, arrived beneath their walls, clamouring for transports to convey them to Palestine to redeem the Holy Sepulchre from the hand of the infidel. No more striking episode is there than this of the fanatical enthusiasm which even seized the minds of the young, and incited them to this wild scheme. There were, too, a few old men and women who followed in this curious train.

When they saw that no transports were forthcoming at their demand, they encamped sullenly under the broiling Italian sun outside the city walls, waiting, they said, like the Israelites of old, until the sea should open a passage for them through its depth ; and thus a week elapsed. The Mediterranean refused to obey the rod of a youthful Moses. The tideless ocean refused to follow the example of the Red Sea, and thus the disappointed enthusiasts grew less heated in their desire for glory in the East. They quietly dispersed, greatly to the relief of the Genoese, who cared not for the turbulent, marauding spirits, who took advantage of this occasion to hover round their walls. Many of these children died from hunger and exposure. Most of them returned to discipline at home, whilst some of them embarked at Marseilles ; and not over well pleased were the Christians in Palestine to receive so juvenile a succour, whose advent was more of an inconvenience than anything else.

Very little better was the Crusade which, three years later, Pope Honorius III. preached throughout Christendom, when he had successfully put a temporary check to the rivalry of the three republics, Venice, Pisa, and Genoa. Throughout the length and breadth of France the greatest enthusiasm prevailed ; whilst the Genoese transported no less than two hundred thousand of them to the siege of Damietta, where the flower of the French nobility fell a sacrifice to the ravages of pestilence and the sword.

In vain did their generals urge them on to deeds of valour ; in vain were wild acts of heroism performed from day to day, Damietta refused to succumb, even as the sea had refused to open its paths to the youthful enthusiasts. At length Genoa sent out assistance in the shape of ten galleys manned with the bravest of her sons. On three successive days, three valiant attacks were made on the walls of Damietta, when French and Genoese, like hungry wolves, hurled themselves against their foe, but without avail. It was not till 1220 that the town at length gave way ; thanks, they say, to the superior engineering skill of the Genoese, who invented wonderful battering rams and stone-propelling engines, before which the infidels were obliged to yield.

But by this one solitary victory the armies of the Christians were exhausted, and powerless to go inland in search of fresh conquests ; and a few months later many of the surviving Christians were slaughtered by the Saracens in their ships.

A wild and touching scene it must have been, and one which echoes the spirit of the times, when before the assembled multitude in the cathedral of San Lorenzo, the Genoese " podestà " broke the seal of the letter announcing the capture of Damietta.

" Amidst rabid and unearthly yells of joy women fainted and wept aloud, old men tottering with years cast away their crutches, and with outstretched arms thanked the Almighty for the mercies vouchsafed." [1] But this, the Fifth Crusade, was at an end, and all this enthusiasm was but a morbid echo of the past, when under the walls of Damietta was buried the chivalry of Europe ; and a terrible earthquake in Cyprus overthrew into the waves the greater part of Baffo and Limeso, as if nature was herself proclaiming that these things should be no more.

[1] Giustiniani annalista.

But for the Genoese the Crusades had wrought everything
on which they had to build centuries of prosperity and wealth.
Commerce in Syria and Egypt, commerce in the Black Sea
and along the coasts of the Mediterranean, were for them the
results. From the Crusades they not only learnt their power, ·
but the way to use it; and both these facts are instanced by
the one feeble crusade which followed these events, wherein
the saintly Louis of France, more fitted for a convent than
a throne, made it the object of his life to arouse this dying
flame.

Again did the Genoese take a prominent part, and again
they were the "carriers" only of the armament. It is from
their contracts for providing the necessary fleet, that we obtain
a faithful picture of the advance the Ligurians had made in the
art of ship-building,[1] after a long period of successful commerce
and voyages of discovery.

The *Gran' Paradiso* and the *S. Niccolò*, the ships which
bore St. Louis on his ill-fated expedition to the coast of
Africa, as they sailed out of Genoa's harbour all radiant with
the flags and banners of this princely host, told of a new
era which was dawning on Europe, and of a new spirit of
enterprise which was awakened amongst men, which would
prove a far more effectual check to Turkish progress, and the
inroads of the Crescent, than the countless ill-organized hosts
who wasted their blood and the resources of their country in
the vain attempt to gain possession of a mystic sepulchre.

Before leaving this subject of the Genoese and the
Crusades, let us glance at another feature of these times, the
fever for which originated in Provence, and spread its con-
tagion far and wide along the Genoese "Riviere." In the
Ligurian capital were born and bred many of those minstrel
troubadours, who in their songs of love and burning passions
tended to form a basis for the growth of language on which
future poets built so noble a fabric.

---

[1] *Vide* ch. x.

Great was the influence of these troubadours on politics ; they would drive a reluctant noble to arm. for the Holy Wars for very shame. Throughout the north of Italy they would excite one town against another in continual strife. Guelphic minstrels visited the towns of Lombardy to excite them against the emperor, whilst a Ghibelline minstrel would not fail to arouse the emperor's adherents against the Lombards. Thus in Genoa we find minstrels lamenting the factions in the city, which prevented a proper utilization of her resources to overthrow the rival Pisa and the rival Venice.

Itinerant minstrelsy was the outcome of the Crusades ; the troubadours were the politicians and the newsmongers of the day, and their control over men's minds was very strong. In Genoa, Folchetto was one of the earliest who abandoned the barbarous Latin, and sang love songs in the native dialect. He was the son of a wealthy Genoese merchant, who resided at Marseilles, consequently Folchetto found himself in easy circumstances on his father's death, and able to indulge his passion for sweet love songs to its full, and gave way to the infectious fever of minstrelsy which then raged in Provence.

He accordingly fell in love, as was the duty of every troubadour, in fact his profession ; and the object of his choice was Adelaide da Roccamartina, wife of Barral del Balzo, Viscount of Marseilles. Barral chased him away from the castle where his love resided, but summoned him again later, on the death of his viscountess, as he wished for a poem to commemorate her virtues and her charms; and no one was better calculated to do so than Folchetto, he thought. The result of his pen, entitled "The Lamentations of Barral," forms one of the principal poems which have been left us by this troubadour.

In after life Folchetto seems to have deserted the follies of his youth, and repaired with St. Dominic to Rome, where he preached energetically against the Albigenses. Richard of England had been one of the most ardent admirers of this erratic poet, also the bard-loving Raimond, Count of Toulouse.   Dante places him in paradise amongst those who had repented of the follies of their youth ; for Folchetto ended his days in a convent, whither he was followed by his two sons, whilst his wife took the veil.   Petrarch alludes to him in his " Triumph of Love," and thus sums up the life of our versatile Genoese poet : " Folchetto gave to Marseilles the honour of his name, which he took from Genoa ; and in his latter days he changed for a holier state both his country and his garb."

Lanfranco Cicala was another of Genoa's love-sick poets, who sang dulcet strains before a court of love at San Remo. Nevertheless, he was made of better stuff than Folchetto, and took a part in his country's affairs, warmly espousing the Ghibelline cause, and occupying the position of judge in Genoa for several years.

Bonifacio Calvi was a good specimen of the wandering troubadour, who, with his friend Bartolomeo Zorsi, left Genoa, and sang sweet music about their country and their loves in foreign courts.   Calvi visited Spain ; and at the court of Alphonso of Aragon he chose the king's niece as the object of his affections and of his song.   But like his compatriot, Christopher Columbus, two centuries later, he suffered much from the jealousies of the courtiers, who hated this Genoese minstrel.   He avenged himself by vituperating them in his songs, and eventually went over to the court of Castille, where he incited the king to make war against the offending Aragonese with the true mischief-making spirit of a troubadour.

Percival D'Oria, a member of that illustrious Genoese family, distinguished himself in the court of Charles of Anjou, who made him podestà of Avignon and Arles in return for his laudatory ditties.   And numerous lesser lights in Genoa, whose works are lost, took up the line of minstrelsy, and are only known by name from the mention of them by some poet of greater fame. Thus did these humble troubadours open the gates by which more brilliant poets entered and crowned themselves with laurels, even as the Crusades paved the way for greater Italian glory in the paths of commerce during the centuries to come.

CHAPTER III.

GENOA AT HOME UNTIL HER FIRST DOGE.

ARE we to dive into heathen mythology for the origin of our town of Genoa ?   Are we to believe with the credulous inhabitants that Janus, the great-grandson of Noah, of the Christian tradition, the old god of the Romans who presided over peace and war, founded the Ligurian capital ?   Are we to put implicit faith in the pompous inscription placed in large gothic letters over the architrave of the cathedral nave, which unblushingly informs the worshippers at S. Lorenzo's shrine, that "Janus, a Trojan prince, skilled in astrology, and seeking on his travels a healthy, strong and secure place to dwell in, reached Janua, already founded by Janus, the great-grandson of Noah, and perceiving that it was well protected from the raging of the sea, increased it in power and renown."

Ingenious etymologists go the length of asserting that the hill of Carignano[1] was his vineyard, and that the hill of Sarzano[2] was his stronghold, and a stranger unaware of this tradition is to-day surprised to see a representation of the double-headed one under each of the city's gas lamps.   But it is certainly more humble-minded, and more within the bounds of possibility to assume that the Romans called it "Janua" because it was the "gate" of northern Italy, or that from its position in the bend of the coast line they named it

[1] Cherem Jani deriv. of Carignano.
[2] Ars Jani deriv. of Sarzano.

from " genu " a knee, after which Geneva, in the bend of Lake Leman, is reported to have been called.

Like the origin of her name, the early history of this commonwealth is cut off from the days of the old Roman municipal city which flourished here,[1] by a dark period of tradition, a period during which nearly all traces of her former civilization faded away before the blighting scourge of Norman and Saracenic invasions, which obliged her, after these early troubles were past, to begin again an entirely new political career.

Like a devastating torrent poured forth from the abyss of hell, writes an old chronicler, was the raid of Hastings . the Norman, and his followers, when they descended from their victorious galleys upon the towns of Liguria. The object of these northern warriors was to possess themselves of Rome, with all her countless treasures; but in their ignorance of geography, they beheld the towers and churches of Luna, near the Gulf of Spezia, and they thought they were then within sight of their wished-for goal.

The treacherous Hastings with peaceful words deceived the trembling inhabitants; he feigned conversion to their creed, he was baptized, he gave the richest of his spoil to the cathedral, begging for a tomb within the cloisters, when his end might come. Thus deceived the inhabitants were entirely off their guard, when a cry of lamentation arose from the Norman camp, proclaiming that the leader was dead, and the archbishop accorded him the burial he had requested before his death. But lo! in the midst of the funeral ceremony the corpse of Hastings arose from his coffin sword in hand; his followers produced weapons from beneath their mourning robes, and Luna was a prey to the Normans—the fairest, and the strongest city along this coast, and with it the rest of the Riviera became an easy prey to their devastation.

But few stones are now left to mark the site of this once

[1] *Vide* Appendix I.

flourishing Roman town ; what remained after the departure of the Normans the Genoese, in after days, and the inhabitants of the neighbouring town of Sarzana, took away to adorn their temples; and in the old churches of St. Mary of the Castle, and St. Mary of the Vineyard, we still see remnants of Luna's glory.   Amidst these ruins Dante wandered and meditated when in exile, and of these Dante thus sang—

> " I was a dweller on that valley's shore
> 'Twixt Ebro and Magra, that with journey short
> Doth from the Tuscan part the Genoese."
> *Paradiso* ix.

> " If Luna thou regard, and Urbisaglia,
> How they have passed away."
> *Paradiso* xvi.

Similar in devastation, and eating up all that the Normans had left, was the Saracenic scourge, perhaps more terrible in its oft-repeated intensity, and more crushing to any outburst of civilization. When the sails of the infidels' galleys appeared on the horizon, the inhabitants at Genoa betook them to their mountain fastnesses, and from them looked down in misery on the smouldering ashes of their homesteads below.

Far from giving way under these frequent raids, which crippled their energies and checked their enterprise, the Genoese grew bolder after each successive blow.   In 936 A.D. we read of galleys being built which enabled them, instead of retreating to the mountains, to hover round their enemies, and inflict some damage in their turn.   It was in this year that tradition says a fountain poured forth for a whole day with blood, prior to the descent of the Saracens on the Genoese coast ; and this year is marked by the first trifling victory which the Ligurians gained over their foes.   Henceforth this kindly fountain was in the habit of giving this timely warning of an attack, and even to this day the street bears the name of Fontanella in which it flowed.

But these, the early troubles of the infant commonwealth,

worked wonderfully for her good. It was in those days that they first learnt the art of building the ships which eventually earned for Genoa the title of " mistress of the seas," and it was in those days of trial that their first walls were built ; and around the slopes of the hill, where now the thick walls and dense crowd of houses crown the eminence of Sarzano, was the first nucleus of Genoa's strength. Here was the citadel, here was the first bishop's palace, and here St. Mary of the Castle, the earliest cathedral of the town, still bears witness in its name to its ancient importance.

The history, too, of this church is lost in the legends of these early times—how here SS. Nazzaro and Celso baptized the first Genoese Christians, after landing on the rocks of Albaro. Out of compliment to this legend, a canon from the cathedral still holds a baptism once a year in S. Maria di Castello. It is a lovely church even to-day, and a museum of Genoese art, endowed as it was by the wealth of the Grimaldi, and adorned by pictures of the best Genoese artists. Here the Republicans of Ragusa built themselves a little chapel, in which to worship when they visited Genoa, though now hidden away behind the high altar ; it is dedicated to S. Blaze, and contains a magnificent inscription, in letters of gold, which tell how the Ragusans claimed to have obtained their liberty from Alexander the Great, and how friendly these Republicans were with Genoa at the time they built this chapel.

The early centuries of Genoa's new life are inseparably connected with her bishops. They were the only fount of law and civilization. In their hands alone were deposited the traces of the old Roman civilization ; the old municipal rights and liberties granted by ancient Rome to Genoa were locked up in their breasts until the " *commune*," over which they presided, at length learnt its own inherent power, and the consuls, a form of government which lingered in Genoa through all her darkness and distress, from being entirely subservient to the sacerdotal authority, became their coadjutors, and eventually their superiors, in the government.

The earlier bishops who ruled in Genoa are known only by name.   S. Salome, lived three centuries after Christ, and S. Romulo succeeded him, to whom S. Remo is said to owe its name and origin.   S. Siro is the first about whom there is any definite account, and he is surrounded by a maze of legendary lore.   He gave his name to the second cathedral, which in its turn was supplanted by the one which is in existence now, and numerous legends are still told of his exceeding piety.   He had a pet blackbird, when a boy, which one day on his return from school he found dead, and brought to life again by a judicious application of saliva; hence his pictures generally represent him with a blackbird, and this bird is allowed to build its nest and rear its young unmolested in his church.

The pious mariner attributes to S. Siro a control over the elements, based on the following claims : once, when walking on the cliffs of Genoa with his father, he beheld a ship making for the port under a steady breeze, he expressed a wish to see it becalmed, when, lo! it forthwith became as if at anchor. Sirus begged leave to go on board, and by expressing a mere wish the ship went on again, greatly to the relief of the merchant to whom it belonged.

A curious legend is attached to the Genoese S. Siro, which in France is told of S. Brise, and is illustrated on an old piece of tapestry at Mompezat. Thus it runs : when officiating as deacon to the Bishop of Genoa, one day, young Sirus gave vent to an immoderate fit of laughter, and after the service was over received the requisite admonition from his superior. To extenuate himself, Sirus related how he had seen, as in a vision, the devil, busily engaged behind a pillar writing down the names of those who did not attend to the mass, on a piece of parchment; before long the parchment became full, and to elongate it his satanic majesty made use of his teeth, when suddenly the parchment gave way, and the devil's head rebounded violently against the pillar, causing him to retire discomfited and badly hurt.

S. Siro is in short a pattern bishop of those barbarous times, whose rule was equable and just whilst he lived, and as a natural consequence, his memory was surrounded by a halo of superstitious awe. His festival is still celebrated with befitting solemnity in Genoa.

From the barbarian invasions from the north, the bishops derived the source of their power and their hold over men's minds. These wealthy prelates were enabled to build castles, and protect the State, when aid from other sources was cut off; the people saw that from them alone could they hope for anything like a good and stable government; and by the exercise of their spiritual authority, in conjunction with a temporal one, their position was unassailable as long as religion meant justice and good government combined.

The bishop's palace, on the hill of Sarzano, was the centre of this political system. Here resided both the consuls of the government and the consuls of the pleas, and when these functionaries entered into office they always took the oath of allegiance to the bishop, and for centuries the ecclesiastic and secular elements worked hand in hand, and worked peaceably for the welfare of the State.

Even as late as 1151 we find the first archbishop a second Sirus, in conjunction with the consuls issuing decrees indicative of supreme authority; and all through the earlier treaties in Genoese history is found a special clause entered in favour of the bishop or archbishop, and his cathedral.

The power of the bishop was externally represented by an officer called the "Cintraco," who collected all dues, and looked after the defences, and represented his master in the general councils. It is to the times of the bishops that we must look for the origin of those "companies" into which the town was divided. They were small societies in which men congregated together, swore to the common defence, and were

E

regulated by their particular consul. This formation of bodies politic within the State is a marked feature throughout Genoese history. It is to this fact that the great strength of certain families is due, and the large army of retainers and kinsmen that a D'Oria or a Spinola could produce in case of war.

These companies in their entirety formed the commune, and, later on, the republic of Genoa, over whom the consuls were the recognized rulers ; at first, merely as executors of the bishop's power, but, as the ecclesiastical influence grew weaker, they gradually got the reins of government entirely into their own hands. Thus was the system of consuls established in Genoa, the very essence of the old municipal system, which had been kept alive by the episcopal influence, the sole depositories of the old régime ; and nowhere was the consular theory more fully carried out than in Genoa. Any body of men to whom self-management was given had a consul ; the archers had their consuls, the colonies had their consuls, and even the body of porters at the Bank of St. George chose a consul from amongst themselves.[1]

At length we find the commune of Genoa, as represented by its consuls chosen at the general assembly of the people, asserting itself after the time of the crusades, and this power growing stronger as that of the bishops grew less. The day. of episcopal rule was over ; they had done their work in preserving the rudiments of good government through a period of darkness, and, by a silent revolution spread over a term of years, the government of the State was transferred from their hands into those of the commune ; and on emerging from a state of barbarism, this commune blossomed into the Ligurian Republic.

One of the first acts of this youthful commune was to do all honour to its cathedral, endow it with gifts and privileges, as if in return for the tender care the bishops had taken of

[1] *Vide* ch. xi.

their slumbering germs of government through a period, when all that had to do with the past was being swept away. Identical with the first sensations of power felt by the people is the origin of the edifice of S. Lorenzo as it stands to-day. Their cathedral served the purpose of council hall for their general assemblies ; here the consuls issued their decrees, here vassalage was sworn by the various lords who entered themselves as citizens of Genoa, here they held their councils of war, and celebrated their victories.

As seen even now the cathedral of S. Lorenzo is perhaps the most striking building in Genoa ; built in courses of black and white marble, covered with carvings and images, all blended together into one harmonious whole by the mellowing hand of time. In scanning the façade of this cathedral, the traveller's eye rests on a perfect museum of architecture. The portals are built in pure Italian Gothic surrounded by a blaze of figure working, in which are seen Moorish designs and Moorish images, whilst the Byzantine element is present in the figure of Christ over the central portal, and in the genealogical tree which climbs up towards it. As the eye travels upwards it rests on some of the best work of the fourteenth and fifteenth centuries—restorations made after a fire, which nearly deprived Genoa of her sanctuary—until at length the Campanile crowns this motley group, finished in 1520, in the stiffest style of the Renaissance. If each of those figures inserted in the walls could give its own history, what a curious network of facts would they produce about Genoa's enterprises, and Genoa's world-wide commerce. Report tells us that those spiral pillars on either side of the central portal, representing palm-trees, came from a Moorish mosque at Almeria, in Spain; the pillars of a loggia, where, according to the original plan, another tower was to have been built, belonged to an ancient church which stood here before the cathedral ; and a grotesque figure of S. Lorenzo on the gridiron, with impish dwarfs blowing vigorously with bellows, came from the same old building;

whilst a legend is attached to a tall thin figure under a canopy on the south corner of the façade, which is commonly supposed to represent the blacksmith who did all the iron-work for the cathedral, and refused to be paid on condition that a statue of himself should be inserted on the walls. And here he stands, with his anvil in his hands, puzzling the heads of antiquarians, who declare him to be a saint, and reject the popular story with scorn.

This church was consecrated in 1118 by Pope Gelasius II., which scene is depicted in a fresco in the archbishop's palace hard by, together with the solemn presentation of it to the saintly hero of the gridiron. Many a strange story could this building tell of bloody deeds enacted before its walls, of oaths taken within to be broken as soon as made; munificent endowments, and concessions of glebe land throughout the length and breadth of the Mediterranean have enriched its hallowed precincts, and each succeeding age has striven to add some mark of beauty to its walls.

Consecrated by the same Pope, and built in the same style as the earliest part of S. Lorenzo, the small black and white marble church of Porto Venere affords us another instance of this early architectural development. The ruins still crown a rocky promontory at the northern end of the Gulf of Spezia. Desolate as this spot now is, it is exceeding rich in its desolation, where the blue waters break themselves on the bright red rocks beneath the frowning Pisan tower and striped Genoese church. Here, 150 B.C., Lucius Porcius, the Roman consul, erected a temple to Venus, which was remodelled and consecrated as above mentioned in 1118. When Charles VIII. of France invaded Italy, in 1494, Alphonso, king of Naples, came down on Porto Venere with fourteen ships, and left it the ruin that Byron and Shelley loved to visit, and that the tourist of to-day casts a hasty glance at if he chance to stay at Spezia.

A second step taken by the Genoese commune in its

infancy was to put down with a firm hand the numerous lords and feudatories with which the Riviera was studded—always at variance amongst themselves, and always giving opportunities for the lawless bands of robbers who haunted the coast and crippled the republic's commerce. The commune obliged them to live within the city walls for a portion of the year, to assist in war, and at the parliaments, and to write themselves down as citizens. Thus came to live in Genoa those

GENOESE CHURCH AND PISAN TOWER, MIRTO VENERE.

troublous, restless spirits, fearing the republic, but not loving it, and bringing with them a new element of feudalism which in its struggles with the democratic element which existed already in the city, laid up a store of evils for ensuing centuries. Counts, viscounts, and marquises from Ventimiglia to the Malaspina near Luna, and inland to Gavi, were enrolled on the lists of citizens, and forthwith used all their influence to overthrow the power of the commune. In vain did the consuls attempt to regulate the helm in this tempest, as their hold on the course of events became year by year more feeble. The factions, for which Genoa was celebrated even in faction-loving Italy, soon took root, and subverted everything inside the walls, until thus hampered at home the Ligurian Republic was unable to grasp the goal which was within her reach of being the most flourishing State in Christendom.

It was not long after their settlement in Genoa that the nobles began to make themselves heard, and to arrange their forces on opposite sides as occasion suited them. Thus, in 1168, the great families of the Castelli and Avvocati were at variance for power. The Castelli took the part of the commune and bishop, hence the Guelphic side, at the time when the cause of Pope and Liberty went hand in hand in Italy. The Avvocati for their assistance went outside the city walls, and became supporters of the imperial cause, and consequently Ghibelline; thus were these fatal names introduced into Genoa, and with this the evil grew apace, until in 1190 a change of government was adopted, and the Ghibelline institution of a foreign *podestà* to superintend the government became the order of the day.

During the consulate were the seeds of all her greatness sown—her influence in the crusades,[1] her expeditions against the Moors in Minorca, Almeria,[2] and Tortosa, the resistance to Frederic Barbarossa,[3] and her earlier successes against Pisa. And with these came the first-fruits of her commerce, which extended even then throughout the Mediterranean. At home during this period the two *riviere* were reduced to obedience, her walls were strengthened, and her city beautified. It was, of a truth, a bad day for Genoa when she abandoned her consuls, and plunged herself into the labyrinth of foreign politics.

The podestà was legally a foreigner ; but on two occasions Genoa set aside this rule, and elected citizens. As a rule they were chosen from Bologna, Florence, Lucca, and the Lombard

---

[1] *Vide* ch. ii.   [2] *Vide* ch. v.   [3] *Vide* ch. iv.

towns ; they were elected by the general council, came into office on the first of September, and remained in it a year. Their oath was stringent, their pay was good, and their conduct was subject to the direction of a council of eight, and the whole parliament of the people. Thus was a podestà, in 1233, pulled up for non-observance of the laws ; and again, in 1237, another of these functionaries, who had in some way mixed himself up in the election of his successor, was exposed to all the fury of an enraged populace. These were the checks on his power ; but he could impose what taxes he pleased. He coined money, he elected the podestà for the colonies and provinces, and also commanded expeditions by sea and by land. It was necessary for him to be a citizen of a free and friendly city, a doctor of law, and of a noble and noted family.

In the selection of their first podestà the Genoese were singularly unfortunate ; he came from Brescia, and was named Tettoccio, but from his severity was nicknamed " Il manigoldo," or the policeman. No sooner was he elected than he appeared in armour in the parliament, and then rode fiercely through the streets on horseback. He levelled to the ground the houses of refractory nobles, and spread terror and dismay throughout the city.

Perhaps to this gloomy precedent may be attributed the fact that the government by podestà never got firm hold in Genoa ; for they constantly returned to their old consuls. And for the next century and a half the supreme command was divided with fluctuating uncertainty between a " podestà," a consul, or a captain ; and hence arose a continual strife between rival parties, and a continued undercurrent of discontent.

Perhaps, too, this system of placing the government in the hands of a foreigner gave rise to another curious feature in Genoa's history, namely, that of from time to time handing over her liberty into the hands of some foreign potentate.

Feeling the want of stability at home, the Genoese were constrained to seek it from without, and hence we frequently find
her rushing blindly from one evil to another, and never contented with her lot.

With such a feeble, fretful state of affairs at home, it is
little to be wondered at that the other towns of the Riviera
were constantly in open revolt against the capital. Savona
was the principal one, and Savona was an object of jealousy
to Genoa from the earliest times. The Genoese hated her
port, and her pretensions to compete in commerce with her
mistress; and whenever Savona revolted, and the times were
not a few, Genoa destroyed her harbour and her forts, and placed
some painful and humiliating obligation on the inhabitants.
No wonder then that Savona was a favourable starting-point
for any foreign lord, were he Milanese or were he French, who
wished to strike a blow at Genoese prosperity.

Crushed and oppressed for many years, at length the voice
of the people was once more heard in Genoa. Tired by the
constant strife between Guelph and Ghibelline (the *"rampini"*
and *"mascherati,"* as they termed themselves here), goaded
into action by the lasciviousness and corruption of their
"podestà," Filippo della Torre, the people in 1257 elected one
Guglielmo Boccanegra to be their captain and defender. His
origin was obscure, but his family was a talented one, his
brother, Marino, being a clever architect and engineer; and
Boccanegra proved himself worthy of the trust placed in his
hands. For the first time was the voice of the people heard
to some purpose; and for the first time was a check put to
the spirit of feudalism which the nobles had brought with
them to the city. But, above all, after generations had to
thank this captain for the splendid commercial treaty which he
negotiated with the Byzantine Emperor, on which the whole
structure of Genoese power in the Black Sea was built.[1] But
it was by his very success that he wrought his ruin; the people

---

[1] *Vide* ch. vi.

grew jealous of the idol they had set up. The joint persuasion of Venice and the supplanted Greek emperor led the Pope to excommunicate Genoa, and the pious Ligurians objected to dying unshriven, the blame of which they put down at Boccanegra's door. They thought he had neglected their interests in Sardinia; but above all they thought he had too much power, and this notion the nobles carefully fanned.

However, during his short captaincy, Boccanegra had wrought a brilliant little episode in the midst of tyranny and oppression at a time when three elements were at strife in the State—the feudal, the ecclesiastical, and the popular, and he glorified the third by keeping in check the other two. But he was obliged to relinquish the reins of government in 1262; and again the Republic returned to the podestà and their tyranny.

It is in this transitory outburst of popular feeling that we find the nobility of the country, as they were called—the Spinola and the D'Oria—associating themselves with the people as against the old nobility, the Grimaldi and the Fieschi. These four families had now grown to an overwhelming pitch of power in Genoa. The Spinola had come into the town from the valley of the Polcevera, where an old viscount, renowned for his hospitality, had tapped (Spillava, Spinolava) his wine casks with such readiness, that he gained for himself this name. The origin of the D'Oria and the Fieschi we will discuss later;[1] whilst to the Grimaldi, the following origin is attributed: Under Charlemagne lived two brothers, Hugh and Ramire Grimaut, the latter of whom fought in Spain against the infidel, and established the Spanish branch of this family, whilst Hugh became Lord of Antibes, and his grandson obtained the lordship of Monaco in 920, by reason of his prowess in driving the Saracen therefrom. In process of time, in common with the other princes of the Riviera, the Grimaldi became subject to Genoa; and during the six centuries that

[1] Ch. xii.

this family continued to give princes to Monaco and citizens to Genoa, they afforded a safe asylum for those whose views of government exiled them from the Ligurian capital. Then, as now, Monaco existed as a plague spot on the Riviera, whither murderers and conspirators would flee to escape justice. Curious is the fatality which has attended this enchanting gem on which nature has lavished all her charms, whilst mankind has endowed it with an heirloom of vice. The Grimaldi were amongst the first to become enrolled as citizens of Genoa ; and throughout their connection with the Ligurian Republic they were staunch Ghibellinists.

After the fall of the imperial cause and the death of Frederic II., the Guelphic and popular adherents, as repre- sented by the Spinola and the D'Oria, were all dominant within the city. Captain after captain was elected from amongst these families, and all the great deeds of the Republic are associated inseparably with them ; whilst the Fieschi and Grimaldi exiles plotted against their country under the Emperor's direction ; and at Monaco the Grimaldi established a hotbed of revolutionary spirits, ever ready to pounce upon Liguria when an opportunity occurred.

The power of this line of captains from abroad was kept in check, firstly, by a podestà, elected as formerly, but now only acting as a supernumerary and head of the judicial de- partment; secondly, by a functionary termed the abbot of the people, an officer whose duty it was to represent the people's interests, and who was elected by the General Council. Com- pared with the various forms of government which appeared before and after, the Captaincy shines out most brilliantly. The abbot of the people was, indeed, a most salutary institution for supporting the popular rights. We first find him men- tioned in 1270. He was a plebeian, and elected by plebeians. He was held in great honour by his electors; they allotted him a house, and paid him well. He sat between the two captains at the general assemblies ; he was in fact a revival of the old tribunes of ancient Rome ; his very name was a popular one, as the "*abbots*" of the mediæval monasteries were the first to offer an asylum and a hope for oppressed citizens, and the first to strike a blow at feudalism. Hence, though entirely unconnected with the ecclesiastical party, the abbot took his name from them as representing the highest conception of freedom in those days.   There were likewise three other abbots, who superintended the popular interests in the neighbouring valleys of the Bisagno, Polcevera, and Voltri.

It is with regret we leave this oasis, so to speak, in the government of Liguria, and turn again to pages of tyranny, which her enemies were plotting for her outside the walls. Prosperous and contented as she was at this time, yet there was a conscious dread of mischief from without, when her annalist, Jacopo D'Oria closed his work about this time, and addressed his native city thus—" O, my country, may you be always thus free from the yoke of slavery !"

A phase in Ligurian history is now brought before us reflecting anything but credit on the Republic. Freer, perhaps, than any other city of Italy from the imperial outbursts which devastated Lombardy and all the east of the Apennines, Genoa was able to hold her own against Frederic Barbarossa, never having admitted his superiority.   In fact, at the time of his greatest power it is that we first hear of Genoa as a recognized republic in her transactions with the emperors of the East.   On the other hand, it is true that from Conrad II., in 1139, she received a diploma for coining her own money, which implies a certain degree of subservience, and certain it is that his initials continued for centuries to adorn the Genoese coins, together with the doge's and griffin's head.

Be this dependence on Germany what it may, they were certainly entirely free from the empire after the death of Frederic II., and it was entirely a voluntary act of theirs which put the management of their state in the hands of Henry VII. of Luxemburg, driven to it, as they were, by their dissensions and the craving for some steady hand to guide them.

After being crowned with the iron crown at Monza, Henry set about the task of visiting the towns of Italy to quell their disorders, and on his way he passed through Genoa. His wife accompanied him, and he was received with all the state and ceremony befitting so august a visitor. When the emperor was once within the city walls,.the Ghibelline party felt their power, and confidently spoke of the coming surrender. And on the 1st of November, 1311, on the piazza of Sarzano, an immense multitude was assembled together to witness Genoa's mighty disgrace.

For twenty-one years, or for the term of his natural life, they conceded to Henry the lordship of Genoa ; and, during his absence, were content to receive an imperial vicar as their governor. It was but a small compensation for these concessions that the D'Oria, and other noble families, were bribed into acquiescence by permission to emblazon the imperial eagle in their shields. The act was one of humiliation, brought about by extinction of patriotism in seeking to further party spirit and party jealousies.

The results of this abandonment of liberty might indeed have been disastrous to the future prosperity of the Ligurian Republic had not an invidious enemy in the German camp carried off their imperial master very shortly after the deed of concession was ratified. Within the gates of Genoa Margaret of Brabant, the emperor's wife, had died of the plague ; and to the same malady, according to some, the emperor fell a sacrifice at Pisa a few weeks later, whilst others assert that poison was administered to him in a sacred wafer at the mass. And thus, according to the contract, Genoa's squandered liberty reverted to herself, and most burthensome it was to her, seeing that for the next thirty years the city was one vast sea of Guelphic and Ghibelline rivalry. They sought the protection of Robert, king of Sicily, in conjunction with Pope John XXII., but in vain ; nothing could quell this terrible party spirit, which shook her to her basis.

The one thing which surprises us, and which proves her inherent vitality, is the fact that Genoa lived through those dark ages, and was shortly after able to proclaim herself the Queen of the Mediterranean, when the first of the doges came forth to rescue her from the toils of faction ; and again did her arms drive dread into the heart of Venice, and again did her commercial name stand forth first in Italy.

By a small fact the latent spark of popular feeling was ignited—one of those small facts in history, the vast results of which turn the channel of events, and give a new tone to a whole country. Philip IV. of France had twenty Genoese galleys to assist him in his wars with Edward III. of England ; when anchored off the coast of Flanders the Ligurian sailors mutinied against their captain, Antonio D'Oria, and, headed by one Capurro, a sailor of Voltri, they sent a deputation to the French king, laying their case before him and seeking redress. Philip, however, chose to take the side of the captain, and ordered Capurro to be put to death, whereupon the sailors returned to Genoa, furious that a king of France should espouse the cause of the nobles against them.

Through the Riviera they passed, raising sedition at each step, and crying, "Alas, poor Capurro! alas, for his children and his widow! and alas, for Voltri, his country! alas, for us, too, a people whom magistrates rule, who satisfy their caprice with the gallows!" At Savona they assembled the people in the church, and stump orators harangued a crowd bent on revolution. When this spirit spread to the capital, it assumed a more systematic tone ; a change there must be, and the assembled multitude determined that the decision, as to what it should be, was to rest with them.

Perceiving the coming storm, the captains—a Spinola and a D'Oria as usual—began concessions, but too late. In the midst of an excited multitude, a gold-beater rose up and said,

" *Do ye wish that I should tell you something for your good?* "
Laughing at the absurd little man, the people with one accord
shouted " No." Nothing daunted, however, the gold-beater
exclaimed, "*Let it be Simone Boccanegra.*" The innocent
object of this haphazard choice was a quiet, demure merchant,
who chanced to be standing by. And, like an Italian crowd
that it was, startled, and amused by the novelty, and perhaps
liking the recurrence of the name of the captain they had
elected a century before, the assembled multitude with one
accord cried out " *Let Simone Boccanegra be abbot of the
people.*"

Taking the opportunity of a hush, prudent Boccanegra
quietly thanked them, and declined. His refusal made them
the more eager, and they cried, "*Let him be our lord*" (signore).
Again Boccanegra declined an honour, the very name of which
smacked of feudalism in liberal nostrils. Then at length a
cry arose, and was echoed from mouth to mouth, " *We wish
him for our Doge.*" To this Boccanegra quietly assented, and
was carried to the palace in triumph by the people, who, wild
with excitement, rushed through the streets crying, "*Long live
the Doge!*" "*Long live the people!*" And the captains prudently withdrew from the town.

Thus did Simone Boccanegra become the first doge of
Genoa, by divine inspiration, they said—rather flattering indeed
to the small gold-beater—and he was to hold the office for life,
whilst a council of wise men chosen from all ranks and classes
of the citizens was appointed to guide and restrain his actions.

For the peaceful quiet merchant it was a bad day when
fortune pitched upon him to rule Genoa. The post was an un-
enviable one, for if at first all went well, with the troublesome
nobles expatriated, and the people all adoring him, he was
not long in discovering that his enemies were not a few. Of
how his armament put down the refractory nobles at Monaco,
and then scoured the Mediterranean, and made the Ligurian
name dreaded throughout its length and breadth, we shall

speak hereafter.[1] From this humble Ligurian merchant the
Khan of the Tartars sought peace, and paid to him a tribute.
In fact, Simone Boccanegra, for a short period after his election, was as powerful as any monarch then reigning on an
ancestral throne.

But the nobles from without, and the nobles from within,
were constantly fanning a discontented spirit, which culminated
in 1345, and Simone Boccanegra descended from his high
estate, and the doge's cap was conferred on one Giovanni di
Murta, whose views were more consistent with those of the
nobles.

In 1356, however, Boccanegra was re-elected to his post of
honour, and ruled this time with redoubled strength.   All
the Riviera was under his control, he was leagued with most
of the leading houses of Italy, he checked the growing power
of the Visconti, and thereby established the balance of power
in Italy.   Thus was his name and fame, and with it the
renown of the republic, established far and wide ; he advanced
commerce and navigation in all its branches, and was in fact
the very man to lead Genoa on to the position of foremost
amongst the States of Italy.   His government represented all
the popular interests of both Guelphic and Ghibelline factions
combined, whilst the more powerful and power-loving nobles
were either exiled or deprived of their posts of honour.

His untimely death, in 1363, draws a veil over this incipient
prosperity.   At a banquet at Sturla, where he was entertaining
Peter de Lusignan, king of Cyprus, who had come to Genoa
in the vain hopes of arousing the old crusading ardour, Simone
Boccanegra was poisoned.   The fatal potion was administered
by a noble Genoese, one Malocello, a favourite and a councillor
of the Cypriot king's ; and after several days of agony the first
doge of Genoa died in the ducal palace.   Knowing that his
end was near, the council thought fit to elect a successor to
the ducal chair ; and as Boccanegra lay in his last mortal

[1] *Vide* ch. v.

agony, he heard the shouts of joy which announced the election of a new popular idol.

This plebeian family of Boccanegra became the object of such fierce hatred and persecution from the nobles on their return to power, that at the end of the fifteenth century not a single member was left in Genoa. A brother of the doge's, Egidio Boccanegra, and his line, were more fortunate. Egidio went with twenty galleys to assist Alphonso XI. of Castille against the Moors, and was appointed admiral of the Spanish fleet, and made count of Palma near Seville, where his descendants continued to reside in possession of this title until quite a recent date. One member of this family was a painter, whose pictures still adorn the cathedral of Granada.

The house in which the first doge was born, and lived prior to his honours, is still seen and marked in Genoa, in one of her busy alleys; also a villa which he possessed at S. Martino d'Albaro; and his tomb still occupies a prominent position on the steps of the university—removed thither from S. Francesco di Castelletto when that church was dismantled. It is in marble, and three lions support his recumbent figure; and an epitaph relates how he died, a sacrifice to his country, by the hand of Malocello. Here he lies in effigy, the first of Genoa's many doges, and perhaps the last who had the interest of the public thoroughly at heart, with his hands crossed over his long tunic, which was of scarlet, and his triangular biretta on his head. It is a peaceful pleasant tomb to look upon, and one which conjures up some of the balmiest recollections of Ligurian history—a sort of oasis in the blank desert of faction.

It was in those days of turbulence which we have thus traversed that the poet Dante was acquainted with Genoa. Early in the fourteenth century he wandered amongst the ruins of Luna, and along the Riviera, and tells us many a little bit which identifies the history of the times. With pious wrath he alludes to the assassination of one Michel

Zante, by Branca D'Oria, in a factious brawl, and in his verses we see the intense feeling of disgust which rankled in his mind at the state of Genoa.

> "Ah ! ye men at variance
> With every virtue, full of every vice,
> Wherefore are ye not scattered from the world."
>
> *Inferno* 33.

It is curious to find authors and poets at vastly distant epochs abusing our Genoese. Virgil thought Liguria almost a synonym for deceit. Dante expresses himself as above ; whilst Horace Walpole thus enunciates his opinion of Genoa : " I hate the Genoese ; they make a commonwealth the most devilish of all tyrannies."

Nevertheless, from his intercourse with the Ligurian republic, Dante learnt much for his pen.[1] He was near Genoa when he wrote about the wanderings of Ulysses. He was acquainted with Andalò di Negro, the great Genoese astrologer and cosmographer, who incited Marco Polo to write the history of his travels ; and the words he puts into Ulysses' mouth breathe the spirit of enterprise of the age. In reading his account of the dread pillars of Hercules, and "the deep illimitable main beyond,"[2] we are carried back to the days of Genoa's early efforts to tread these unexplored ocean paths, which led to the discovery of America by a Genoese.

---

[1] The difficulty of reading Dante is enhanced by the frequency with which he introduces Genoese words unknown to the rest of Italy. A shrill hissing dialect is that of Genoa, and in cases well suited for poetic expression. The poet himself thus passes his judgment upon it. "If the Genoese, through forgetfulness, should lose the letter 'z,' it would be necessary for them to remain mute, or else to find another means of elocution." Dante introduced into his vocabulary, amongst other Genoese words, the following : " chiappa," for " ardesia," a slate—chi-che is pronounced as in Spanish and English in Genoa—" Potevam sut montar di chiappa inchiappa " (*Inf.* 24) ; " barba," for " zio," an uncle—" L'opere sozze del barba e de fratel." (*Parad.* 19) ; " a randa," for " rasente," close to—" Quivi fermammo i piedi a randa a randa " (*Inf.* 14).

[2] *Inf.* Cant. 26.

F

CHAPTER IV.

GENOA AND HER PISAN RIVAL.

THE old commonwealth of Pisa, rich in historical lore of early maritime development, of ardent crusading enterprise, of firm adherence to the imperial cause, in her day was one of the foremost leaders of Italian spirit.

> " The proud mart of Pisa,
> Queen of the western waves,"[1]

was, for several centuries, the strongest bulwark of Christendom against the infidel.   Through her instrumentality was brought about what kings and emperors had failed to achieve—the recovery of the island of Sardinia from the Saracen.   There she had judges, and there she had bishops under her, and there it was that she first came into contact with Genoa ; this island was at once the scene of her greatest successes and the origin of her doom.

How Pisa, in 1063, burst the chains of the harbour of Palermo, and from the rich booty gained therefrom built her glorious marble cathedral ; how, a century later, her Saracenic-looking baptistery, and her leaning tower, were placed as its fitting companions ; and again, how yet another century saw the Campo Santo added, as if by magic wand, to the fairy trio, every Italian traveller is well aware.

[1] Macaulay.

" There is a sacred place within her walls . . .
Where yet remain apart from all things else,
Four, such as nowhere on earth are seen
Assembled." [1]

Genoa, in her grandest days, could never do for art what
Pisa did ; yet Genoa, in her weakest days, held her own against
the Queen of the Arno ; and when she gloried in all the pride
of her riches and her strength, it was destruction and ruin
which Genoa carried into the very heart of her rival ; through
Genoa's instrumentality the commerce was driven from the
mouth of the Arno, and the diadem of that river was removed
from the head of Pisa to that of Florence.

In this deadly rivalry between Genoa and Pisa we see all
the subtle influence at work which made Italy what it was—a
heterogeneous mass of rival towns. In the first place, there
was the natural rivalry of commercial and colonial projects engendered by the crusades. This might have been wholesome,
and easily kept in check, had it not been for influences which
worked upon them from without. It was the policy of the
emperors to pit one hated republic against the other ; it was
the policy of the popes to keep them separate, for fear of
raising up too powerful a body on Italian soil.

Thus situated, no power existed to part the Griffin and
the Fox, the rival emblems of the rival republics, in this
deadly war, in which one of them must succumb ; and for two
centuries the contest fluctuated with varied success, until the
fatal day of Meloria left Genoa in a position to dictate the
terms of her rival's downfall.

During the early depredations of the Saracens, Pisan and
Genoese fleets acted in unison, to rid the Mediterranean of the
scourge which troubled both ; but when it happened that the
Lombard cities preferred the port of Genoa for their disem-
barkations, and the German emperors showed a marked preference for that of Pisa, a sort of rivalry sprang up, a rivalry

[1] Rogers.

which developed itself into a struggle for the mastery of the " western waves."

But it was Pope Benedict VIII. who threw the real apple of discord between the two republics in 1015, by granting the possession of the islands of Corsica and Sardinia to whichever of them should first drive out the infidel. Then, in the annals of Pisa, side by side with their contests against the Saracen, appear the more fatal ones with their sister republic and Genoa's modest but useful ally, the commonwealth of Lucca. It was this papal grant which wove the first threads of the net in which the Pisan fox was captured and enchained.

Thus event after event occurred which tended to rouse the jealousy of Genoa. Pisa became all powerful in Sardinia. Pisa strove likewise to become all powerful in Corsica ; and Urban II., in 1091, out of affection for the Pisan bishop Damberto, and out of love for that "dearest daughter of the blessed Peter," the Countess Matilda, gave Corsica as a perpetual donation to Pisa, and moreover raised Damberto to the rank of an archbishop, with full power of consecrating all the Corsican bishops. The Corsicans, however, a wild and independent race, spurned this wholesale treatment of their welfare, and stuck faithfully to the Genoese cause, with what results to themselves the course of after events will show.[1]

This was the firebrand which the popes cast between Genoa and Pisa, and a contest, fraught with all the horrors of civil war, between two neighbouring cities was the result. If Genoa was strong, and if she held her own against Pisa, mattered not just then ; neither of the belligerents were in a position to strike a decisive blow. But it was of far more importance to the Genoese cause, when a pope, Calixtus II., took their part. He had passed through Genoa, consecrated their churches,[2] and had been fawned upon to a degree highly pleasing to his dignity. Moreover, it was grievous to him, that, owing to the quarrels between the rival republics, the two

---

[1] *Vide* ch. xv.   [2] *Vide* ch. iii.

props of Italian Christendom, the Saracens should be allowed to carry their ravages even to the very gates of Rome. So Calixtus determined to call together a council at the Lateran, the first that bore that name, with the ostensible motive of bringing about a peace, and with the ulterior one of assisting Genoa.

From Genoa came the annalist Caffaro as her representative, and Pisa sent her hot-headed Archbishop Roger to plead her cause. An old document still exists in the archives of Genoa, which shows how the Ligurian Republic was accustomed to gain her ends. Seven thousand marks were given to the Pope, three hundred marks were distributed amongst the cardinals, and smaller sums to various influential bishops; in fact, it was a delightful network of bribery. No wonder poor Pisa was vanquished in this underhand fray; no wonder her enraged Archbishop Roger cast down his mitre and his ring at the papal feet, and with these words of indignation prepared to leave the conclave: " I will no longer be your archbishop or your bishop." The enraged pontiff spurned the mitre and ring from him with his feet, and with undignified rage shouted to the retiring archbishop, " Thou hast done wrong, Roger ; I promise thee thou shalt live to repent it."

With sorrowful heart and evil forebodings Roger betook himself to the banks of the Arno, and the hearts of the Pisans sank within them at his hasty return, and at the tale he told ; whilst Caffaro brought back gladness and joy to the hearths of Genoa at this hollow victory. Thus ended the Council, and thus again the war broke out with redoubled vigour.

But Pisa now fought under grave disadvantages. She was under the papal ban, and the more formidable attack of the papal allies hemmed her in on every side. Her ships were wrecked and beaten, her commerce was cut off from her, and her enemies everywhere victorious. Her success was no better when she tried to meet her rivals with the secret weapons of bribery, when another Pope, Onorius II., occupied the papal chair.   The Genoese were always first in the secret chambers of the Vatican, and always first in every undertaking, from Sicily even to the fair fields of Provence.   At length Pisa, overcome by stress of circumstances, and Genoa sufficiently exultant with her successes, consented to listen to the more pastor-like advice of Pope Innocent II.

This Pontiff was ably backed up in his pacific intentions by St. Bernard, the celebrated abbot of Clairvaulx.   His Holiness keenly desired to recover his territories, which were in the hands of an antipope ; and St. Bernard, actuated, perhaps, by stronger feelings of humanity, penned a letter to Genoa, which he concluded in the following strain : " If the love of war actuates you, O Genoese, if it is grateful to you to prove your strength, let not the impetus of your generous ire be directed against your neighbours and your friends, but against the enemies of your Church."

Thus were Genoa and Pisa pacified in 1133.

Out of this struggle Genoa gained an archbishop's mitre for her metropolitan ; and the two rival republics, thus placed on religious equality, divided the cure of Corsican souls between them, and then joined in fighting the battles of a Pope whose wisdom had pacified them.

The second contest in which Genoese met Pisan was echoed from across the Alps, when Frederic Barbarossa left his German home and brought destruction and tyranny into the plains of Italy.   Portentous of coming woe was that celebrated Diet of Roncaglia, whither each city sent its representatives to do homage to the grasping Teuton.

On the road to the Lombard plain we see the annalist Caffaro again despatched with presents to appease the imperial wrath—silks brought from the fall of Lisbon,[1] parrots, ostriches, and two lions from Africa—a goodly proof of the world-wide riches of the Ligurian Republic.   Caffaro returned

---

[1] *Vide* ch. v.

home with soft messages and goodly promises, the hollowness
of which Genoa was not long in realizing, when the fiery
German scourge was let loose on the rest of Northern Italy.
Forthwith her councillors prudently set to work to build walls,
to form alliances with Barbarossa's enemies in the shape of
William, King of Sicily, and the weak and terrified Emperor
of the East. And thus was Genoa busily engaged at home.

Men, women, and children, halt and lame, all assisted in
the arduous task of surrounding Genoa with a strong defence.
The archbishop melted down his chalices of gold ; women
brought their jewellery to be melted down, and in eight days
Genoa was girt with a handsome wall, traces of which are even
now to be seen in the very heart of the town. In the densely
populated quarter of St. Andrea rises the gateway of that
name, with its Gothic arch and bastion towers, and on either
side of it extend massive walls, now dimly fading away into
the squalid houses built upon, against, and underneath the
venerable fortification ; whilst inside the gateway is still read
an inscription which tells of its erection. From the arch of
this Porta di St. Andrea until quite a recent date, was hung
part of the chains brought from the Pisan harbour, both gate
and chains existing here in the very centre of Genoa, as a
testimony of how the Ligurians fought and conquered in their
day the proudest of Germany's emperors, and his republican
ally.

In Genoa thus defended and begirt, Barbarossa found the
strongest resistance to his arms in Northern Italy, so that at
length he was constrained to temporize with the Ligurians,
whose courage on this occasion had warded off the fate which
had befallen most Italian towns ; and intent as he was on his
conquest of Sicily, it occurred to him that it might be expedient to obtain the Genoese galleys for this purpose by peaceful
means. Not long was it before they had cause to rue any
overtures of peace they might have made with this treacherous
emperor ; for no sooner did he perceive that he could get his

galleys from Pisa with equal ease than he entered into a treaty with that republic, promising her broad acres of Genoese territory if she would declare war against her rival, and provide him the fleet he required. And by this stroke of policy he again plunged the two Republics in deadly strife. Intent on his conquest of Sicily, he cared little about his republican allies or his republican foes; it was sufficient for him to have thrown a new apple of discord between them, as the Pope had done in the first war. Probably he looked on with intense satisfaction ·at the mischief he had made, as thereby two troublesome powers were too much occupied in their own affairs to oppose his schemes.

It was not only in Italy that Pisan and Genoese carried on their rivalry; wherever their commercial enterprise took them there was sure to be some dispute—in Palestine, in Provence, and, above all, in Constantinople, where, says the annalist Caffaro, ten thousand Pisans attacked three hundred Genoese and burnt their warehouses. In this fray a young Genoese noble was killed with barbarous outrage, and those who escaped home swelled the list of complaints against the hated rival.

During these years of conflict and scenes of horror the aged Caffaro passed away (1163), and in him we lose a valuable assistant in threading the maze of crime and bloodshed, which he relates with a simplicity and truthfulness which brings each fact more forcibly to view. It is pleasing to find that he could close his annals with some details of improvement and progress in Genoa. He relates how the Borgo di Prè was beautified with a new street, which led down to the busy quays—the venerable Borgo di Prè which still exists as a portion of Genoa, and which earned its name in the days when shiploads of booty (prede) returned from the sack of Saracenic towns; and here, in the open space before the venerable church of S. Giovanni, the treasures were meted out to the deserving.

Meanwhile Frederic Barbarossa was busy with his Sicilian wars, and from time to time, by sending peaceful messages to each republic, secretly added fresh fuel to the fire of rivalry ; until at length an enterprising genius in Sardinia managed to gather around him the threads of this contest, and made himself the object for which the rivals fought. Three rulers, or judges, in those days superintended the welfare of the island, under the eye of Pisa. Of these the judges of Cagliari and Torres thought fit to seize upon the territory of the third, Barrisone, judge of Arborea. Promptly did the exiled judge betake himself to Genoa, where he was sure of obtaining aid. The Republic promised him money, gave him advice, and sent him with a goodly array of followers to Crema, where Barbarossa held his court, and recommended him boldly to demand the throne of Sardinia for himself ; and again did Genoa outwit her rival by a prompt outlay of money which induced the emperor to further her schemes.

With a king of Sardinia in their possession, and at their beck and call, the Genoese were exultant, and the Pisans again trembled for their very existence in the island. In vain did they protest against a vassal of theirs being raised to the regal estate. They could do nothing but join their forces with those of the other Sardinian judges, and prepare for war.

But poor King Barrisone found his affairs not over flourishing when it came to actual war. The Genoese had promised him four thousand marks, with which to buy his crown from the emperor ; but those Ligurian merchants were very cunning, and very slow in parting with their gold. They held back in their payment, and they tried to get Barrisone to pay as much of it as he could himself, until the emperor was furious when he found his marks not forthcoming, and threatened to carry the newly elected king with him as prisoner to Germany. On his knees Barrisone implored the compassion of the Genoese consul, who at length promised that the money should be forthcoming within four months, and after much difficulty the emperor was induced to wait.   Hard and stringent were the conditions imposed by the republicans on this wretched king —immediate repayment, a war subsidy, and a handsome donation to the cathedral of San Lorenzo, recognition of the archbishop of Genoa as primate of Sardinia, and other concessions, which would make Barrisone a mere puppet in the hands of Genoa ; and when he had signed this treaty, he was provided with a few ships and his four thousand marks, the price of his kingdom.

Many a long day were the Genoese creditors before they saw their money.   Beyond the empty name of king, Barrisone got but little in Sardinia, whilst the Genoese only established for themselves a hopeless and endless dispute with Pisa ; and for years this suicidal war continued, in which now a Genoese took a Pisan ship, and now a Genoese castle fell into the enemy's hands, to be reconquered in a few months.   This war with Pisa was a lengthened scene of rapine and bloodshed ; and if for a moment peace was established, internal faction would spring up ; and then came pestilence and famine in the train of all this misery.   Nothing can prove more clearly the intense vitality contained in these mediæval commercial cities than the fact that they not only continued to exist, but after the fiery trial burst out into greater magnificence than before.

This is the picture we have before us, and a melancholy, tedious drama it is.   Frederic Barbarossa, like Jove, ruling the destinies of men, hovers at one time over Italy, at another time he is across the Alps, when his absence causes men to breathe more freely.   On the narrow stage of the Mediterranean stand the two combatants, Genoa and Pisa, fighting for the possession of Sardinia, their archbishops and their puppet kings put forward as the *casus belli*, whilst the wretched inhabitants of these two republics fall stricken and decimated by the continued struggle.

Gradually the more youthful republics of Lucca and Florence got dragged into the fray; the contest was one of diplomacy rather than strength, and the Genoese were always the readiest with their purse-strings. Perhaps they had longer ones, perhaps they did not spend so much on lovely churches as the religious Pisans, who showed their lack of the wisdom of this world in spending their gains thus, instead of filling the coffers of the emperor, and purchasing allies.

Hemmed in on all sides, yet not giving way, the brave Pisans must have hailed with satisfaction the unanimous outcry of christendom for peace, in 1175, in order that all might unite in the third Crusade. According to the terms of this peace, Genoa was allowed to keep all her conquests in Sardinia, and full power to maintain her claims on the meagre exchequer of King Barrisone. Thus a thousand Pisans and a thousand Genoese swore to maintain eternal friendship, and to further the interests of christendom. But in this pacification we can but trace the effects of the German emperor's occupation elsewhere; for in giving Barbarossa enough to do in the north of Italy, the Lombard League removed the existing evil, and enabled the ardour of rivalry between Pisa and Genoa to cool down. In 1183, the peace of Constance broke the power of the emperor, and brought peace and contentment to the hearths of the rival republics, and when at length he of the red beard breathed his last in eastern climes, Italy was again able to attend to her internal discords, perhaps better thus than employed quarrelling with her neighbours at the suggestion of a foreign prince, who hoped thereby to crush them one by one without expending his own men and money in so doing.

Out of this contest Genoa had gained far more for her commerce and her fame than at the time she realized—an undisputed position in Corsica and Sardinia, undoubted superiority along the coasts of the Riviera, whilst her

cathedral was enriched by rich glebes in Sardinia. There is
still to be seen a curious old map done in fresco on the walls
of the archbishop's palace in Genoa, which marks in red the
castles and territories in Sardinia handed over to the Metropolitan Church, from which tribute was due; and thus has
Genoa, in her own peculiar way, proved to posterity the extent
of her power, and corroborated the statements of annalists
by indelible statistics posted up on her walls.

A desultory series of wars and peaces, to be broken al-
most as soon as made, ushered in the thirteenth century for
Genoa and Pisa, each republic snatching at every straw with
which she hoped to strike a blow at her hated rival. It was
with this intent that Genoa warmly espoused the cause of the
Pope, and Pisa as warmly espoused that of the Emperor
Frederic II., in his wars against the pontiff. Hence we find
Genoese galleys employed in transporting the prelates who
were to figure at the Lateran Council for the deposition of
Frederic, and in Genoa was held a congress of these worthies
prior to their embarking for Rome. Whilst, on the other
hand, at Pisa, in 1241, were assembled the imperial forces, and
a fleet to oppose the pontiff's plans.

From the port of Genoa, the poor prelates started on their
luckless errand. Contrary winds drove them into all the ports
along the Ligurian coast, and the Genoese squadron at length
was confronted by the Pisan and imperial fleet at Meloria,
and was hopelessly routed, and the terrified priests found themselves the prisoners of the German Emperor. The Genoese
at home were awestruck at this defeat, more especially as
they were expecting daily a large fleet heavily laden with
eastern merchandize, and far more anxiety was felt for its safe
arrival than for the fate of the unhappy prelates in the conqueror's dungeons. Their forebodings, however, were turned
into joy when the sails of the looked-for vessels were seen on
the horizon, and they put into the harbour amidst shouts of
joy; for the nonce the well-to-do merchants shook their well-

lined purses, and for the moment forgot their pontifical ally and his troubles.

A new outburst of interest in this dreary struggle was awakened in Genoa when a Genoese cardinal, Sinibaldo Fieschi, was raised to the pontifical dignity and assumed the name of Innocent IV. These Fieschi[1] were already great in Genoa. They had vague claims of descent from some Bavarian prince; but all that is definitely known of them is that they were counts of Lavagna, a family well known to Dante, and who, after fighting well for Genoa against Pisa, were taken into the family circle, so to speak, and took a leading position for weal or woe within the city walls.

The Cardinal Fieschi had been a firm adherent and a trusted friend of Frederic II.'s, before his elevation to the papacy, and, on hearing of his election, the emperor exclaimed that he had lost a most friendly cardinal and had gained a most hostile Pope. So indeed it proved; for no pontiff was better calculated to break the power of this powerful Teuton than Innocent, backed up as he was by Genoa, by France, and by all that was free and noble in Italy, which influence no one knew better than he how to use.

Very hurried was this pontiff's election at Anagni, whither the trembling cardinals had repaired when they heard of the disaster at Meloria, and short was the breathing time allowed him before the German emperor was at the city gates. A hasty messenger was forthwith despatched to Genoa to implore aid, and twenty-two galleys were manned under pretence of proceeding against the Saracens, but secretly they turned into Civita Vecchia, and the hunted pontiff breathed again the air of safety on his country's galleys.

Though Genoese by birth, and the successor of the fisherman saint, Innocent took by no means kindly to the mighty deep. So ill was he from the effects of a storm, that he had to be landed at Porto Venere, and from thence proceeded to

---

[1] *Vide* ch. xiii.

Genoa by land.   Great were the rejoicings in his native
city at the arrival of the Pope.   They decked the carriage
which brought him with cloth of gold and rich silks ; they
strewed rich tapestries and flowers along the path which led
to his lodgings in the archbishop's palace, where now, on the
dingy mouldering walls, Innocent's cynical countenance looks
out from a dingy mouldering fresco, telling how he fought
and how he crushed the Teuton emperor.

Enraged was Frederic when he learnt of the Pope's escape.
"I had well-nigh checkmated him," he exclaimed, "and
Genoa has removed the chessmen." With this sage remark
he hurried to Pisa, there to see to the arming of fresh galleys,
whilst Innocent busied himself in calling a council at Lyons.
But the Pope's frame was enfeebled by his trials, and at Sestri
di Ponente, five miles from Genoa, he had to rest to recoup his
strength.   Though pressed much by his Genoese advisers to
take the sea route to France instead of the land one, poor
Innocent determined not again to encounter the horrors of
the deep, preferring rather to hazard, with Genoese assistance,
the dangers of the land.   So he threaded his way through
the network of marquises and counts who lived like bull-dogs
along the Riviera, in the emperor's pay, until he reached the
city of Lyons.

The Genoese took the opportunity of this visit from their
native Pope to adopt for themselves a new and magnificent
seal.   They placed their griffin—the mystic animal under
whose protection they fought, and the animal whose name
their citadel then bore—over a crouching eagle, and a still
more crouching fox, with the claws of the triumphant griffin
deeply embedded in their flesh, thereby symbolizing their
victory over the high-flying Emperor and the crafty Pisa.   All
memory of this is now lost, save the old seal of the Commune,
and the inscription still legible in the Bank of St. George ;[1]
and if rather premature, nevertheless the wish, which had

[1] *Vide* ch. xi.

been father to this offspring of their proud brains, was soon to be realized.

From the Council of Lyons Innocent fulminated his celebrated anathemas against the emperor; and these, coupled with the unwearying zeal of the Genoese pontiff in opposing the arms of Frederic at Parma and Piacenza, soon brought about his downfall. It was a rapid one; and with his death Italy was again relieved from her German tyrants. Thus did the Genoese griffin, in the shape of her native pontiff, checkmate the eagle; and before the close of this century we shall see the fox of Pisa, bereft of her Ghibelline allies, falling a sacrifice to the same foe.

" Pisa, renowned for grave citizens,"[1] had indeed cause to look doubly grave when she saw, not only Genoa, but Florence and Lucca, arming against her; and at the compact made between these three republics her doom was sealed.

The Pope, meanwhile, on hearing of Frederic's death, hastened by way of Genoa towards his capital. No honour that a grateful people could heap on a beloved citizen was spared as Innocent passed through their town. The chief magistrates met him outside the walls, and his entrance recalls the triumphant processions of ancient Rome. For days Genoa was *en fête*, whilst crowds of Guelphic ambassadors came to congratulate the pontiff on his return to Italian soil. Though worn out by illness the old man was still eager to follow up his advantages. He pursued the luckless house of Swabia out of Naples, and did not relent his bitter enmity against them until death carried him off, anathematizing with his last breath the successor of his foe. He was indeed an intrepid man, and a staunch upholder of what he deemed the rights of the Church.

Against overpowering odds the commonwealth of Pisa now contended; but spiritedly she manned her galleys, and courageously she repaired her castles, one of which, at Lerici,

---

[1] Shakespeare, *Taming of the Shrew*, act i. sc. i.

bears to this day this scornful defiant inscription over its
portal in boastful patois—

> " A mouth emptier for the Genoese,
>   A heart breaker for the Porto Venerese,
>   A purse stealer for the Lucchese." [1]

To follow the events of this war would be a thankless
task, with its details of strife all through the Mediterranean,
centred in the sister isles of Corsica [2] and Sardinia ; so

LERICI.

let us hurry on to the climax of 1284, which Genoese historians write down as the most glorious year in their annals,
the Pisans as the most humiliating, and the rest of Italy as
the most disastrous, when two of her brightest stars met in
deadly conflict. In this year the battle of Meloria was fought,
and in this year much of the best blood in Italy was shed.

By prodigious exertions Pisa got together seventy-two

---

[1] " Scopa bocà al Zenese,
      Crepa cuore al Porto Venerese,
      Streppa borsello al Lucchese."
[2] *Vide* ch. xv.

galleys for the combat, which with some smaller vessels were put under the command of Alberto Morosini, a Venetian by birth, and a relation of the reigning Doge in Venice. It is surprising that, even though on intimate terms with Pisa, Venice raised not a helping hand to save her. She paid the penalty of her folly hereafter, by having to fight Genoa single-handed.

This fleet was manned by the flower of the Pisan nobility, and as it lay in the Porto Pisano looked a goodly and invincible armada. On the dawn of the 6th of August, at the rumour of the approach of the Genoese, the Pisans hurried to their ships; the archbishop came down to bless them before they started, the townsfolk came down to give them a parting cheer and take part in the benediction, when lo! evil omen that it was, an omen which damped the heart of the bravest, the handle of the archbishop's cross gave way, and the figure thereon was swallowed in the waves. Amidst the awe-struck, speechless Pisans, an impious voice was heard to exclaim, "Take courage, O Pisans! why fear ye? Let Christ be in favour of the Genoese, if the wind be in ours."

A circumstance in this war is curiously illustrative of the etiquette of mediæval warfare. Morosini, with his Pisan galleys, entered the gulf of Genoa, and finally cast anchor off Chiavari, into which town he cast silver arrows, which in those days was considered a deadly insult, and calculated to inspire the opponent with a dread of their enemy's opulence and resources. But his taunts were unavailing to bring the Genoese to close quarters. A richly-dressed emissary was sent to him with the following polite message: "The Genoese, my lord, send you greeting, and beg of you to bear in mind that but little honour can accrue to you by bidding them defiance, as long as half their fleet is at a distance, and half not ready for sea. Return to your port, and rest assured that ere long we shall visit you."

G

In compliance with this request Morosini returned home, and failed to strike a blow which, though a breach of international honour, would then have been decisive in Pisa's favour.

Meanwhile the Genoese had strenuously prepared for the coming death-struggle. Thirty galleys under Benedetto Zacharia, and eighty under Oberto D'Oria, met off the promontory of Portofino, and hastened in the direction of Pisa together, with Oberto D'Oria as admiral of the whole. He formed his ships into the shape of a triangle, of which he led the van himself, having on his left the galleys of San Matteo as the D'Oria's own special property, and on his right the ships of the Spinola family and their dependents. Thus arranged, the Genoese directed their course towards the rock of Meloria, and D'Oria thus harangued his men :—"Here is that rock of Meloria ; a Genoese defeat has rendered it famous,[1] a victory would render it immortal. For more than two centuries we have fought against the Pisans, and for the last two years we have received convincing proofs of the justice of our cause. Now is the moment ; in the conflict which impends, country, liberty, and the safety of our families are at stake. Let us conquer, O Genoese! and we shall have gained all."

On this address, with one accord the sailors raised the shout of St. George, and fell to their oars to make good the distance between themselves and their foes.

The port of Pisa was defended on the south by this rock of Meloria, and another rock called Montenero to the west shut in the harbour, across which a mighty chain was stretched to prevent ingress or egress against the will of the defenders. It was about sixteen miles from the city and eight from the mouth of the Arno, and opposite to this spot the heated animosity of the two rivals was let loose in fearful and terrible earnest.

[1] *Vide* ch. iii.

Of mediæval naval warfare the battle of Meloria is a good instance. Every known invention in the art of war was here brought into play. Arrows, lances, spears and battle-axes darkened the air; burning oil mixed with soap flowed in every direction, and a dense hissing noise, as if the gates of hell were loosened, maddened the suspense of the trembling Pisans, who watched their fate from the shore. The blue waters of the Mediterranean were tinged with the blood of the slain, and around the contending ships seethed a heaving mass of corpses, and drowning men fighting with their last desperate breath even here, until the sea covered them over, and locked in deadly embrace they sank to rise no more.

Around the standard-bearing ships the battle raged the fiercest, now one, now the other almost grasped the longed for prize, until at length the Pisan standard fell, stricken by a mighty blow. But the cause of their defeat lay not so much in this loss as in the fact that an ally of theirs, Count Ugolino della Gherardesca, was but lukewarm in his ardour, hoping by a cunning manipulation of affairs to obtain for himself the lordship of Pisa. In the heat of the contest this treacherous count deserted, with his galleys, the Pisan fleet, and hurrying to the city, told the senators that all was lost.

Disheartened by this defection and the loss of their standard the Pisans' courage gradually gave way. Their admiral, Morosini, fell into Genoese hands, together with the seal of the Commune, an imperial eagle round which was written, " Seal of Alberto Morosini, Podestà and Generalissimo in war by sea and land of the Commune of Pisa."

In the disorder and confusion which ensued the Genoese took twenty-nine galleys, sank seven others, and the rest retired, crestfallen, within the chains of the harbour. At the fall of night the Ligurian fleet beat a retreat homewards, having suffered so severely themselves that they were prevented from following up their victory, and possessing themselves of the almost unprotected town. The loss had been

terrible on both sides. " If Pisa 'mourned," ran the saying,
" Genoa did not laugh." And Pisan and Genoese differ hopelessly about the number of the slain; but by the lowest
computation Genoa is stated to have taken home on her
galleys no less than 9272 prisoners, which was a goodly loss
on one day for a single city, together with her slain.

All the Pisan nobility, seventeen judges, and their podestà,
swelled the numbers of the captives and the slain, and thus
ran the proverb of the day, " He who would see Pisa must go
to Genoa." A piteous sight it was to see the nine thousand
dejected Pisans disembarked in chains on the quays of Genoa,
alive with joyous inhabitants, who forgot their mourning and
their grief in this moment of exultant triumph. And thus
ended the day of Meloria ; and thus was Pisa crushed never
again to hold her own as a leading commercial town in Italy.

Venice requested the liberation of Alberto Morosini as
her own subject, and it was granted him on condition that he
never returned to the Government of Pisa ; but the other
prisoners were not so fortunate, and languished in their
dungeons down by the quay until their friends at home,
anxious to release them, offered to concede to the Genoese
the castle of Sangro and broad lands in Sardinia ; but the
patriotic captives with one accord refused to accept their
liberty on such terms, and a secret message was despatched
to the senate at home positively declining to be released at so
grave a loss to their country. So they continued to endure their
misery and privations until peace restored them to their homes.

On seeing Pisa thus stricken, her enemies all eagerly came
to the fore to demand her further humiliation, whilst her
friends were slow in offering assistance. Florence and Lucca
entered into a further compact with Genoa not to leave a
stone unturned until Pisa was thoroughly crushed. These
two inland republics were to keep a brisk attack by land,
whilst Genoa carried on her operations by sea. And this
league was soon swelled by minor satellites—Prato, Pistoia,

Volterra, and others—who all swore solemnly not to put down their arms till the glory of Pisa was no more ; and each of them looked forward to some castle or sum of money out of the proposed dismemberment of.the pride of the Arno.

A desultory warfare of four years ensued, in which Pisa's greatest safeguard was the desire each of the allies manifested to throw the onus of the war on each other's shoulders. At last Genoa took an opportunity to pause from hostilities, and made peace with Pisa on the following conditions : That Pisa should desist from assisting the Corsican rebels, that she should hand over the capital of Sardinia to the Ligurian Re-public, and should pay the expenses of the war, and likewise consolatory sums of money to the members of the League. Then were the prisoners restored to their homes, and the cat-like Genoa allowed her mouse-like foe just two years of rest, before she pounced upon her again with redoubled fury, and squeezed the very marrow out of her tortured bones.

In 1290, without any apparent reason for breaking the peace, without any offence from humbled Pisa, Genoa made a new compact with Lucca for another combined attack by sea and land. Conrad D'Oria, the son of the victor of Meloria, was deputed to ruin the Porto Pisano, whilst Lucca, advancing by land, ruined Leghorn and almost razed it to the ground.

No difficulty presented itself to Conrad D'Oria in his attack on the harbour; he pulled down its towers, its bridge, and its forts ; he cut the chain which secured the entrance to the harbour, and carried it back with him in triumph to Genoa ; and, for the assistance rendered by a blacksmith, Carlo Noceto, in this last exploit, the company of ironworkers in Genoa were ordered to celebrate a mass for his soul in the church of S. Sisto, in Genoa, in memory of his prowess, and in honour of the saint on whose day Meloria had been fought.

The chains thus taken to Genoa were hung about the town. A portion adorned the bank of St. George, another portion hung from the centre of the gateway of St. Andrea.

In this way did Genoa perpetuate her triumph ; and it was considered, some few years ago, an act of restored friendship and good feeling, when Genoa and Pisa entered the fold of Italian unity, that these mementos of former rivalry were restored to their former owners—a hollow mockery indeed, when her port was gone, and when the deserted streets of Pisa attest to the struggle she has had with ruin for centuries. But there they hang, in the Campo Santo, in that glorious sanctuary of mediæval art, with an appropriate inscription telling how generous Genoa restored these cruel reminders of hateful wars to Pisa, as a token of her everlasting and sisterly affection in this their happy union.

A singular marble monument is still visible in Genoa, re-

SLAB COMMEMORATING CAPTURE OF PORT OF PISA.

presenting the towers and battlements of the once almost impregnable port 'of Pisa ; it is let into the corner of a house just out of the woolstaplers' street (Via dei Lanieri), and it relates to unmindful posterity of how the great Conrad D'Oria destroyed this port almost six centuries ago.

Not satisfied with the destruction of her port, Genoa determined on cutting off all communication with the sea from her fallen rival. Huge blocks of stone were taken from the island of Capraia to block up the mouth of the Arno, so as effectually to stop the entrance of any large craft. As Dante expresses it :

> "Let the Capraia and Gorgona move,
> And make a hedge across the mouth of Arno,
> That every person in thee it may drown."
>
> *Inf.* 33.

It was thus that the Italian republics fought. Pisa had sacked and ruined her sister republic of Amalfi; she tore from her the precious Pandects of Justinian in 1135, and two years later returned to complete the work of devastation from which Amalfi never recovered. In the following century Genoa ruined Pisa at Meloria, and a hundred years later Venice fought a duel to the death with Genoa; and what Venice left undone the Visconti of Milan accomplished for the ruin of Ligurian liberty.

For the future Pisa was condemned to drag on her weary existence as an inland town. Even yet she might have succeeded in somewhat recouping her fortunes, judging by the vitality of other mediæval cities, and the grand superstructure which Florence built on her ruins. But by her disasters Pisa was thoroughly demoralized; her government became factious and tyrannical, her commerce was neglected, and never again could she raise her head against her Ligurian rival, until at last she became engulfed in Medicean tyranny; and to-day one sees nothing of the once proud queen of the Arno save

> "The towers
> Of Pisa, pining o'er her desert stream."
>
> ROGERS.

CHAPTER V.

GENOESE COMMERCE IN THE MEDITERRANEAN.

TRADE and commerce are by no means indigenous; they are the outcome of national intercourse, and a proof of civilization. Who, then, taught England how to trade, and how to traverse the ocean paths in search of the products of other climes? We answer unhesitatingly, the Flemish wool-staplers and the Portuguese navigators were our forerunners in those commercial fields. This to a certain extent is true; yet the commercial development of our isles was rather contemporary with that of those countries. We were, so to speak, the younger sister of those maritime nations from a commercial point of view, claiming as our common sire the republics of Italy—Genoa and Venice—and with the former of these our intercourse in those mediæval days was the greatest, as we shall hereafter see.

In the pedigree of commerce Italy's republics played the part of Noah in preserving through the deluge of barbarism a knowledge of the paths of civilization and national intercourse in which the Romans, Carthaginians, Greeks, and Phœnicians had in their generation respectively trodden. The bishops and ecclesiastics of Italy formed the depository, the ark of safety, so to speak, amongst whom alone reposed a knowledge of all that had gone before; and the Crusades played the part of Mount Ararat, from which all the contents of this ark poured forth its treasures to resuscitate the crushed but purified minds of men ; and from this date we fix the birth of modern development.

The sequel to those Holy Wars is best read in Italy, and in her republics. Whereas elsewhere the absence of monarchs, the drain on their exchequers, and the loss of the bravest and best blood wrought misery and discontent, in Venice and Genoa the Crusades formed the very fount of their political existence, and the commerce which flowed into them through Asiatic channels quite changed their character from marauding and freebooting communities to substantial bodies of respectable tradesmen ; and the study of Genoa's history for the three centuries after the Crusades is the study of one of those steps in the ladder of modern progress, on the present summit of which we ourselves now stand.

It was from the first Crusade to the fall of Acre, in 1291, that the Italians had it all their own way in Syria, and reaped the advantages of their assistance in raising up the crazy fabric of the Kingdom of Jerusalem. From this period to the discovery of the Cape of Good Hope, they shared the produce of the Indies with other Mediterranean towns ; and after this event commerce passed outside the pillars of Hercules, and was for ever lost to its originators.

During the first of these periods Italians strove keenly amongst themselves for streets, warehouses, and banks in all the ports of Syria, by means of which they were enabled to carry off and disperse through Europe the rich produce of the caravans, which, starting from the centre of Asia, gathered like snowballs on their way all the wealth of those Eastern countries.

Two treaties with two Christian princes, form the basis on which Genoa laid her commercial superstructure. One of them we have seen, when in 1105 Baldwin granted them streets in the principal towns of his kingdom,[1] and further

---

[1] *Vide* ch. ii.

promised to respect the property of Genoese in every part of his kingdom, and likewise that of the towns on the Riviera, Noli, Albenga, and Savona ; and four years later Genoa did a good stroke of business for herself in Tripoli, in Syria, which Raimond, Count of Toulouse, had won with their aid.   His son Beltrame met with some difficulty in getting possession of this from a relative, who had seized his patrimony during his absence in Toulouse.   With the assistance, however, of the brothers Embriaci, Ugo and Niccolo, the sons of Guglielmo, he recovered the town, and showered down his blessings on Genoa. Ugo Embriaco was presented with the feud of Biblos, Genoa was presented with a third part of the maritime dues both in Toulouse and Tripoli ; and to the cathedral of San Lorenzo he gave all Gibelletto and immunities for traders throughout all his provinces.   On the walls of the archbishop's palace in Genoa we still see the fresco which represents the monks on their way to Gibelletto to take possession of this gift in the name of their cathedral ; and eventually it was conceded to the veteran Guglielmo Embriaco, who farmed it, and paid the metropolitan a large annual rent. Thus was the road towards Egypt opened to them, and great were the profits that ensued therefrom.

When Guy de Lusignan was, in 1190, raised to the throne of Jerusalem, from the assizes of Jerusalem we gather that the following extensive privileges were enjoyed by the Genoese in the three great maritime ports of the kingdom, Sidon, Tyre, and Acre—

1. Absolute liberty of merchandize, and warehouses necessary for carrying it on.

2. The privilege of their own laws, tribunals, and consuls, in all except criminal cases.

3. Faculty of regulating weights and measures.

4. Exemption from all taxes.

5. A third share in the maritime dues.

As time went on, and the power of the Christians grew

less, Acre became the very stronghold of the kingdom, and
the centre of commerce ; thither flocked men of every nationality, and each mercantile nation had there its street, its warehouses, and its government building. In such a motley collection as this but little was required to foment disputes
amongst the rival merchants. Genoese and Pisans we find
early at work, but the King of Jerusalem favoured Pisa, and
the Genoese cause in Acre was rather injured thereby. But
their days of prosperity in Acre were numbered by a contest
with the Venetians, who having kept out of the fray for some
time, at length joined in.

Each republic had its separate storehouses and palaces ;
yet they had but one church in common, namely, that of
S. Sabbas, and struggles for precedence in officiating in this
formed a constant and fertile source of dispute.

One day, in the sacred edifice, Genoese and Venetians had
a regular hand-to-hand fight. The Genoese were worsted,
fled in confusion, had their warehouses burnt, and finally were
compelled to sign a treaty which excluded them from trading
here for three years ; and hence the centre of Genoese commerce was removed to Tyre. Here their consul resided, and
here they awaited until their three years of banishment from
Acre had expired. Marble pillars from S. Sabbas were sent
in triumph to Venice, which are still to be seen, with their
quaint devices, at the door of St. Mark's towards the ducal
palace, and still tell their tale about the bitter rivalry between
the two Italian republics. But the Genoese never properly
regained their footing in this last stronghold of Christendom
on the shores of Palestine ; and when—through the internal
squabbles of the Christians, in which the Knights Templars
and Hospitallers joined, instead of combining together against
the infidel—Acre fell into the hands of the Sultan of Egypt,
in 1291, the Genoese were not so much affected thereat as
their rivals. Tripoli had fallen some years before. Tyre and
Sidon fell also about the same time, and on a Genoese ship

the wretched remains of the Lusignan dynasty were carried to the island of Cyprus.[1]

In Antioch, too, and Laodicea, the Genoese did a handsome traffic under the protection of the six princes of the house of Bohemond. As early as 1098 they got large concessions for defending them in their wars, and the treaty which ensued therefrom is perhaps the first of the numerous list of commercial immunities which the Italians won for themselves in Asia. The brothers Embriaci fought also, and obtained large concessions. In Antioch, and after the siege of Antioch, they paid their men partly in peppercorns instead of gold, knowing of no commodity more prized than this, amongst the many spices and drugs which now began to travel westwards.

But this extended commerce in Syria and Asia Minor was destined to an early destruction from the hands of the infidel. And with this doom hanging over them we see both Genoese and Venetian traders making comfortable treaties for themselves with the Sultan of Egypt, in spite of Christian remonstrance. Cairo was the emporium of the road to India by the Red Sea and Arabia, and when the merchants recognized that there was no hope of getting possession of Egypt through Christian instrumentality, they set to work to gain for themselves a sure footing in this realm.

A treaty was made with Egypt, in 1177 ; but before this there are proofs enough of an extended commerce there, so that when Benedetto Zaccharia, that lawless Genoese rover of the seas, seized an Egyptian ship laden with merchandize and conveyed it home, the merchants of Genoa were exceeding wrath with him, and obliged him to take it back to the infuriated sultan. For a century after this the Genoese were not received well by the Mussulmans; and it was not till 1290 that a satisfactory treaty was concluded, just one year before the fall of Acre into the sultan's hands.

---

[1] *Vide* ch. vii.

This document is still preserved in the university library at Genoa, and is a curious testimony to the spirit of the times, proving how little the Genoese cared to whom Palestine belonged, so long as their commerce was secure, and likewise giving us an insight into the commodities with which they traded and the value in which each was held.

Along the coast of Northern Africa many were the points where Genoese merchants drove a lucrative trade. The centre of this department was Tunis, which was conveniently situated for rapid visits from Genoa, and the consul at Tunis had jurisdiction over all the coast of Barbary. But Tripoli on this coast was also a great mart, whither the Genoese repaired, and is often alluded to in their annals. On its voyage from Tripoli Shakespeare's merchant of Genoa, the unfortunate Antonio, lost his ship, the *Argosy;* and amongst the later annals of their dealings with Tripoli occurs a story which aptly illustrates the marauding spirit which infused itself into the republican admirals, when out of work.

No sooner did a Genoese admiral find himself in possession of a fine set of galleys, with no particular object in his view, than he set to work to disturb and rob his more peaceful neighbours. Thus it was with the Embriaci after their crusades ; thus it was with Andrea D'Oria four centuries later, and thus it was with Philip D'Oria in 1347. Having suffered a repulse off the coast of Sardinia, and not quite liking to return home in disgrace, D'Oria set sail for Tripoli, where a blacksmith had managed to usurp the sovereign power. Since Genoa was on good terms with Tripoli at this time, D'Oria was well received. A banquet was given him, and the town did all honour to the Genoese admiral, as their guest. Towards evening the Genoese returned to their ships under plea of an immediate start. However, in the dead of night when the Moors were asleep, they fell ruthlessly upon the town, massacred many, and carried off a large cargo of booty, jewels, etc., to Genoa, and demanded further aid to establish the banner of St. George on the walls of Tripoli.

With unusual probity the governors of the day chose to
disapprove of this proceeding, and ordered D'Oria to take
back his illgotten gains and make amends. This, however,
was not pleasing to the admiral: he preferred to retain his
spoil, and to sell the city and its contents to the Saracens, for
which piece of treachery he was compelled to wander about
as an exile for the remainder of his life.

A later episode in the connections between Genoa and
Tripoli, told us by Leo Africanus, satisfies us that the Tripolines hereafter were a match for the grasping Ligurians. The
town on one occasion was surprised and sacked by a Genoese
fleet of twenty sails ; when the king of Fez, then ruler of
Tripoli, heard of this, he gave the Genoese fifty thousand
ducats upon the consideration that he might enjoy the town
in peace. But when the Genoese had surrendered the town,
they discovered on their journey home that most of their
ducats were counterfeit.

There lies a small island not far from the coast of Africa,
the name of which is Tabarca, which, in the palmy days of
Mediterranean commerce, was a great rendezvous for ships on
their passage to and from the East. Here the Pisans had a
strong fort, and large coral fisheries along the coast. In both
of these they were succeeded by the Genoese, who made
great use of coral in their commerce. In common with the
rest of those parts, it was early swept over and devastated by
the Turkish scourge, and it is not till the sixteenth century
that Tabarca again appears in Genoese annals, when Andrea
D'Oria got it as the ransom of a captured pasha.

Tabarca was then sold to the Lomellini family, who retained the lordship of it for two centuries, and made much
money out of the coral fisheries, of which wealth a substantial
memorial stands to-day in Genoa in the shape of the church
of the Annunziata, on which the Lomellini lavished all that is
glorious in marbles, in gold, and in frescoes, making it a perfect paradise of florid art, which is aptly summed up in the

simile of Sismondi, who likens it to an illuminated snuff box.

From time immemorial the Genoese had been celebrated for their coral, which Dante describes as "of pallid hue, 'twixt white and yellow." It is surmised that from these coral fisheries of Tabarca the fishermen of a place called Cervo, on the Ligurian coast, amassed amongst themselves great wealth, a melancholy testimony to which is seen still in an unfinished church ; for these pious sailors vowed to the Madonna a portion of their gains from these fisheries with which to build it.

One day, however, before its completion, the men of Cervo started in quest of further gains, leaving only their wives and children behind them, never, alas ! to return ; and at one fell swoop the whole male population of this village was swept away. The secret of their discoveries was buried with them in the waves, and the church they had vowed to their all-powerful Madonna remains unfinished to this day, as if to rebuke her for her neglect in their hour of need.

The island of Tabarca was a perfect Naboth's vineyard to the neighbouring states. In 1632 the French governor of a fort on the coast of Barbary, M. Sanson, tried to seize it by treachery ; he bribed the three bakers of the island to poison the bread, so that he might the more easily possess himself of it, when its defenders were dead or dying. Luckily, however, the Genoese governor discovered the plot, and when the French arrived they were easily driven off, and the baker trio were publicly impaled as a warning to all such traitors.

A century later, under pretence of a friendly visit to the Lomellini, the Bey of Tunis managed to seize it, made the inhabitants slaves, and annexed it to his dominions ; and thus did Genoa lose this important port for her ships.

Passing along the coast of Northern Africa numerous names appear on the lists of Genoa's trading ports : Bugia, Garbo, Morocco, and Ceuta ; but of these the last named was by far the most important, situated as it was at the

threshold of the gates of Hercules, and from the fact that in
her contests here for possession Genoa first set on foot the
celebrated system of "Mahones," which culminated in the
establishment of the Bank of St. George, and the very essence
of her financial system.[1]

That Genoa tráded here as early as 1203 is proved by an
annalist, who states that a ship was sunk in the harbour
during a great storm "with a cargo of money for the Saracens
of Ceuta." At this time the town was governéd by a khedive,
under the Emperor of Morocco. Another Moorish sovereign in
Seville was anxious to possess himself of it in 1231 ; and had
it not been for timely aid from Genoa he would have annexed
it to his dominions. From this expedition the Genoese gained
a handsome treaty, and ships full of booty to gladden the
hearts of their friends at home.

Only three years after this the " men of Navarre," jealous
of the footing Genoa had gained in Ceuta, preached a crusade
against it, and started thither with an armament, under pretext of planting the Christian flag upon its towers, but, as said
the Genoese, with the real intent of seizing their warehouses,
and their quays.

Thus it behoved the Genoese to arm them a fleet ; and to
do so they adopted the plan of selling a portion of the public
revenues, be it the tax on salt or on some other commodity,
to capitalists who would advance money for the expedition.
These capitalists were called " monisti," and in the Genoese
dialect their loan was called a " maone " or " mahone." Con-
cerning the origin of this word, *mahon*, I think it is no stretch
of imagination to consider it of Carthaginian origin. Mago,
brother of Hannibal, took the Balearic Isles, and after him
the chief town was called Portus Mago, now Port Mahon.
From thence Mago went to Genoa and besieged it and established himself there. Genoa was in constant communication
with the Balearic Isles and the old points of Carthaginian

[1] *Vide* ch. xi.

resort. What more possible that the Genoese monetary system and our English title of Lord Mahon both owe their origin to Hannibal's brother ?

In this manner were these early expeditions of Genoa brought about by the simultaneous concourse of two different forces, namely, persons acting, and persons contributing. On an appointed day all those who were to serve as soldiers arrived at Genoa, each receiving one "soldo" per diem, and a right to share in the booty, on which a tax was laid for the benefit of the first galley which boarded the enemy's fleet. At the same time societies were formed to advance money for victuals and galleys in the public service. Probably this system was adopted prior to this expedition to Ceuta ; but it is here that we find it first in proper working order.

To one Mahone there might be any number of subscribers, large or small capitalists, merchants, workmen, religious corporations, and so forth ; in fact any one who felt inclined to speculate on the success of the expedition, and, if successful, they got their share of the booty, tribute, etc., or, as not unfrequently happened, grants of land. As an example of this the Giustiniani became lords of Chios, which they held for several centuries.

This system of Mahones may be said to be the key of Genoa's success and prosperity. In speaking of the Bank of St. George,[1] we shall have occasion to trace the development and progress of the system until it became the pattern from which the European schemes of banking took their origin.

Of this expedition to Ceuta it is sufficient to say that it was successful ; but it had more importance to after generations from the system on which it was carried on, and the system which it inaugurated.

Genoese commerce with mediæval Spain is full of incident and life. It gives us an insight into the gradual development

[1] *Vide* ch. xi.

of that great nation from the chrysalis state of barbarism. It gives us an insight into their long contests with the Moors ; and moreover shows us how the crusading spirit which was dying out in Palestine, burnt here with a healthier vigour, inasmuch as it was for their hearths and their homes that the Spaniards fought.

Not only in the Eastern Crusades was it that the Genoese lent a helping hand. Many an Alphonso and many a Sancho of Spain was thankful to hire galleys from the Ligurian republic at the sole expense of handsome commercial grants and large shares of booty. Perhaps the best known of the Genoese expeditions to Spain, and probably the first, was that against Almeria, in 1146. They had some years before driven the Saracen marauders from their strongholds in the Balearic islands ; and, at the solicitation of Spain, they were induced to follow up their victories on the mainland.

Caffaro, the annalist, went with the twenty-two galleys despatched by Genoa ; and with these the Ligurians laid waste this famous centre of Moorish commerce, and came home well stocked with booty and honours. But the Moorish power was not thus easily crushed ; and three years later we find Alphonso VII. of Aragon, the kings of Castille and Navarre, applying for aid against the Saracens. The Pope, to whom their first application was made, referred them to the Genoese, and the Genoese responded right willingly to the call, since the odour of sweet booty was still strong in their nostrils ; and in the cathedral, where a general concourse was held, the consuls could scarce repress the enthusiasm of the populace who wished forthwith to proceed to victory. Nowhere could the eagerness for revenge on the infidel be found keener than in Liguria. From San Remo to the Gulf of Spezia, each village has still its watch-tower, and each village had then its tale to tell of ruined homesteads, of wives and children, household goods, and everything carried off on Saracenic galleys. Before the altar of their patron saint, all quarrels were rapidly adjusted, the factious rivals embraced one another, and a regular crusade was at once voted. Ladies gave their trinkets and priests their plate, and cowardly was he who refused to join the fifteen galleys prepared by the Genoese as quickly as time would permit to join her allies in Spain.

On reaching Almeria, the Genoese found none of their allies there to meet them. Single-handed they had to contend with the Infidel; but nothing daunted, their captain, Ansaldo D'Oria, urged them on to the attack, and so expert, says the patriotic annalist,[1] were the Ligurian sailors, that the havoc amongst the Moors was complete, and the Genoese were "like a lion amongst a flock of sheep." However exaggerated this victory may be by their ardent historians, certain it is that it was sufficient to raise the drooping spirits of their Spanish allies. Alphonso soon came and assisted them in laying siege to the walls of Almeria. Here again, as at Jerusalem, the prowess of the Genoese in constructing towers and battering rams rendered the greatest assistance, and on the 26th of October, 1149, a valiant attack was made on the city; and Almeria fell, with all its countless stores of Moorish wealth and its thousands of prisoners, into the hands of the allies.

Of the ship-loads of booty taken home by the Genoese glorious accounts are given by contemporary writers. Still we see those twisted pillars on the cathedral façade, the bronze gates of the baptistery, and all those Moorish images and carvings which adorn Genoese churches, of which no records are left; but we can only surmise that from the ruins of Almeria they were taken. Likewise also they brought home with them a taste for Moorish architecture and Moorish buildings which blends so curious with the Lombardo-Gothic, and Byzantine. Impossible is it at this date to estimate the influence of this contact with the south of Spain. There exists to this day much that is Arabic in the Genoese dialect,

[1] Guglielmo Pelli.

and their intercourse with a hated race may be said to have
been inaugurated by this expedition to Almeria.

The chain of events which led up to and developed this
intercourse is curious.   Saracenic marauders devastated
Genoa when it was little more than a fishing village.   This
caused them to build their watch-towers, their walls, and
their ships, until Genoa gradually developed herself into a
strong maritime city.   Then in their turn the Genoese assisted
in driving their enemy out of Corsica and Sardinia.   Single-
handed they drove them from the Balearic Islands, until at
length the time for revenge came, when they could attack
them in their homes.   They besieged them, they conquered
them, and they made treaties of commerce with them.   They
admired, learnt, and adopted the high refinement of Moorish
civilization.   For a time they were content with their virtues
and avoided their vices ; and, as if led on by the spell of
destiny, the Genoese boldly passed through the Straits of
Gibraltar.   They coasted West Africa and discovered the
Madeiras,[1] until at length a Genoese put the crowning point
to all this by setting foot on American soil.

But to return to Almeria ; for Genoa, out of this victory
excellent commercial treaties were forthcoming, being as she
was the chief instrument in the Moorish defeat, amongst which
figure prominently an exemption from all taxes and dues
for her ships and resident merchants in Almeria, and the
customary concession of an annual tribute to the Cathedral of
S. Lorenzo.   Of more import, however, than these was the
reputation her arms acquired thereby.   To the standard of
the allies now flocked numerous crusaders, English Knight
Templars and others, all eager for fresh victories over the
infidel.   Forthwith they marched on Tortosa, which fell, after
fluctuating success, in 1150.   And thus was an enormous field
opened to the Genoese after a few years of honest war.
Freedom of toll in all cities which Alphonso recovered from .

---

[1] *Vide* ch. x.

the Moors, and in those at the capture of which Genoa assisted in person she was handed over a third part of the maritime dues by way of payment.

It was in this year that Lisbon fell into the hands of the Spanish crusaders, and with it was introduced a new field for exploit and discovery, the importance of which will appear when we discuss Genoa's voyages and dealings with the Portuguese.[1]

If prudence is a virtue essential to all who would thrive, it was one with which the Genoese were richly endowed ; for not only did she covenant with the Christian kings of Spain for immunities for her commerce, but she likewise took the prudent course of seeking to maintain them, even should these cities fall back into the hands of Moorish masters. With the Moorish kings of Murcia and Valencia treaties were formed, in 1149, for commerce, and for the safety of their countrymen in Almeria in case this town fell again into the old hands. In the dominions of these kings they had their allotted warehouses, and as early as 1160 we find the Genoese introducing the wool trade into Europe by way of Murcia— a vast field for future development and riches for coming generations.

It mattered but little to the Genoese whether Moors or Christians were lords of Seville and Cordova. In each place they had large immunities from taxation under both dynasties, and their ships were ever ready to carry the silks of Spain to exchange for the skins of Russia and the produce of India. Whether these goods were made by Spaniards or by their Arab instructors, it concerned them little.

In many instances the Ligurians preferred dealing with the peaceful and civilized Moors of the south, to transacting business with the more energetic and warlike inhabitants of Northern Spain. The Catalonians, for example, were at daggers drawn with the Genoese throughout the greater part

[1] *Vide* ch. x.

of the Middle Ages. This hardy, lawless race scoured the Mediterranean with just a little more disregard for the laws of nations, and with just a little more piratical disposition than the Genoese themselves. Hence constant rivalry was the result between the two. The first open warfare between them occurred in Pisan waters in 1291, and after this many were the struggles in different parts of the inland sea.

A band of these Catalonians was in the pay of the Sicilians against the Angevins at the time of the Sicilian vespers ; and it was a curiously savage band, too—each man with his rough, short tunic, girdle, and leathern cap, a pouch on the shoulders for food, at his side a short sword, and in his hand a spear. They knew no discipline, no fatigue, and had no pay, but wandered about like hungry wolves in search of booty, of which a fifth part was religiously set aside for their king. They were almost more skilled for action by night than by day ; more at home amidst forests and rocks than on the plain. They scoured the country without baggage, and if their supply of food fell short they could subsist well on herbs. Theirs was the strength of a horse, and their nature was but little removed from that of brute beasts.

Under a certain Roger de Flor these Catalonians wandered over sea and land in search of booty ; they enriched themselves in Palestine, they remorselessly laid waste towns in Asia Minor, until the odour of an easy victory attracted their greyhound noses to the neighbourhood of Constantinople. With the Genoese colony at Galata [1] they soon came to high words. Suspicious that Roger de Flor was aiming at the imperial crown, the weak Emperor Andronicus invited him to a banquet, and there had him massacred, and many of his followers with him. A cry of revenge arose amongst the survivors, which was echoed by way of Sicily to their comrades at home ; and in Northern Spain was prepared an armament which should crush the emperors of the East, and

[1] *Vide* ch. vi.

place their newly-elected leader, Berengarius D'Entenza, on the throne.

On the news of this impending storm, Andronicus, in his dire distress, sent hastily to Genoa for assistance ; and Genoa, true to her interests, which could ill brook the establishment of this lawless race at the very threshold of her Black Sea colonies, despatched Edoardo D'Oria with sixteen galleys to oppose them.

With blandishments and fair promises the Catalonians tried to dissuade the Genoese from taking a part in the quarrel, which they affirmed was none of theirs. But D'Oria prudently sent to inquire of his countrymen at Galata what their wishes might be, and learning that the Catalonians had misrepresented many of the facts of the case to him, he determined at once to have no more dealings with this perfidious race, and threw in his lot with the Greeks. And the Catalonians were vanquished in 1302. All their ships were taken, and the leader, who had hidden himself in the hold of one of the ships, was dragged out by his conquerors, and sent to end his days in Genoa.

Thirty years later, when Boniface VIII. gave Sardinia and Corsica to James II., King of Aragon, on condition that he would abandon his claims on Sicily, a band of Catalonians was sent to substantiate the Aragonese pretensions to the latter island. Pursuing their usual predatory tactics, they straightway descended on all the towns along the coast of Liguria. Chiavari was laid waste, and a raid on the promontory of S. Chiara carried devastation up to the very walls of Genoa. Mentone was burnt, and at Monaco all the vines and trees were cut down—in short, the days of the Saracens were renewed in the depredations of these barbarians of Northern Spain. They had no honour in warfare ; they impaled their prisoners ; and for three days the Genoese coasts were subject to continual alarms.

At length Salagro di Negro was armed with a force sufficient to carry the war into the enemy's country, the result of which was a speedy peace. These treacherous Catalonians were cruelty itself when victorious, but barbarous in the extreme when driven home. In 1336 peace was again restored, and her Corsican possessions and her Spanish commerce were no longer molested by Catalonians.

Of Genoese commercial dealings with France there are endless reminiscences. From her close proximity to the

S. CHIARA, NEAR GENOA.

Gulf of Lyons, Genoa was constantly brought into communication with all the commercial activity of the towns of Provence, which marked the Middle Ages. Marseilles at this time was more of a rival than a friend—a rival carrier of pilgrims and crusaders to the East, a rival also in commerce in those Eastern fields; and in each treaty made with Marseilles, clauses were inserted, referring to rights of *meum* and *tuum*, which were not always scrupulously observed. For example, in 1245 these rival trading towns busied themselves in burning all the ships belonging to each other to be found in their respective ports, not to mention frequent instances of disputes and insults offered to one another on the high seas and in foreign harbours. "Never did the men of Marséilles right loyally love the men of Genoa," says a Genoese historian, and never could they be brought to understand how enormous were the mutual advantages of good terms.

We are amply provided in the commercial archives of Genoa with volumes of treaties, lists of consuls, exchanged commodities between the Ligurian and Provençal merchants of Narbonne, Montpellier, Aiguemorte, etc., each similar to the other, and the whole breathing the intense spirit of activity, which in those mediæval days resounded throughout the length and breadth of this lovely coast.

By far the most interesting episode in mediæval commercial life is afforded us by watching the Genoese at the celebrated fairs of Champagne. There the merchants of Italy, Spain, and France congregated. From far distant climes the Genoese transported thither bales of goods ; and busy traders came to meet in open market the infant efforts of Belgian manufacturers from Yprès, Douai, and Bruges. Burgundy sent cloth, Catalonia leather, and the Genoese and Florentines brought silks ; and at all the seaports along their coast vast cargoes were unshipped and placed on the backs of mules to wend their way to the place appointed for the fair.

These fairs would begin with the sale of cloth, perhaps for seventeen days ; then the cloth merchants would settle their accounts prior to the silk merchants entering on their bargains. In the middle of it all the great cry "Ara" was raised, as a signal for the money-changers to take their seats, and for four weeks they sat for the benefit of the various nationalities who wished to realize their gains in their native coin.

After the conclusion of the fair, a busy time of fifteen days was set apart for those who had not yet settled their accounts, and to rectify disputes, which was extended in favour of the representatives of more distant people who wished to go home and return before finally completing their books. Thus we find the Genoese bursar at these fairs had always a month allowed him before settling his account.

But these fairs in Southern France were not without their political significance. Besides bringing hither their merchandize, the Italian traders imported into these towns their spirit of independence and their love of republicanism. It was from the South of France that the seeds of liberty, equality, and fraternity spread northwards. No greater stronghold of the rights of the third estate existed than at Marseilles. To this day the influence of this fact is strong on the politics of France. And the principles inculcated by the independent traders of Italy took deep root here under the eyes of despotism, and found a truly favourable soil in which to develop. The French revolution, and the state of France as it is to-day, may owe their first source to these very times, when a Genoese merchant would repair to these fairs, proud and boastful of his own freedom, of his vote in the general council, and of a government which owned no royal master, and all this could be said with a sneer at the people over whom the banner of the lilies held despotic sway.

Along the coast of Western France, past Bordeaux, La Rochelle, and the Isle of Olerón, the Genoese found their way to the Low Countries. Here they exchanged the goods of the south for the carpets, tapestries, and woollen goods of Flanders, and at the Dutch fairs they shook hands with their successors in the commercial world, the men of Holland and the men of England.

Bruges was the grand emporium of all this wealth, owing about as much allegiance to their Brabant liege lord as the Genoese did to the distant Emperor of Germany. Here Genoa had warehouses and foundries ; also at Antwerp, where, in 1468, on the event of the marriage of Margaret of England to Charles the Bold, we read of the emulation of the foreign merchants in doing honour to the occasion. In the procession which went forth to meet the bride, appeared Genoese and Venetian banners side by side with the Hanseatic and German companies. The Genoese company was called "La Spinola," from the name of that noble Genoese family, who figured largely in those northern countries as extensive merchants and money-lenders, holding much the same position as hereafter the Fuggers of Augsburg and the Rothschilds held.

Larger ships were built purposely in Genoa for meeting the terrors of the Bay of Biscay and the German ocean, which carried their intrepid mariners to all the Hanseatic towns of the far north, to Wisby in the island of Goltand, and to the coasts of Russia, to participate in the fair of Novgorod.

"You whose ships have free course in the ocean, and in the Euxine, and before whom peoples and monarchs tremble. From Tapobrana to the Fortunate Isles, to the unknown Thule, to the extreme confines of the northern and western world your pilots safely guide their crafts." Thus wrote Petrarch of them in 1351, when he sought to heal the hostilities and factions in the rival republics of Genoa and Venice. With impassioned vehemence he reminds them that "no sea exists in which the echoes of your triumphs do not resound. The ocean itself dreads you. The Indian sea is rejoiced for once to be released from your triremes." But the laureate's enthusiasm was of small avail. The evil which he strove to check was the one bane of their prosperity and success. In vain was it that they filled their coffers with gold if it was to be squandered on internal quarrels and contests with a rival.

CHAPTER VI.

GENOESE COMMERCE IN THE BLACK SEA.

THE products of India, China, and the East, poured into Europe by three channels throughout the Middle Ages. There was the Egyptian channel, highly convenient, but highly precarious as long as Christian and infidel continued to break lances over their creeds. There was the Syrian channel, which for the same reasons offered but an uncertain field for enterprise after the fall of the Christian kingdom of Jerusalem. And, lastly, there was the Black Sea Channel, perhaps the most secure of all, and offering the further advantage of being the mart for the skins and animal productions of Russia, and of this channel Genoa had almost an undisputed monopoly for two centuries. She ruled in the Black Sea, in Constantinople, and in the Greek Archipelago, with almost as firm a hand as we to-day rule in India ; and if, as we have seen, her commercial schemes elsewhere were vast and lucrative, yet it is along this high road to the East we must look to grasp the nucleus of it all.

As the foundation on which Genoa's supremacy in the Black Sea was built consisted in their dealings with the decayed Byzantine empire, we must for a moment trace her intercourse with it before entering the Black Sea, and visiting the numberless Genoese colonies which were dotted along its coasts.

From a treaty with Emmanuel Comnenus, in 1178, we

gather that even at this early period Genoa trafficked through-out the empire, with Constantinople as the emporium of her commerce ; but Venice at this time was the ruling spirit in the Eastern capital, and not until Venetian traders by their high-handed insolence had made themselves hated and feared . in Constantinople were the Genoese able to step in and usurp their power, their warehouses, and their quays.

Great intimacy existed between Emmanuel Comnenus and the Ligurian Republic on the subject of Frederic Barbarossa, both hating this German barbarian, and both fearing to be swamped in his schemes. The emperor sent a certain Deme-trius to Genoa with a large sum of money to help them in building their walls, but when he saw the Ligurian Republic somewhat wavering in its allegiance, and almost on the point of transporting Frederic and his troops to Sicily,[1] he was ex-ceeding wråth, and wreaked his vengeance on the luckless Ligurian merchants in Constantinople, and repented him in his weakness of the concessions he had given them. All were plundered, some were murdered, and the rest banished ; but it was only in his weakness that he repented, for when the Genoese were gone, a large portion of the precious tribute which vessels paid was gone too, and realizing that as crusade after crusade failed, nothing could save his empire but these maritime republics, and that the road of commerce through the Caspian, Erzeroum, and Persia was his only mainstay, he was not slow to re-establish the Genoese in his favour again.

During the Latin dynasty in Constantinople the Genoese never gained the first place in the commerce of the Black Sea. Treaties indeed were ratified not only with the Latin emperor, but also with the Flemish lords, who after the fourth Crusade were dotted about in small principalities over Roumania and Greece. But it was Venice who held the key of all this com-merce, at Constantinople ; when, after diverting the whole course of the fourth Crusade, she induced Christendom to

[1] *Vide* ch. iv.

waste its energies on subduing the Greek empire for her benefit.

With the exiled Greek dynasty, however, the Genoese were always on the best of terms, at Trebizond, Nicea, and in Roumania; and recognizing that as long as the Latins were all-powerful in Constantinople she would have to relinquish the cream of the Black Sea commerce to the Queen of the Adriatic, she at length determined to strike a bold stroke and replace a Greek again on the throne.

The weakness of the Latin line favoured her plans. The Emperor Baldwin the Second was so reduced in circumstances as to be compelled to pull up the floor of his palace to make himself a fire, and furthermore had been forced to sell "the crown of thorns" to France to raise money. And Genoa burned to revenge the insult received at Acre [1] from Venice, and she burned to some purpose, as events will show.

Michael Paleologus, the tutor of the young John Vatace, Emperor of Nicea, was a spirited, enterprising young man; to him the Genoese unfolded their plans, and at length, with Genoese aid, he made boldly for the diadem of Constantinople, and won it without a blow. Baldwin II. ignominiously fled on some Venetian galleys, and spent the remaining thirteen years of his life in vainly trying to urge the Venetians and other powers to regain him his country, and in vituperating the Ligurian Republic; but all aid sent by Venice was effectually combated by Genoa, for at this time the Queen of the Adriatic was not at the pride of her strength and power, and moreover her interests were more directed towards the commercial channel of Syria and Cyprus.

On the strength of their assistance given to Michael Paleologus, the Genoese obtained the treaty of Ninfeo, in 1261, which firmly established their influence in the Black Sea, which only the Turkish wave two centuries later could swallow up and annihilate.

[1] *Vide* ch. v.

. Many of the expatriated Greeks, who at this time were in Genoa, got them joyfully to their galleys at this good news, and returned home, except one, the Duke Isaac, who remained behind, and whose tomb is still seen in the cathedral. Thus did the brave mariner-town of Genoa turn the scale of the vast, but rotten, Eastern Empire ; and her reward was manifold. The grateful emperor gave her streets and quays in Constantinople, immunity from tribute, and a free passage for her commerce ; and he gave her a Venetian monastery called Pantocratore, which intensely gratified her jealous hatred of her rival, for she removed it stone for stone to Genoa, and eventually used these to build the national bank of St. George, which, as it now stands, is a living memorial of the uncompromising hatred which existed between the two republics.[1]

In addition to these excellent terms in the treaty of Ninfeo, the emperor conceded to various Genoese private families numerous islands in the Archipelago. Thus the Embriaci were established in Lemnos, the Centurioni in Metilene, the Gatilusii in Enos. The Zaccharia first got Negropont, which was afterwards exchanged for Chios, with the title of admiral and grand constable of the Eastern Empire. The Catanei got Phocea, and the rich mines of alum. These little island lordships changed hands from time to time. We will presently glance at the fortunes of Chios under her Genoese lords as a fair specimen of the rest.

But the great nucleus of this power was the streets, churches, and quays in Constantinople which were allotted to the Genoese, and formed a vast emporium of strength and commerce, which must have eventually led to entire possession of Constantinople, had not the "podestà," or ruler of the Genoese colony ·there, thought fit, from personal motives, or from large offers made to him by the Venetians, to attempt a restoration of the Latin line. His name was Guglielmo

[1] *Vide* ch. xi.

Guercio, and his influence about the emperor was great. His conspiracy was discovered, and the Genoese were sent away in a body to Eraclea. However, on representation from home that it was none of their doing, and that Guercio had been acting entirely on his own account, the emperor yielded in perpetuity to the Genoese the town of Pera, on the sole condition that the governors should do him homage, that they should bend their knees twice in his presence, once on entering, and once halfway up the hall, and that they should kiss his feet.

Thus were the Genoese established in this commanding position ; here they had a separate government of their own, from here they ruled the road of commerce from China to Europe ; and, taking advantage of the weakness of the emperors, they were able to do much as they wished about building fortresses and palaces, with gardens to the water's edge ; and thus from Pera, with its citadel of Galata behind it, they were enabled to dictate what terms they pleased to ships passing to and from the Bosphorus, and, by a secret treaty with the Emperor Cantacuzene, a little later they were allowed to build a second castle on the opposite coast of Asia, which, with its European *vis-à-vis*, were known as " the keys of the Black Sea."

Having thus firmly established our Genoese in Pera, let us, with their permission, enter the Black Sea, and glance at their numerous possessions therein.

From time immemorial the small tongue of land now known as the Crimea, then as the Tauric Chersonese, was the mart towards which all the caravan trade of Asia was directed by this northern road, and upon this tongue of land sprang up a group of noble cities which, until finally seized by the Turks, were without exception Genoese property. Of these, Caffa was the chief. When this city was built on the ruins of Theodosia, and by whom, is somewhat shrouded in mystery. Certain it is that Genoa had a colony here soon after the first

Crusade, as their treaty with Emmanuel Comnenus proves; and certain it is that the well known Genoese name of Caffaro was largely mixed up in the early Black Sea commerce, and that this family had seignorial rights in Caffa, which eventually passed into the family of Dell'Orta. It is therefore no great stretch of imagination to surmise that a band of crusaders, under one Caffaro, on their return from the Holy Land passed by here, saw the advantages of the position, and founded a colony. Caffaro, as we have seen, was the historian of the crusade; and Caffaro is to-day the name of the leading Genoese newspaper, whilst the once noble city of Caffa is a mere fishing village, with naught save ruins of stately towers to testify to its quondam glory.

With its excellent harbour and its fertile surroundings it soon assumed the position of first importance in Genoa's commerce in these parts, and but little disturbed the even tenor of its ways, until the arrival of the Mogul Tatars, who obliged the rich merchants to open their purse-strings in 1240, and to pay a tribute as the price of possession. But far from injuring Caffa's trade, the influx of the Tatars added doubly to her importance, for the Tatars had influence far into the centre of Asia, and they at once realized how convenient it was to have a destination for their caravans and an active people like the Genoese to transport their goods to distant countries.

Then it was that thousands of houses grew up around the port. Feeling a security before unknown, the merchants built themselves palaces, towers, and forts; and when, in 1261, the treaty of Ninfeo further secured their commercial position, numerous families flocked from Genoa, and this colony of Caffa poured endless wealth into the purses of her merchants.

In 1288 the government, which had hitherto entirely rested in the hands of the Dell'Orta family, was entrusted to a consul and a parliament, and a long list of minor officials; one of the D'Oria family was the first consul, and when at home the government was torn by factions, that of Caffa went on in a most peaceful groove. Not only did the Caffese hold their own against all intruders, but they were enabled, in 1289, to send a subsidy to assist Tripoli in Syria against the sultan. In 1268, Caffa had been made an episcopal see, and in 1316 John XXII. raised it to the rank of a city.

So important did Caffa become that the Genoese found it necessary in 1398 to grant its inhabitants more share in the government. Prior to this, the Caffese had only sent four representatives to the council of twenty-four, whom the Genoese sent out to govern the affairs of this colony. In this year they were allowed to fill half of the twenty-four places themselves, and their consul was to rank above and to have control over the other Genoese consuls in the Black Sea.

The following is a remarkable instance of the power and resources possessed by a wealthy merchant in Caffa. A Genoese, Megello Lercari by name, resided at Caffa, and traded constantly with the imperial city of Trebizond. One day Lercari was grievously insulted by a page of the Greek Emperor, Alexius III., who struck him in the presence of the court. He appealed to the emperor for redress, but Alexius refused to punish his page, so Lercari withdrew, vowing vengeance on the imperial court. With the sole assistance of his personal friends and kinsmen at Caffa and Genoa, Lercari succeeded in fitting out a fleet far superior to the emperor's; he ravaged the coasts of Trebizond, he destroyed the Greek commerce and captured the imperial galleys. By way of revenge he cut off the ears and noses of all the prisoners he took, and sent a barrel full of them to the emperor, with the threat that he should continue to exact similar tribute until he obtained full satisfaction for his insult.

Alexius was hence obliged to deliver up his page, whom Lercari magnanimously scorned to punish, but at the same time secured for his country ampler commercial treaties than they had previously enjoyed. Such were the Genoese of

Caffa, and such was the power possessed by a single citizen of this wealthy town.

There are but few reminiscences to be seen now of the wealth and prosperity of this town. The Turks on their occupation did but little to destroy them. They turned their churches into mosques, and utilized their fortifications ; but the Russians, when they became masters of the Crimea, remorselessly pulled them all down; they built barracks out of the cathedral, and pulled down the palaces to make forts, so that to-day the visitor sees but two of the old churches, one of which was given up to the Roman Catholics, and the other to the Armenians ; and of the forts and ramparts but one tower remains, in which is an inscription to the memory of Pope Clement VI., to whom the tower was consecrated when he preached a crusade against the Tartars, who at that time threatened the colony.

All these Genoese colonies were kept in check and in allegiance to the home government by a body of men appointed to superintend all their commerce. This body was called the " Gazzeria," and it had full jurisdiction and a final appeal from all these ports. The members were appointed at home by lot ; and it is from the documents of their sessions, which are still preserved in the archives of St. George, that we learn all particulars about these flourishing colonies and their government. So beneficial was this system found, that as time went on, the jurisdiction of the Gazzeria was extended outside the Black Sea ; and the laws which they passed, and their judicial sentences furnish us with a complete museum of Genoese maritime law. They superintended also the armies and navigation of galleys in those parts with sound rules and regulations.

Second only to Caffa in importance, and better known to us by name, was the town of Crim, which gave its name eventually to the whole peninsula, which originally it had got from the Crim Tatars. Crim, in the days of Genoese glory, was indeed a goodly city to look upon—well stocked with palaces and towers, and, from its proximity to the isthmus, was the recognized destination of the caravans, shoals of which daily arrived from the East. Prior to its cession to the Genoese, it had been the residence of a Tatar emperor, and when the Genoese obtained it they enlarged and beautified it to such an extent, that report extravagantly says that a good rider could not go all round it in a day. Crim, like Caffa, was under a Genoese consul ; there were two colleges there, and it was the centre of Crimean learning in the Middle Ages.

Soudak, or Soldaia, was another opulent city on the Chersonese which owed its origin to the Genoese, or rather its revival under a Genoese form, for near here once stood the ancient town of Cherson. But Genoa, " that proud mistress of the seas," imposed a tax on all vessels going to Cherson, which wrought its ruin ; and, invaded by barbarians and crushed by Genoa, the inhabitants left it to the mercy of the oppressors, and the once flourishing depôt of commerce under the emperors ceased to exist except in its Genoese offspring, Soldaia; and to future generations the ruined walls and towers of Cherson were known as Sebastopol. There, too, the Genoese had a consul; and Soldaia and Sebastopol, with their magnificent port, until Turkish occupation, continued to bring in much wealth for the merchants of Genoa and Caffa. Soldaia still has left a monument which attests to the Genoese rule. It is a fountain, over which a bas-relief represents St. George and the dragon, and a scutcheon of Doge Adorno over the gateway hard by, with the date of 1385, and the consul's name ; whilst, as at Caffa, the churches and houses, with few exceptions, have been pulled down to build barracks for the Russian soldiers.

We must mention two or three more towns in connection with the Genoese in the Crimea which were governed by their respective consuls in those days, and the names of which send a thrill into every English heart : Cembalo, the Balaclava of the Turks, and Inkermann. The former had an excellent fort, which overlooked the harbour, and so important did it grow under Genoese influence, that Eugenius IV., in 1432, saw fit to make it the see of a bishop.

Great as was Genoa's prosperity in the Black Sea, she had occasional disputes with her Tatar neighbours, which increased in intensity as time went on, and decay set in in all her colonies. A short war occurred in 1374 with the Tatars, arising from a petty quarrel between a Genoese and a Tatar. In this the Genoese were successful ; but they were not so fortunate in 1432 ; and though an armament was sent out from home under Carlo Lomellini, Caffa was sacked, and for the rest of its existence had to pay a heavy tribute to the Khan of the Crimea.

Of Genoese colonies on the Chersonese, Kertch was about as flourishing as any—now a mere fishing village, with nothing to attest its grandeur save a few marble fountains and a fortress, a goodly array of bas-reliefs and a Venetian stone lion of St. Mark, taken from the rival republic, and here set up over the entrance to the fort as a proof of triumphant jealousy. Numerous other colonies are dotted all along these coasts, each with a history and name to be read in Genoa's archives.

Though the commodities in which Genoa traded in these parts represented all variations of the animal, mineral, and vegetable world, the skins of Angola, Russia, and the far East, drugs and spices in countless numbers, salt and precious stones, yet of these none was so lucrative to them as their traffic in that branch of the animal world represented by their own fellow creatures. Dark-eyed, lovely girls were torn from their homes in the Caucasus, and borne off to stock the harems of the Turks, or for purposes equally nefarious in Liguria. From Cilicia they drove down hordes of able-bodied men, who were taken to Egypt to serve as mamelukes, and in exchange for these cargoes of human flesh they received sugar, spices, and precious goods from Arabia and Upper Egypt. But from the books of the Gazzeria we are glad to learn that this horrible traffic was strenuously put down · towards the end of the Genoese reign in those parts, as inconsistent with humanity and the laws of civilization, and in 1449 it was no more carried on, as far as the Genoese were concerned.

Here then, in this narrow tongue of land which we now call the Crimea, was the kernel of Genoese prosperity. As long as she flourished here she flourished at home. And when at length the Turkish scourge swept over this peninsula and swallowed up her colonies, the Ligurian Republic, by a process of slow decay, withered like a sapless tree.

To enumerate the towns where Genoese consuls ruled over small merchant-colonies in Asia would be an endless task. At Trebizond she had a large emporium. At Toris in Persia, whither roads led to Muscovy and Turkey, Genoa's consul governed the commerce of Southern Asia, whilst in Armenia their centre was Kars. As early as 1257 the traveller, Marco Polo, was struck with the number of Italian merchants who frequented each of these towns ; and as years rolled on the intercourse increased. It would be hard to realize the terrible change it must have been for Genoa when all this was cut off. Perhaps it was for them as it would be for England now, were she to lose her India, her Australia, and her Canada. Though Genoa's territory was small, it was thickly populated, and the want of a field for her surplus population must have been severely felt. No wonder she exhausted herself in civil commotions ; and it was only the wealth accumulated through so many centuries which kept her from succumbing before she did.

We have seen how the islands of the Greek Archipelago were dealt out to Genoese families like a pack of cards : of these Metilene, with its marbles, wines, and flocks, became the property of the Gatilusii in this wise. Young Francesco Gatilusio was a bold and enterprising Genoese. He possessed a couple of galleys, with which he roved the seas in search of adventure. One day he found himself at the island of Tenedos, whither had fled John Paleologus, the emperor, from Cantacuzene, the usurper. Gatilusio met the expatriated monarch, talked with him, encouraged him, and finally they settled to make an attack together on Constantinople by night ; and as a reward for his services the Genoese was to receive the island of Metilene and the emperor's daughter in marriage.

Accordingly they repaired to Constantinople one evening, and when the inhabitants were in bed seized the imperial palace, and then overcame Cantacuzene's guard, whilst his subjects were utterly callous about the whole affair, and arose next morning quite content to find a Paleologus again at their head. This circumstance proves at the same time the utter rottenness of the Byzantine empire, and the influence Genoa exercised over it.

Towards the middle of the fifteenth century the curtain of Turkish slavery falls over this fair picture of Genoese prosperity ; all this splendid network of commerce was thereby broken, and all which remains to verify it to-day are the mouldering annals piled in confusion in the archives of St. George, volume after volume labelled Caffa, Pera, or Crim, containing the minutest details of their government and the trade.

Though Timour the Tatar had infused dread into the hearts of Greek and Genoese alike, his was not the arm destined to destroy them ; it was reserved for another and more fearful scourge, namely, the Turks, to effect the overthrow of both, with their commerce and their household gods. Vile as the Greeks had become, there still remained a few sparks of patriotism in their breasts as this cloud appeared. But though the Genoese seem to have been the strength and mainstay of the empire, it is hard to understand their total inactivity as this crisis presented itself. Perhaps they thought the Turks would be as beneficial to their commerce as the Tatars had been ; perhaps they had grown so accustomed to treating with Turkish and Moorish princes that they hoped to enjoy their immunities undisturbed even should a Mussulman rule in Constantinople ; and engaged as they were at home with their internal troubles and Corsican war, they hoped that their flourishing Black Sea colonies would be able to take care of themselves.

Caffa and Pera, the centres of Genoese power in those parts, both entered into amicable negotiations with the Sultans Amurath and Mahomed prior to the fall of Constantinople ; and we shall see that if the Genoese in the fort of Galata had chosen to raise a finger in the defence of Constantinople, its fall, for a time at least, might have been averted.

The affairs of Europe, too, prevented any co-operation to avert the fall of the Eastern Empire. Venice had her own possessions securely outside the Bosphorus, and trusted to the power of Scanderbeg in Albania to check the Turkish onroads. The Pope did not love the Greeks, and cared not to use his influence to arouse Christendom in their defence, and contented himself with sending a cardinal and a handful of priests to their aid.

Genoa too, busy as she was at home, only despatched three hundred archers, and a few boat-loads of men to the assistance of a city eighteen miles in circumference ; and it was not until Mahomed stood before the very walls of Constantinople that the Doge, Pietro Fregoso, at length becoming alive to the necessity of action, so far managed to heal the internal quarrels in Genoa that a little fleet of five galleys was got ready and despatched eastwards ; but, owing to contrary winds, did not arrive at the mouth of the Bosphorus until it was completely blockaded by the Turks.

The story of the bravery of these five ships is, if true, worthy of being placed side by side with the defence of Thermopylæ. How they reached the Bosphorus only to discover that two hundred Turkish galleys were therein assembled, and the banks lined with Mahomed's mighty army; how they held a hurried council of war, and determined not to retreat; how they advanced boldly, overcame the Turkish galleys which opposed them, even though Mahomed, with rabid fury, spurred his charger into the very waves, until at length they reached the city; all savours strongly of romance. Yet at the same time the existence of this story proves how the Genoese reproached themselves for not taking measures which could have effectually preserved for them their colonies, and for the emperor his crown.

In his last hour of distress the bravery of the Emperor John Paleologus was most praiseworthy. Around him he gathered all that was still left of courage in the enervated Greeks. But not so was his Genoese admiral Giustiniani, who, taking advantage of a wound, left the fray before the last desperate moment, and retired within the walls of Galata; and not so were the Genoese in Galata, who are under the everlasting blame of having suggested to Mahomed the very plan by which he took the city, namely, by carrying his ships across under the walls of Galata into the inner harbour. Certain it is that if they did not suggest it they could easily have prevented its execution; but instead, they remained in sullen silence, spectators of the scene, and rumour adds, that when a brave Italian proposed a plan for burning the sultan's ships, the men of Galata revealed it to the Turks, and thereby rendered the scheme abortive.

Mahomed II. did not, however, reward the men of Galata according to their expectations, for a few days after his occupation of Constantinople, he levelled to the ground their walls, and though many continued to linger in the haunts of their former greatness, this nest of commerce was lost to Genoa for ever. Most of the inhabitants took flight to Caffa, or their mother city, and almost the only relics now left to Genoa of the once lordly Pera are a small Byzantine picture of the Madonna, presented to the church of St. Mary of the Castle by a merchant as a thank-offering for his escape, and which hangs there still, and a quaint old " pallio " or flag of silk, one of which was sent by the Greek emperor annually, as a token of his respect to the Genoese archbishop. One is still preserved in the "palazzo civico," representing S. Lorenzo in the act of introducing Michel Paleologus into the Genoese Church.

Great was the consternation at home when the news spread of the fate of Galata. Unable to cope with the general dismay, the rulers of Genoa determined on the plan of conceding their Black Sea colonies to the management of their celebrated Bank of St. George,[1] which then in Genoa represented the only lasting and stable form of government. The protectors of this rich firm entered into the final contract with the Government on the 15th of November, 1453, and with praiseworthy efforts came to the rescue of the checkmated signory. All and singular the corporeal and incorporeal rights, and full jurisdiction over the Black Sea colonies, were thereby handed over to the protectors. This important document is still kept, amongst others of this eventful period, in the bank's archives, all of them breathing a spirit of fear and trepidation at the doom which was hanging over them.

Galleys were armed in due time, and the doge was deputed to write for assistance to all the potentates of Europe. To the king of England he wrote on the 7th of April, 1456, to the king of Portugal on the 3rd of September. But Pope Pius II. and the Genoese seemed alone to realize the dangers of the situation ; the rest of Europe turned a deaf ear to their entreaties, and finally, finding resistance utterly impossible, the Genoese relapsed again into inactivity, and quietly awaited the turn events might take.

But it was the degeneracy of the very men of Caffa which conduced to the final overthrow of those flourishing colonies ; for under the protection of the Khan of Tartary the Crimean

[1] *Vide* ch. xi.

Chersonese at least was comparatively safe. The Genoese governor, Uberto Squarciafico, at Caffa, not content with superintending the affairs of Caffa, chose to mix himself up in the contested appointment to a neighbouring satrapy, wherein the ambitious widow of the late satrap wished to gain the nomination of her son to the exclusion of the newly-appointed one, Emineces by name.

Hoping thereby to gain for himself some advantage, the governor of Caffa took the widow's gold, and sent her some assistance. Whereupon Emineces repaired to the Sultan, who was on the point of starting with a fleet that he had got together for the siege of Crete. Mahomed at once gave orders that the armament of four hundred and eighty-two sail should be sent against Caffa, which, after a gallant defence, was taken by the Turks in 1475. Most of the Genoese senators were slain, including the governor, and fifteen hundred Genoese boys were sent to serve amongst the janizaries, and the rest were taken to repeople a street in Pera. Thus fell the rich city of Caffa, and in her train all the rest of Genoa's colonies became Turkish property, whilst the mother country was groaning under the tyranny of Galeazzo Sforza, who threw every obstacle in the way of an armament being sent to their relief. All these colonies, indeed, fell without a struggle worthy of note, except the one rock fortress of Mangoup, which offered a brave resistance and which is further remarkable from the fact that here fought some Goths, almost the last mentioned of these warlike northmen in history. A tribe of Gothic-speaking people had lived in the Crimean mountains, unmixed with the other inhabitants, for centuries, subject to Genoa since 1380, when, by a treaty with the Khan of Kaptchak, "*La Gotia con i svoi Casai*" was annexed to the Genoese possessions, and here, at the siege of Mangoup, fell two Gothic brothers, the last of the hero warriors from the North.

When Mahomed II. threatened Otranto, a feeble league

was got up in Christendom to resist him, in which the Genoese played a conspicuous part, and voted four hundred and fifty ducats and twenty-one galleys for the expedition ; and the death of Mahomed kindled hopes in their breasts of regaining a portion at least of what they had lost. The protectors of the Bank, and the governors of the Republic held grand councils, and moreover a monk, Domenico di Ponza, preached a crusade in Genoa, but all of no avail ; for when Otranto was relieved and Mahomed was dead the ardour of her allies quickly faded away, and thus were the riches of the Black Sea, with Pera and Caffa to boot, for ever lost to Genoa and to Christendom.

Some lingering traces of the extent of Italian influence on the coasts of the Levant are still left in the frequent occurrence of the Italian language. Last century all the treaties between Russia and Turkey were written in Italian. At Pruth, for instance, in 1711 ; at Belgrade, in 1739; and for a traveller along this coast a knowledge of the Italian tongue is still an inestimable blessing.

Before leaving this corner of Genoese commerce, let us pay a visit to the island of Chios, and look at some of the vicissitudes it underwent under its Genoese masters. Chios was the most important of these island dependencies ; and occupied a position of great consideration for the well-being of the Genoese Black Sea colonies ; and with Chios in friendly hands, the inhabitants of Pera and Caffa had no cause to dread competition from the side of Venice.

We have seen how the Zaccharia became lords of Chios, in 1261, for their assistance given to Michael Paleologus in establishing himself in Constantinople. Some say Benedetto Zaccharia won it by his own prowess, others that he got it by way of dower with one of the emperor's daughters whom he married. Be this as it may, the Zaccharia rule in Chios was hard, and it was short ; and the Emperor Andronicus, backed up by the solicitations of the Genoese in Galata, who grew jealous of their compatriot's successes, deprived them of it, and for some time the island fell under Venetian rule.

At length, however, when the early days of incipient liberty under their first doge[1] urged the Genoese to deeds of valour, in 1349, a fleet was sent into the Greek Archipelago, under the command of Simone Vignoso, and provided for by another of those popular loans, entitled the "Mahone of Chios," and the recovery of this island was the result. No more honourable man appears on the pages of Genoese history than this admiral Simone Vignoso ; he refused Greek gold, and positively forbad any of his soldiers to touch so much as a bunch of grapes on the island under pain of a public flagellation.

His son scoffed at such stringent orders, and to prove his nonchalance, advanced amongst his comrades eating some grapes that he had plucked. His enraged father forthwith commanded that he should receive the penalty he had ordered, and, in spite of the entreaties of the Greeks and Genoese, young Vignoso was soundly whipped, as a warning to all who should dare to break the admiral's commands.

Before leaving the island Simone Vignoso left five hundred ducats, to be distributed amongst the young ladies of Chios on their marriage, by way of compensation for any real or imaginary damage that his troops might have inflicted.

When the Ligurian republicans possessed themselves of Chios, they forthwith gave it to those who had advanced the money for the expedition by way of repayment, and amongst these were some of the ancient family of the Giustiniani, who claimed in some way to be descendants of the Emperor Justinian. Recognizing the advantages of such a name in a Greek country, the shareholders in the Chian loan with one accord took the name of Giustiniani, a custom by no means uncommon in Genoa, where families often clubbed together in companies or "alberghi," sinking their own name for the advantages accruing to them from belonging to a sort of guild.

[1] *Vide* ch. iii.

Once established in Chios, the family or guild of the Giustiniani continued to hold the island for two hundred years.
In 1409 they became tributaries of Mahomed I., paying four
thousand scudi per annum as the price of their peaceful possession of Chios. This sum Mahomed II. raised to ten thousand scudi after the fall of Constantinople, for he did not see
fit to turn out these Genoese from their island dependencies ;·
and on payment of the above sum the Giustiniani were allowed
to retain their own laws, and their own religion, provided no
ringing of church bells or sound of chants were raised to disturb the followers of Mahomed.

The island of Chios was very rich and very loyal in its
devotion to its mother country. The Giustiniani, from all
accounts, well merited their name. From the numerous families of this name in Chios a council of a hundred was chosen,
which council from amongst themselves elected a body of
officials who had the charge of the government. After paying
their tribute to the Sultan, the residue of their gains was
divided amongst the Giustiniani according to their respective
rights. Their army consisted of three hundred youths of the
Giustiniani guild, with other resident Greeks and Genoese, and
formed a tidy little force, which was often swelled from the
mother country by men who found it convenient, for political
reasons, to absent themselves from home for a while.

The island was well stocked with churches, convents, and
schools, from whence missionaries were sent into the Turkish
dominions ; and furthermore, Chios was a harbour of refuge for
Christian slaves who had escaped from their Turkish taskmasters, and a special magistrate was elected to watch over
them. Food and lodging were given to the fugitives in a
retired spot in the island, until an opportunity occurred to
send them to their homes, and the ships which brought them
were burnt, so as more effectually to conceal their presence in
the island. Sometimes in one year more than a thousand
would thus be liberated, and it was a frequent cause of com-

plaint for the Turks; but the Giustiniani knew how to give hush-money judiciously, and not till the days of Solyman the Magnificent were steps taken to put a stop to this.

This sultan was greatly annoyed when the Giustiniani, from their constant intercourse with Constantinople, were able to give the knights of Malta timely warning of his impending attack; and his rage against the lords of Chios was further aggravated by their instrumentality in the escape of certain Spanish slaves. Upon these double grounds of complaint Solyman determined to remove these obnoxious Genoese from so close a proximity to his capital.

Orders were given to his admiral, Piali Pasha, to surprise the island one day in Holy Week, when the inhabitants were busily engaged with their devotions. Accordingly, under the appearance of a friendly visit, the Pasha arrived at Chios, disembarked his janizaries, and when he saw a favourable opportunity, he seized the town in the name of the sultan. The Giustiniani were shipped off in large bodies to Constantinople, together with the treasures of their temples. The ships which bore the latter, however, says the chronicle, sank unaccountably in a calm sea, as a judgment on the infidel.

Some of the Giustiniani remained on the island, and became merged in the Turkish ·and Greek element, others returned to Genoa, where a piazza, a street, and a palace, named after them, attest their residence to this day; and others again spread over Europe, where an opening occurred for further commercial enterprise. The unfortunate prisoners who were taken to Constantinople were shortly removed to Caffa, where they languished three years in bondage, but were released eventually at the intervention of Charles IX. of France and Pope Pius V.

There is a horrible story current in Roman Catholic circles, but not much accredited thereout, of the martyrdom of some young Giustiniani boys. It runs as follows: eighteen boys, the eldest of whom was sixteen, sons of the captives taken to

Constantinople, were seized and conducted to the Seraglio, where, after being duly circumcised, they were ordered to be brought up in the Mahomedan faith. But neither threats nor flattery could induce them to abandon their religion. At length they were threatened with death. One of them was killed, by way of example, before the eyes of the others ; but still they continued firm, and their mothers, in disguise of washerwomen, entered the Seraglio, and exhorted them to maintain their constancy through all their tortures. Whilst the most excruciating agonies were being inflicted on them, whilst their skin was being torn from their hands and limbs, riches and honours were offered to them as an incentive to apostacy, but without avail ; all remained firm, and died under the torturer's irons, except the three youngest, who recanted. But this apostate trio, when grown up, managed to effect their escape, and lived honoured lives in Christendom, one of them entering a convent. Genoa honoured these young martyrs with a picture, which once adorned the chapel of the " Palazzo pubblico," but was burnt with the rest of the building.

Thus, with the fall of Chios, Genoa lost every vestige of her footing within the Eastern Empire. In the whole of her annals her Black Sea commerce forms one of the most illustrious pages, in perusing which one is led to wonder how that narrow strip of Ligurian coast, and the narrow limits of one single city, could attain so great an influence—an influence indeed which could turn the scales in the destinies of an empire, and could unite the extreme corners of the then known universe with the gilded threads of commerce.

CHAPTER VII.

THE GENOESE IN CYPRUS AND IN ENGLAND.

IN proportion to the disasters which attended the Christian arms in Palestine so did Cyprus grow in importance as a commercial centre, and thither must we follow our Italian traders, who carried along with them their jealousies and their contentions, with which to increase the difficulties which hung around the uneasy crown that the Lusignans wore.

As a first record of a Ligurian footing on this island we note that, in 1208, Pietro Gontardo, the Genoese envoy, was sent to negotiate terms for his country with Elizabeth, the Cypriot queen, the fruits of which embassy were various immunities from taxation for Genoa's merchants, and a plot of ground in Nicosia on which to build them warehouses. With the progress of time and the progress of the Genoese in commerce, these terms were periodically enlarged, until, in 1232, Henry I. of Lusignan gave the Ligurian traders most excellent terms—ingress and egress free of toll for their ships in all the ports of his kingdom, streets and warehouses in various towns, and thereby formed the pattern for all the transactions hereafter held between Genoa and Cyprus, and thereby was laid the foundation stone of that ambition which prompted Genoa in after years to aim at entire control over this island kingdom.

So long as the ports of Syria remained in Christian hands Cyprus was merely a convenient trading centre at which the galleys eastwards and homewards bound would halt to ware-

K

house or disperse through Europe the rich produce of the
caravans; and though valuable enough as a receptacle, or
mart, it was not till the close of the thirteenth century that
the real importance of Cyprus asserted itself. When, however,
in 1288, Benedetto Zaccharia, the Genoese " rover of the seas,"
brought the remnants of the conquered garrison of Tripoli
in his galleys to Cyprus; and when, three years later, other
Genoese galleys conveyed thither the titular king of Jerusalem
from Acre, his last stronghold on the coast of Palestine,
then was the whole of the Eastern commerce centred there.

Various and fluctuating as were the fortunes of Cyprus for
the next hundred years, the Genoese and Venetians always
remained firm to their object of commerce. It mattered little
to them whether the lawful heir or a usurping uncle sat on
the throne, so long as they secured for themselves streets,
warehouses, and extensive immunities from taxation. Inasmuch as the island was the stronghold of Christendom against
the Turks, fleets without end from Genoa were constantly
entering her harbours. The energetic Pontiff Nicholas V.
sent one to act against the infidel, under the command of
Emmanuel Zaccharia, with Tedisio D'Oria as vice-admiral,
both from Genoa. This enabled the merchants to put in
their claims for further advantages under Henry II. of
Lusignan, for this prince had been driven away from his
kingdom by Prince Amaury, of Tyre, and it was to Genoese
aid that he owed his restoration; and at the festivities
incident on his return to Cyprus, no " loggia " was grander
than Genoa's; and throughout his reign no warehouses were
better stocked with merchandize than theirs.

But throughout this prosperous period, prosperous alike
for Genoa and her Cypriot allies, a secret undercurrent of
jealousy was striking at the very root of their good-will. The
Ligurian sailors when from home were by no means renowned
for their good feelings. They quarrelled with the Venetians,
they quarrelled with the Pisans, and, moreover, not a few times

were they engaged in brawls with their Cypriot hosts. Added
to this they acquired for themselves a reputation for robbery—
probably well founded, as the complaint seems to have been
universal—and for some cause they chose to countenance
robbery in others, for one of the most formidable complaints
against them was that they favoured rather than otherwise
the frequent descents of the corsairs on the Cypriot coasts.

Thus were the Venetians and the natives drawn into a
closer bond of union, and out of this sprang a long disastrous
war, which ruined Cyprus, which exalted Genoa above all due
limits therein, and which paved the way for the final subjection of the island by the Turks.

During the reign of Peter I. of Lusignan this animosity
against Genoa grew more open. Men hated the insolence of
our Ligurians; street brawls, destruction of property, and
constant uneasiness were the result ; and when the king saw
fit to perpetrate an outrage on some sailors then in port, all
pretensions at friendship were at an end. It was in this wise
King Peter planned an expedition against Setalia. To swell
his troops he ordered a small handful of Genoese to join him.
They flatly refused to do so, whereupon the king had them
publicly whipped, their ears cut off, and thus maimed and
battered they went home to tell their tale to the enraged
citizens at Genoa.

After much difficulty and loss of life a peace was again
established, which outwardly continued to exist till 1369,
when King Peter was murdered—through Genoese influence
men said—and his infant son Peter II. reigned in his stead,
under the control of his uncles, who used all their power to
fan the anti-Genoese feeling amongst the inhabitants. Venetians and Cypriots were in closer league than ever. Not
unfrequently would the darkness of the night be illuminated
by the burning of Genoese warehouses ; not unfrequently
would a wealthy merchant be knocked down in the streets,
his house ransacked, and his stores carried off. No insult was

left untried upon them, and it wanted but a flagrant outrage to excite an open war, and this was forthcoming at the youthful monarch's public coronation in 1373. A grand banquet was given to celebrate the event in the town hall of Famagosta. Thither were bidden Venetians and Genoese, and over the festive board Venetian and Genoese came to open blows, and the Cypriots having thrown in their lot with the former, the unfortunate representatives of the Ligurian Republic got grievously worsted. They were hurled out of the windows into the square beneath, and those of them who escaped with life from this by no means insignificant fall, were set upon by the rabid populace below, so that not one of them escaped alive. It was in vain that the Genoese "podestà" at Famagosta remonstrated at this breach of treaty. All the Ligurian goods to be found in the city were seized ; every merchant there resident was killed, and from this terrible massacre escaped only one, so says the historian,[1] to relate his tale of woe at home.

All was rage and consternation in the Ligurian capital. A council was hastily called ; an armament was at once voted to chastise this youthful scion of the Lusignan house ; and before many days had expired, Pietro Campofregoso sailed forth from the harbour of Genoa with a goodly fleet of over forty galleys, and the bravest of Genoa's sons were thereon, "embarked with such loud reason for the Cyprus wars."[2]

At this period of her history Genoa was at her best and proudest ; her standard was all dominant throughout the Mediterranean. Pisa was crushed, Venice was weakened by her frequent losses, and hence was unable to assist her Cypriot ally very substantially. Not a power existed in those days to keep her in check, and therefore we are not surprised to see that disasters fell fast and thick upon the Cypriots. And out of this war Genoa added fresh laurels to her crown, and founded, as her historians are pleased to call it, "her royal

[1] Accinelli. [2] Shakespeare, *Othello,* act i. sc. i.

greatness," inasmuch as kings were conquered by her, and kings became her vassals.

By way of further assistance to their cause, the Genoese obtained an award from the Pope entitling them to recover all their lands and goods from the young king of Cyprus ; and, moreover, the king's own mother, Queen Eleanora, favoured the cause of the Genoese, disliking the avuncular influence which excluded her from any hand in the govern- ment or in the management of her young son. The grand- master of Rhodes tried in vain to arrange a peace ; Genoa was too intent on revenge to listen to his mediation. And well she might be.

The forty-three galleys at length reached the island of Cyprus. They brought with them wondrous instruments, the product of skilful Ligurian brains, called *Troja*, calculated to throw large stones a hitherto unprecedented distance— another instance of this peculiar skill evinced by the Genoese in developing the then but youthful talent for producing instruments of death.

Damiano Cattaneo landed with the vanguard, whilst a priest was entrusted with a letter to the king, stating how the Genoese had come to carry out the Pope's award, solely from a sense of duty, which would not allow them to neglect the pontifical injunctions. At Famagosta the king heard of the advance of his enemy ; he heard of the fall of Limesso and of Paphos, and in his weakness he could do nothing. Genoese annals state how just and honourable Damiano Cattaneo was towards the conquered inhabitants ; how he told his soldiers to respect the honour of women, as it was not against them they were sent to fight. But Cypriot annals tell a different tale ; and a pilgrim of strong Venetian proclivities relates thus, in the allegory of a dream, the distress of the Cypriots : "But alas now for the kingdom of Cyprus! Through the tyranny and oppression of those who bear the red cross on the white ground—the Genoese I mean—all the merchandize has disappeared, all the inhabitants are become savage, and appear more dead than alive." [1]

Towards the close of the year 1373 the Genoese army appeared before the walls of Famagosta, the king's stronghold. Again the grand-master of Rhodes took upon himself the office of mediator, and through his instrumentality a peace was brought about, for the king was without the sinews of war. And, according to the terms of this peace, he consented to hold his crown as a tributary of Genoa's, to disburse within twelve years over two millions of golden florins, and to grant the Genoese free egress and ingress into his kingdom, whenever and wheresoever they desired ; and the town of Famagosta was to be handed over to them in full sovereignty ; and as a pledge of good faith, he gave them his uncle, James de Lusignan, the heir presumptive to the crown, who, together with his wife, was sent as a hostage to Genoa.

Thus was the Genoese war in Cyprus drawn to a close, and thus was the curtain drawn over the prosperity of the once flourishing house of Lusignan ; and over the towers of Famagosta the most prosperous city in the island, floated for a century the banner of St. George.

On the return of her victorious troops and her triumphant admiral, great rejoicings took place in Genoa. Campofregoso, the republican conqueror of a king, was honoured as befitted his deserts. For his lifetime he was freed from the payment of every tax, and a handsome palace was presented to him by a grateful senate just outside the city walls—a palace which in after years was Prince Andrea D'Oria's Naboth's vineyard, and the home of his latter days ; and on this spot did Andrea, after the old Cypriot hero's fabric had been destroyed by the French, erect the palace which is now visited as one of the sanctuaries of Genoese art. Thus did Genoa requite her deserving citizen ; whilst every 11th of October it was ordained that a golden offering should be made to the

---

[1] Philip de Maizières.

church of St. Francis with a fitting number of waxen tapers as a pious acknowledgment of mercies received.

Meanwhile, in Cyprus the state of affairs was by no means so cheery, though a brother of the doge's was sent to re-organize the defences and legislate for Famagosta; yet the Genoese, here as elsewhere, were hard taskmasters, and had but little mercy on a fallen foe. Again our old pilgrim takes up his allegorical dream, and puts into the mouth of an old beldame, who was sent as a messenger from the island of Aceldama (as he is pleased to term Cyprus) to the Queen, this dirge: "What more," says the hag, "can I say, O Queen, in thus renewing my weary tale? Those mortal enemies of ours, the Genoese, came to Nicosia, and without regard for the divine majesty, they publicly robbed the Cathedral of St. Sophia and all the other churches, Catholic, Greek, and schismatic alike; and from the holy Mother Church they stole away her vessels, her relics, her jewels, and her holy chalices; and, what is worse, the pavements of the churches themselves are red with the blood of priests vilely slain, to the confusion of the Catholic faith and their own damnation." In this allegory the pilgrim continues to pour down accusations of every baseness on Genoese heads. Though, as we have seen, his proclivities were Venetian, nevertheless it is more than probable that he had good grounds to go upon in his assertions, for certain it is that ever afterwards the commerce and prosperity of Cyprus gradually disappeared. The Genoese, by their exorbitance, destroyed the goose which had laid so many golden eggs for Christendom; and then, when Venice had got all the gleanings left by Genoa, after the weak reigns of James the bastard of Lusignan and Catharine Cornaro, the island of Cyprus became an easy prey to the Sultan of Egypt. "Venetian fishermen, indeed," sneered two English lords in the reign of Henry VIII., when talking of Cyprus; "expert enough in filching what belongs to others."

With so large a sum of money to advance, and with so

little to advance it from, King Peter was obliged to come to Genoese and other traders for assistance. To them he sold a large portion of the revenues of his kingdom, as security for the sum advanced, and thus was established one of Genoa's best known "mahones," or public loans, got up on the principle of numerous others in which mediæval Genoese capitalists so largely embarked. This debt was placed under the immediate protection of Genoa, and when, in 1408, all the several loans were united into the one Bank of St. George, the Cypriot company had consigned to them, as security for their advances, all the revenues and credit of Famagosta ; and though virtually merged in the great bank, this loan main-tained its identity and its several privileges, and was separately mentioned in various treaties, as may be gleaned from the archives of St. George.

Genoa had now a sort of monopoly over the Cypriot trade, and nothing was more ruinous to the island than this. Every branch of industry, every branch of commerce, was heavily taxed by the Génoese governors, in accordance with the extortionate system on which the Ligurians treated their various dependencies. The natural result of this was intense dissatisfaction throughout the island, constant insurrections, and constant endeavours to throw of the yoke ; and when Genoa was weak at home, troubles in their island dependency was the natural result. Unable any longer to control these affairs, the government of Genoa, in 1447, handed over their interest in the island to the protectors of the Bank of St. George,[1] and here, as elsewhere, the mercenary rulers of this great bank tried to squeeze thereout everything they could, and introduced a system far harder than before, which ground down the wretched inhabitants to the lowest depths.

But to return to the fortunes of the royal house of Lusig-nan. The king's uncle James and his wife were meanwhile languishing in their Genoese prison. They had tried to effect

---

[1] *Vide* ch. xi.

their escape, but only succeeded in making their jailors more strict than before, so that they were removed to the castle behind the lighthouse ; and here Caroline de Lusignan presented her husband with his firstborn son, and out of compliment to the traditional origin of their Genoese jailors, they christened the infant captive " Janus," trusting perhaps that this complimentary name, coupled with the mythological notion of peace therein contained, might soften the hearts of the persecutors of their land.

Almost identical with the birth of the infant Janus came the news that the youth King Peter of Cyprus was no more ; and thus, as he left no issue, the titular kingdom of Jerusalem, and the almost titular one of Cyprus, devolved on the head of James de Lusignan, who was so closely guarded between the four walls of a Genoese prison.   The doge, Niccolò Guarcio, at once repaired in great state to the prison with this joyful intelligence, and proposed that James should at once assume his inherited honours, previously having signed a document by which Genoa was to reap numerous additional advantages. To ensure the protection of Famagosta, and her absolute sovereignty therein, two leagues of land all round the town were to be conceded to Genoa, numerous forts in the neighbourhood also were to be handed over to the Ligurians, which secured for Genoa entire command of the port ; and after agreeing to these and many other favourable commercial pacts, the doge conducted his prisoner in state to the ducal palace, and there, amidst great display and before the assembled multitude, the doge placed the crown of Cyprus on James's head.   Curious indeed must have been the scene, and humiliating in the extreme for the descendant of the haughty crusader, Guy de Lusignan, to receive his crown from the hands of the simple burghers of Genoa.

A banquet was given to the new king and queen of Cyprus by the doge of Genoa, prior to their departure for their island realm.   Much was said thereat about mutual affection and regard, but little of which can have existed, inasmuch as, on pretext of the dangerous state of the island, the doge insisted on retaining the youthful heir in Genoa, as a pledge of good faith ; and when king James and his wife set off on ten of the republican galleys, they only exchanged their prison for the leading-strings of the Genoese captain of Famagosta. Throughout the remainder of his reign James was but a tool in the hands of Genoa. The doges treated him with the utmost contempt, when he wrote to complain of the insults offered to him by the captain of Famagosta, and by all the Genoese throughout the island. History affords us examples of but few crowns which were more uneasy to wear than his.

When young Janus went to Cyprus to inherit his father's crown, he too went under Genoese auspices ; but Genoa, during his reign, was not so strong, and not so able to control his footsteps, and the king bore but little regard for his native and namesake Genoa. He did all he could to take Famagosta, but without success. Throughout his island kingdom there was no organization, no sinews of war, and Janus in himself was one of the weakest of his weak line. He hesitated to throw himself into the protection of Venice ; he groaned under the yoke of Genoa; and whilst he hesitated and groaned, the Sultan of Egypt came one day and actually carried him away captive, in 1424. Poor young monarch—the offspring of a Genoese prison, the football which Genoa, Venice, and Egypt kicked mercilessly about—he did again recover his freedom, but only on the payment of a large ransom ; and on his return to Cyprus he could do little but live as a sort of wandering bandit amongst his mountain domains ; and shortly afterwards this troubled namesake of the god of peace breathed his last in poverty and distress.

It was Genoa's internal decay which eventually brought about the downfall of her prosperity in Cyprus. Their French despot, Boucicault, ruined her with fortifications and armaments both at home and in the island, and with the increase

of their difficulties the Genoese squeezed harder than ever
to get what they could out of Cyprus; so that when, in 1447,
Famagosta was ceded in full sovereignty to the Bank of St.
George, their exorbitance was so great that this once flourishing mart of commerce was completely ruined, and after twenty-
nine years of this oppression became an easy prey to James,
the bastard king of the house of Lusignan, and his Venetian
allies. Thus it was that Genoese influence in Cyprus passed into
the hands of the Queen of the Adriatic. It was a thoroughly
disgraceful influence indeed which she had exercised therein ;
and Venice, following in her footsteps, left naught but the
rotten carcass of this once great stronghold of Christendom to
fall into Turkish hands.

Let us now follow Genoa into other climes, and to another
page of her history which unites her more closely with ourselves, and with the infant efforts of England to become a
mercantile nation. In their commercial intercourse, mediæval
Genoa and mediæval England offer much of interest. In
England it was that leather and steel were produced cheaper
than elsewhere ; her woollen goods rivalled those of Flanders,
and thither did Genoa bring the silks and velvets of the south,
the drugs and aromatics of the Indies to exchange for these
commodities ; and, as incipient ideas of luxury began to
develop, this intercourse became more marked, and Genoese
families found it by no means unprofitable to establish commercial houses in London, and to have warehouses along the
Thames, as they did in Constantinople, Cyprus, and other
centres of commerce.

We have seen how close the intercourse was between
Genoa and England during the Crusades,[1] how Richard
Cœur de Lion carried home the banner of St. George, and
how his followers tarried in the Ligurian capital on their way
eastwards. These perhaps were the seeds which did not
grow up and become mature until the commercial-loving

---

[1] *Vide* ch. xi.

Edward III. aimed at establishing on our isle a commerce which should rival and eventually surpass that of Flanders. Thus, during the most flourishing period of Genoese story, and during the period of youthful development in England, we find many points of interest which bound together these commercial powers, of which the small Italian republic was to pave the way for much of the greatness of the other.

A slight difference which occurred between the Genoese and the English in the reign of Edward II. goes far to prove how much intercourse there had been between the two countries for some period before. Two Ligurian merchants, Simone Dentone and Emmanuele Mangiavacca by name, had, on their own account, assisted Robert Bruce in Scotland by selling to him galleys and materials for war. Edward II. wrote a remonstrance to the Republic about this, dated July 18th, 1316, from Westminster, and begged Genoa to punish the delinquents. Not only did the rulers of the Republic see fit to do this, but also, six months later, we find Leonardo Pessagno sent with five galleys, armed at the expense of the Republic, to assist Edward in prosecuting his Scotch wars; and in the following year Edward wrote a letter of thanks to the podestà of Genoa, couched in the most cordial terms.

This Pessagno family is curiously mixed up in Genoa's mediæval annals of commerce. Again and again they appear in her books as carrying on a brisk traffic with England in woollen goods; and from this noble house came forth numerous brave sailors, who acted for a century as admirals under the crown of Portugal,[1] superintended her maritime adventures, and undoubtedly by their prowess paved the way for the discovery of the Cape of Good Hope.

On the accession of the third Edward, the demonstrations of friendship between Genoa and England were still more marked. When, on one occasion, some Genoese merchant ships

[1] *Vide* ch. x.

were seized on the coast of Essex by one of the Despencers, Niccolò Fieschi was sent by the Republic to demand reparation from the king. This was readily granted, Edward writing himself to the Republic, expressing his regret for the misfortune, "in consideration of the friendship and goodwill with which our ancestors and your commune reciprocally did honour to one another, and which we desire in our time to increase." This same Niccolò Fieschi was appointed special ambassador for the Republic in London, and was held in great friendship by the English king.

Amongst curious documents lately brought to light, none is more overwhelming to our preconceived notions of English history, and to the story of Edward II.'s sad death in Berkley Castle, than a letter from one, Manuele Fieschi, notary to the Pope at Avignon, addressed to Edward III. of England, and lately discovered in the archives of Herault.[1] It lacks in itself much to substantiate it and make it accepted as an historical truth ; yet, in comparing English and Genoese history at this time, and in identifying the writer of it, it is placed conveniently within the bounds of probability if not of certainty. It runs as follows :—

" Let it be in the name of the Lord, what I have here written with my own hand, I have gathered from the confession of your father, and so I took heed that it should be notified to your lordship. In the first place, your father said that, seeing England raised against him at the instigation of your mother, he fled from his family, seeking refuge at the castle of Chepstow, which belonged to the grand marshal, Earl of Norfolk ; and at length, becoming alarmed, he embarked with Hugh Despencer, with the Earl of Arundel, and with some other lords, and landed at Glamorgan, where he was made prisoner by Henry of Lancaster, together with the said Despencer, and Master Robert of Baldok. Your father

---

[1] By M. Le St. Germain ; the document is now in Paris.

was then conducted to Kenilworth, and his followers were sent to different places ; and thus he lost his crown at the petition of many.

"Subsequently, at the coming feast of Candlemas, you were crowned, and the prisoner was finally removed to Berkley. But the servant who held him in custody, after the lapse of a little time, thus addressed him: 'My lord, Sir Thomas Gournay and Sir Simon Ebersfeld, are come here to slay you. If it is pleasing to you, I will give you my clothes that you may escape.' In short, at nightfall, your father, in this disguise, got out of his prison and arrived at the last gate without meeting any resistance, and without being discovered. Finding there the porter asleep he forthwith killed him, and, having possessed himself of the keys, got out into the open country, at liberty to go where he wished. Then the knights who had come to kill him, learning too late of his flight, and fearing the wrath of the queen, and for their own lives, took council, and determined to put the corpse of the above-mentioned porter into a coffin, and bury it at Gloucester as if it had been the body of the king. First of all they cut out the heart, and cunningly presented it to Queen Isabella, and made her believe it was her husband's.

"Your father, however, when he got out of Berkley Castle, fled forthwith with a companion to the castle of Corfe, where the keeper, Thomas, received him without the knowledge of his lord, who was John Maltravers, and there he remained concealed for the space of a year and a half. At length, hearing how the Earl of Kent had been beheaded for asserting that he was not dead, your father and his companion, by the wish and advice of Thomas, embarked on a ship and sailed for Ireland, where they lived nine months. Fearing, however, to be recognized, your father at last determined to dress himself in a hermit's dress, and thus passed through England ; and having reached the port of Sandwich, crossed from thence over to Sluys. From thence he travelled through Normandy,

and from thence he crossed through Languedoc, until he
reached Avignon, where, slipping a florin into the hands of
a pontifical servant, he got a letter consigned to the Pope,
John XXII. His Holiness having summoned your father into
his presence, secretly, but honourably, lodged him for fifteen
days ; at the expiration of this time, after various projects
and considerations, he went to Paris, and from Paris to
Brabant, and from Brabant to Cologne, on a pilgrimage to
the tomb of the three kings. On his return from Cologne he
crossed through Germany, and thence into Lombardy. From
Milan he went to a certain hermitage in that diocese, where
he remained two years and a half, until a war broke out, and
then he removed into another hermitage in the castle of
Cecima, belonging to the diocese of Pavia,[1] and there he
remained in strict seclusion for about two years, living a life
of penitence, and praying God for us, and other sinners.

"In testimony of the truth of all I have narrated to your
lordship, these presents are stamped with my seal.

"Your devoted servant,

"MANUELE FIESCHI, Papal Notary."

By referring to the Genoese story at this time, the writer
of this letter can be well identified ; for in the annals of the
Fieschi family this Manuele is entered as having been nominated papal notary in 1337 ; and before this we gather that
he had enjoyed a benefice, which belonged to the diocese of
York. Hence his intimacy with England, and with her deposed
king can in a measure be accounted for. And, moreover, from
the will of his brother Gabriele Fieschi, signed 29th January,
1326, we gather that this "canon of the Church of York"
was furthermore presented with a rich canonry in the diocese
of Arras. Thus have we Manuele Fieschi clearly identified,

---

[1] Cecima was originally dependent on the Bishop of Pavia, and was
renowned for its strong position. To-day it is a commune in the Godiasco
division.

not only as closely connected with England, but also as a man of some note in the Church ; and, at the very time of writing this letter, his kinsman, Niccolò, was in London, in high favour with Edward III.

The decapitation of Edward II.'s brother, the Earl of Kent, on the 19th of March, 1330, comes in as a sort of supplementary proof to this assertion of the escape of the king from Berkley Castle. In a letter to the Pope, written by Edward III., and to be found in Thomas Rymer, the king accuses his uncle of "wishing to disturb the peace of the kingdom by proclaiming that my father, who had been dead three years, at whose obsequies he himself had been present, was still alive." Who more likely than his own brother to know of the escape of the exiled monarch ? If this letter from the Genoese be correct, what a revolution it makes in our preconceived belief in English history ; and it is somewhat pleasant to have an excuse for disbelieving the awful story of the red-hot iron, which every one believes to have pierced the second Edward's vitals, and thus to have one more stain wiped off the pages of our annals.

It is, however, unsatisfactory to have to believe that his tomb at Gloucester is apocryphal, and that the bones of our unfortunate monarch lie mouldering amongst those of some old Italian monks cast together in some long-forgotten charnel-house.

Let us now pass on to facts better ascertained than this, which are of greater interest to the English student of his native poet, Chaucer, and which lead us to believe that in addition to our lessons in commercial enterprise, it was in Liguria that our earliest poet, the morning star of our literature, learnt one of his sublimest stories under the tutelage of Petrarch, and in the land where Dante loved to roam.

In 1347, Edward III. hired Genoese galleys for his wars, and in 1372 the king appointed Pietro di Campofregoso, brother of the doge, as commander of the Genoese vessels in his service, with Sir James Pronan, an Englishman, as his lieutenant. A mission was sent three years later to settle, as some say, about a port for their factory in England, or as others say, to negotiate for a further supply of galleys. Be this as it may, Sir James Pronan, accompanied by Giovanni De'Mari, a Genoese, and Godfrey Chaucer, were despatched to Genoa in 1375. Thus far we can satisfactorily trace our poet to Liguria ; whether Petrarch was there at the time or

PORTOFINO PROMONTORY, FROM THE PRISON OF FRANCIS I. IN CERVARA MONASTERY.

not we cannot say. Certain it is that he stayed more at Genoa in his later years than anywhere else in Italy, and certain it is that his old friend Guido Scettem, his college friend, his friend in France, and the friend to whom he addressed many of his letters, was at this time reposing in the monastery of Cervara, which he had built as a resting-place after years of toil in his diocese of Genoa.

Exceeding fair even now in its ruin is that monastery of Cervara, amidst the olive-clad hills of the promontory of Portofino, with the tomb of its founder still resting in its graveyard, and with its reminiscences of the fallen French king Francis I., who, after the battle of Pavia, passed two nights here, in a little room which is still shown, overshadowed by a palm-tree and commanding heavenly views over rock and cliff, pine-trees and olives, washed by the blue waters of the Mediterranean.

This was the spot where Petrarch passed his days when on a visit to Genoa ; here it was that he would discuss with the old archbishop the troubles of Genoa and of Italy, how to heal them, and how to bring about that peace in men's minds which reigned in theirs ; and what more likely than that here Chaucer, on his mission to Genoa, learnt from Petrarch's lips the story of the patient Grisaldis.

For it is scarcely probable, judging from the politics of the day, that a friendly embassy from England to Genoa would proceed to Padua, then in close union with Venice and at war with Genoa. And since we have proof of his being at Genoa, and proof that during these years Petrarch was often at Genoa on visits to his friend, and there is none that either of them were at Padua, in fact presumptive evidence to the contrary, one can only suppose that he spoke figuratively of his clerk of Oxenford, who—

> " Lerned at Padowe of a worthy clerk,
> Francis Petrarch,"
>> *Cant. T.* v. 79.

the story of Grisaldis, mentioning Padua as a place where learned Italians were likely to be met, whereas busy commercial Genoa would hardly be the place for his learned clerk, who would—

> " Lever have at his beddes head
> A twenty bokes, clothed with black or red,
> Of Aristotle, and his philosophie,
> Than robes riche, or fidel, or sautrie."
>> *Cant. T.* v. 296.

whilst Padua, the leading Italian university of the day, would offer every attraction to the representative of the English Oxford.

This indeed was a wonderful storehouse for Chaucer to have opened for him, and over the future of the English language this journey to Genoa had an unlimited influence. Petrarch and Boccacio much esteemed this story of the patient Grisaldis. They considered it as one of their gems in literature ; and the fact of Petrarch's having imparted it to Chaucer when on this visit, shows how friendly must have been the reception given by him to the English poet. In fact, Petrarch seems to have had a special like for Englishmen, and to have met many of them at the papal court of Avignon. Amongst others, he twice met there the peace-loving Richard de Burgh, once in 1331, when he came to treat about the question of Queen Isabella, and in 1333, when he was sent to settle some disturbances between England and France,[1] and with him as with Guido Scettem, Petrarch discussed his topic of peace in an age when they knew no peace.

On returning to his native land, Chaucer delayed not to put pen to paper, and gave to the world perhaps the most pathetic and the best known of his Canterbury tales.

Around the rocky promontories of the Ligurian coast numerous are the spots where poets of various ages have found a suitable haven for their vivid thoughts, and one con-genial for the flight of their imaginations. About seventy years before Chaucer visited Genoa, Dante likewise came on an embassy to the Republic from his native Florence, and during the long period of his exile he passed much time near the ruins of Luna, at Sarzana, with his friends the Malaspina. His acquaintance with this rocky coast is aptly thus ex-emplified—

> 'Twixt Lerici and Turbia, the most desert,
> The most secluded pathway, is a stair
> Easy and open, if compared with that.
>
> DANTE, *Purg. Cant.* iii.

---

[1] " Libraria Visconti " at Pavia.

Whilst amidst the same scenes, centuries later, Byron penned his " Corsair " upon the blood-red rocks of Porto Venere, and Shelley wrote near Lerici, inspired by the gentle rippling of the Mediterranean waves, in whose subtle embrace he breathed his last.

Before referring to the part played by the Genoese at the battle of Crecy, we must take a glance at those well-trained troops of archers for which mediæval Genoa was so justly celebrated. No greater protection had Genoa, both at home and abroad, than these regiments of archers. They were celebrated in the Crusades, they were celebrated in the Black Sea, in France, and in Spain, in short, in every spot where the large Ligurian merchant ships traded—each with its attendant troop of bowmen, sometimes fifty strong, to defend them against marauders.

Every year, in January, the doge and council would appoint two trusty men well skilled in archery to search throughout the dominions for youths who would swell the number. Four times a year in some of the principal towns in Liguria, prizes of silver cups were awarded to successful amateurs, and from amongst the competitors at these meetings, the best shots were chosen ; and it was a much envied post to occupy, for the pay the archers received was exceedingly high, not only at home, but also in the service of foreign monarchs, who hired them to fight their battles. Fifty of these archers, kept at the Republic's cost, formed a body-guard for the doge, and each castle and fort throughout the long coast line of Liguria had a regiment of archers quartered therein, varying in numbers as circumstances required.

When the Milanese laid siege to Como, in 1116, they set the example of hiring these archers ; and this fact gave a great impetus to the pursuit of archery in Genoa, for, in 1118, after the Pisan war, they were thoroughly organized into a regular body, under their own especial consul, and the archer contingent became at once Genoa's stronghold, and the dread of her enemies.

When, in 1346, the Grimaldi and their comrades were driven from Genoa,[1] and were hard pressed by their fellow country-men in Monaco, they passed, as a matter of course, into the service of Philip of Valois in his wars. Antonio D'Oria and Carlo Grimaldi had the title of admirals, and did great service in the wars between the houses of Blois and Montfort, in Brit-tany, and to their expertness was due the capture of Nantes and Hennebon ; hence when Edward III. of England invaded France, Philip eagerly sought the assistance of these able exiles of Genoa to aid him in his struggle, and glad enough were the nobles of Monaco to enlist in the service of a monarch who fought against the ally of their mercantile fellow-countrymen.

On the eventful day of Crecy no less than fifteen thousand Genoese archers are said to have fought under the banner of the lilies. They came up, so runs the story, wet and tired after a heavy march through rain and mud, yet Philip, yield-ing to the jealousy of the French and his own impetuosity, ordered them at once to proceed to action ; in vain did they represent that they were worn out by a six-league march, and that their bows were spoilt by exposure to the rain ; in vain did they ask to be allowed to postpone their attack until the morrow. The Duc d'Alençon reviled them as mercenaries, who fought only for pay ; and thus, stung by reproach, they hesitated no longer to make a gallant attack ; but their efforts were in vain, their war-cry availed them little against the English archers, who were fresh and met them with well strung bows ; at last, pushed on by advancing French, and confronted by advancing English, the unfortunate Genoese were cut to pieces and beaten back. But it was in vain to retreat ; Philip, with unnatural cruelty, ordered his own troops to fall upon the "*canaille Genoise,*" as he termed them, and in the very

---

[1] *Vide* ch. ix.

face of their advancing foes, the French set to work with right good will to execute their inhuman orders.

Thus came about the rout of Crecy, and thus the almost entire annihilation of this troop of archers. Those who escaped were few, but sufficient to excite indignation in the breasts of all Genoese, whether nobles or of the popular faction, and no more Ligurians were found to support Philip in his wars; on the contrary, the bond of union between England and Genoa was thereby more firmly cemented. Large commercial immunities were given to the D'Oria, Spinola, and Fieschi in England, and a sort of perpetual alliance was brought about through their instrumentality between the Republic and the English king.

During the fourteenth and fifteenth centuries large loans were from time to time negotiated by the kings of England from Genoese capitalists, and in return Ligurian merchants obtained the right of importing wool free of charge, and not unfrequently the Genoese were employed to furnish letters of change payable in Rome to acquit the annates of the English bishops with greater ease ; and in London a Genoese consul was in perpetual residence to superintend the interests of their British society of merchants, and in those days most of the English export was done on Genoese bottoms.

A curious tale is told by the Genoese annalist Giustiniani, which, if true, does not reflect much credit on our maritime skill in 1416. In those days some Genoese ships were fighting in the Channel in behalf of France against Henry V. One of these, under command of Lorenzo Foglietta, got detached from the rest, when it was suddenly fallen upon by seven heavy English ships, commanded by the Duke of Warwick and manned by fifteen hundred men. In the ensuing encounter the Genoese, according to their annalist, behaved most bravely ; and when, by means of a pontoon, some English with their standard managed to board the Genoese galley, a sailor cut the bridge with a knife, so that many English with their standard, were captured and many others drowned. Staggered by such valour, the other ships kept aloof, and the Genoese galley effected its escape, with the prisoners and standard to boot.

However this may be, certain it is that in 1421 Henry V. formed a peace and league with Genoa, and the commercial intercourse between the two countries continued with undiminished vigour throughout the succeeding reigns, and little is said of Ligurian fleets in northern waters fighting against the British flag.

A branch of the family of the "rob neighbours," as some assert is the derivation of Pallavicini, had been settled in Genoa since 1353, when John Visconti sent Guglielmo, the marquis, from his home on the banks of the Po, to act as his vice-regent in Genoa. To this family of Pallavicini many noble sons were born, who distinguished themselves in war and in council, but above all in the mercantile line ; consequently their riches increased and multiplied, and even to this day the Marquis Pallavicini is one of Genoa's richest and best known nobles, with his palace and pleasure-grounds at Pegli, where every branch of fantastic landscape gardening has been brought to assist the natural beauties of the spot, from surprise shower-baths to mock cemeteries, amidst lakes, grottoes, and Grecian temples.

Horatio Pallavicini was born in Genoa to this rich branch of the Lombard family; his uncle was Cardinal Pallavicini, famed as the historian of the Council of Trent. Young Horatio, however, developed a taste for travel, and lived in the Low Countries for some time, but eventually crossed over to England with letters of recommendation to Queen Mary, who forthwith made him the collector of the papal taxes in England. On the accession of Elizabeth, Pallavicini found himself with a large sum of money in his hands, and every opportunity afforded him for pocketing the same ; being a thrifty Genoese, he lost no time in doing so, and made himself so agreeable to our maiden queen that she quite overlooked his theft, naturalized him in 1586, knighted him the following year, and borrowed large sums of this stolen money at different intervals and at a high rate of interest.

Thus flourished Horatio Pallavicini when transplanted into English soil; he built himself a fine Italian mansion, with its "loggia" and courtyard, and he owned Baberham, near Cambridge, where he generally lived. An epitaph written in doggerel verse, presumably for his grave, and found in an old manuscript by Sir John Crew, sums up his life thus crudely—

> " Here lies Horatio Palavazene,
> Who robb'd the pope to lend the queene.
> He was a thief : a thief ! thou lyest,
> For whie? he robb'd but Antichrist.
> Him Death wyth besome swept from Babram (Baberham)
> Into the bosome of oulde Abraham ;
> But then came Hercules with his club,
> And struck him down to Beelzebub."

However, Sir Horatio acquired a reputation in other matters than in pilfering a pope, for he commanded an English ship against the Spanish armada, and gained for himself great renown thereby, and a portrait, amongst the other heroes of that occasion, in the borders of the tapestry of the House of Lords. Twice did Sir Horatio marry, and the second time to the daughter of a Dutch merchant, who presented him with three children.

This lady, on the demise of her husband in 1600, waited but a year and a day before she consoled herself by marrying Sir Oliver Cromwell, grandfather of the " Protector." So pleasing was this union to the three young Pallavicini, that they forthwith fell in love with and married three young Cromwells, children of their stepfather,[1] and hence the great Oliver had no less than two Genoese uncles and one Genoese aunt. Perhaps this may in a measure account for the protector's love for the Ligurian Republic. The result of this kindred spirit

---

[1] Noble's " House of Cromwell."

was that he saw fit to do so much honour to the Genoese ambassador, that a remonstrance from the representative of Spain was drawn forth. " Do you not perceive," replied Cromwell, " that England and Genoa are both republics ? hence thcy wish to do themselves mutual honour, being as they both are under the protection of St. George."

With the decline of Genoa's commerce her intercourse with England becomes less marked, and but little of moment occurred between the two countries until Napoleon's days, when Genoa was at her last gasp.[1]

[1] *Vide* ch. xviii.

CHAPTER VIII.

GENOA AND HER VENETIAN RIVAL.

IN order better to realize the importance of the long struggle between Venice and Genoa, let us for a moment place ourselves under the guidance of Francis Petrarch, who lived during the very heat of the contest, and in his peacemaking capacity wrote long letters to the doges of both Republics, showing the lively interest that he, from his retreat at Avignon, felt in the welfare of each. But alas! whilst he occupied the position of unbiassed and respected arbitrator, his sage prophecies about the ill effects of civil war fell, like the warnings of Cassandra, on unheeding ears. In vain he shook his laurelled head, and echoed presages of woes to come on Italy; yet these gloomy forebodings provide posterity with the keynote of Italian politics of the day.

" Do ye wish," he wrote to the doge of Venice, " that this most flourishing Republic which is entrusted to your charge, and all the fair fields of Italy between the Alps and the Apennines, should become the prey of foreign wolves, whom nature has beneficently separated from you by the Alpine ridges and the sea? Do ye wish that the shepherds of the Italian fold should turn upon each other? The foreign wolves are rabid with hunger. Do not persuade yourselves that if Italy be lost Venice will be safe, for she is but a part of it, and it is the nature of the part to follow the whole."

To Genoa he writes even in fuller terms; he chides her

for her internal quarrels, he chides her for her hostility to Venice instead of directing her strength against the common enemy, the Turk, reminding her of her former and present greatness, and threateningly adds, "Rome could not be conquered except by Rome herself. The fate which befell that mighty republic of antiquity will be yours also if you do not apply yourselves to uniting the minds of your citizens, especially now whilst the breath of fortune smiles upon you."

Thus were the "two great lights of Italy," as Petrarch terms them, rushing eagerly to war, regardless of Turk or Saracen who approached their colonies, regardless of the foreign monarchs who smiled to behold their discord. At the outset of the struggle Genoa, perhaps, was the strongest ; she had the largest internal resources, and the greatest ability for action. But Genoa was rotten at the core ; her nobles and her people were the most factious in Italy, and hence, when at peace she had no respite from war. Venice, on the contrary, was constitutional stability itself, and in this lay the secret of her success, and this finally gave her the upper hand over turbulent Genoa.

But, as Petrarch foresaw, this was all gained at the risk of Italian freedom. Italy, and then Venice, fell a prey to the hungry ultramontane wolves, and, as centuries went on, all the poet's worst forebodings were realized to the letter. This struggle between the sister republics tended perhaps more than any other circumstance in mediæval history to alter the aspect of European affairs. It made Italy the battle-field of nations. It was a long weary struggle which lasted over three centuries ; in modern times it might have lasted only as many months. But the results were the same, only the thread of events was thus rendered more complex and difficult to follow.

The first actual encounter between Venice and Genoa which we can honour with the name of war took place in 1206. Their sailors had had frequent collisions before this, in

Palestine, in the Black Sea, and elsewhere, and the seeds of
rivalry, as between Genoa and Pisa, took their origin in the
very outset of their commercial career.

This "affair of Candia," as it is termed, arose out of the
complications incident on the fourth Crusade, in which
Venice, to suit her own ends, directed the forces of Christendom against Constantinople, instead of the Turk. Out of
this Venice gained for herself a fourth part of the Eastern
Empire, and old Dandolo, her doge, has received much praise
for not placing on his own head the imperial diadem, for
recognizing that his republic had not inherent strength enough
to maintain him there, and for accepting, in lieu of an empire,
large maritime possessions better suited to promote the commercial interests of his people. Amongst these was the island
of Crete, over which at this time a certain Arrigo Pescatore,
Count of Malta, held a sort of doubtful lordship.

The Count of Malta was of Genoese origin, and lost no
time in repairing to the Ligurian Republic to demand assistance, which was readily granted him ; and then for the first
time Genoa and Venice found themselves at open war.

Affairs went badly for Venice at the outset. Her general,
Rainieri Dandolo, fell into Genoese hands and was hanged.
Crete was conquered ; and had it not been for the contest with
Pisa, at that time raging, Genoa might easily have established
herself in this advantageous station for eastern commerce.
But as it was, affairs occupied her attention nearer home, and
in 1212 Crete fell again into Venetian possession without a
blow.

The hollowness of the peace patched up in 1218 beween
the rivals is attested by the frequency with which it had to be
renewed during the next forty years; small acts of depredation,
such as seizing each other's merchant ships on their way from
the East, kept the flame alive. It is curious to see such
intense jealousy existing between two such small republics.
No question of confines could arise, for they were both hedged

in by nature within the smallest limits, the one by precipitous mountains which left them but a meagre unfertile coast-line, the other was but a mass of houses rising out of the waves. They solely fought through envy, they fought for the empire of the seas and exclusive privileges of commerce ; they rivalled each other in the advance of industry, development of manufacture, and ship-building ; they rivalled each other in the field of travels and discovery, and were then ready to fight to the death, regardless of everything save satisfying their respective jealousies.

When Genoa was driven from Acre, and by her *coup de main* got the upper hand in Constantinople, and, by the treaty of Ninfeo in 1261,[1] found herself installed in much that Venice had previously enjoyed, the occasions were provided for a second war. And this contest illustrates admirably the inherent defect in the Ligurian Republic, namely, her want of unity within herself which stood in the way of her establishing an indisputable superiority over her rival. And this contest likewise prominently displays the weakness of Venice, which prevented her from taking proper advantage of the factions in which her rival was plunged.

To maintain her newly acquired influence in the East, Genoa sent forth a fleet under the joint command of Pierino Grimaldi, a noble, and Perchelto Mallone, the people's representative. They encountered the Venetian squadron at Malvasia which was greatly inferior to their own. But as the combatants were just warming to their work, Mallone, actuated by party spirit, withdrew his ships and sailed away.

The Venetians could scarcely believe what they saw ; they anticipated some deep laid stratagem, and withdrew for a while from the contest. When however they beheld Mallone's galleys fairly under sail, they wonderingly attacked Grimaldi and his thirteen ships and obtained an easy victory. Grimaldi fell at his post. "He died," says an annalist,[2] in a few ex-

---

[1] *Vide* ch. vi.   [2] Scriba.

pressive words, "but he will live for ever, as far as the glory of the Republic is concerned."

This fatal day of Malvasia might easily have secured Venice her lost place in the Black Sea had she been able to follow up her victory, but with inexplicable want of vigour she remained inactive. She had not helped Pisa three years before,[1] and now she let slip the opportunity of checking Genoa's power in the East.

Meanwhile in Genoa all was blank dismay and confusion. It was in vain that they passed sentence of death on the delinquent when the deed was done. The only course by which the nobles saw they could get unanimity of action was by condescending to elect a popular admiral over the fleet. Accordingly, from amongst the people they chose one Simone Grillo, and his election was heralded with delight by the populace ; he was carried in triumph through the streets, and the trembling nobles feared a general *émeute* was at hand. Grillo, however, relieved their minds by appearing unarmed in the Council Hall and protesting his loyalty. On this he was permitted to join the fleet, and sailed out of the harbour amidst the hearty cheers of all parties.

With unanimity to secure his success, Grillo hastened at once into the Adriatic and waylaid a rich squadron of merchant ships, on its way to Venice from Egypt, off Durazzo, in Albania. After a short but severe conflict the whole of this immense wealth fell into his hands, and thereby the loss of Malvasia was more than repaired, and Genoa's interests in the East were again firmly secured. Simone Grillo returned home with his booty, and modestly resigned the command of the armament which had been entrusted to him.

It surprises us immensely to find how for the next thirty years Genoa was able to keep up a desultory warfare with Venice, when she was at the height of her struggle with Pisa ; and it surprises us still more that Venice raised not a hand to

[1] *Vide* ch. iii.

assist Pisa, though she was on most friendly terms with her, and when by so doing she could have ruined Genoa. But so it was; this opportunity was allowed to escape, and the penalty for such short-sighted policy was a single-handed contest with Genoa for many a good year.

It was in this same desultory warfare with Venice that Oberto D'Oria, the victor of Meloria,[1] earned for himself a reputation as a rising admiral, and added another to the list of D'Orian heroes, almost invariably invincible by sea. We see him throughout his active career scouring the Mediterranean from East to West; from Canea in Crete he brought the bells which he hung in his family church of S. Matteo; at another time he pounced upon a merchant fleet bound for Venice, and retired quietly to Messina to divide the spoil.

Under the very eyes of Venice, Genoa at this time carried on a brisk traffic in the Adriatic. Three times a year Bari, in Apulia, was the busy scene of one of these great international fairs, and numerous accounts are extant of Ligurian merchants and their transactions at this mart. Going northward from Bari, the Genoese were on most intimate terms with the Republic of Ancona, and several treaties between Genoa and Ancona point to a sort of mutual protection and defence against Venice.

After the fall of Pisa at Meloria, in 1296, Genoa could transfer her attention with all the greater vigour to her contest against Venice. Four years after this victory men's minds were again bent on war. Venice cared not to pay a tax to her rival on all ships which went to Caffa, Genoa resented the treatment she had received in Cyprus, and thus the rivals prepared for another and more determined contest for supremacy.

As usual, during a cessation of foreign wars, Genoa busied herself with her internal factions; but it was fortunate for her that she had at this time two influential men within her walls,

---

[1] *Vide* ch. iii.

who used their power to quell the disorders. Oberto D'Oria, the victor of Meloria was one, and a monk, James of Varagine, who was afterwards beatified for his virtues, was the other; the latter preached peace and good-will amongst men, whilst the former used the forcible argument of expediency, and together they contrived to pacify the city.

An armament was voted by the council, and Oberto D'Oria was elected admiral. In his official capacity he took up his pen and addressed to the Venetians a singular epistle, which gives us an insight into the convenient arrangements they had for carrying on mediæval warfare. He therein chided them for their continuous assaults on Genoese property; he represented to them that the Genoese would ·stand it no longer, and stated that on this account they had prepared an armament. He then proceeded to propose that for the convenience of both parties their respective squadrons should proceed to the coast of Sicily, and there decide the dispute by force of arms.

Having despatched this challenge, D'Oria proceeded with his ships to Sicily, but waited in vain for the arrival of an enemy. Venice was unprepared for war, and wisely deferred a contest until a more favourable opportunity presented itself. Oberto D'Oria was thus forced to return home, and soon afterwards died; and on the loss of his influence, Genoa again returned to her factions with redoubled energy.

At length Venice saw her opportunity for striking a blow at her adversary. A fleet was sent to operate in the Black Sea, fire was set to the houses of Galata, irreparable damage was done to Caffa, and in the Archipelago everything Genoese was burnt, and then off they sailed for Cyprus, whilst the Genoese were squabbling amongst themselves. With much trouble the many rulers of Genoa succeeded at length in adjusting their difference, and a goodly array of seventy-six galleys was entrusted to the care of Lamba D'Oria to punish the Venetians for their depredations. "Go," said the captain of the people, "go, brave man ; thy country entrusts you with her forces, hasten to curb the pride of our enemies, and show yourself a worthy successor of the D'Oria."

Much larger was the force Venice produced for the contest, and when the combatants met off Curzola, amongst the Dalmatian islands, the Genoese were anxious to come to terms, and sought them, but the Venetians haughtily refused. In the arrangement of his forces amongst the islands, Lamba D'Oria showed much tact, and on the eve of the contest, September 8th, 1298, addressed his men in thrilling terms, reminding them of the burning hearths in Galata and Caffa, and of their recent victory at Meloria.

At the outset of the battle ten of the Genoese vanguard were cut off by the enemy in breaking their way through to join the rest of their forces, and they sustained a heavy loss. Amongst others fell a fine young man, the son of Lamba D'Oria. Petrarch tells us of the touching scene when the admiral stooped down to see whether life was extinct; he uttered not a word of lament, but, taking up his dead son in his arms and folding him to his breast, he exclaimed, "If thou hadst died in the bosom of thy country thou couldst not have had a more splendid burial than this!" and clad in armour as he was and still warm, Lamba D'Oria cast his son from the ship's turrets into the waves.

This battle of Curzola was a sharp and vehement struggle, and resulted in terrible loss to the Venetians, four of whose galleys alone escaped to tell the tale to their terrified countrymen, who beheld from afar how events had gone. Had Lamba D'Oria but driven the contest home, Venice was ill-prepared to meet him ; as it was, he determined to sail off to Genoa, taking with him the Venetian admiral, blind old Andrea Dandolo. Chained to the mast of his own vessel, and unable to sustain the effects of his humiliation, there, as he stood, Dandolo dashed his head against the mast and died.

Great were the rejoicings of Genoa on their admiral's

return, and **Lamba D'Oria's** praises were widely sung. A grateful senate gave him a house in the Piazza S. Matteo, and he died in 1323, a much honoured citizen. On the church of S. Matteo a long Latin inscription is still to be read, on the

FAÇADE OF S. MATTEO.

black and white marble façade, testifying to the service he had rendered his country ; and his remains were placed in an old Roman sarcophagus, likewise still to be seen fixed upon the same façade.

The natural result of such a victory was a most favourable peace for Genoa, signed under the direction of Matteo Visconti, lord of Milan, in 1299; and thus the century closed on Genoa as without doubt the most powerful state in Italy, and unquestionably the mistress of the Mediterranean; Pisa was no longer a maritime power, and Venice was for the moment at her feet. What a glorious future might have been in store for the Ligurian Republic; but again, to quote the words of Petrarch, "Civil conflagrations are the death of nations, and you Genoese are an example of it." The truth of this assertion required but two more centuries to verify.

The next outbreak of war between the two Republics had its origin in the occupation of the island of Chios, in 1349,[1] which both parties considered essential to the development of commerce in the Black Sea. Angry messages and useless demands, which neither felt it consistent with their dignity to accept, passed between them. Venice could not forget that she had once held Chios, Genoa could not help taking every opportunity to use her position for molesting her rival. Thus constant acts of hostility were the upshot. For instance, in 1350, Philip D'Oria, in command of a few galleys, left the port of Chios and proceeded to the Venetian stronghold of Negropont, which he put to the sword, and carrying back with him the keys of the town hung them on the walls of Chios by way of trophy.

Venice could ill brook such insults as these, and set to work to get up an alliance against Genoa, which for a moment appeared overwhelming. Cantacuzene, the Greek emperor, did not love the Genoese in Pera; he felt probably like France did when England held Calais, and eagerly accepted the opportunity afforded him for picking a quarrel with Genoa.

But Cantacuzene had a wife Anne, a daughter of the house of Savoy, a house at that time on terms of close intimacy with Genoa, and she hoped by Genoese assistance to place

[1] *Vide* ch. vi.

her son on the imperial throne in his father's stead ; hence the want of union in the Greek court made them but poor allies for Venice.

But not so was their other ally, Peter, king of Aragon, who agreed to keep a fleet of at least eighteen galleys winter and summer to assist Venice ; and eager as he was to establish his rule in Corsica and Sardinia, he did not break his promise, and came bravely forwards.

Niccolò Pisano was the Venetian admiral entrusted with carrying on the war, and Pagano D'Oria was the admiral of the Genoese fleet. In spite of D'Oria's endeavours to prevent the allies from joining, he was unsuccessful, and found himself confronted by thirty Venetian and thirty Aragonese galleys on his arrival at the mouth of the Bosphorus.

Without delay, however, he determined to fight, knowing well the dangers of the spot, and feeling convinced that the Spaniards at least were ignorant of the sunken rocks and pitfalls which surrounded them. Of all mediæval sea-fights, none equalled in intensity of horror this engagement, which was named after the Bosphorus. Shortly after the commencement a fearful storm arose, and the sea dashed the conflicting vessels against one another, and against the hidden rocks in frightful confusion. Neither party could retreat, and through the livelong night they fought with the nearest enemy they could find, by the next wave to be dashed with destructive violence against a friendly galley, then both would sink in the waves. In such dire confusion as this the Spaniards, through entire ignorance of the place, and perhaps less skilful sailors than the maritime republicans, were nearly all lost, and dawn broke on a scene of the wildest possible horror. The sea, now a little calmer, was one seething mass of corpses and wreckage, whilst cries of despair from drowning and wounded rent the clear morning air.

Taking the opportunity of the return of day, the Venetians extricated themselves from this scene of confusion, and sailed away to the neighbouring port of Terapia, leaving the Genoese on the field to count the number of their slain. To Genoa has been attributed the victory by all contemporary writers, but it was a sorry one. Most of the flower of her nobility was left in the Bosphorus, and the return home of her battered squadron was attended with far more mourning than joy.

For the time, however, the results were satisfactory for the Ligurian interests in the East. Cantacuzene, making a virtue of necessity, wrote on his submission, "It is necessary to humble myself before the lords of the sea." And again the Black Sea commerce was secure.

From Petrarch's letter to Genoa after this contest, we can realize how deeply he was moved by the disastrous effects of this battle on both his beloved Republics. He spoke as follows: "The Mediterranean worships your standard, the ocean fears it, and the Bosphorus is still tinged with your blood. Who can without shuddering read and listen to the details of your success in this last battle, in which three powerful nations fought? Who can describe all the horrors of that fearful day, the whistling of the winds, the clash of ropes and iron, the shock of vessel meeting vessel, the blasting of trumpets, and the hissing of flying arrows, the groans and yells of the dying? Who can paint in words that night which followed the day, a night like that which Virgil described in the burning streets of Troy? No centuries gone by furnish us examples of so obstinate and bloody a conflict."

Through the force of party spirit, Pagano D'Oria was removed from command on his return home. Men said, and perhaps with reason, that he had been ruthlessly wasteful of life in hazarding an engagement with a storm impending in so dangerous a locality. But the appointment of Antonio Grimaldi in his stead only brought disasters on the Genoese arms.

Alghero, in Sardinia, was besieged by the Aragonese, and Venetians; Grimaldi was despatched to relieve it, but he was

piteously and hopelessly repulsed. He fled to Genoa with
nineteen galleys, but through the influence of his party he
escaped the punishment he so justly merited; and to the
same influence he owes a handsome Gothic tomb erected
to his memory, which still adorns the cathedral walls.

ANTONIO GRIMALDI'S TOMB.

After this repulse a hopeless state of confusion reigned in
Genoa. Unable herself to curb the factious spirit within
her walls, she cast away her fair liberty, and entrusted her
government to the hands of the lord of Milan, a folly for

which she had cause to repent too late, when a peace was brought about by Milanese intervention, and she had breathing time given her to realize the ill effects of the steps she had taken.

Venice meanwhile, elated by the victory of Alghero, heeded not the cooling words of peace breathed into her assemblies by Petrarch. He was civilly answered by the doge, and addressed as "Man of high virtue and constancy, to whom God has given the faculty of wisdom, and of speaking choice words." But this was the only heed they paid to them, and they quickly manned a fresh fleet under Niccolò Pisano to carry on their victory.

Genoa had the wisdom on this contingency to heal her quarrels once more, and re-elect Pagano D'Oria to the command. And these heroes of the Bosphorus once more met for a trial of strength off the island of Sapienza, near the Morea, and a signal victory was gained by the Genoese, which wiped off all former stains, and made the name of Pagano D'Oria honoured amongst men. This worthy admiral was presented with a house, still standing amongst the other mansions of this family in the Piazza S. Matteo, and his name and honours are still written up on that stone volume, the façade of the D'Oria's church.

On the 29th of September, 1355, a peace was ratified with Venice, by which the Queen of the Adriatic agreed to pay down a handsome sum of money, promised to abandon her Black Sea commerce, and a mutual exchange of prisoners took place. Thus again was Genoa undisputed mistress of the seas, and a few years later we shall see her within an ace of grasping the very lagunes on which her rival was built. Such was the greatness won for her by brave men and true. Such was the greatness won for her by her inexhaustible wealth. She won Cyprus,[1] and thereby kings were her prisoners. Yet with the same hand she presented her own

[1] *Vide* ch. vii.

freedom to Germany, to Milan, to Monferrato, and to France ; and each time, when she had cast off her self-imposed yoke, she returned to her petty jealousies and quarrels, only to fall into another yoke even harder than the first.

Let us glance for a moment at the respective positions of the two rival Republics before we see them once more, and for the last time, openly and independently contesting for the mastery of the Mediterranean. Both, after a long course of commercial success, had reached an enormous pitch of wealth and prosperity. In addition to her hundred miles of lagunes, and coast line along the Adriatic, well studded with islands and cities, Venice was mistress of many other provinces on the coast of Dalmatia, Friuli, and Istria. She ruled in Crete and Negropont, she had extensive concessions in Constantinople and Cyprus. In Egypt she held a position of the greatest importance to her commerce with the Indies. The Black Sea was her one Naboth's vineyard, and the tribute she had to pay to the Genoese for the use of the harbour of Caffa went sorely against her grain ; for Venice had a colony on the Don, to reach which she had to pass by Caffa, and this was a constant source of annoyance to the proud merchants of Venice. In the Adriatic and Ægean seas Venice held numerous islands, and here Chios was her eyesore, all chance for the recovery of which was lost on the day of Sapienza.

Genoa, on the other hand, besides her narrow coast line of a hundred and sixty miles, held Corsica and many important posts in Sardinia. There were her Black Sea colonies, her town of Famagosta in Cyprus, and numerous settlements along the northern coast of Africa. Thus, externally, Venice and Genoa were fairly matched ; internally the difference of power lay in their constitutions—a difference which in the long run told in favour of Venice, and left her rival struggling on in inglorious confusion.

Thus matters stood in 1370, and but a small spark was wanted to ignite the trains of discord which lay across their paths at every turn ; and of these the first which was destined to explode and light the whole was ignited by the wretched emperor of Constantinople, with whom the two Republics played many a ruthless game and then squabbled over the results.

Tenedos was in those days an object of cupidity to both the Republics. Except for the sacrifice of Iphigenia, Tenedos was a place of small importance ; yet though sterile, and harbourless, it was an island much sought after as commanding an entrance to the Hellespont, and hence each Republic tried to manœuvre for its possession either by fair means or foul. The following are their respective claims to it, over which they fought their last fierce battles, and shed the blood of Italy's bravest sons.

The emperor, John Paleologus, had two sons, of whom he preferred the youngest, and destined that he should succeed him in the empire. Andronicus, the elder brother, considered this sufficient grounds for a revolt, which however proved unsuccessful, and the enraged father ordered his son's eyes to be put out. This, however, was done so clumsily that a Genoese physician succeeded in healing him as he lay in prison, and at the same time infused into his mind pleasant dreams of revenge, to be gained with the aid of the Ligurian Republic, who for their reward asked no more than the possession of the island of Tenedos.

Thus it happened ere long that Andronicus, with aid from Genoa, succeeded in supplanting his father, and consigned him to the same prison where he himself had been languishing. John Paleologus, however, in his youth had made love to, and won the affections of a certain woman called Petronilla, who tenderly watched over him in his dungeon, and sought for a means for his escape. There chanced to be a young Venetian adventurer in Constantinople at that time, Carlo Zeno by name, and to him Petronilla went and begged him to invent a plan for the emperor's release. Zeno repaired to the prison with all sorts of appliances for escape, but at the last moment the emperor's heart failed him : he cried like a child, and Zeno left him in disgust. Repenting, however, of his folly, the old emperor again, through the medium of Petronilla, implored Zeno's aid ; and to excite the Venetian's interest in his own behalf, he drew up a document, by which he bound himself to deliver up Tenedos to Venice.

This correspondence, however, was discovered, the emperor's guard was increased, and Zeno with difficulty escaped to Venice with his valuable document, which, when placed before the senate for discussion, was decided sufficient grounds to go upon, if ever the Genoese were to be kept in check, if ever Venice was to humble her rival.

Thus out of the weakness and petty quarrels in the East sprang this relentless war. The Genoese felt they could never sleep safely in their houses at Pera and Caffa with the Venetians at Tenedos, and the Venetians felt that they might never again get so favourable an opportunity for striking a blow at their rival.

The opening scenes of this war were unfavourable for Genoa. Vettor Pisano, the Venetian admiral, attacked the Ligurians in their own waters, taking captive to Venice a merchant squadron, under command of one Luigi Fieschi, by which he got a good haul of booty. Moreover, the Visconti of Milan joined Venice against Genoa, and caused many of the towns along the Riviera to revolt, including Albenga and Noli. And the free company, known as the " Company of the Star," under Bernabò Visconti, made a raid up to the very walls of Genoa, sacking Sampierd'arena, and would not retire until he had had a large sum of money laid down.

At length the Ligurian fleet, as usual under the command of a D'Oria, put in an appearance in the Adriatic. Luciano D'Oria took up his position at the port of Pola, and by a stratagem concealed the number of his fleet, and by this means surprised and captured a Venetian squadron on its

way from Sicily, laden with grain, and accompanied by a
strong escort. This was a most signal victory, and opened a
direct way to Venice. But in the heat of the contest D'Oria
was struck down. In order not to dishearten the troops, his
death was concealed by dressing up another man in his
armour ; but on the discovery great was the general lamentation, for Luciano D'Oria was indeed a worthy scion of his
house—a worthy successor of Oberto, Lamba, and Pagano.
His qualities as a commander were equalled by his generosity.
On one occasion, when money fell short for payment of his
troops, Luciano distributed every coin he possessed in his
private purse amongst his men. And when a poor oarsman
complained that he had received nothing, D'Oria took off the
golden buckle from his coat and presented it to him. Amidst
the general rejoicings, the Genoese felt deeply the loss of
this worthy man ; his heirs were provided with handsome
allowances out of the public treasury, and all honour was
done to his name.

Fresh galleys were forthwith placed under the command
of Pietro, another of the noble D'Oria family ; and before
the eyes of all Genoa, and after the benediction of the archbishop, the fleet sailed from the harbour, and a great cry was
raised from roof to roof, and from window to window, and
each alley and each street re-echoed it with enthusiasm, " to
Venice ! to Venice ! "

On arriving in the Adriatic, Pietro D'Oria joined the fleet
already there, and prepared for his attack on Venice. These
were pitiful days for the Queen of the Adriatic, the days of
her greatest peril and humiliation. The Lord of Padua
joined the Genoese ; the King of Hungary sent troops, as did
also the Marquis of Friuli, and all seemed lost to her both by
sea and land. Everywhere within the city was misery and
dismay. Through the narrow streets processions of all the
Venetian priesthood wended their weird way by night and day,
who undertook, as their part of the defence, the prayers of the

faithful, for which the faithful had now but little spare time, as they worked night and day with their fortifications and their chains across the harbour.

To possess himself of Chioggia, which was twenty-five miles distant from Venice, was D'Oria's first plan. It was the key of the capital, commanded the entrance to the harbour, and cut off any assistance which might come from Lombardy. Chioggia was very strong in itself, defended by bastions on all sides; its weak point lay in being built on two sides of a river, which was spanned by a large wooden bridge. It was the first care of the defenders to block up the mouth of this river.

After a few days of gallant defence, and a few days of gallant attack by sea and land, the defenders of Chioggia were reduced to the last extremity. The entrance to the river was broken open, and the bridge, which for some time was a stumbling-block to the besiegers, was destroyed with all the soldiers upon it by the bravery of a Genoese sailor, who took a boat laden with tar and wool and other combustible materials, and set fire to it, escaping by means of swimming. The defenders having thus perished in the flames, and Chioggia being taken, the triumph of the Genoese was at its height.

It now seemed as if Pietro D'Oria had but the word of command to give, and Venice would have met with the same fate as Pisa had but a century before. But with this the fortune of the Ligurians began to wane. One small cannon of leather, with a wooden car, brought from Chioggia as a trophy to Genoa, is all that exists to-day to testify to their victory ; and but few travellers of the nineteenth century to these rival towns would ever dream that Venice, with all her inexhaustible proofs of wealth and power, had, in the year 1379, been almost at the mercy of that town on the opposite coast, whose treasures in the way of mediæval art and greatness, only call for a side glance as the traveller hurries on his road to Venice.

Let us picture to ourselves the horror in Venice at the news of the fall of Chioggia. The great bell of St. Mark rang out a dull funereal peal both night and day. Scared faces, and trembling senators in eager converse, filled the Piazza of St. Mark, then glowing in all the magnificence and brilliancy of its first brightness. They decided upon taking Luigi Fieschi out of prison, and five other influential Genoese, and sending them as a deputation to the victorious D'Oria at Chioggia.

It was a mournful message, and it was worded with all the humiliation of fallen fortune. It appealed to the generosity of Genoa and concluded thus: "We Venetians, constrained by your prosperity and our adversity, demand peace from you on whatever conditions you may deem just; we will unhesitatingly restore all Genoese prisoners; and here is a blank sheet of paper—We implore you to write thereon our fate as mercifully as your heart and your humanity can dictate." With these words Piero Giustiniani, the spokesman of the embassy, stood silently, but firmly, awaiting his country's doom.

In haughty, insolent words Pietro D'Oria trampled thus on his fallen foe: "We do not wish to deny you the peace you crave, but we cannot entertain thoughts of it until those horses of yours are bridled which stand on your Piazza of St. Mark. Take back to their prisons my fellow citizens, whom you have brought with you to release, and before long I shall come in person to deliver them."

Thus did Pietro D'Oria, with this reply, dash away for ever the chance of even a favourable peace. He roused to the utmost the indignation and the courage of Venice. Every effort at defence was put forward; every sinew, every nerve was strained. New nobles were elected from amongst the rich tradesmen. A patent of nobility could be bought by an aspiring baker or a fishmonger, provided his purse was long enough to contribute to the public defence.

Vettor Pisani, who since the defeat at Pola had languished in prison, was brought out by unanimous consent, and before an assembled multitude he quietly and modestly accepted the position of saviour of his country. A great shout went up of "Viva Vettor Pisani." He quietly rebuked them and said, "Cry rather, Viva la Republica, Viva San Marco! May God make the Venetian Republic everlasting." And all that could be was effected to make secure the harbour and the canals.

The one saving point for Venice lay in the arrival of a few ships from Constantinople, which our old friend Carlo Zeno had under his command, endeavouring to make a diversion in the favour of the Venetians at the Eastern capital. Pending the return of this fleet, the Venetians made an attack on Chioggia. And an additional gleam of hope raised the spirits of Pisani's men in the disaffection of the King of Hungary from the Genoese cause; and gradually, as if by the magic hand of a fickle fortune, Pietro D'Oria found himself and his troops besieged in Chioggia, instead of going on his way to Venice as he had himself prophesied.

But the Genoese position was still too strong, and Pisani found it hopeless to attempt to dislodge them; his troops became restless: they wished to return to Venice, though they had sworn never to go back thither except as conquerors.

It was in this moment of dire distress that the ultimate resort was vaguely whispered from the Venetian Council Hall to the Piazza. A solemn decree was passed, "that if within four days the succour from Carlo Zeno did not arrive, the fleet should be recalled from Chioggia, and then a general council should be held as to whether their country could be saved, or if another more secure might not be found elsewhere."

Then did the law-givers of Venice determine that on the fifth day the lagunes should be abandoned, and that they should proceed *en masse* to Crete or Negropont to form for themselves a fresh nucleus of power on a foreign soil. It is indeed hard to realize that the fate of Venice, associated with all that is Italian, the offspring of the hardy few who raised the city from the very waves, once hung in such a balance. But so it was, when towards the evening of the fourth day sails were descried on the horizon, and Carlo Zeno arrived to save his country from so great a sacrifice.

Meanwhile, at Chioggia the Genoese were day by day becoming more careless; they felt their position so strong, they talked merrily of fixing the day when they should bivouac on the Piazza of St. Mark. Little did they dream of the net of misfortune into which they were being drawn so fast.

Besides reinforcements by sea, assistance by land flocked in towards Venice. Barnabò Visconti, and his company of the Star, a roving company of Germans, and the celebrated Breton band under Sir John Hawkwood, the Englishman, all hurried to assist the fallen banner of St. Mark.

Pietro D'Oria did all he could to maintain discipline amongst his troops; but when he fell one day in an engagement, through being struck by a Venetian arrow, a general demoralization set in, and their only thought was how to save themselves and abandon Chioggia. On the death of Pietro D'Oria, Napoleone Grimaldi assumed command of the panic-stricken Genoese at Chioggia. He endeavoured to keep up their drooping spirits, and sent a message to sue for peace at Venice, which was repudiated as Pietro D'Oria had rejected theirs but a few weeks before; and as a few weeks before the Venetians had looked for succour to Carlo Zeno, so now did the Genoese look for the arrival of assistance from home, which at length came under Matteo Maruffo, but the Venetians were too strong to allow of his forming a coalition with Grimaldi. On the 18th of February, 1380, the Venetians made another gallant attack. Both sides fought with desperation, the Genoese for life, their rivals for their country and their country's fame. Fearful slaughter occurred amongst the Genoese, and they were obliged to retire within the walls; and thus were they cut off from all communications with home, from all hope of safety, surrounded as they were, by sea and land, by hostile troops. And here, in this isolated town on the Adriatic, were the soldiers from whom the haughty Venice but a few months before craved for peace, now in their turn obliged to humble themselves before their rivals.

A deputation under Tazio Cibo was sent to Venice to seek for a safe passage home; but the Venetians replied that it was an immutable decree of the senate that they should all be imprisoned; and so, driven to extremities, on the 22nd of June in that year, four thousand Genoese were taken to the public prisons in Venice to swell the number of those whose liberty they had refused so short a time before. Then again did the Piazza S. Marco behold another striking scene, this time one of exulting triumph, for amidst a wild display of flags, feux-de-joie, and rejoicing, stood the four thousand Genoese, stripped naked to the very skin, and heavily laden with chains, to be exposed to the taunts of their victors before being cast into prison. Thus all was lost for Genoa. Her resources were exhausted by the effort she had made, and the flower of her army was now languishing in Venetian dungeons.

Carlo Zeno and Vettor Pisani drove every trace of the Ligurians from the Adriatic, and before the year was out all that was left to testify to Genoa's successes and Venice's disgrace was what can be seen by the curious of to-day in Genoa, namely, two stone lions of St. Mark, which came from Pola, and are still stuck up on their walls, one of them down near the harbour on the sailors' church of S. Marco, and the other in the heart of the city, let into the walls of the Giustiniani palace. These two stone lions, with their wings and their open Bibles, are now but a satire on all around them ; it was once considered right to restore them to the city of the Lagunes ; but they still remain to testify to the bitter jealousies of mediæval Italy.

Since both parties were tired of war, and weakened with these extreme efforts, it was no difficult matter to establish a peace. Amadeo VI. of Savoy, ancestor of the present master of both, superintended this peace. Tenedos was to be dismantled, and allowed to return to its desolation and its reminiscences of the unfortunate Iphigenia ; and here all open war was at an end. The veil is drawn over this rivalry, and here the prophecy of Petrarch was soon verified. The hungry wolves from across the Alps were soon heard to howl around Italian homesteads.

Genoa fell a prey to French intrigues, and Venice found enough to do to contend with the house of Hapsburg. But more especially, the fall of their joint power in the East tended to extinguish this rivalry, when the Turks deprived them both of the objects for which they had fought.

A curious proof of the lurking spirit of distrust which existed between Venice and Genoa as late as 1623 is thus brought out ; when it was agreed that a Ligurian force should be sent to assist the Venetians in war. However, when it was rumoured that Venice still held to her pretensions of pre-eminence at sea —the Genoese annulled their decree, and the promised succour was never sent.

In 1866, however, when Venice was united to Italy, Genoa, as a token of her welcome to the Queen of the Adriatic, and as a pledge of affection, sent busts of the two admirals, Vettor Pisani and Pietro D'Oria ; and, in return, Venice sent back portraits of Marco Polo and Christopher Columbus, done in Salviati's mosaic glass, and which now adorn the hall where the Genoese town council meets.

CHAPTER IX.

GENOA AT HOME TILL THE DAYS OF ANDREA D'ORIA.

THE century and a half of Genoese story which we are about rapidly to traverse, is one long and melancholy tissue of internal and external troubles, coming faster and faster upon one another as the inherent vitality of the Republic grew weaker. Prominently before our notice stands out the monopoly of the dogeship during this period by four families, the Adorni, Fregosi, Guarci, and Montaldi, who thence acquired the name of the "Cappellazzi" families. Of these, the first two gradually became all dominant, and though they produced many high-spirited and beneficent rulers, the general tendency, nevertheless, was one of oppression.

In the second place, during this period we have a constant and unhealthy craving for foreign masters, be they Marquises of Monferrato, Dukes of Milan, or the more formidable subverters of freedom, the kings of France. And thirdly, we are brought face to face with some brilliant spirits who sprang up from the lower ranks of life, and who made brave struggles to free their country from the yoke of slavery, and whose end was generally the scaffold.

The old nobility, the Fieschi, D'Oria, and Grimaldi, had likewise their own line of policy during this period. Finding themselves unable to rule at home, and jealous of men they considered their inferiors, they gradually learnt that their policy was to further the claims of foreign taskmasters ; and the court of France was always well supplied with these noble malcontents; and this unpatriotic game played by them eventually blossomed forth in the hands of Andrea D'Oria, and ushered in a new era for the Republic. These are the chief characteristics of this period, and the whole may be summed up as a path of *decadence*, which conducts us through scenes of poverty, pestilence, and war: from the brilliant fields of Genoa's mediæval career, from the days of Meloria, Chioggia, and the Black Sea supremacy, to the time when the so-called freedom established by Andrea and his successors was another word for Austro-Spanish despotism, to the time when France and Germany fought hard for the dry bones of Genoa; and Andrea D'Oria, by throwing in his lot with the latter, sealed the fate of his country and drove her commerce from her shores.

The dogeships of Antoniotto Adorno, for he occupied the ducal chair no less than four times, give us a good idea of what occurred in Genoa during the earlier part of this period. Though elected as a popular representative, he acted throughout unscrupulously for his own ends. He tried to make himself arbitrator in the papal schism; he tried to induce Urban VI. to take up his residence in Genoa; and through his dealings with this demon-like successor of St. Peter, he made his country the scene of the massacre of the six cardinals.[1] So great was the disgust against Adorno for this act, that he found it necessary to use excess of cruelty to maintain his position, and, as a diversion, to arrange an expedition against Tunis. But all this was of no avail: hated and threatened on all sides, in 1390 Adorno secretly left Genoa, but only to return again and to be re-elected doge when an opportunity offered itself.

In 1396, however, Adorno, finding himself unable to tyrannize as he wished, decided on handing over the government to Charles VI. of France. In this he was ably backed up by many members of the old nobility, as the signatures to

[1] *Vide* ch. ii.

the treaty testify. The king was to be entitled "Defender of
the Commune and People," and was to respect in every way
the existing order of things. So on the 27th of November in
that year the great bell in the tower of the ducal palace was
rung, the French standard was raised by the side of the
red cross of Genoa, and in the great council hall, where her
rulers had sat for centuries, now sat enthroned the French
ambassadors, whilst Antoniotto Adorno handed over to them
the sceptre and keys of the city. These symbols of government were graciously restored to him, with the admonition
that he should no longer be styled "doge," but "governor"
in the name of France. Thus did Adorno sell his country for
the love of power, preferring to be the head of many slaves,
rather than to live as a subordinate in a free community.

The first two governors sent by France after Adorno's
death, were unable to cope with the seething mass of corruption they found within the city walls, until the Marshal
Boucicault was sent, whose name was far famed for cruelty
in Spain against the Moors, in Bulgaria against the Turks,
and in France against the rebels. The Genoese had once
done him a good turn when a prisoner in Turkey : they had
effected his release ; and in return he had helped them
against the Turks ; so there was a sort of bond of union
established between them, which Boucicault turned to his own
advantage for establishing a system of tyranny to which his
predecessors had not aspired.

He ordered at once two popular leaders to the scaffold,
one of whom, Dei Franchi, managed to escape by rushing into
the crowd, almost as his neck was on the block ; the other, a
member of the popular Boccanegra family, was not so fortunate;
he had a violent struggle with the headsman, but was put to
death—and under these auspices did Boucicault inaugurate his
government. To keep the people quiet he drafted off crowds
of them to foreign wars in the East. Cyprus was conquered
by him, and at home he built extensive fortifications, which

drained the Genoese resources and wellnigh ruined the credit
of the Bank of St. George. Furthermore, he attempted to make
the Genoese follow the fortunes of the French candidate in
the papal schism, a policy which the Republic highly resented.
Benedict XIII. was invited by him to Genoa, grand *fêtes* were
ordained, and the city was compelled to do honour to the
French favourite. In short, everything that was galling to a
naturally free people was imposed upon them.

An undercurrent of discontent was not long in manifest-
ing itself, and the Marquis of Monferrato was invited to
supersede the hated Marshal. Dei Franchi, the man who had
so lately escaped from the jaws of death, was the chief mover
in this arrangement, and the Marquis entered Genoa in 1409,
whilst Boucicault was at Milan exacting homage in his
master's name from the lords of that city. Great was his
wrath when he heard how affairs were in Genoa ; but it was
futile : he was obliged to return to France, where the war
with England was then raging. He fought at Agincourt, and
was there taken prisoner, and ended his days in captivity in
London. His name is handed down by the Genoese as the
most hateful of her many tyrants.

It was but for a brief period that the Genoese submitted
to the Marquis of Monferrato ; they preferred to return to their
doges and internal quarrels. The old nobles on the one side
were opposed to the Adorni and Fregosi, backed up by those
who wished for a thoroughly popular government on the
other. Thus did a severe contest rage within the city walls,
and the battle-field was in the narrow streets and piazzas,
and in the very houses themselves, which were joined together
across the streets by wooden bridges, and throughout the city
nothing was heard but the din of arms. Brother fought
against brother, father against son, and for the whole of an
unusually chill December, in 1414, there was not a bypath
in Genoa which was not paved with lances, battle-axes, and
dead bodies.

In vain did men implore, for a truce, in vain did the artizans assemble and elect eight from amongst themselves to attempt to pacify men's minds. The mad fury of faction raged above all restraint. The priesthood attempted by processions and carrying relics between the combatants to still their wrath; they would wait reverentially, with hats off, whilst the Host passed by, and then set to work to fight again with redoubled fury. Matrons and young children crowded the churches, and cried for peace and pity. A three days' fast was ordained, and prayer, but alas! this brought no peace. The fires of burning houses, and the gleam of swords lit up the cold night air. And not till men were worn out and prostrate by contest could anything be done towards peace through the whole of that gloomy December.

Out of this fiery trial Genoa at length emerged with Tommaso Campofregoso as her doge, one of the few bright lights which illumined Liguria during the early part of this century. This new doge was received with unmitigated delight by all parties; he was *fêted*, he was caressed, and he showed himself right worthy of the confidence placed in him. Out of his own private means he gave sixty thousand golden ducats towards ameliorating the condition of affairs; and he extended the city walls so that a circuit of six miles was now enclosed. One of the most important public works he executed was the increasing and clearing out of the dockyard (d'arsena), which had been originally constructed out of the proceeds of the booty taken from the Pisans in 1283; the entrance of which had become blocked up, and the depth was not sufficient for the larger vessels. Eight hundred men were employed in this every day until completed. A quaint old picture, to be seen still in the "*Palazzo del municipio*," illustrates this work—one which was of lasting good for Genoa—and now the old red battlements and turrets of her d'arsena form a conspicuous object along the coast-line of the harbour.

To raise money for all these works, the doge was constrained to sell Leghorn to the Florentines. It was unquestionably a great loss to Genoa and her commercial interests, and it was vehemently opposed in the senate by one Luca Pinelli, but the doge thought it was necessary, and the people agreed with him. To remove the dissentient voice from amongst them, masked men were sent in the dead of night to Pinelli's palace; he was dragged from his bed, and crucified in the Piazza dei Banchi. When men rose next morning they found his dead body hanging to the cross, with these words written beneath—" Because he has uttered words which men may not utter." In this way did the rulers of Genoa remove from their path all opposition.

The Genoese arms during this time of quiescence again shone forth with something of their ancient brilliancy. Corsica was subdued, and a substantial league was formed with Henry V. of England, which was signed at Westminster on October 20th, 1421, by which perpetual friendship and peace by land and sea was sworn. Short, however, was the period during which Genoa could rest contented at home. Campofregoso was driven from the dogeship, and Filippo Maria, Visconti of Milan, was appointed protector of the Republic, and through this allegiance the Genoese were drawn into an unprofitable war for the succession in Naples, in which the Duke of Milan and the Pope supported the claims of Queen Joanna and her adopted son, Louis of Anjou, against Alphonso of Aragon.

A goodly fleet left the harbour of Genoa under the banner of St. George; but it was no longer a D'Oria who was admiral, it was no longer to Venice, Pisa, and the East, that her course was directed; and the minds of the men were uneasy and dissatisfied at the change. Perceiving this, the Milanese admiral, Torello, lowered the standard of St. George and sent it to Milan. Great was the disgust of the Ligurians at this, and numerous were the attempts to free themselves from their self-imposed yoke; but without avail, for in 1435 we find the Genoese again arming a strong fleet in the service of the

Duke of Milan, and again busying themselves in opposing the advances of Alphonso of Aragon.

Gaeta was undergoing a vigorous siege at the hands of the Spanish claimant, and the Angevins therein were reduced to the last extremities, when the Genoese fleet appeared in the horizon, under the command of Biagio Assereto, a lawyer by profession, but, like all his fellow-countrymen, well versed in the affairs of the sea. Alphonso in person commanded the hostile fleet, accompanied by his three brothers, and numerous Spanish grandees ; moreover, he had on board a large quantity of gold, silver, and valuables, coming, as he thought, to certain victory, and to establish himself in possession of the crown of Naples. Remonstrances against Genoese interference were of no avail. Alphonso was obliged to fight ; and with a long harangue Assereto addressed his men, as a D'Oria would have done, infusing valour into their hearts, and reminding them that this was not the first time they had fought against kings, and been victorious.

On the 4th of August, 1455, the two fleets came into action near the island of Ponza. Alphonso himself was in the heart of the contest, and much bravery was displayed on either side ; but eventually Ligurian skill proved more than a match for the Spaniards, and the proud king of Aragon was constrained to deliver himself as a prisoner to the Republic. He begged to be allowed to deliver up his sword to one of the Giustiniani, a noble from Chios, who chanced to be in the contest, as the most fitting and least humiliating process, and the request was granted.

Thus did the Ligurian Republicans, whilst in the service of the Duke of Milan, get into their hands two kings—namely, Alphonso, and his brother the king of Navarre, the heir-apparent to the throne of Aragon—and many nobles and hoards of wealth. It was indeed a proud day for Genoa; slightly, however, tempered with mortification at having to consult their ducal master as to what should be done with the august prisoners.

And this mortification the Duke of Milan, unwisely for his cause, fostered ; for he was somewhat jealous of the signal success gained by his subjects ; and with the Machiavellian policy then so much in vogue in Italy, he chose, with all the trump-cards in his hand, to try and dictate what terms he pleased to the other players in the political game. He ordered Alphonso to be conducted to Milan by way of Savona, and treated the captive monarch as a guest. The Genoese, with indignation and chagrin, found the fruits of so much valour and so much blood cast away and unrequited by their lord.

The city boiled with indignation when the duke ordered them to man galleys at their own expense, and conduct Alphonso home as if he had been on friendly terms with them. Their anger was now thoroughly aroused, and the Milanese governor, Opizzino d'Alzate, fanned it by the grossest cruelty. The duke recalled him and promised reform. But before the hated Milanese governor could leave the city gates, he was seized by the populace and torn to pieces, his mangled remains being left on the threshold of the church to which he had fled for safety, as a warning to the new governor Trivulzio, who prudently withdrew to the castle, and only saved his life by a timely capitulation.

So ended the Milanese rule ; for an army sent under the command of Niccolò Riccinino, the leader of a celebrated free company, could not succeed in reducing Genoa ; and Genoa forthwith returned to her doges, and a rapid succession of Adorni and Fregosi, who kept alive the internal animosity, relieved only by a desultory war with king Alphonso, who now was in possession of Naples ; and during the period of weakness which ensued from these internal and external struggles, she saw the Turk advancing on her colonies in the East without raising a blow in their defence.

More and more closely was this net of foreign despotism being wound around Liguria, when the attack came from the side of France. As soon as the king of Naples thought that the hour was come for avenging the defeat of Ponza, he mixed himself in Genoese politics and espoused the cause of the Adorni against the Fregosi; and the latter, to prevent exile and loss of their property, saw fit to put the Republic under the protection of Charles VII. of France, on the same stipulations and conditions that his father had held the lordship of the city before him.

At this time there lived in Genoa a wonderfully warlike prelate, the archbishop Paolo Fregoso, who was afterwards raised to the cardinalate. He was, moreover, a pattern bishop of his times—far more skilled in handling the sword than the prayer-book, and better versed in martial law than in theology. To serve his own ends he carefully manipulated party feeling, and by joining his family partizans together by aid of his influence in the confessional, he succeeded in driving out the French and in dressing himself in the ducal toga, more suited to his tastes than the cassock. But he possessed the dogeship for a brief time only, and again we have another Milanese Protectorate in the person of Francesco Sforza, the condottiere duke, who ruled the Genoese with more moderation and tact than her other foreign rulers.

Not so did his son Galeazzo, of whom the Genoese soon acquired a wholesome dread, for a man who in his own country had once cut off a man's hand for jealousy, had starved a priest to death who had prophesied him ill-luck, and at another time had obliged a peasant, who had been convicted of poaching, to eat raw, skin and all, the hare which he had stolen, could hardly be expected to be a lenient ruler of the ever fretful Genoese ; and it does not surprise us that insurrections against his rule were frequent, and that when Galeazzo Sforza fell by the assassin's hand, the Milanese were soon driven from the walls of Genoa, and again the Adorni and the Fregosi squabbled for the dogeship.

The cardinal archbishop, Paolo Fregoso, was elected now for a second time to the dogeship. He was indeed a wonderful man, whom one day we find fighting against a fleet of French who threatened the city, killing fifteen of them with his own hand, and another day leading the attack against the Turks at Otranto. He was well versed in all the wiles of a subtle age —a restless, unquiet spirit—and it was for the peace of the world when he died at Rome, in 1498.

The dawn of evil days was now fast approaching for restless Italy and factious Genoa. The hungry wolves from across the Alps were now to be let loose in all their wildness on her troubled soil. No hope of unity, no hope of peace was there for centuries to come. Genoa was humbled to the lowest degree. Her colonies had gone, her bank was almost ruined by its attempt to maintain them, and it was without a blow that she succumbed to the successive lordships of two French monarchs, Charles VIII. and Louis XII.

There is no more melancholy picture than that represented by the Ligurian Republic for the next thirty years. It is the last step in our path of decadence, on which Andrea D'Oria, backed up by his wealth and his ability, erected the fortunes of his family, than which Genoa had never produced a more powerful or a more proud. The Medici had done the same in Florence, and other princely houses had done the same elsewhere, but they maintained their power differently, and under a different name it assumed a different form. Virtually speaking, Andrea D'Oria was as much lord of Genoa, as Cosmo de' Medici was lord of Florence, and so were his successors; but they never assumed the name, but chose rather to govern by their influence and their wealth, backed up by foreign assistance, than which there was no more insidious foe to the well-being of the State.

The meteor-like descent of Charles VIII. into Italy, in 1495, had but little effect on Genoa. She was constrained for the time to do his bidding, and never raised a hand to check his rapid advance. She lay there stranded on her own Ligurian shore, the wreck of her former self, so weary of war that she scarce cared who tyrannized over her. Of the bitter fruits of the French invasion of Italy, Genoa felt but little : the whole seemed to pass over her like a dream ; and perhaps better for her that it did so, for by mingling herself up so little in the contest, she escaped the fate of others who took a more active part.

One feeble attempt at war was roused in her breast by the piteous appeal of Pisa, whom Charles VIII. had freed from Florence without giving her the means of support. It must have been a melancholy sight to see the embassy of the once proud rival of Genoa seeking aid in their dire extremity from the victors of Meloria. Thus this deputation spoke :—" The long tyranny of Florence has deprived us of the words to express our wants ; we are become plebeians whose only object is to cultivate our fields, and to pay our tribute. King Charles has given us our liberty, and told us to find means to preserve it ; but without you we cannot ; it rests with you whether we live or die."

The hearts of the senators were melted by this appeal. They were strongly moved to witness the depths to which their rival had fallen, and a small armament was sent to her assistance ; but it lacked the vigour of ancient days, and Pisa soon fell back into Florentine hands.

The days of Louis XII., and his ambitious claims on Italy, brought further foreign complications for Genoa ; for Louis was not so foolhardy as young Charles VIII. had been : he preferred making a firm basis for his operations in Northern Italy. So Genoa came more under his especial notice, and of his campaigns and visits to Italy, Genoese history affords us much information. On succeeding to the French crown, and on his successful occupation of the duchy of Milan, Genoa found herself compelled to submit herself gracefully to Louis XII. ; she had not the wherewithal to resist him, more especially as the old nobility were all in favour of a French occupation.

Thus was it the concluding act of this century, when, on the 26th of October, 1499, Philip von Ravenstein, in the name of Louis XII., received the oaths of fidelity, and swore to govern Genoa to the honour of his king and in accordance with the statutes of the Republic, even as the former kings of France had done. Gian Luigi Fieschi, for his interest in the cause of France, was invested with the government of the two Riviere, and others of the old nobility received favours according to their deserts. It was indeed a gloomy close of the century for Genoa, and with but little glory to look back upon as compared with the last, and with but little brightness to look forward to for the future.

In 1502 Louis XII. came down into Italy, and paid a visit to Genoa, where he was received with fitting honours. Everything that could contribute to attest to their loyalty was attended to in the streets; festoons of flowers and tapestries adorned the thoroughfares through which the king should pass.

A characteristic dispute arose for precedence at the ceremony of reception between the nobles and the people. The former maintained that every noble, as being of more honoured blood, should take precedence of the people; to which the people responded that they had held the state the longest, that the nobles had only been admitted within the walls at a later date, and added, with a spice of sarcasm worthy of a better cause, that if the question were of blood, pigs ought to take precedence of all other animals, as theirs was the most savoury. The French governor, on being referred to, wisely decided on giving the preference to the people, as most averse to the French cause, and hoping to gain their favour thereby.

During this visit the French monarch was sumptuously entertained at the Fieschi's mansion on Carignano,[1] and tarried eight days in the city, amidst a succession of banquets and

---

[1] *Vide* ch. i.

festivities. Here he met many of the exiled princes whom Cesare Borgia and his father had driven from their homes. They talked with Louis a good deal about restoration and revenge; but Alexander VI. was too good a friend to be interfered with, and pleasing conversation around the Fieschi's hospitable board was all the good they gained from Louis' visit to Italy.

Some external influences were brought to bear on the natural dissatisfaction the Genoese were sure to feel after a few years' experience of a foreign government. Julius II., the new pontiff, had his plans for driving the wolves out of Italy; and though he did not ostensibly promote sedition in Genoa, he lent it many a secret help. The Della Rovere family, moreover, had great influence on the Riviera, as they hailed from the village of Celle, near Savona, where the father of Sixtus IV. lived, and from whence the future pontiff used to carry into Savona the products of his father's garden, and sell them in the market there. Julius II. was the nephew of this mushroom pontiff, and hence his influence in Genoa and along the Riviera was not a little.

Added to this anti-Gallic influence, came up the inevitable question of Savona, which was always a bone of contention between French and Genoese. Under the favouring wing of France, Savona grew insolent, and sought to break through the shackles of dependency to Genoa; and France hoped to humble and impoverish Genoa by setting up Savona as a rival port.

Again the Pisan question was one on which Genoa and her lord disagreed. It is certainly curious to see the anxiety which Genoa felt to assist her old foe against Florence. But two centuries had elapsed, and Florence was now a more formidable commercial rival. And it is still more curious to see how readily Pisa came and laid herself at Genoa's feet. But so it was. Rather than submit to Florence, Pisa offered to put herself unconditionally under Genoese protection;

there was even much talk of removing Genoese families to
Pisa, and Pisan to Genoa, so as more thoroughly to amalgamate the two. This was pleasing to the people and senate,
but not pleasing to Louis XII., and consequently vehemently
opposed by his faithful slave, Gian Luigi Fieschi, and the old
nobility.

Hence, with so many rocks of which to fall foul, the
French government could hardly hope long to steer a clear
course in restless Genoa. Discontent grew apace. In private
and in public angry meetings were held; the name of noble
was again unsavoury to plebeian nostrils; and the French
government daily grew more detested and insupportable.
Calamitous indeed was the vial of wrath poured forth on the
head of Genoa after the insurrection which ensued and one
which for ever broke the last remnants of freedom which
lingered in the breasts of the Ligurians.

For generations the citizens had divided themselves into
nobles, merchants, and artizans—the two latter always forming the popular side—and thus did the factions of the
"bianchi" and the "neri" form themselves. For long we find
in state appointments, such as governors of provinces, etc, an
equal distribution of "whites" and "blacks," but after the
French occupation the former had gained such a preponderance that but few of the latter were honoured with
appointments.

This growing discontent was fostered by the arrogance of
the nobles. In their breasts they carried poniards with the
motto, "It chastises the people" engraved thereon, and at
every available moment they used them with right good
earnest. For example, a poor peasant of the Polcevera
valley was one day selling mushrooms to a Fieschi; unable
to get them for the price he wished, the noble struck the
peasant a blow with his fist, and made his nose bleed. At
this the mushroom vendor was naturally not a little enraged,
and used stronger language than was befitting. A butcher,

who chanced to be passing by, took up the cause of the injured man, whereupon the Fieschi and their retainers became mingled in a desperate brawl with all the butchers and bakers who came to hand.

The French governor took up the question, and did his best to pacify the discontent ; but the root of the evil was there, and it wanted but a few more of such encounters to make it blossom forth into open rebellion.

As the populace paraded through the streets with shouts of " Liberty ! " and " Long live the people ! " the nobles would look down from their palace windows, and jeeringly inquire, " Are ye bands of flagellants ? Are ye a pack of religious fanatics ? " But they paid dearly for their jokes, and had soon to flee the city, and in doing so lost not a few of their number. The French governor hastily gave the insurgents all they demanded. But it was too late for concessions ; he likewise had to abandon Genoa to the unbridled will of the populace.

In accordance with the natural order of things on such occasions, the lowest of the people, the riff-raff of Genoa, who had nothing to lose and everything to gain, now came forward, whilst the respectable merchants held aloof, and repented them of the turn they had given to affairs. The " *capetti*," as the rebels called themselves, an exact parallel to the " *ciompi* " of Florence, and the more modern communists, repaired to S. Maria di Castello, and there elected themselves tribunes, and a perfect reign of terror set in. Many of the ships in the harbour belonging to the nobles, and full of rich merchandize, were sunk ; and any wayfarer who chanced to be in Genoa at the time was treated as a French spy, or an agent for the exiled nobles.

Thus, like a troubled ship in a mighty tempest, without a helm to guide her, the Republic of Genoa was dashed to and fro by the conflicting waves, until finally it was decided to renew the dogeship in the person of Paolo, a dyer, of Novi, a man who throughout these disturbances had given proofs of judgment and ability.

On the 10th of April, 1507, a council was called, and Paolo da Novi swore to govern Genoa according to her constitution, and then ascended the ducal throne, whilst all the people present bowed in homage to him as at once their saviour and their lord.

Paolo at once set to work to drive the French out of the castle, and to reduce the Riviere to order. His rule was most salutary, for he appeased the disturbances within, whilst at the same time he prepared for active measures without; namely, to assist Pisa, and to re-establish the fallen name of Genoa along the coasts of the Mediterranean. A right noble man was Paolo da Novi, worthy to be classed amongst Genoa's bravest sons, and in his adversity, as in his prosperity, he showed himself worthy of the confidence reposed in him—for adversity was not long in following this transient gleam of prosperity.

Louis XII., with a mighty army, crossed the Alps; Gian Luigi Fieschi and the exiled nobility flocked to his standard, and marched on Genoa. The "*capetti*," craven-hearted sensationalists that they were, were filled with terror; they left Genoa and fled to the mountains. The doge alone, with the tribunes and a few brave spirits, remained to meet the coming storm. Paolo da Novi took every means within his power for the defence of the city : he distributed arms to all : he occupied and defended the deserted palaces of the nobles ; but all in vain. The French carried all before them, and were already in possession of the forts overhanging the city. Men's hearts gave way for very fear, and to prevent the sacking of the town, an embassy was sent to crave for pardon in the most humble words.

Stefano Giustiniani and Battista di Rapallo were chosen as its mouthpieces, and these men gave up everything that the victorious monarch chose to demand, and on the 28th of April Louis reached the city gates. Unsheathing his sword

O

with an ominous frown, he said, "Proud Genoa! with this I have subdued thee," and with a look that presaged no good for the conquered, he entered the city. Stefano Giustiniani, with a band of followers dressed in mourning, went forth to meet him. They prostrated themselves on the ground and implored the royal clemency for their unfortunate city. Without deigning to reply to this obsequious embassy, Louis, accompanied by the Fieschi and the nobility in gay attire, went straight to the cathedral to offer up a thanksgiving for the victory; to meet him came a band of six thousand virgins, dressed in white and carrying branches of olive in their hands, and with their lamentations and moans made the temple re-echo with an agonizing prayer for mercy.

They say that Louis was much moved by this appeal, but his after conduct shows but little signs of its having made a deep impression upon him. Scaffolds were erected right and left throughout the city, and at every corner was crucified some unfortunate malefactor who was marked as a seditious character. A relative of the obsequious Giustiniani was raised aloft upon a scaffold, in spite of his kinsman's entreaties, and with the agonies of death thus staring him in the face, he denounced many of his accomplices, and received pardon, whilst at the same time he provided materials to satisfy the French monarch's thirst for blood.

On the 11th of May, in the public piazza, a great dais was raised, in the centre of which was a throne; there sat Louis XII., surrounded by five cardinals, numerous princes and ambassadors from Italy and elsewhere; and there before the assembled multitude the rulers of the people did him homage and craved pardon for their sins. This was graciously accorded them, on condition that the rebellious commune paid the expenses of the war; that on their coins, where the emperor Conrad's head had appeared for centuries, that of the French monarch should be substituted; that a large force of Swiss and other mercenaries should be received within the walls as a permanent garrison; and, as a climax to their humiliation, that a fort should be erected, where now the lighthouse stands, to receive a strong French garrison, and this Louis playfully termed "the Bridle" (la Briglia) with which to keep the Genoese in check.

This was the pardon Louis granted to Genoa; for this had Stefano Giustiniani grovelled in the dust, and for this had the comely band of virgins implored his august pity.

But what of Paolo da Novi during this time, the doge who had fought so well and planned so bravely for his country? When all hope was lost, he fled from Genoa; his house was levelled to the ground, and a large sum of money found therein appropriated by the French. He fled to Pisa, on his way to Rome, where Pope Julius II. would doubtless have cordially given him an asylum, but the Corsican captain of the ship which bore him, induced by a bribe, sold him to the French for eight hundred ducats, and he was conducted back to Genoa to await his trial. And a mock trial it was, with every hand against him; he was sentenced to be beheaded, and his body cut into four quarters, to be posted about the town as a warning to all others who might wish to murmur the word of "liberty." Nobles and people all assisted at the execution in the public piazza; not a murmur was heard when he mounted the scaffold with a firm step and addressed a few terse words of vindication before he died; after which the sentence was carried out on his mutilated remains.

But the French affairs in Italy did not always proceed thus prosperously, and from the Vatican came echoes of relief from this foreign yoke, which encouraged the Fregosi and the popular leaders in Genoa once more to drive out the French. Then followed the brave attack on "the Bridle," in which Andrea D'Oria distinguished himself;[1] and, after the final overthrow of Louis XII.'s cause at the battle of Novara, Ottaviano Fregoso was elected doge of Genoa.

[1] *Vide* ch. xii.

This new appointment was a good one, for Ottaviano was a generous, high-spirited man, who inaugurated his dogeship by a course of good legislation for the people. He took the hated fortress of "the Bridle" from the French garrison, and razed it to the ground. His rule was essentially popular, and had he been able to maintain it longer, much of the old spirit might have been revived in Genoa; but as it was, the Ligurian Republic, crippled in resources, and with an empty exchequer, could not, without foolishly losing all, resist the claims of Francis I. of France, who, on his accession, assumed the name of "Lord of Genoa" amongst his other titles, and his victorious troops in Italy soon obliged Genoa to recognize a French master.

But experience had taught prudence to the French, the result of which was the continuation of Ottaviano Fregoso as governor under the king; and under Fregoso's temperate rule Genoa spent three peaceful, happy years. The means he employed were popular; he was no grasping Boucicault, nor tyrannizing Ravenstein, and the French king was rewarded for his choice by an unusual quiescence in his Genoese dependency.

But a storm was brewing for her in the east of Italy—a storm which devastated the city, than which none more terrible had ever burst over Genoa; and the perpetrators of it were her own citizens. The Adorni and the Fieschi combined in hating the supremacy of Fregoso and the French, inasmuch as they were deprived of all share in the government, and they repaired to the court of Charles V., the emperor, intent on revenge, be the price of it the ruin of their country.

Charles, ever ready to strike a blow at his rival, lent a willing ear to their advice. "If Genoa will not take Genoa no one else can," he exclaimed, and forthwith he put his saying into practice. Pescara, with a large force of Spaniards and Austrians, under the guidance of the unpatriotic lords, was sent to lay siege to Genoa. The governor, Fregoso, in his weakness and alarm, called in vain to France for aid. The enemy was at their gate before any help could arrive ; the enemy was within their walls almost before they had had time to prepare proper defences, and all the horrors of a conquest were wreaked on the unfortunate inhabitants—palaces, churches, men, women, and children, were plundered, robbed, and ravished, a mode of warfare which had hitherto been unknown to Italians.

Not even the aged archbishop, or noble matrons of spotless ancestry were secure from their brutal violence·; and foremost among the list of persecutors was Gerolamo Adorno, himself a Genoese. He headed an onset against the canons of the cathedral as they stood prepared to defend their treasures to the last drop of blood. Ottaviano Fregoso was seized, and, mounted on a mule, was carried through the town, and subjected to all the taunts and opprobrium of the foreign soldiery ; he was conducted as a prisoner outside the walls, then put on board a vessel and taken to Naples, where he died shortly afterwards of poison, and thus perished the last distinguished member of this noble house. His brother Federigo, and a few nobles, sick at heart, and mourning for their country, took sail together with Andrea D'Oria, and entered the service of the French king.

Other and more important affairs led Charles's army away from Genoa, for at the time the contest with the French king was at its height, and under the dogeship of an Adorno, Genoa dragged on a weary existence for the next few years, crippled, dismantled, and pest-stricken.

At Madrid, when Francis I. was granted his liberty, after his capture at Pavia, all that was allotted to him in Italy was the county of Asti and the commune of Genoa, over which he might exercise his seignioral rights. So low were the fortunes of Genoa fallen, that her consent to this arrangement was barely asked. With meekness she received a French garrison, and thus did the curtain fall over her prosperity. She slept, as it were the sleep of death, to awake again under a new form, and to commence a new era as different as may be from her glorious days of old—and the hero of the future was Andrea D'Oria.

CHAPTER X.

GENOESE VOYAGES AND DISCOVERIES.

CORRESPONDING to the advance of the Crescent, and the disasters which fell on the cause of the Cross, was the impetus given to the minds of Venetian and Genoese merchants in discovering fresh commercial paths, and new fields for their enterprise.

When the Genoese and Venetian met and quarrelled in Cyprus, and when, at Curzola, Genoa conquered her rival in 1298,[1] one of the captive Venetians, who lay in a Ligurian dungeon, was destined to arouse within the breasts of his jailors that yearning for discovery and adventure which was consummated by Christopher Columbus when he discovered America.

This prisoner was Marco Polo, the patriarch of mediæval travellers, who, whilst in prison in Genoa, compiled his volume of travels,[2] which throws so much light on early voyages in the East. Marco Polo seems to have enjoyed great literary advantages in his prison, for there he met the astrologer Andalo di Negro, the friend of Dante, and one Rasticiano, a Pisan compiler of romances, who had been captured at Meloria. And when to-day we look upon those mosaic glass portraits of Marco Polo and Christopher Columbus in the Council Hall of Genoa, we behold at once the Alpha and Omega of Italian enterprise.

---

[1] *Vide* ch. viii.   [2] Chronicles of Giacomo D'Acqui.

When they heard and read how Marco Polo had penetrated into the inmost recesses of China, with the double object of seeking treasures and converting the grand Khan of Tartary, the Genoese merchants were moved to their very souls with dreams of precious stones, shining silks, and aromatic spices. Yet these worthies were wise and prudent in their generation ; they rushed not headlong into danger, but rather preferred that missionaries should go before and pave the way for them. So when Fra Giovanni da Monte Corvino brought back word of the amicable tendency of the Tartars, and when he himself received the archbishopric of Cembalu, or Pekin, from the hands of the Pope, those anxious to amass the goods of this world quickly followed in his train.

Apart from the stimulus given to Genoese enterprise by Marco Polo, we find a spirit of restless excitement pervading their commercial world in those days ; and Benedetto Zaccharia, of a noble Ligurian family, is an apt example of the same. He was the dread of the Pisans, inasmuch as he had helped to conquer them at Meloria ;[1] he was in the pay of the king of Castille for his services against the king of Morocco ; and he was bosom friend of Aitone II., king of Armenia, with whom he negotiated a most favourable treaty for Genoa. From his dealings with the Eastern emperor, he gained for himself the lordship of the Island of Chios, and he ruthlessly plundered Egyptian ships when he met them on the high seas. In fact, the Mediterranean was becoming too narrow for Genoese enterprise, and cautious ambition pointed beyond. But before following these intrepid mariners outside the Pillars of Hercules, let us gather together what traces we can of their adventures in the East.

As above mentioned, it was from the missionaries that we have the first notice of travel in the further East; and these missionaries were in the habit of relating their travels with an exceedingly long bow when they returned home.

[1] *Vide* ch. iv.

A certain Fra Tommaso di Tolentino,[1] says the chronicle, suffered martyrdom in some remote part of China. In quest of his bones, Pope Clement, in 1321, sent Fra Giordano and a young nameless Genoese. Having secured the body of the now sanctified martyr, the travellers returned in haste to the coast of Coromandel. On their way the Genoese fell ill of dysentery, and was cured, so says his companion, by drinking a glass of water in which one of S. Tommaso's teeth had been well steeped.

Another Genoese missionary, Oderico da Pordenone, tells us how in 1317 he went to Java, "where the king had a palace of massive gold and silver." However extravagant these missionaries may be in their details of what they saw, they all agree in one point, that the centre of their exploits was Cembalu, the modern Pekin; and this fact alone proves the wide extent of their enterprise.

As an instance of a secular adventurer in these unknown regions, let us take one, Luca Tarigo, a Genoese, who in 1374 started from Caffa with a small craft and a few men, and entered the Don. Having gone up this river a good way, they disembarked, dragged their boat over to the Volga, and from thence to the Caspian Sea, where they made numerous raids on the neighbouring towns; and having carried off as much as they could, they set off homewards, but were waylaid by a nomad tribe, and robbed of their ill-gotten gain, so that they reached Caffa with only a few jewels which they had secreted amongst their clothes.

In accounts of early Scandinavian adventure, this plan of drawing ships over from the Don to the Volga is often referred to. Thus did the Varangians reach Constantinople, and Genoese adventurers followed their example.[2]

The spirit of enterprise was, however, taking a much more extended turn westwards, and by far a more important one for the destinies of the world at large. The year before the

[1] Waddingo.　　　[2] Rambaud's "Histoire de Russie."

fall of Acre, we have seen the Genoese entering into a treaty with the sultan of Egypt,[1] probably with a view to reaching the desired haven of India by way of Arabia, when the Syrian channel should be closed to them. Moreover, in the town of Genoa itself, Arabic was largely studied, for as early as 1274 we read of Asmet Beraderamen, of Tunis, who acted as tutor and interpreter for those who had dealings with the African coast.

By reason of the part they had taken in the Crusades, and by reason of the extended commerce incident on them, the Genoese had made vast progress in the art of ship-building. Numerous dockyards lined the Riviere on either side of Genoa, and numerous contracts are still extant in which the Genoese engaged to supply foreign sovereigns and merchants with the transports they required.

Of these, perhaps the most conspicuous about this time were two made with Louis IX. of France for the ships to carry his troops to the ill-fated Crusade in 1251. Particulars about the construction of the *Gran Paradiso*, which was built in this year for the saintly monarch, are still preserved; but more minute and clear are those which relate to the building contract for a vessel called the *S. Niccolò*, in 1268, for the same monarch and for the same purpose. And from comparing these two contracts, we can fairly well picture to ourselves a thirteenth-century Genoese ship of the highest class, as it would sail out of the harbour in quest of adventure or commerce.

Seven sails in all was the *Gran Paradiso* to have, one of canvas, six of cotton, with nine yardarms, seven anchors, twenty cables, and one hundred sailors, including twenty archers, and two expert helmsmen. Not more than one hundred pilgrims were allowed on board, and none of them were permitted on the deck between the mainmast and the poop ; whilst the twelve merchants who had contracted for

[1] *Vide* ch. v.

the ship had sufficient room allotted them to carry their merchandise.

The *S. Niccolò* was to have one mast, forty-seven cubits in height, and from ten to eleven hands in circumference, six sails of Marseilles cotton, and two other smaller masts; two rudders of oak, eight hands in width, twenty-four iron anchors, each weighing seven hundredweight, and twenty-eight cables for each, together with the necessary cordage. There was also to be an attendant craft with three sails, and two small rowing-boats.

Probably the greatest ornaments to these old ships were their castles, all turreted and battlemented, of which the *S. Niccolò* had two, and their bridges, from which they fought; whilst the whole, as it issued from the harbour, was one blaze of streaming banners and festoons, producing an effect indicative of wealth and power, with which even our old black and white ships of war, picturesque according to modern notions, will ill compare. The *S. Niccolò*, moreover, was to carry stabling for as many horses as might be required, and barrels of water for the whole campaign. The whole cost a trifle over one thousand pounds sterling.

The Genoese plan for building ships was to divide the responsibility into several shares, and hence the interest in an expedition was divided amongst a large number of citizens.

Besides these contracts we find elsewhere various descriptions of other ships enumerated, many of which can now be only known by name, but proving how advanced were the Genoese in all branches of ship-building. There was the *Taride*, with two masts, six anchors, two rudders, and a boat; there was also the *Bucio*, for carrying merchandise; the *Sagitta*, or arrow-boat, so named from its speed; the *Panfilo*, a simple sailing boat; and others, the names of which are points of discussion amongst nautical archæologists.

It was towards the close of the thirteenth century, when affairs looked threatening in the East, that the Genoese first conceived the plan of coasting along the west of Africa, perhaps in vague hopes of reaching their commercial paradise of India by this route, whilst Marco Polo and the Venetians were busily engaged in the East. Be this as it may, two brothers, Vadini, manned two galleys in 1291, and shortly afterwards, Tedisio D'Oria and Ugolino Vivaldi joined them, and together they set sail, passed the dreaded Pillars of Hercules, and plunged into that unknown and fearful expanse of sea whose paths hitherto were utterly untraversed.

This brave little fleet, however, was destined never to return. Yet it is to this the Genoese attribute the discovery of the Canaries, and there are very valid grounds on which to substantiate these claims.

Though French, Portuguese, and Catalonians all lay claim to this honour, they all deny that they were discovered before the fifteenth century; whereas Pope Clement V., in 1344, awarded them to Louis of Spain and the Portuguese. Barros tells us that in 1400 they were well known to Europeans.

The most substantial argument in favour of the Ligurian claims is, that on their registers are ascribed two ships to the above-mentioned Tedisio D'Oria, the *S. Antonio* and the *Allegrancia*, in the year 1291. So there can be but little doubt that these were the ships on which he started on his voyage; the name of one of the Canaries is also Allegrancia.

Furthermore, another of the Canaries is called "Lancellotto," which, the French say, was discovered by one of their countrymen, Lanzelode Maloysel; whereas a Genoese cosmographer drew a map in 1455, and put a Genoese flag at the spot intended to denote the Canaries, and under it wrote "Maroxello Lanzerotto." This family of Marocello was a well-known one in Genoa, and there is evidence of a member of it, Lanzerotto, living at the time when Tedisio D'Oria and his friends left for their voyage. Genoese writers unhesitatingly claim this honour; but it is probably one of those points which never will get satisfactorily proved.

Speaking of Vivaldi's voyage, Humboldt says, " It is of the more interest as preceding by nearly sixty-five years the voyage of the Catalan, Don Jayme Forrer."

Of this ill-fated expedition little is known. Probably they were wrecked on the coast of Africa, as we shall presently see one of their descendants turning up unexpectedly one hundred and sixty years later in the very heart of the " Dark Continent." There are those who affirm that the Genoese likewise discovered the Madeira island, and called it " Legname," from its wooded appearance, which was translated into Madeira by the Portuguese. Probably they did discover St. Helena, for it was originally known as " Braxe," a genuine word of Genoese origin, likewise meaning wood.

Let us now pass over one hundred and sixty years, and hear the fate of the Vivaldi expedition from the pen of their fellow countryman, Antonio Uso di Mare, whose *itinerario* has thrown so much light on these early expeditions, and which document, having travelled almost as much as the author of it, now reposes in the Genoese university library.

Antonio Uso di Mare was of a noble consular family in Genoa, which had attained great renown, as its name implies, for maritime and commercial enterprise. Luckily for posterity, Antonio was a great spendthrift, and was obliged to travel to avoid his creditors ; moreover, the letters that he wrote to them throw additional light on his wanderings.

In the year 1454 Antonio Uso di Mare met a Venetian, Cadamosta by name, at the Cape Verde Islands, and together, they agreed to go in search of a new road to India ; for the year before, Constantinople had fallen into the hands of the Turks, and the Genoese were trembling for their Black Sea provinces, and enterprise of some kind was felt necessary to obtain some other outlet for their commerce.

Accordingly, these representatives of the rival republics undertook to push their way together as far as they could along the broiling shores of Africa. They first essayed to land at a river called Gambia, but the natives shot at them with poisoned arrows, and they were obliged to proceed to the states of a certain "nobile Signor Negro," who presented Uso di Mare with thirty-one head of slaves, elephant teeth, parrots, and a few civets, and moreover, sent a secretary with him to appease the wrath of the men of Gambia.

At this point Antonio states that he was but three hundred leagues from the home of Prester John,[1] and that he there met five men from "Prete Janni," one of whom was of Genoese origin, the descendant of one of the Vivaldi who had been wrecked on the coast of Guinea one hundred and sixty years before; the last, affirmed the man, of this strangely transplanted race. Marvellous indeed is this fact, if true, and showing how near the Genoese were to grasping geographical secrets which even in these days of exploration and adventure are only beginning to unravel themselves.

The journal that Antonio Uso di Mare wrote is a most curious document, of about thirty pages in length, and divided into three parts. The first treats of legends which the author had found inserted on an old map of that period. In the second, he gives us a compendium of geography describing Tartary, India, Æthiopia, and the territories of Prester John, supplying what he had not seen himself out of Marco Polo and others. And, in the third, he describes the "principal islands of the world," in which are related wonderful things about Ireland, Scotland, and Norway, much after the style of Herodotus, though on a more ambitious scale.

Many points in this *itinerario* are well and faithfully told, and, as far as his own expedition went, are confirmed by the writings of his fellow traveller, Cadamosta. At Java, for instance, he relates how they had ships called "gionchi," junks, with sails of hemp and palm-leaves.

---

[1] Prester John was an imaginary Christian priest and king, a Will-of-the-wisp, or wandering Jew, everywhere and nowhere—in India, Abyssinia, and China. No traveller thought fit to return home without having in some way heard of him.

One of the most interesting points in it is that in which he identifies the mythical islands of St. Brandan, which were supposed to play bo-peep with mariners. He describes them as "of exceeding pleasantness." St. Brandan, according to the legend, was a pious abbot of Ailech, who lived in the sixth century, and had three thousand monks under him. He and St. Maclou, or St. Malo, together set off in quest of some island in mid-ocean, where they could exercise their religion undisturbed. The legend says they reached the Madeira islands, and this Uso di Mare states as the current belief in Genoa and amongst the inhabitants in his day. An old map of this period, by Cardinal Zurla, also shows this island, with a picture of the saint in the act of stepping towards it.

Perhaps the most important feature in Antonio's voyage is the fact that it paved the way for Vasco di Gama's discovery of the Cape of Good Hope half a century later. In fact, though the Portuguese have all the credit of this discovery, it was from the Genoese that they learnt the art of navigation.

From 1317 to 1448, a Genoese family, the Pessagni, held the post of admirals in Portugal, with their own Genoese officials under them. From a certain Emanuele Pessagno, whom king Diogenes the Liberal elected as his admiral in 1317, to Lanzerotto Pessagno, who died in 1448, this family superintended the navigation of Portuguese ships, and it is more than probable that, on the death of the last capable member of that family, Antonio Uso di Mare occupied the same post on his return from his voyages, for he remained until his death in the pay of Prince Henry the Navigator. Of the Pessagno family, descendants are still living in Portugal, under the name of Pessanha ; and of the deeds and honours of this family the time-mellowed church of S. Stefano, in Genoa, is a lasting memorial ; for there, on the white marble streaks, now grown yellow by years, we read the names of these admirals, who had brought honour on their country in distant lands.

What Antonio Uso di Mare had done, and the wonders
that he related, greatly stimulated the Portuguese ; more especially when a Camaldolese monk, Fra Mauro by name, made
a map, marking all the discoveries Antonio had made, and
expressing an opinion that there was a passage to India round
the Cape of Good Hope.   This map the wise Prince of
Portugal, in his palace on the barren promontory of Sagro,

CHURCH TOWER OF S. STEFANO.

had copied and widely circulated throughout his brother's
dominions, and the stimulus thus given to adventure was
crowned by the ultimate discovery of the Cape of Good Hope.

We are told by Cardinal Zurla, in his map, that
Antonio di Noli, a Genoese, discovered the Cape Verde
Islands, but this man is terribly mixed up with the more
illustrious Antonio Uso di Mare, and nothing but uncertainty
can result from the accounts of him.   The probability is that

the Genoese, during this period, flocked in crowds to the Portuguese court, and that under the direction of the worthy Pessagno family most of the discoveries in that direction were made by Ligurian merchants and adventurers.

Almost coincident with the rounding of the Cape of Good Hope, Christopher Columbus, the greatest of Genoa's sons, set foot on American soil—the great Christopher whose name fills every Ligurian with the profoundest respect ; and though his actual birthplace is unknown, and a mystery hangs over his sepulchre, yet the Genoese are no sceptics, and refute with scorn any attempt to deprive them of their creed with regard to their distinguished fellow-citizen.

But in studying Genoese history there is much to be gathered, which will elucidate facts in the discoverer's career —a few crumbs, so to speak, which have fallen from the well-stocked tables of Washington Irving and succeeding biographers, in taking his life from a purely Genoese point of view.

In the first place, we are accustomed to be surprised that the son of a poor woolstapler in Genoa could have encompassed so great an end ; but his father, Domenico, was far from being a poor man, woolstapler though he were. He had a comfortable house outside the Porta S. Andrea, which he got as the dower of his wife ; and, moreover, he was eligible to all the honours of the Republic. As in Florence the guild of the woolstaplers produced many of the leading men of the day, for from the so-called low origin of trade sprang the Medici, the Strozzi, and others, so it was in Genoa, when in 1339 a doge was elected from amongst the butchers ; and the haughty families of Adorno and Fregoso were respectively descended from a butcher and a woolstapler.

Domenico Colombo had a widely extended trade along the Riviera ; he was constantly on the road from Genoa to Savona, on the registers of which latter city his name is seen, as attesting a will, some years after his son discovered America.

As many towns in Liguria fight for the honour of being his birthplace as in ancient Greece claimed to be the birthplace of Homer. However, since Domenico lived in his house close to the Porta S. Andrea from the time of his marriage until 1477, years after the birth of Christopher, as documents belonging to the monastery of S. Stefano testify, there is more reason to give Genoa the proud title than her neighbours ; for wherever a family of Colombo lived, and there were not a few dispersed about Liguria at this time, there they assert to be the birthplace. Cogoletto, Rapallo, Quinto, and Savona have each their arguments to produce, and believe in them, however vague.

> " How young Columbus seem'd to rove ;
>   Yet present in his natal grove ;
>   Now watching high on mountain cornice,
>   And steering now from a purple cove.
>
> " Now pacing mute by ocean's rim ;
>   Till, in a narrow street and dim,
>   I stay'd the wheels at Cogoletto,
>   And drank, and loyally drank to him."
>   TENNYSON, *The Daisy.*

This is the vision our laureate saw when at Cogoletto, and if this village's claims to notoriety on Christopher's account wrought nothing else, they gave our poet an excuse for refreshing himself with a glass of wine, and afforded him food for two pretty stanzas in his poem.

Thus we see the young Columbus introduced into the world in a position highly favourable for his advancement in life. His father, a shrewd man of business, doubtless as a man of business would do now, gave his son a good education, which fell not on stony ground. We can easily imagine a spirit like that which Columbus afterwards displayed, eagerly drinking in all that fell from the lips of the Genoese mariners, with whom, in the pursuit of his trade, his father must have had close intercourse. And at this time nautical enterprise was at its height in the Ligurian capital ; thither flocked the cosmographer and the astrologer, to assist the mariners in deciphering the ocean paths. For in those days Genoa was in great trepidation ; she felt that the influence which she had held in the East was fast passing from her, and to hold her own in commerce and in arms new lands and new fields must be discovered.

Young Columbus thus could hear all their speculations and their theories. He heard how mahogany and sponges were washed up on the shores of the Madeira ; his natural inference was that there were other lands beyond that vast expanse of sea, and his dauntless spirit determined him to start on a voyage of discovery.

In following up his history we find that the fact of his being a Genoese, which in the first instance was of so much advantage to him, as placing him in the centre of nautical experience, told seriously against him in his after career ; and to the nationality of the great discoverer may be traced the jealousy and hatred of the Aragonese against him, and the almost martyrdom he passed through in his efforts to organize his colonies in the New World. Were not the Aragonese always at daggers drawn with the Genoese in Mediterranean commerce? Had not they fought over Corsica and Sardinia for generations? And we have seen how, in 1435, at the battle of Ponza,[1] Alphonso of Aragon, grandfather of Ferdinand the Catholic, to whom Columbus owed allegiance in virtue of his employment, was taken prisoner by the Genoese.

Furthermore, if the researches of Cav. Bossi in the archives of Milan are reliable, Columbus himself, in 1475, was captain of a galley in the service of Réné II. of Anjou, and shortly before had commanded a small Genoese galley for the purpose of driving out the Aragonese from Naples.

Hence it was to Isabella of Castile that he owed every-

[1] *Vide* ch. ix.

thing, even the very ships in which to start ; whilst from first to last he was trampled upon by the Aragonese, who were jealous of his strength of mind, jealous of a hated Genoese obtaining such distinction, and it is for his bravery in withstanding such opposition that he deserves praises equal to those bestowed upon him for his discoveries.

Instances of this interline every page of his biography, and would be here superfluous; but we may add that not only was his nationality a misfortune for himself in this case, but it was even a greater one for the Spaniards, who, instead of setting foot on American soil under a captain who had full authority over his men, were in mutiny before they got there, and Columbus had no influence to prevent them from pursuing their greedy researches after gold. Thus at the very outset they sowed the seeds of that policy which enraged the natives, and brought forth a plentiful harvest of misfortune for the Spaniards, unable as they were to staunch either the love of the glittering ingots engendered in themselves, or the constant hostility of the aborigines.

That the Ligurian Republic was not the discoverer of America was not the fault of Columbus, for when he had matured his plans, in 1477, he laid them before the Genoese government before going elsewhere ; but so great were their difficulties at home at this time, and so empty was their treasury, that they were obliged to forego grasping the golden prize. At the time when Columbus visited his native town she was gnawed to the heart's core by the Adorni and Fregosi factions, the former supported by Milan, and the latter urging on the Corsicans to revolt. The people of the Riviere, too, were excited to complaints by the excess of the taxes and the insinuations of the Fieschi. Thus it is hardly requisite to add that they were unable to accept his proposals, and had to forego the glorious career which was open to them.

After his many wanderings, and shorn of even the honour

of giving his name to the continent he had discovered by a
sort of evil genius which seemed to follow his footsteps,
Columbus breathed his last at Valladolid in 1506; whilst
Amerigo Vespucci, the Florentine adventurer, handed down
his name to posterity—thanks to the instrumentality of a small
printer in the town of St. Diè, in Lorraine, who compiled a
short account of Vespucci's travels, and not knowing what
other name to give the land to which he had wandered, called
it "terra Americi," and thus perpetuated the name.

The history of the ashes of the Genoese hero are almost
as mysterious as the facts attending his birth; and only by
the light of a recent discovery has his last resting-place been
definitely determined.

From a protocol of the monastery of Las Cuevas we
gather that his remains were removed from Valladolid to
repose in greater splendour in the Certosa of St. Anna,
near Seville, where a tomb was put up attesting to the fact
that for Castille and Leon "Colon" had discovered a new
world.

But, in accordance with the defunct admiral's wishes, in
1537, the widow of his son Diego got leave to transfer them
to the cathedral of San Domingo in the West Indies. The
superintendence of this removal was given to Luigi Colombo,
the admiral's grandson; but this youth was a *mauvais sujet*,
and shortly after he had taken his grandfather's bones to San
Domingo, a sentence of banishment was passed upon him for
having three living wives, and he was obliged to flee his
country before he had erected a fitting monument to his
grandsire's memory, and from this fact poor Christopher's
remains were well-nigh lost to the world.

When, in 1795, the Spaniards ceded San Domingo to
France, and thought fit to remove the ashes of their great
discoverer to the cathedral of Havanna, a magnificent tomb
was prepared to receive them, with this inscription: "O
remains, and image of the great Colon, for a thousand cen-

turies may you be guarded in this urn, and in the remembrance of our nation."

But when they had recourse to San Domingo, nowhere could the desired remains be found.   High and low they sought without success, until at length they broke open the tomb of his grandson Bartolomeo, which is now empty, and removed his bones to Havanna.   Nothing more occurred to make the deception known until the year 1877, when some priests were busy digging in the choir of the cathedral of San Domingo, and came across a curious lead coffin, on the lid of which was written, " D. dela A. P^{ero} A^{te}," which would read, "Descubridor dela America Primero Almirante."[1]   On the left of this coffin was a C, on the front a C, and on the right side an A.   On lifting the lid they discovered the following inscription: " Ill^{tre} y Es^{do} Varon D^{n} Christobal Colon,"[2] besides twenty-eight fragments of bones.

Thus, in birth, in life, and in death, the great discoverer of America has been a problem not easily solved.   Sufficient, however, it is to know that Christopher Columbus, a Genoese, did discover America, and by this wrought the final death-blow to his country's prosperity, and by drawing off the commerce from the Mediterranean he inaugurated that history of decay the results of which we see to-day.

This very year, curiously enough, another relic has ˙come to light in the shape of an anchor discovered off Point Arenas, Trinidad, bearing the date 1497, the place at which and the date when Columbus on his third voyage is known to have lost his.   Will America give it to Genoa ?   For Genoa has not been unmindful in these later years to claim the shreds of honour accruing to her from the fact of being the discoverer's birthplace.   A handsome statue in white marble has been erected to overlook the busy haunts of men near

---

[1] Discoverer of America, first admiral.
[2] " Illustrious and esteemed man,
   Don Christobal Colon."

the Genoese railway station; it is interesting as a study of incidents in his life, represented in bas-reliefs around the pedestal, yet melancholy to look around and behold the signs of departed grandeur, and to feel that so great a man unconsciously wrought so great a ruin.

Side by side, on a house along the quay, stand statues of Christopher Columbus and Andrea D'Oria, with bas-reliefs above and below to illustrate their great deeds. Certainly of Genoa's sons they were the greatest, and certainly to Genoa's prosperity no two men ever brought greater harm; the former by discovering other channels by which Genoa's commerce was not destined to pass, and the latter by stagnating internally every drop of free blood which flowed in Genoa's veins.

It has been recently made known to the world at large, chiefly through the instrumentality of M. d'Avezac,[1] that John Cabot, the father of Sebastian, who brought such honour on the English flag under Henry VII., was a Genoese by birth, a Venetian by adoption, and an immigrant to Bristol.

John Cabot was in the habit of leaving Bristol with two or three ships in the hopes of discovering the "island of Brasil," which was probably St. Helena or Braxe, the name Brasil being but a Portuguese translation of the Genoese, *Braxe* or "wood." But he never succeeded in reaching his destination.[2] The ambassador of Ludovico Sforza in London, the Abbot Raimondo, in writing to his master, speaks of him as a Genoese.[3]

In identifying him as such there is some little difficulty; but in Savona the name Cabutto, coupled with the Christian name Sebastiano, was common in those days, so the probabilities are that this Genoese explorer came from the Republic's troublesome dependency.

Though John Cabot himself never reached the longed-for

[1] "Les navigations Terre-Neuviennes de Jean et Sabastien Cabot."
[2] Archives of Simancas. [3] Archives of Milan.

transatlantic haven, he evidently shared Columbus' belief that it did exist. And, besides, in the account of Columbus' voyage to England, as related by his son Ferdinand, it is mentioned that he had frequent intercourse with the English, more especially those of Bristol. And it is not improbable that in this town the two great Genoese explorers met and talked over their respective plans, and perhaps then made much improvement in the use of the magnetic needle, the discovery of which kindly biographers have attributed to each.

Before leaving the subject of Ligurian discoveries, we must glance at some of her explorers whilst Genoa was in her decline.

Worthy contemporaries of Columbus were Gerolamo Adorno, and Gerolamo di S. Stefano. In 1495 they together made an exciting travel through Egypt and the Red Sea, round the coast of India to Ceylon and Coromandel, where Adorno died. S. Stefano proceeded further to Sumatra, where the king deprived him of most of his goods. However, he managed to escape with his ships, and reached the Maldave Islands, where he waited six months for fine weather, apparently without success, for he was shipwrecked immediately afterwards, and after floating about for twenty-four hours on some wreckage, was saved from a watery grave by another of his ships. Columbus alludes to him as a brave mariner, in one of his letters, and in 1499 S. Stefano wrote an account of his travels to the king of Portugal, showing the intimacy which still existed between Genoa and this seafaring country.

More learned are the works of Giorgio Interiano, who visited many parts of the interior of Asia, and wrote about them. Angelo Poliziano mentions this Genoese as a "learned seeker into recondite matter;" and his account of Circassia, where he lived for many years, is amusing. In 1501 he presented Aldo Manuzio, the celebrated Venetian printer, with the products of his pen, apologizing for their imperfections, and begging the printer to correct mistakes in orthography.

Of the Circassians he thus writes:—that they professed Christianity, and had a Greek ritual; but their nobles never entered a church until they were sixty years of age, because, as they lived by rapine, they were deemed to desecrate the sacred edifices.

After they had attained this respectable age they gave up brigandage and attended church, having previously only been allowed to listen to the distant hum of sanctity on horseback outside the porch.

Their priests appear to have been ignorant, illiterate men, performing the Greek ritual without any knowledge of the language. When a child was born to a Circassian family, it was straightway carried to the nearest river, in spite of ice or cold, to receive its first ablutions and its baptism at one and the same time ; and to the shivering infant was always given the name of the first person who chanced to enter its mother's tent after it had seen the light of day.

Even more celebrated were the exploits of Cassiano Camilli, who died of the plague in 1528. He reached a high pitch of renown as a cosmographer ; and his eulogistic biographer tells us,[1] "not only did he know the ports, promontories, gulfs, islands, rivers, mountains, and the most celebrated cities, but every little castle he had at his fingers' ends ;" and then proceeds to say that he had travelled through all the countries of Asia, Egypt, and Africa, not to mention Spain, Germany, France, and England. Indeed, if his knowledge of the countries he had visited were as extensive as his biographer would have us believe, before him a Livingstone or a Stanley must sink into insignificance.

When, in 1519, the Portuguese discoverer, Ferdinando Magagliano, set foot on the Molucca Islands, he had on board his little fleet of five ships no less than twenty-one Genoese mariners, and five other Italians, one of whom, Leon Pancaldo, of Savona, on his return home, did not wish

[1] Cardinal Gregorio Cortesi.

to hide his candle under a bushel, so affixed up over his house a lengthy inscription [1] as a pompous testimony to posterity of the travels he had made and the wealth he had acquired thereby.

Almost last, but not least, in the long programme of Genoese heroes of discovery comes one, Paolo Centurione, who was employed by the Grand-Duke Basilius of Russia to discover a better means of bringing goods from India, for the Portuguese, owing to the long sea voyage, often turned out their wares much the worse for an admixture of salt water.

Centurione went through Astrakan and the Oxus valley, and on his return home represented to the Grand-Duke that a passage could easily be effected, but at a great outlay of capital. At this time the Muscovites were not over ready with their purse-strings, and this fact, combined with the inherent jealousy of the Russians at employing a foreigner to treat with the various tribes, prevented them from opening out a road to India, and thereby they lost an opportunity which the Russians of to-day must bitterly regret. And thus early in the seventeenth century was India saved from Muscovite rule.

Amongst the dying embers of Genoese enterprise we find an East Indian Company formed towards the middle of the seventeenth century ; and England sought the greater ex-perience of her forerunner in commerce to aid her in establishing her incipient colonies in India. In the state archives of Genoa are numerous letters written in 1655 from one Thomas Skinner, who was deputed by Cromwell's government to form a contract with Genoa to colonize a vast island

---

[1] Io son Leon Pancaldo Savonese
Che il mondo tutto rivoltai a tondo
Le grand' isole incognite, e il paese
D'Antipodi già vidi e amor giocondo
Pensava rivederlo ; ma comprese
L' invitto Re di Portugal che al mondo
Di ciò lume darià : pero con patti
Ch'io non torni mi diè due mil ducati.

in the East to the intent to secure the British traffic in those parts, which was so much interfered with by the Dutch.

But these negotiations, as far as Genoa was concerned, came to but little, and this, her last flickering breath in the commercial world, soon expired with the events which rose out of her contest with Louis XIV. of France.[1] No more could she think of travels or commerce in distant lands; it was now for bare existence on her restricted Ligurian territory that she fought. But she had done her work nobly in her day, and from none is more tribute due to her bravery and her enterprise than from the British nation, which has followed in her steps, and has been one of the principal gainers by her discoveries. It is but a faint, but remarkable echo of ages long gone by, that the Italian Antarctic Expedition, which has just started on voyages of vague discovery in the Southern hemisphere, sailed from Genoa.

[1] *Vide* ch. xvi.

CHAPTER XI.

THE BANK OF ST. GEORGE.

THE Bank of St. George, its constitution, its building, and its history, forms one of the most interesting relics of mediæval commercial activity.   Those old grey walls, as seen still in Genoa, begrimed with dirt and fast falling into decay, are the cradle of modern commerce, modern banking schemes, and modern wealth.   In those old halls were first mooted the development of capital, the funding of money and interest, which the advance of mercantile ingenuity has so perfected and unravelled.

Thus Machiavelli, in his history of Florence, alludes to this bank—"An example indeed most rare, by philosophers in all their imaginations and conceptions never found, is that system of administration adopted in Genoa in the 'compere' of St. George. . . . So that if it could happen that this city (Genoa), full as it is of ancient and venerable customs, might fall entirely into the possession of the Bank of St. George (which doubtless with the process of time will happen), it will then be a republic of greater importance than even that of Venice."

This Bank of St. George is indeed a most singular political phenomenon.   Elsewhere than in Genoa we search in vain for a parallel for the existence of a body of citizens distinct from the government—with their own laws, magistrates, and independent authority—a state within a state, a republic within a republic. All dealings with the government were voluntary on the part of the bank. Over their deliberations the Genoese government and senators could exercise no influence, nor could they interfere with their general assemblies without violating the most stringent oaths, and without destroying the very basis of the constitution.

But, far from working without harmony, we always find the greatest unanimity of feeling between these two forms of republics within the same city walls. The government of Genoa always respected the liberties of the bank, and the bank always did its best to assist the government when in pecuniary distress. And whilst the state was convulsed by continued revolutions from within and tyrannies from without, the Bank of St. George, or the institution of the " compere," always kept an equal course, never deviated from its paths of justice, grew in riches and credit—in short, was the heart of the Ligurian Republic.

To define an exact origin for the bank is difficult ; it owed its existence to the natural development of commercial enterprise rather than to the genius of any one man, or the shrewdness of any particular period in Genoese history.

The Crusades, and the necessary preparation of galleys, brought into Genoa the idea of advancing capital for a term of years as a loan to the government on the security of the taxes and public revenues ; but in those cases the profits were quickly realized, and the debts soon cancelled by the monarchs who incurred them.

However, the expeditions against the Saracens and the Moors were otherwise, and were undertaken at some risk to Genoa herself. We have seen the system inaugurated by the expedition to Ceuta.[1] Now large sums of money were advanced the profits on which were not spontaneous ; it was more an investment of capital for a longer term of years, which was secured by the public revenues, but the profits of which depended on the success of the expedition.

[1] *Vide* ch. v.

In 1148 was the first formal debt incurred by the government, and to meet the occasion the same system was adopted which continued in vogue, subject only to regulations and improvements which were found necessary as time went on, until the days of the French Revolution.

The creditors nominated from amongst themselves a council of administration to watch over the common interests, and to them the government conceded a certain number of the custom duties for a term of years until the debt should be extinguished. This council of administration elected their own consuls, after the fashion of the Republic governors. Every hundred francs was termed a share (*luogo*) and every creditor a shareholder (*luogatorio*).

Each shareholder's separate amount of shares was summed up as "a column" (colonna), and entered in a book called "cartulario." Each separate loan was termed a "compera," and these loans were collectively known as the "compere of St. George," which in later years became the celebrated bank.

Each loan generally took the name of the object for which it was raised, or the name of the saint on whose day the contract was signed; and when an advance of money was required, it was done by public auction in the streets, when the auctioneer sold the investment to the ever ready merchants, who collected outside the "loggia," or other prominent position chosen for the sale. In a loud voice was proclaimed the name and object of the loan, and the tax which was to be handed over to the purchasers to secure its repayment.

So numerous did these loans become by 1252, that it was found necessary to unite them under one head, with a chancellor and other minor officials to watch over them. And as time went on, so great was the credit of Genoa, and so easy was this system found for raising money, that the people began to grow alarmed at the extent of the liabilities. So, in 1302, commissioners were appointed at a great assembly, two hundred and seventy-one articles and regulations were drawn up to give additional security to investors, and henceforth no future loan could be effected without the sanction of the consuls and the confirmation of the greater council of the shareholders.

These consuls of the debt were always interested therein, and bore the name of "Sapienti," or assignees of the shares. Numerous were the minor officials under them, such as key-bearers, visitors, etc., who superintended the various branches of the scheme. And owing to the frequent changes in the national government it was necessary to adhere most stringently to all their regulations about the payment of interest and capital at the appointed times, so that the credit of Genoa might be un-flinchingly maintained.

In 1336 a singular instance of the means employed to raise money occurred. Cardinal Fieschi assigned to his creditors for the advancement of a considerable sum, the times and seasons for repayment of which were carefully specified, no less a treasure than the "sacred basin," the Holy Grail, or whatever they chose to call it ;[1] and this contract bore the title of the "Cardinal's loan on security of the sacred Parossidis."

During the days of the first doge, Simone Boccanegra, great changes were to be effected in the working system of the "compere of St. George." To this date many have assigned the origin of the Bank of St. George, but it will be seen only to be a further consolidation of the same system, which had already been at work two centuries.

In 1337, accordingly, a large loan was raised for the purpose of crushing the refractory nobles in their lair at Monaco and for regaining the Island of Chios (Scio) from the Venetians, and it was called the "Mahone of Scio," by that curious Genoese name which served to denote a large advance of money by "maonisti," or men ready to advance money, the derivation of which term is obscure. In like manner, some years later, we have the "compera" for the reconquering of Corsica, and a goodly list of loans bearing the titles of Finale,

---

[1] *Vide* ch. ii.

SS. Peter and Paul, Monaco, Cyprus, and "the great peace with Venice."

In 1339, however, at the popular revolution, all the old books were burnt, and a new commission appointed to regulate the "compere;" for the government expenses had been so great, and the treasury so exhausted by the twenty-six galleys they had sent out, that the doge and council had been obliged to concede a very large portion of the public revenues to meet the demands of their creditors ; and the results of the conquest were all ceded for three years to the shareholders, and the loans all consolidated into one whole under the newly appointed commission.

Instead, therefore, of being the origin of the bank, it was only another step in the growing wish for consolidation, which the expanding tendency of the " compere " rendered necessary ; which consolidation took final effect in 1407, when the Bank was thoroughly organized on the same footing which lasted till the end.

Every year and every event tended towards this system of blending the loans together, to which fact is due the extensive power which the directors of the bank eventually wielded, when all interests and all petty disputes were merged together in one. It was naturally exceedingly beneficial for the shareholders in weak transactions. It was beneficial also to the shareholders in safer ones, that no failures should take place in connection with the system, and that the credit of the Ligurian Republic should be universal.

And here we have the development of this financial republic inside a democratic one. Development, I say ; for it was not yet mature, and the system had to steer the course of Genoa through many troubled waters before its power became entire, and before the sovereignty which appertained to the universality of the shareholders was clearly established. And then we have the marvellous picture presented to our view of two republics, one within another—one poor, turbulent, racked by sedition, and torn by discord ; the other, rich, peaceable, well regulated, and maintaining its ancient probity —a unique example both within and without of public good faith.

During the political disturbances which troubled Genoa towards the close of the fourteenth century, a wonderful scheme was conceived by a shareholder in the bank, of the multiplication of interest, which was to have great influence over the commercial world for future ages.

At this time, so great was the distress, that the government was reduced to placing taxes on some of the most outrageous things, such as dead bodies, etc. No possession, no industry or traffic, was untaxed ; cart-loads of sand and rubbish could not be carted away without a tax ; a man could not even sweep snow from his doorstep without paying for it. And thus did the government and the people struggle hard, the one to sustain their country, and the wretched inhabitants to sustain bare existence.

At this critical moment a worthy man stepped forward to save his country ; a name almost lost to history, but who deserves a renown far wider than that of Andrea D'Oria, and claiming far higher merit as a statesman-patriot than many of those whose lives have called for volumes.

Francesco Vivaldi was a man of exceeding modest habit. His apartments were neither sordid nor gaudy ; he ate to live, and only wore such garments as decency required. No one knew him as a charitable man, only as a keen man of business, always at his desk, and counting his gains, with a tendency to hoard rather than to distribute his earnings. In short, he was without ambition, and had entirely escaped the praise or obloquy which falls to the lot of greater men.

In the year 1371, at the time when the Genoese sufferings were at their height, and the loans of the "compere" in the greatest request, and commerce and industry were felt to be fast disappearing from hitherto prosperous Genoa—at this time, Francesco Vivaldi came forward and saved his country.

On the twelfth of April in this year, the generous old patrician came down to the council hall in his usual mean attire, his threadbare coat, and with his thoughtful, searching eye. All men held their peace as he entered, for he had previously given out that he had some weighty points to communicate, touching the welfare of the State ; and amongst hushed voices he thus spoke, as we gather from an old document in the archives of St. George :—

"Sirs, I recognize the wants of my country, and I feel the burden of our debt, as it is befitting a good citizen should. I have carefully kept for you the value of my shares in the Bank of St. George, since they belong to you, being the governors and administrators of the people ; use them in accordance with the design I have now in mind as I offer them to you. These shares are inscribed in my name inviolate and sacred, and so they shall remain as I despoil myself of them. Those of you who have the charge of the "compere," seek to draw the interest from this sum never later than the fall of each year. With this interest I purpose that other shares be bought, to bear fruit also in their season ; and thus fresh fruits and fresh gains may multiply with the course of years, until a sufficient sum is accumulated to pay off the shareholders in the loan you call 'of the great peace.' This accomplished, the capital must be employed in laying by interest to pay off all the other loans, be they heavy or be they light. Nor must you ever stop as long as a single debt remains in the Republic, and whilst you read in the books a single subsidy which weighs on you and on my fellow-citizens. This is my will, and if it is transgressed, or in part neglected, I will cancel the gift, either myself if alive, or by the hands of my successors if I am no more."

Thus was the contract executed between this noble citizen and the directors of the "compere." Thus was a noble course of heroism initiated, in the steps of which many followed hereafter, for the benefit of their country. It is to be regretted that Francesco Vivaldi, the inaugurator of this system of public relief, should have been honoured with nothing but a statue of an inferior kind which now stands, scarce discernible for dirt, in an isolated corner of the building. Francesco Vivaldi is eclipsed by larger donors, and larger liberality in more prosperous days caused the sacrifice he made to grow dim ; and thus the man who stemmed the current of decay by one single act of generosity became forgotten.

Meanwhile the credit and interest of the bank grew apace. Hospitals, churches, and confraternities, all placed their capital in it. All corporations and civil establishments here deposited their possessions with the administrators, who employed these funds to the best advantage. If a family chose to build a church, or a bridge, or some other public work, they assigned so many shares in the bank as an endowment in perpetuity.

After the example of Francesco Vivaldi, founders of benefices not unfrequently took care to order that the shares they contributed should not be applied to their destination until a certain epoch or concurrence, in order that the accumulated produce in reserve might serve for the purchase of fresh shares to increase the inalienable capital. But though it worked well in Vivaldi's case, and saved the credit of the Republic, and gave men an insight into the manipulation of interest, yet these frequent " multiplications " often impoverished the State when carried to excess, by keeping money out of profitable and useful channels.

As time went on, and the French governor, Boucicault, weighed on the treasury the burden of fresh fortifications,[1] and an expensive war ; when Corsican troubles, and the Turks in the East, caused the advance of money to be frequent, an assembly of all the shareholders in all the loans decided that an entire reorganization of the public debts should take place.

Nine men were elected to draw up a new scheme, in 1407,

---

[1] *Vide* ch. ix.

and by their instrumentality all the shares were united ; the interest for all was to be seven per cent., and fresh officials were appointed to superintend the now thoroughly constituted and re-named " Bank of St. George." And at length we behold this celebrated bank. Its credit never failed, and no anxiety was ever felt by any shareholder about his annual income, until the days of the French Revolution.

An agreement between the shareholders and the government was drawn up, by which ample authority was given to the newly appointed " protectors." Every right of passing judicial sentences without appeal, all prerogatives of self-government, were conceded to them, and the government of the State vowed never to interfere with the government of the bank.

This Bank of St. George was essentially one of the times, and not one which could have existed on modern ideas of credit; for it was a bank which would only issue paper for the coin in its actual possession, and would hardly suit the dictates of modern commerce. It was not a bank for borrowers but for capitalists, who required enormous security for immense sums until they could employ them themselves. A sign, indeed, of great opulence at the time ; but also a sign of an industry which was approaching stagnation.

In this year of 1407 a new constitution was given to it. Out of thirty-two notable citizens, chosen by lot from amongst those most interested in the " compere," the ballot was to extract eight, whose interest in the bank should never be less than one thousand Genoese florins ; and these were the protectors. They must not have any special interest in any special tax, and into their hands was consigned the chief executive power.

These eight protectors were given different offices to superintend in the working system of the bank. There was the president, treasurer-general, superintender of the sale of shares, and the three judges, who saw to frauds and the general management of the building, and two secretaries, who all remained in office for a year.

But though re-organized, all the old rules and customs were maintained, as far as was compatible with the new order of things. The general council of four hundred and eighty controlled the protectors, and to this everybody over eighteen, and whose interest was over ten shares, be he Genoese or foreigner, was eligible. The election took place by ballot, and to this council was referred the question of every new loan, or any new regulation which was deemed advisable.

As a matter of course, in so large a concern there were numerous minor officials : the syndics, who acted under the judges, with whom all complaints were lodged ; the consuls, who sold the shares at public auctions ; and a large staff of advocates and lawyers, one of whom always sat at public meetings to see that the protectors were not at fault in their law. Then there were the chancellors, who acted under the secretaries in writing out the deliberations of the council, and in keeping the books with all the lists of the proprietors of shares. All these were indexed, and open to public inspection ; so that it was easy for an inquisitive Genoese to form a pretty good estimate of how much his neighbours possessed, as deposits for money outside the precincts of St. George were almost unknown.

With the advance of time the growth of the absolute power possessed by this bank became still more marked. For example, in 1425, safe conducts granted by the government of Genoa did not hold good for debtors to the government of the bank ; and in 1528 it was decided that no person who held an appointment under the Genoese government could hold an appointment in the government of the bank.

A curious instance of a floating debt occurred soon after the establishment of the bank in its new form, perhaps the first on record in modern annals. When in 1456, owing to the defence of Caffa against the Turks, the directors were

obliged to reduce their rate of interest on certain shares they
then sold, and to retard the repayment of the same for three
years, so as not to alter the annual system of the "columns,"
they were written apart, and called "entered debts." In the
fourth year they paid the account due the first year, and in
the fifth year that of the second, and so on in perpetuity.

To quiet the consciences of various ecclesiastics, who were
participators therein, and consequently thought themselves in
a measure responsible for the honesty of the bank, these loans
had to be authorized by bulls of Calixtus III. and Sixtus IV.,
since it was looked upon as little short of usury—that hated
usury, the fear of which haunted mediæval enterprise, and any
approach to which, except by Jews, was thought totally inconsistent with humanity.

A hundred years later than this, during the dogeship of
Andrea Giustiniani, when corn had all to be brought from
Sicily, and there was the greatest distress in Genoa, a large
portion of the debt was made irredeemable. The government
of Genoa, for a large loan negotiated for them by the bank,
agreed to hand over to their creditors the taxes on certain
commodities in perpetuity; and no further tax was to be
placed on them without the consent of the shareholders.
Prior to this the tax had only been conceded for a term of
years, until the portion of money advanced, and the interest
thereon, had been paid off; now, shareholders were secure
of a substantial rate of interest extending over an unlimited
amount of years.

One of the most interesting features in connection with
the dealings of the bank with the Genoese government, and a
conclusive proof of the perfect accord which existed between
them, was the cession from time to time of various colonies
and provinces to the directors of the bank when the
government felt itself too weak and too poor to maintain
them.

In this manner were the colonies in the Black Sea made

over to the bank[1] when the Turkish difficulties arose. Corsica and Cyprus, also towns on the Riviera, such as Sarzana, Ventimiglia, Levanto, found themselves at various times under the direct sovereignty of the bank, and the banner of St. George was seen to float over their towers in lieu of the republican red cross. For a parallel to this in later history we have not to search far afield, for our own cession of our East Indian colonies to the East India Company was almost exactly executed on the same principle. In fact, the powers and independence enjoyed by the Bank of St. George throughout remind us forcibly of our East India Company in its dealings with our government, only the jurisdiction of the latter was at the other end of the world and not situated in our very midst.

However well regulated the home concerns of the bank may have been, they were singularly unsuccessful in their dealings with these colonies allotted to them. Young, inexperienced, and grasping men were sent out to govern them ; to ensure some profits thereout the deputies of the bank ground down the unfortunate Corsicans and Cypriots to the last penny ; and when at length they found that no more was to be got out of them, and that to hold them longer would rather entail a loss, the directors of the bank modestly returned them to the Genoese government in a far more hopeless state of confusion than they were before.

The old system of the "compere," of stated times for payments, of publicly negotiating loans at the street corners by means of their auctioneer, continued so long in vogue that, though essentially acting as a bank, it was not till 1675 that the directors recognized the necessity of adopting a more convenient mode of transacting business by means of separate branches about the city, where loans could be negotiated, and money drawn after the fashion of a modern bank. Then, and not till then, did the old name of the "compere" disappear

---

[1] *Vide* ch. vi.

and give place entirely to the title of "bank." In this year the directors received from the government an allotment of four different places in the city for transacting business, which were found highly convenient for the merchants whose business lay in different parts of the town. And thus did the old word "compera," which had existed since Genoa's merchants supplied the first sinews of war to fight the Saracens and the Moors, disappear, and survives now only in a street in Genoa, which smacks strongly of Genoa's ancient mercantile power both in its buildings and in its name, the "Strada delle Compere."

During the last two centuries of its existence the Bank of St. George had frequently great trouble to provide for all the exigencies of the times. After the French and Savoy invasions the government was compelled to raise forced loans, independent of the bank, with which to build up fortresses, which still surround the city in a semicircle from the Bisagno to the Polcevera valleys ; and hence were established public pawn loans, called "monte," each bearing the name of some saintly protector—for example, the "monte of the Madonna," the "monte of St. Bernardo," etc. Each of these loans had its separate government, on the system of St. George, but were kept apart from the bank, and when the emergency was over were speedily paid off by the instrumentality of the bank.

It is a curious relic of ancient days, when a high rate of interest was reckoned a most heinous sin, altogether usurious, that all the pawnshops in Italy should rejoice still in the euphonious title of "mounts of piety." For in those days, when the leading commercial nations of the world lent money at a higher rate of interest than was deemed compatible with honesty, they did so under the kindly veil of religion, as if to disarm all who assailed them with religious weapons by their very name.

The Bank of St. George, after the terrors of the Austrian

invasion, when most of its gold was carried off to the tents of the invader,[1] established a " monte of preservation," in which they wrote down all the interest and sums of money they found it inconvenient to pay at the time by way of a further loan at a higher rate of interest. When the Austrians had gone and things righted themselves again, all this was paid off; and thus did the bank manage to get over its difficulties, but not without imposing new taxes on commodities, which must have fallen somewhat hard on the Genoese, who were thus forcibly obliged to lend their income for the public weal.

It is melancholy to have to draw a veil over the career of this illustrious bank with the Revolution of 1798. The new order of things which Genoa had learnt from France deemed it inconsistent with liberty that the taxes, the property of the Republic, should remain in the hands of the directors of St. George; it was voted a tyranny on a small scale, and the directors were compelled to surrender them ; and inasmuch as the taxes represented the sole source from which their income was derived, they soon discovered that their bank notes were useless, and the building was closed shortly afterwards.

In 1804 and 1814 attempts were made to resuscitate the fallen fortunes of St. George, but without avail; and so this bank, the origin of which was shrouded in the mysteries of bygone centuries, fell under the sweeping scythe of the French Revolution.

The history of this bank is the preface to all the leading commercial undertakings of Europe ; it is the sanctuary of the merchant, and the shrine of the banker, and compared to the consuls—the protectors and directors of this bank—the managers of our own Bank of England and the Rothschilds are but *parvenus*.

St. George, the mystic knight-priest of Cappadocia, has indeed been a name under which commercial enterprise has flourished. It is singular to find his name associated with,

---

[1] *Vide* ch. xvii.

and his protection claimed by, one of the most flourishing systems of mediæval Europe ; and again to find St. George for merry England, the patron of Anglo-Saxon colonists in all parts of the globe.

The reported deeds of chivalry and piety attributed to this saint were dear to the crusaders of old. His spirit was supposed to fight for the Genoese before the walls of Jerusalem, and Richard of the Lion's Heart carried his banner home, out of compliment to his Genoese allies. And in the same manner we find most of the maritime people of the Mediterranean adopting him as their patron saint. At Venice, indeed, he was eclipsed by the superior merits of St. Mark and his lion ; but in Genoa, St. George, with his white banner and blood-red cross, and his legendary victory over the dragon, held his own nobly against St. John the Baptist. In the dark slate-marble of Lavagna his knightly form was depicted over hundreds of Genoese lintels, in his contest with the dragon, whilst the king's daughter and the flocks, with their attendant shepherds, are placed near in many of them, looking on in grateful recognition of their release from the monster's jaws. In maritime Portugal also St. George was the cry raised in battle, for it was at the decisive battle of Aljuberrota, in 1385, that the Portuguese, under John II., effectually threw off the Castilian yoke to the cry of St. George for Portugal.

It strikes one as curious that a soldier saint should have found so much favour with maritime people. For Venice and Genoa he was the miraculous stiller of the storm and tempest, no less than their stalwart ally in battle and in siege. Some twenty miles from Genoa the lovely little fishing village of Portofino lays claim to the possession of the largest portion of St. George's scattered body. They got it, they say, direct from Palestine, and hence chose St. George as their patron saint. Every 24th of April they do him homage, whilst he in return, say the pious mariners, wards off their pestilences and stills their storms. Thus do the Portofinese fishermen sleep peacefully beneath their olive-clad hills, which scarcely leave room for the narrow line of houses surrounding their tiny land-locked harbour, under the protection of the same

CHURCH IN PORTOFINO.

saint whom every Englishman invokes by way of a gentle oath.

The palace of St. George, as it still stands in Genoa, amply repays a visit and careful attention. Though the mere shadow of the once noble building which in its day has contained the fortunes of millions, still much is left to testify to its bygone glory, and to rake up reminiscences of the past.

Venerable indeed is the old Gothic building, down near the port, handed over as it is to all the filth and squalor of an Italian custom-house ; and though it has been a much mooted question by the present government whether it should not be pulled down to make room for a handsome modern street, the Genoese have nobly stuck to this relic of their former wealth.

The very stones of which it is built, tradition says, were brought by the Genoese from Constantinople, in 1260, when Michael Paleologus gave them the Venetian fortress of Pancratore in recognition of favours and assistance received. Three lions' heads, which adorn the Gothic portal, indicate very ancient and rude Eastern art, and go far to prove the truth of this piece of spiteful folly from which one would gladly free the Genoese ; but here, too, were hung part of the chains of the Pisan harbour, and it looks much as if the façade of this building had been intended as a museum of triumphant jealousy.

This palace was erected much in its present exterior form in the days of the first captain of the people, Guglielmo Boccanegra, in 1260, as is attested by a tablet in the interior, which reads as follows :—

"Guglielmo Boccanegra, whilst he was captain of this city, ordered, in the year 1260, that I should be built. After this was decreed, Iva Oliviero, a man divine for the acuteness of his mind, adapted me with great care to whatever use should then or ever after be applied to me by the captain."

Boccanegra recognized the necessity of erecting a suitable building for the transaction of the ever-increasing monetary affairs of the Republic, and this was the result.

It requires much courage and determination to ascend those dirty marble stairs, to withstand the jostling of garlic-eating Italian porters, but on reaching the summit of the staircase the reward is complete. On every side the visitor is greeted by statues of worthy men, some well executed in white marble by eminent Genoese artists.   They line the walls of the entrance hall, they line the walls of the council hall, each one a testimony to some magnanimous citizen, who gave a portion of his patrimony towards relieving some pressing distress.

> " We loved that hall, tho' white and cold,
> Those niched shapes of noble mould ;
> A princely people's awful princes,
> The grave, severe Genoese of old."
>
> TENNYSON, *The Daisy.*

One of these worthies had founded a hospital, another had bought off a tax on provisions which pressed heavily on the poor, another had left shares in the bank to provide a dower for poor maidens, another had left his whole fortune to improve the port or strengthen the fortifications.   There they stand in this noble hall, thirty-five benefactors of their country, all robed in the loose flowing dress of mediæval Italy, each with his quaint " beretta " on his head, a stone slab underneath each, relating to their many virtues and their liberality.   In fact, this old building contains a perfect museum of Genoa's worthies, scarcely to be distinguished from the dirt which covers them, a perpetual shame to their descendants who allow such oblivion to cover the deeds of their ancestors, far nobler than themselves.

These statues are all arranged in an order peculiar to themselves, suited to their various grades of liberality.   For those who only bequeathed twenty-five thousand francs to the state, a simple commemorative stone was thought sufficient, whilst their more liberal brethren, whose donation amounted to fifty thousand francs, were honoured with a half figure bust. All those who gave up to one hundred thousand francs, were represented standing in a row over the heads of the most generous of all who exceeded this sum, and who were placed in a sitting posture close to public gaze and admiration. It was this fact which caused Francesco Vivaldi's great liberality during a time of distress only to receive a memorial of the second order, and to remain neglected in an upper corner.

Before leaving this hall, let us turn our eyes to an old inscription, which is still legible over one of the doorways, though the image, which once stood above it, is gone. Triumphant in her victory over the combined forces of Pisa and Frederic II., Genoa wrought a new seal, and a marble image representing the griffin of Genoa trampling beneath her feet the eagle of Germany and the fox of Pisa. As seen to-day, the inscription runs thus—

> " As thus the griffin doth its prey devour,
> So Genoa doth her foes o'erpower."

Of the small marble image, all that is left is the pedestal and the inscription, and the old seal of the commune, which was a copy of it.

In this grand council hall, with its surrounding statues, was the tribune in which sat the old president of the bank, with a picture over his head, which still hangs there, representing the Madonna supported by SS. John the Baptist and George, by Domenico Piola. Here the full council of four hundred and eighty was held. Around the room were placed the desks of the clerks, with their books, and indexes of the shareholders in alphabetical order. And in this hall were initiated some of the most important steps in commercial enterprise.

A visit to the archives of this old bank will well repay the curious. Here lie piled together the many volumes of the proceedings of the bank, now principally used as a place of research by those interested in making out their pedigrees ; but what are, perhaps, of more interest to the world at large, are here deposited—the records of Genoa's dealings with her colonies. Here is a copy of the old colonial codes, the Gazzaria,[1] by which she governed her Black Sea possessions.

[1] *Vide* ch. vi.

Here are books without end, labelled Caffa, Scio, Famagosta, etc., all full of lore about her colonies in her palmiest days.

In wandering through these deserted halls—deserted in fact they are not, for they are redolent with everything that can offend the senses, but bereft of their former splendour— one is confronted at every turn with some interesting inscription, some lovely black marble carving, or some fast fading fresco. In one corner we see holes in the wall where the letters for the various magistrates were put over four hundred years ago; in another we see a long list of important duties on various commodities throughout the Riviera. In a room downstairs all criminal cases were tried, as an inscription attests, while above, in an upper room, is the ballot-box with which elections were decided centuries ago.

It is a melancholy sight to see and realize how great Genoa once was here in the very centre of her greatness— faded, indeed, like that gigantic fresco which faces the sea, in which Lazzaro Tavarone represented St. George on the façade of this his own palace. An apt simile of the fortunes of Genoa is this fresco, scarce now discernible from its continued exposure to the very element which won for Genoa her fame; whilst the bell in the old clock tower is now for ever silent, and no longer reminds the busy Ligurian mariner of the motto inscribed within it, "Divide thy time, like the measured striking of this bell."

Of the many benefits conferred by the Bank of St. George on mercantile Genoa, none perhaps was more substantial than the erection and establishment of the buildings of the Porto Franco. In olden days every ship which entered the harbour paid "a tenth of the sea," as it was called, to the archbishop, and hence many vessels used to anchor in neighbouring ports, and unship their cargoes elsewhere.

To obviate this difficulty, in 1595, a Porto Franco, or free entrance, was proclaimed for three years by way of experiment, which proved so beneficial that it was extended in perpetuity by the government, and the management of it handed over to the Bank of St. George, as most interested in the affairs of export and import.

Forthwith the directors built large warehouses for the goods which now flocked into Genoa on a spot granted them by government. And now we see the three hundred and fifty-five bonded warehouses, as they were originally erected, surrounded by lofty walls, and with gates towards the sea and the city. Without special permission the military, priesthood, and women were not admitted within its precincts. Nevertheless, the Jesuits contrived to possess themselves of one of the richest of these warehouses for the aromatic drugs, and other precious products, which arrived for them from Spain, Portugal, the Indies, and China.

Materially the Porto Franco was a circle of shops in the public keeping, and under the keys of the custom house. Thither all merchandise from abroad was gratuitously admitted, and thence it could be sent by sea or land without tax or duty of any kind. It was the secret of Genoa's later prosperity, and kept for her the nucleus of trade when her colonies and possessions had passed from her.

In connection with the Porto Franco a curious regiment of porters was maintained by the legacy of a wealthy citizen. They were called the " Company of the Caravans," originally only twelve in number, but afterwards they were raised to three hundred. Two out of this body were annually elected as consuls, who punished delinquents and thefts, and had a sort of little jurisdiction of their own. They wore their own distinctive dress, and were exclusively connected with the custom-house. As Genoese were alone admitted, it was an exceedingly comfortable berth for many a hard-working Ligurian. It was a sort of almshouse, conducted on active principles, to enter which interest was required. It is only a few years since this body of porters was abolished.

To one of these porters of the Porto Franco, towards the

close of the last century, was born a child of surpassing musical genius. He astonished his rough parents by playing the violin from ten to twelve hours daily. And when at seventeen he was taken from his amusement for a more active occupation, as befitted a labourer's son, it was only to lay aside the violin for a more convenient season. This youth was Niccolò Paganini, whose fame went throughout Europe, and whose violin is still treasured in the Genoese council hall.

> " The pale musician of the bow
> Who brought from Italy the tales, made true,
> Of Grecian lyres, and on his sphery hand,
> Loading the air with dumb expectancy,
> Suspended, ere it fell, a nation's breath."
>
> LEIGH HUNT.

We have now sketched the history of this bank and its principal bearings on the history of the Republic; in fact, without this, the history of Genoa would be an entire problem. Her resuscitations after overpowering disasters; her extraordinary vitality, which led the Emperor Charles V. to say that "No one could crush Genoa, if Genoa did not crush herself;" all these had their centre in the Bank of St. George, its wonderful constitution, and its world-wide fame.

CHAPTER XII.

HOW ANDREA D'ORIA CAME TO RULE IN GENOA.

FEW families have served their country better than the D'Oria of Genoa. In few countries do we find a family for centuries producing members victorious in war, pre-eminent in council, so that scarcely a name can be read on their long pedigree which does not recall some point of interest in Ligurian history. Hardly is there a boast in Genoese annals which was not effectuated by one of them.

Every visitor to Genoa pays a hurried visit to their sanctuary, the small church of San Matteo, and here on the black and white marble façade he may pause and learn the glorious deeds of each from this, the perpetual testimony to their valour :—how Oberto D'Oria, in 1284, defeated the Pisans at Meloria ; how Lamba, in 1298, routed the Venetians at Curzola, whilst that curious old Roman sarcophagus under the window on the right is a relic of his victory in which his son Lambino buried his honoured father's remains ; how Filippo D'Oria fought bravely for the French banner in the Gulf of Salerno ; how, in 1352, Pagano routed Venetians, Greeks, and Catalans in the Bosphorus ; how Luciano died conquering the Venetians at Pola, in 1379.

All this and much more is learnt from this marble volume. But perhaps it is in Andrea D'Oria, the greatest of this great house, that modern interest in this little church chiefly centres. Under his direction it was beautified by Montorsoli ; here his venerable bones were laid, and here, over the high altar, stands the sword given him as a token of respect by Pope Paul III.; whilst in the adjacent cloister, with its hundred light double pillars, stand the remnants of two colossal statues erected by an obedient people to the memory of their masters, the great prince Andrea and the son of his adoption, Giovanandrea D'Oria, but decapitated and cast down during the French Revolution and carried hither, like the mortal remains of the men they represent, to receive honoured sepulture amongst the graves of the ancestors of the D'Oria.

Every house in the little square which surrounds this church speaks of the D'Oria. Here is the palace which a grateful commonwealth allotted to Lamba, and another to Pagano; whilst in a retired corner is the one which was presented to Andrea by his country in 1528. In the "loggia," or raised platform, which occupies the centre of this square, the busy D'Oria merchants were wont to meet their clients, and from here Andrea addressed the assembled populace, in 1528, when he came to give them that much-talked-of but doubtful gift of liberty, the nature of which we will presently discuss.

No less romantic than its after acquired fame is the story of the origin of this family. One Arduin, Viscount of Narbonne, came to Genoa prior to embarking for a Crusade, and was lodged in the house of a widow della Volta, of a noble Genoese family; here he fell ill, and was tenderly nursed by the widow and her fair daughter Oria. On recovery, he found himself deeply enamoured with the girl, and after fulfilling his vows in Palestine, he returned to Genoa to demand her hand. Soon after they were married, and Arduin took up his residence in Genoa, and merged his nationality in that of his wife. In Andrea D'Oria's palace at Fassuolo there still hangs a picture illustrating the betrothal of the fair Oria della Volta to the knight of Narbonne; and from this marriage sprang all this illustrious line. Their children were called D'Oria, and the property which Arduin bought was called Port'Oria, to-day a substantial portion of the Ligurian capital.

Of the numerous heroes of this family we have had many details in these pages, but now we have to treat of the greatest of them all, the warrior-statesman Andrea, whose life of ninety-three years is about as eventful as any in history, and whose character is one of the most striking the world has produced. On the firm basis of an iron will and an iron constitution were grafted the cunning of a Borgia, talents of the highest order for both naval and military affairs, and that entire disregard of principle, so essential for the statesman of those days. Before him emperors and kings trembled, for they recognized in him their superior. Italian politics of the day consisted in the maintenance of a balance of power between France and Germany, and of this Andrea D'Oria was the keystone.

Undoubtedly he did much for his own special country, but though he gave Genoa an unhealthy brilliancy during his lifetime, it was but the hectic flush of the doomed, it was the signal for her downfall and her ruin. During the two centuries and a half that the aristocratic government instituted by Andrea continued in Genoa, a slow decay set in in her commerce; her haughty, purse-proud nobility ground down all within her that was generous and free, until her liberty mouldered away and became extinct; and though Andrea D'Oria bore the proud title of "liberator of his country," and the constitution he established was looked upon as the very essence of liberty, yet, as read by the light of after events, it appears more to resemble an iron fetter which Spaniard and Frenchman drew tighter and tighter round the Ligurian Republic until Napoleon squeezed thereout the last remaining spark of vitality.

In himself Andrea was undoubtedly a glorious man; the emperor Charles V., on whose dominions the sun never set, was controlled by him, fawned upon him, and implicitly trusted him. Francis I. of France, "the most Christian king," recognized Andrea's power, but by a mistaken policy sought to keep it in check, and thereby lost him to his cause.

One of the most curious features in Andrea's career is that he was a comparatively insignificant personage until his sixty-third year. He had, it is true, lived the life of a successful *condottiere*, but by no means more successful than numerous other members of his family had been before him; until at length, when he had attained an age at which most men seek for rest from their labours, by a *coup d'état* he became master of Genoa, left the service of King Francis I., and for the remaining thirty years of his life held the casting vote in most of the affairs of Europe.

Another feature in Andrea D'Oria's character, absent in most of Genoa's heroes, was the love he displayed for art, which hitherto had been greatly neglected in Liguria; and in his palace at Fassuolo, which we will visit presently, he gathered together some of Raphael's and Michael Angelo's most accomplished pupils to adorn his dwelling with some of the most vivid conceptions of their school.

Andrea's person and frugal habits are thus portrayed by Richer:[1] "He was tall, well built, and of an agreeable countenance; his eyes were searching, and his memory so excellent that he never forgot what he read. He was most religious, and daily said his litany to the Virgin. He had only two meals a day, and always diluted his wine with water. He was fond of the fair sex, but never allowed them to interfere with his duties." This was the man under whose sway Genoa now fell.

It would certainly be interesting if more of the facts of his early life, during which such grand abilities were nurtured and matured, could be brought to light. Unfortunately his earlier career is as devoid of narrative as his later days are abounding in it.

[1] Andrée Richer, "Vie des plus célèbres marins."

We are told how he was born on the night of S. Andrea, in 1466, to one Ceva D'Oria, a younger branch of this noble family, who lived on his property at Oneglia, on the Riviera, whither he was obliged to repair for political reasons, and from the emptiness of his pockets. Andrea was his second son—a daring, wild youth, full of spirit, and addicted to the habit of running away from home, and being brought back in disgrace ; and so much did the spirit of enterprise evince itself, that a maiden aunt left him some money only on condition that he should abandon his vagabond tastes, and settle down to a steady life.

Andrea was early left to his mother's charge, his father dying when he was still a boy, and infinite was the trouble he gave her. On one occasion, when an uncle took away his elder brother for a more active life, poor Andrea was so disgusted at his uneventful lot that he took to his bed and wept, requiring all the blandishments of his mother to rouse him from his state of despondency.

At length, at the age of twenty-six, he was able to leave home with empty pockets but eager heart, and rushed headlong into that life of activity and danger for which his soul craved. By the influence of his kinsman Niccolò, he became man-of-arms in the service of the Genoese Pope, Innocent VIII., of the house of Cybo ; and in this pontiff's behalf, he fought many a battle against the infidel, for Innocent was especially strong in this line. In the archbishop's palace at Genoa is a fresco illustrative of Saracenic subjection and papal aggrandizement, illustrating the Genoese Pope with his foot on a Saracen's head. Innocent was the jailor of that unfortunate Prince Djem and master of Andrea D'Oria at one and the same time. Hence Andrea was well trained in hatred of the Saracen.

On the accession of Alexander VI., the licentious Borgian pope, Andrea quitted the Vatican, and retired to Urbino, where the duke received him into his service, and where

Andrea fell violently in love with the duchess. Some years later, he was enabled to save this lady from the clutches of Cæsar Borgia, with a cunning that matched his own. At the siege of Sinigaglia, Andrea sent off the duchess in disguise, and placed an image of her in her bed. This, Andrea carefully showed to Borgia to disarm all suspicions ; but when the escape of his prey at length dawned upon him, Cæsar Borgia, they say, was more hurt than at the loss of a battle.

At the court of Naples, Andrea D'Oria was introduced to all the horrors of despotism, cruelty, and bloodshed, which may have greatly influenced the formation of his character ; for whether in Genoa, Corsica, or against the corsairs, Andrea D'Oria was proverbial for his cruelty, and his hot-headed persecution of a rival or a foe.

A pilgrimage to Jerusalem, and the tutorship of the young duke of Urbino, Francesco Maria II., occupied some of Andrea's subsequent years, until he reached the age of thirty-six, and found his interests in the world no further advanced, and his pockets, if possible, emptier than they were when he left his mother's roof.

Again did his kinsman, Niccolò D'Oria, lend him a helping hand, and got him an appointment in the Corsican army, of which he was at that time in command, fighting on behalf of the Bank of St. George, against the rebels ;[1] and when Niccolò was summoned elsewhere, Andrea obtained sole command of the army. This is the first time we find him in anything like a responsible position ; and here his character came out. With uncompromising cruelty, he put every person that came into his possession in the island to the sword, sparing neither age nor sex in his sweeping commands. He burnt their houses ; and at length, with dogged determination, he succeeded in starving out the Corsican leader, Ranuccio, in his fastnesses, and finally reduced the island to order.

During all the earlier years of his military career, Andrea

---

[1] *Vide* ch. xv.

seems to have had but little to do with the politics of his native country. The Fregosi and the Adorni might dispute to their hearts' content, nobles might quarrel with the people, but Andrea's time was not yet come. At the age of forty-six, we find him in Genoa, and ready to accept an active post under Gian Luigi Fregoso, who had possessed himself of the city by means of a handful of Swiss. To Andrea he gave the captaincy of a few galleys, and thus, from being a soldier and a *condottiere*, he turned into a naval officer; and though somewhat advanced in life for so important a change, he nevertheless soon proved himself equal to gaining laurels for himself by sea.

Soon after he had adopted this new mode of life, Andrea took part in an escapade of which Genoese annals are justly proud. In 1513, the French, and their Adorni allies, held the lighthouse, or " Briglia," with its command of the entrance to the harbour. After a long siege the garrison was on the point of surrender, when, to the dismay of the senate and the Genoese besiegers, a ship was seen making for the lighthouse, from the side of France, with provisions and ammunition for the beleaguered garrison. Thereupon one Emanuele Cavallo presented himself to the senate, and promised that if he might choose thirty comrades, and have a galley given him, he could prevent the vessel from having communication with the garrison.

To this request the senate cordially acquiesced, and amongst the chosen number was Captain Andrea D'Oria. This brave band at once set out to attack the French ship. Emanuele Cavallo was the first to board her; many of his comrades were slain, and others wounded, but eventually they succeeded in capturing the ship, and in taking thirty-two Frenchmen back with them in triumph to Genoa as prisoners. For this deed Cavallo received great renown, and immunities such as were but seldom granted to a citizen, and Andrea D'Oria then received the only wound he ever had in his long life of war, and his first experience in nautical warfare.

Recognizing the talents of their kinsman, some two or three years later, some of Andrea's relations set him up with four galleys with which to start his roving, seafaring life; and for the next few years we see him wandering through the Mediterranean, the terror of the Saracen, the ally of the French, and the bugbear of the Imperial cause. At Tunis, in 1517, he dislodged the infidel, at a great loss to the Christians, but with great honour to himself, and then set sail for Monaco, where he was implicated in a dark affair which, if report be correct, reflects but little credit on his name. ᾽It runs as follows :—

A Grimaldi in Monaco murdered his brother about this time, and in his turn was disposed of by one Bartolomeo D'Oria, who seized the principality. Just at this concurrence Andrea D'Oria turned up, avowed his dislike to the step his kinsman had taken, and privately arranged with Archbishop Grimaldi, brother of the two murdered princes, that Bartolomeo should be also put out of the way. This thread of murders, report says, was all instigated by the cunning of Andrea. That the last was, there is sufficient proof ; and the sequel to the tragedy, namely, that Andrea possessed himself of Monaco without a blow, and then handed it over to his royal master, Francis I., looks much as if he had laid the train of these events to accomplish his ends.

During these days Andrea managed to make himself invaluable to the French monarch in his war with the emperor Charles. He did good service for him at Marseilles; he killed the Prince of Orange, the imperial admiral, for him, and before the battle of Pavia, through Andrea's instrumentality, France was predominant in the Mediterranean, more especially as the Barbary corsairs were kept in check by Andrea and his nephew Philippino.

But Andrea was not content to remain a mere instrument

for the aggrandizement of France. Out of the rivalry between the heads of Europe he planned to reap for himself no small advantage. After the fatal battle of Pavia the prisoner-king, Francis I., was conducted by way of Genoa to the monastery of Cervara, a lovely spot near Portofino, which had been built two centuries before by Guido Scettem, an archbishop of Genoa, Petrarch's friend. To-day there stands a fine palm tree overshadowing the room where the French king was imprisoned ; and this monastery of Cervara is a charming rest for the eye as it wanders along the steep olive-clad hills and bold rocks and fortresses which line the coast.

Here slept king Francis, whilst Andrea D'Oria and his galleys were reposing in the little land-locked harbour of Portofino, scarce two miles distant. At one blow he could have released his royal master from his prison, if such had been his wish ; but his plans were otherwise laid, probably far too deep to be fathomed after this lapse of time. But certain it is that after this arose a marked coolness between Andrea and the French king, and for the next few months Andrea fought under the papal banner, and not under that of the lilies.

It was during his dealings with Pope Clement VII. that this great admiral, of whom the Genoese are so proud, and who gave them their liberty, they say, actually found himself laying siege to his native town and the Spanish garrison therein. Scarcely three years afterwards did he treat the French, whom he now introduced as lords of Genoa, in the same way. What versatility for a liberator of his country, and what curious means to obtain that liberty !

After the sack of Rome, and Clement's disgrace, Andrea again found himself in the immediate service of France. He seems, in fact, to have had great dislike to sticking by a friend in distress ; and his friends were always those from whom he could reap the greatest benefit. Thus, with French aid, did he manage to drive the Spaniards out of Genoa, and impose that very yoke upon his native city for removing which, in 1528, he was crowned with everlasting laurels, and hailed as the saviour of his country. It is a striking instance of the system of politics carried on in Genoa that the future host of the

HARBOUR OF PORTOFINO.

emperor Charles should be the person to introduce into her assembly the French governor Teodoro Trivulzio.

During all these busy scenes of politics and war, Andrea D'Oria found time enough to pay attention to his domestic affairs. In the year 1526, when sixty years of age, he took to himself a wife, one Peretta by name, an elderly, highly respectable woman, whose chief recommendations were of a domestic nature, for which alone did Andrea marry her, being actuated neither by beauty, riches, nor the hope of offspring in making this choice of a companion for his declining years. Throughout his long career the character of Andrea D'Oria escaped the slur of scandal, in an age when vice itself was almost looked upon as a virtue; and beyond an attachment to the Duchess of Urbino in his younger days, Andrea's name is never coupled with that of any of the fair sex, until he took Peretta to his home, and together they began life as it were at the wrong end.

Daily the coldness between Andrea and his master, Francis, was increasing. Diligently enough D'Oria collected troops to assist the French king in Naples, but Francis was dilatory in coming forward, and Andrea's impetuosity could not stand it; so off he set on an expedition of his own to Sardinia; but not with his usual success did he attack the Spaniards in this island. However, all failure was more than compensated for by a signal victory the two D'Oria, Andrea and his nephew, gained over the imperialists at Capri.

A great and terrible battle of a truth was that of Capri, and mainly to a device of his own did Andrea owe the successful issue thereof. To his slaves he promised liberty, and a galley all for themselves, with the D'Orian flag, if they should win the day. Under this incentive, they rushed with one accord into the water, with knives in their mouths, and caused such havoc and confusion amongst the imperial galleys that when Andrea came upon the scene he was enabled to strike a decisive blow.

Be it said to his credit that he gave his slaves their liberty and their galley, on condition that they should burn it on reaching Africa. We know not if their part of the contract was fulfilled.

This victory at Capri was for Andrea D'Oria the great turning point in his life. It alarmed Francis I. to find himself

under the control of his powerful admiral; it made the
emperor obsequious and ready to come to terms with Andrea
at any cost. And thus, after Capri, judicious Andrea paved the
way for changing his allegiance from France to Austria, and
with it the allegiance of his country.

It is a curious historical drama, this freak of Andrea
D'Oria's, but when read with a view to the politics of the day,
it was clearly the wisest course he could have pursued. He
recognized that Francis was jealous of his transcendent
power, and would crush him if he could. He recognized not
only that his own downfall was being aimed at by the French
monarch, but also that of his native Genoa. For, by setting
up Savona as a port with franchises greater than those of
Genoa, Francis hoped to overthrow Genoese commerce.

Moreover, Francis hit Andrea hard on a sore point; for the
admiral was exceedingly fond of money, and the king gave
him nothing for his capture of the Prince of Orange, instead
of two hundred thousand ducats, as he had originally promised. And although Francis sent him the much-coveted
order of St. Michael, he never gave him a property he had
promised him in Provence; and such want of faith as this,
more especially when his own pockets were concerned, Andrea
was not the person to leave unrequited.

By way of a further indignity to his victorious admiral,
Francis was induced by jealousy to supersede him by appointing a man called Barbesieux to command the Mediterranean
fleet, a man whom Brantôme tells us " scarce knew what a
sea, a port, or a galley were." And this appointment was
coupled with instructions, if possible, to get Andrea into his
power and bring him to France.

But Andrea was not to be so easily caught. He was aware
of the machinations of the French king, retired to the castle
of Lerici, and refused all Barbesieux's solicitations for an
audience on the French galleys. He was too ill, replied the
cunning Andrea; Barbesieux might come and speak with

him at his bedside. But Barbesieux's guilty conscience would not allow him to trust himself within Andrea's four walls, so the audience never took place.

The French monarch, however, when he had gone too far, began to repent him of thus alienating the allegiance of his admiral. In vain did he make specious offers and promises of amendment; Andrea wisely recognized that an injured monarch would not be so easily appeased, and that a perjured monarch would take the first opportunity of again breaking his word.

Who then can blame Andrea D'Oria for deserting a cause which not only struck at his own downfall, but at the downfall of his country? more especially when we take into account the politics of the age, and consider that he was but

> " Like a true Ligurïan born to cheat,
>   At least when fortune favoured his deceit."
>   VIRGIL, *Æn.* xi.

How valued Andrea was by the French, and how keenly the loss of his aid must have been felt by them, is shown by Brantôme, who says, "that amongst the good admirals of the emperor Charles V., Andrea D'Oria was the best, who formerly had served the king (Francis) faithfully . . . and if Andrea D'Oria had not departed from us, no one would have prevented us from taking Naples; but the king alienated him from us."

On the 19th of June, 1527, Andrea sent his cousin, Erasmo D'Oria, to Madrid, and there an open treaty, which had previously been drawn up, was ratified; and on the 2nd of August, Andrea raised aloft the emperor's banner over his galley, which but a short time before he had captured at Capri.

The following were the advantages gained by Andrea from this treaty: Genoa was to be freed from the French yoke, and to govern herself in the form of a republic; all her dominions, including Savona, were to be restored to her, and she was to enjoy large commercial advantages throughout the

empire. Andrea himself was to be made captain and lieu-
tenant-general of the imperial navy for life ; he was to have a
slave and a condemned criminal in return for each prisoner
he gave up, and a pension of ninety thousand golden scudi
per annum, besides a handsome list of smaller privileges.

Here we in a measure conclude the brilliant side of
Andrea's career.   In his transactions with crowned heads, we
can but admire his astuteness and independence, how he
roved the seas in the service of king, pope, or emperor, careless of the smiles or frowns of each.   But when we turn to
his dealings with his native country the case is far otherwise.
Whether we praise or blame him for his versatile conduct with
regard to rival potentates, we cannot help recognizing that
his dealings with Genoa were entirely mercenary.   He wished
for a *pied-à-terre* where to deposit his galleys, his slaves, and
his wealth ; he was glad of the opportunity afforded him by
Genoa's fine harbour and still finer bank ; he could have been
doge for life or king of Genoa if he had wished ; but he who
could control kings was satisfied with a place in the council,
and the entire submission of the Ligurian Republic to his
plans.

Let us now look closely into his dealings with Genoa
seriatim.   No sooner had he entered into the emperor's service
than he found it necessary to dislodge Trivulzio and the
French garrison in Genoa, which three years before he had
placed there.   At the time the city was stricken by a plague,
the streets were empty, the French garrison decimated ; what
more fitting opportunity for a *coup de main ?*   At the Porta
dell 'Arco no resistance was offered to him, and he proceeded
staight to the D'Oria quarters around S. Matteo without a
single impediment, and there from the "loggia" he addressed
a small handful of men, for the public buildings were all con-
verted into pest-houses, and men feared to meet each other
save in the open air.   To his harangue the people feebly
responded an assent.   What cared they for his elaborate

reasonings about deserting the French cause? All life was gone from the city which once had been the mistress of the Mediterranean, and whose sons had discovered new worlds for others.

In Genoa hitherto the nobles could shake the constitution without being able to control it. The people often ruled, but never really governed, and were every moment ready to entrust their lacerated liberty into the hands of strangers, with a view to regulating it, and then they would take back again their gift, like a capricious child with its worthless toy. From her miserable delirium Genoa never could recover, and now she had found a master who knew how to enslave her.

The much-vaunted liberty of 1528 was as iron a chain of aristocratic tyranny as could well be wrought. Henceforth the very revolutions change their character, and instead of being the result of rivalries between free citizens, they are the upshot of some foul plot. Of these the Fieschi revolt was the most respectable; but those of Vacchero, Della Torre, and others, all emanated from debased natures and sordid plans.

With the cry of "Liberty and St. George," Andrea D'Oria soon succeeded in arousing the people to assist him in driving out the French governor who was established in the castle. The infected council hall was hastily cleaned out, and thither Andrea proceeded with what senators he could gather together, hurriedly to dictate the reforms which, under his substantial patronage, took such deep root in Genoa that it required the force of a Napoleon to break them.

But what of these reforms and their liberal principles? They were based on the system of the exaltation of the family. For centuries this system had been in vogue in Genoa, as a means whereby the nobles, by uniting together with their retainers and their kinsmen, were enabled to keep the populace in check. At first they had been termed "companies," now they were known as "alberghi." Andrea D'Oria limited the number of these to twenty-eight, obliged every one to enroll himself in one, and made it necessary for the family who gave its name to an "albergo" to be descended from the old consular families, and to have six open houses in Genoa; and all those who became merged in these companies were to take the name and arms of the one in which they were enrolled.

From the order of the nobility the members of the great council of four hundred were to be chosen by an elaborate system of balloting; and thus, whilst all the turbulent spirits were divided judiciously, and made to live under the eye of an "albergo," both greater and lesser nobles were pleased at the amount of power they found in their hands. The people, in their turn were satisfied, because much was said about liberty after a bad time. Spaniards and French were driven from their castles, Savona fell before D'Oria's arms, whilst the most factious of the nobility were driven to take refuge in France. And, moreover, they looked upon Andrea D'Oria, the chief mover in this new order of things, as a sort of demi-god. What magnanimity it was to refuse the dogeship for life, which a grateful council offered him, and to be content with remaining a simple syndic! This had great effect on the popular minds, and the day on which the new statutes were promulgated, the 12th of September, was kept as an annual festival until 1798.

The senators, in the plenitude of their gratitude, presented the hero of the day with a handsome black and white marble palace, close to his family shrine, which still satisfies the curious, with its large Latin inscription, that it was presented to Andrea D'Oria, the liberator of his country, as a public offering.

What Andrea D'Oria did for his country, he did for Italy at large, for by destroying the balance of power between France and Austria, which Lorenzo de Medici had worked for, and which had been the aim of all Italian politicians of

S

the day, Andrea gave undue preponderance to the Austro-Spanish cause. During his own lifetime he was able, with his wealth and with his galleys, to keep the Spaniards out of Genoa; but they got Naples, whilst the Austrians advanced in the north, and thus was wound round Italy a coil of foreign despotism from which she has never recovered; and Andrea D'Oria, the liberator of Genoa, the patriot, the magnanimous, was the chief instrument in bringing it about.

Poor Genoa! within her walls he introduced a system of aristocratic tyranny which by a process of slow decay undermined her prosperity.

Andrea was indeed a great captain and a great statesman, inasmuch as he understood the intricate politics of that most designing age; but he was a bad citizen, and looked upon his country more as a savings bank for the deposit of his enormous wealth, and as an excellent starting point for his various schemes. As far as he himself was concerned, Andrea was almost invariably successful; as far as his country was concerned, he brought about a temporary blaze of prosperity, and introduced a new era, a brilliant dazzling era for the thirty years that he survived the new order of things, but it was the brilliancy as of an angry setting sun, with dark tempests lowering in the distance, and abject rottenness at heart.

During Andrea D'Oria's rule in Genoa, no town in Italy was gayer, nowhere were the people entertained so lavishly with festivities and processions. Into his palace at Fassuolo, Andrea introduced some of the best artists from all parts of Italy to adorn its walls. Montorsoli and Pierino del Vaga had fled from Rome after the sack of the eternal city by the Cardinal Bourbon. Shortly after this Andrea was anxious to build himself a palace outside the walls of Genoa, where one of the Fregosi had lived; and whilst the former of these artists designed the building and erected statues in the vigorous style of his master, Michael Angelo, the latter covered the walls of this palace with frescoes worthy of comparison with

Raphael's *stanze* in the Vatican. In an upper hall we see all
the heroes of the D'Oria family depicted on the walls in the
dress of ancient warriors; the ceilings recall the triumphs of
Scipio side by side with the triumphs of Andrea D'Oria over
the Saracens.[1]

In a hanging garden behind, now severed by the railway
from the palace, Montorsoli erected a colossal statue of
Andrea as Jupiter, which still looks down in naked silence on
the busy station of Genoa and the haunts of men. Towards
the sea, terraces and fountains adorned the grounds, where the
emperor Charles V. wandered,[2] and where Philip II., when a
gay young prince, was entertained with all the lavishness of
old Andrea's wealth, and all the magnificence of the artist's
skill. Subterranean passages led down to the water's edge,
and here Andrea had his galleys anchored, twenty in all,
whilst from the terrace above his keen old eye would watch
them going to and fro laden with precious goods from all
parts of the world. It is said he had twenty thousand men
at his disposal—soldiers, sailors, and slaves, all counted; and
beneath the vaulted halls of his princely palace may still be
seen the dungeons which were always well stocked with slaves
for his galleys.

Barely a century after the completion of this palace,
Evelyn visited it, and thus described it in his diary : "One of
the greatest palaces here for circuit is that of the Prince
D'Oria, which reaches from the sea to the summit of the
mountains. The house is most magnificently built without,
nor less gloriously furnished within, having whole tables and
bedsteads of massy silver, many of them set with agates,
onyxes, cornelians, lazulis, pearls, turquoises, and other precious stones. The pictures and statues are innumerable. To
this palace belong three gardens, the first whereof is beautified
with a terrace supported by pillars of marble. There is a
fountain of eagles, and one of Neptune, with other sea-gods,

[1] *Vide* illustration in last chapter.   [2] *Vide* ch. i.

all of the purest white marble. They stand in a most ample
basin of the same stone. . . . . One of the statues is a colossal
Jupiter, under which is the sepulchre of a beloved dog, for the
care of which one of this family received of the king of Spain
five hundred crowns a year, during the life of that faithful
animal."

The history of Andrea's thirty years' supremacy in Genoa
naturally divides itself into two periods—before the great
Fieschi revolt, and from that to his death. During the first
of these periods Andrea was still, though old, in possession of
all the vigour of youth; and under his banner, and for the
imperial cause, Genoa fought bravely against the Turk, and
the elements of discontent incident on Andrea's reforms had
not yet had time to develop.

The French were naturally much disconcerted at the loss
of their hold on so advantageous a spot as Genoa, and sent St.
Pol, with a considerable force, to try and restore their power, but
without avail. They nearly, however, succeeded in catching
Andrea, who had just removed to his new palace outside the
walls; but his soldiers were on the alert, and gave the admiral
warning just in time to escape, but not in time to don a befitting garment, and the Genoese received him within their
walls draped only in the scanty folds of his night-dress. The
old palace of the Fregosi was razed to the ground, and
Andrea had therefore to begin it again on the new designs
made for him by Montorsoli.

Shortly after the repulse of the French, the emperor
Charles V. paid his first visit to Genoa, and was lodged by the
municipality for forty-four days at the cost of seventy-five
thousand ducats. Most magnificent were the festivities, and
for Andrea this was the proudest moment of his life. He
had brought the emperor from Spain in his galleys, which
proves the confidence placed in his versatile admiral by
Charles, who refused to listen to the admonitions of his friends,
who thought the step a rash one of entirely entrusting himself

to the tender mercies of a man like Andrea who had only lately left the service of his arch enemy, King Francis.

However much the Republic spent on this imperial visit, all the benefits thereof were showered on the head of Andrea, and a goodly catalogue they were. A purse of twenty-five thousand scudi, the order of the Golden Fleece, together with the more substantial possession of the broad lands of the principality of Melfi, with its attendant title of prince ; also various confiscated goods were heaped upon him, and when Charles left Genoa, the name of D'Oria was still more powerful, and the liberty of the Republic still more circumscribed.

In the war against the Turks, which followed soon after Charles' passage through Genoa, Prince Andrea D'Oria was again to achieve a great success, not only for his imperial master, but for Christendom at large.

Whilst Solyman the Magnificent was threatening Vienna, Barbarossa, his able admiral, was laying waste all the coasts of the Mediterranean. The very centre of Spanish commerce, Cadiz, trembled at the boldness of this infidel marauder, and Liguria too had great cause for alarm at the frequent Saracenic raids on her long coast line.

Prince Andrea at once threw all his energies into this campaign ; he conquered Barbarossa, who had gathered around him all the strength of Islamism, and thus relieved Cadiz from the hands of this cruel red-bearded admiral, the son of a Lesbian potter. Eight hundred prisoners and much booty was the result of this victory. But Andrea tarried not ; he hastened to follow it up by attacking the Turks in their home. He sailed for Greece and, by a second sea-victory at Corone, entirely changed the tide of affairs. Solyman was obliged to relinquish his attempt on Vienna, and to the success of his admiral in the waters of the Mediterranean, rather than to the emperor's prowess in his campaign in Hungary, is due the fact that the Austrian capital and the whole of Christendom were saved from the impending destruction.

From his victory in the Gulf of Lepanto, Prince Andrea took home a large cannon, and piously had wrought thereout a statue of the Madonna for his chapel down by the quay.

Shortly after this triumph over the infidel, Charles paid a second visit to Genoa, and was this time lodged with all that was luxurious at the palace of Fassuolo, then blooming in all its fresh magnificence.[1]   But it was not long that the emperor had to tarry with his old admiral ; the French troubled him on one side, and the Turks on the other, and with disgust Europe beheld the most Christian monarch of France and the most infidel sultan of Constantinople working hand in hand in attacking the mighty fabric of Austro-Spanish grandeur.

In the history of Genoa these wars into which she was dragged by the vast connexions and ambition of her mammoth citizen were uninteresting and of little importance, except that thereby her treasury was drained, and all the glory was heaped on Prince Andrea's head.

When Charles and Francis came to terms at Aiguesmortes, an interesting interview occurred between Prince Andrea D'Oria and his former master.   The French king in lofty language addressed D'Oria thus:—"We are content, at the intercession of the Emperor, to restore you to your ancient place in our grace and friendship."   "It will be well," replied Andrea with emphasis; "for whilst I served your Majesty *I* never was wanting in respect or in fidelity."

Fearful of higher words, the emperor judiciously led the French monarch and his touchy admiral away to view the beauties of his galley.   And troubles with the corsairs soon called for Andrea's attention elsewhere.

A celebrated corsair was Dragut, his fame went through the length and breadth of the Mediterranean ; mothers terrified their children to obedience with the mention of his name. His origin was obscure, but his talents for naval warfare were transcendent.   His fine figure and manly bearing soon gained

[1] *Vide* ch. i.

for him a reputation amongst the Turks, and under Barbarossa he commanded nine galleys, and therewith swept the seas.

Andrea D'Oria sent his adopted son Gianettino, the son of his cousin Tommaso D'Oria, to secure this fire-brand ; and after a long and weary search amongst the bays of the Mediterranean, the corsair was taken by a stratagem, put in irons, and conducted to Andrea's palace at Genoa. Here the Princess Peretta, Andrea's wife, took a great fancy to him, and wished him to be released. However, she thought it advisable not to take the responsibility on herself, but despatched him to her husband, who was then at Messina. Prince Andrea was greatly embarrassed at the presence of so great a prisoner, surrounded as he was on all sides by the corsair's friends eager for an opportunity to release him ; so he offered him forthwith to the emperor, who refused, for where Dragut was there were the Turkish troops gathered together. At length, in a weak moment, Andrea liberated him at the ransom of thirty thousand ducats, which Barbarossa willingly paid, and Dragut went forth from his prison to become a worse scourge than ever to the Christian coasts, and bitter were the reproaches heaped on old Andrea's head in after years for having let go such great quarry.

Prince Andrea was now approaching an age which few succeed in reaching, and if they do so, cease to mix in worldly affairs.

In the year 1545, when the patriarchal D'Oria was in his eightieth year, he conducted an expedition to Algiers for his imperial master. It was perhaps one of the last lingering signs of Andrea's ancient shrewdness, which led him to attempt to dissuade the emperor from this ill-starred expedition. Certain it is that ever after this the aged admiral lost his prestige, and spent the remaining years of his life in constant trouble at home, and in seeing his expeditions ill-managed by less competent successors.

But it is in these last years of his life that his dealings with the Ligurian Republic are more marked and better exemplified. Insurrection after insurrection proves their dissatisfaction with the reforms Andrea had instituted.   And we have but to scan the closing scenes of his long life to realize the hollowness of that liberty about which poets have sung, and eulogies have been written to extol the great name of D'Oria.

CHAPTER XIII.

THE FIESCHI CONSPIRACY.

PERHAPS in itself, the conspiracy of Gian Luigi Fieschi against the power of the D'Oria would have passed away and sunk into oblivion had not the importance of it been world-wide, and had not Andrea D'Oria held, as he did, the keys of European politics in his hands. Moreover, the facts themselves have much of the sweet savour of romance about them, which poets, from Schiller downwards, have loved to hover over and exaggerate.

There was the patriarchal D'Oria reposing, like an aged war-horse, under the laurels of countless campaigns; and there was the young and handsome Gian Luigi, the Alcibiades of Genoa, as he was termed, courting the favours of fortune, with everything to make him attractive to the fickle goddess. But for once she was true to her old love; for once she was content to smile on a life which covered all but a century with scarce the shadow of a frown. These were the leading actors in our drama; and when we have as accessories the mighty emperor Charles V. attracted from his persecutions of the Protestants in Saxony by this sudden outbreak in Liguria against his aged admiral, and when we have the French monarch eagerly looking on for an opportunity to recoup his fallen fortunes in Italy, and the old Farnese, Pope Paul III., one of the greatest plotters for temporal power and nepotism, we cannot wonder that this conspiracy has been a favourite theme, with Europe for the stage and her greatest potentates for the chief actors.

By way of preface, let us glance at the Fieschi, and the position they held in Genoa. We have had much to do with them in the course of these pages. We have seen the power they had, and how they used it ; we have seen how they originally became merged in the commune of Genoa with Ghibelline interests. The founder of the family, it is said, collected an emperor's fiscal revenues, and hence called himself Fisco. We have seen, too, how it had been the policy of this house to fight against popular interests, to prefer being the most powerful vassal of a French king to being subordinate in a republic; and how Gian Luigi Fieschi, the grandfather of the hero of this conspiracy, had ruled both Riviere, and had amassed enormous wealth under the favouring wing of Louis XII. of France.

Sinibaldo, his son, had so far deviated from the policy of his ancestors as to espouse the cause of Andrea D'Oria in throwing off the French allegiance. He was on terms of the greatest intimacy with the old admiral, and on his death left him guardian of his sons. Sinibaldo had the character of a spendthrift ; he loved gorgeous displays, and lived in his palace on Carignano with little short of regal magnificence ; but he died in 1532, whilst his eldest son, Gian Luigi, was still a boy, leaving an impoverished estate and a widow of unbounded ambition. She was born a della Rovere, a niece of the proud pontiff Julius II., and inherited all the love of power so characteristic of her race.

Forthwith the widow retired with her numerous family to the castle of Montobbio to bring them up in seclusion; and in this castle, and from his mother's lips, Gian Luigi was first imbued with a thirst for power and a hatred of the D'Oria. She gently infused into his mind the bygone glories of his house—how two popes, Innocent IV. and Adrian V., had gone forth from it, seventy-three cardinals, and full three hundred mitred bishops. It was not only spiritual but temporal grandeur which illumined their ancestry. Even though it was but for a short time, nevertheless, Giacomo Fiesco had been invested by his uncle, the Pope, with the kingdom of Naples, and had worn a crown. At various times and seasons the Fieschi had been lords of independent cities along the Riviera, and to their family belonged the saintly Caterina of Genoa, who had died in 1510, after a life of piety. In her youth she had been married to an Adorno to please her

FROM PONTE CARIGNANO, GENOA.

parents; but the joys of piety had more charms for her than those of married life. Many are the stories attached to her memory of the days she spent in hospitals, and of the treatise on purgatory that she wrote, and even still her name is dear to the pious of Genoa.

Such had been the Fieschi; but now, impoverished and shorn of honours, they were treated almost as the D'Oria's subjects. And such were the seeds which the widowed Fieschi poured into the mind of her son, and they fell not on

sterile ground ; for Gian Luigi hated the D'Oria, especially
Prince Andrea's haughty, overbearing, adopted son, **Gianet-**
tino, whom report said was only awaiting his kinsman's **death**
to assume the lordship of Genoa.

"Moreover, who were these D'Oria?" asked his **mother.**
"Was not Andrea himself the offspring of a younger **and**
impoverished line, with none of the blood of the heroes **of**
Meloria and Curzola flowing in his veins? And as for
Gianettino, his father had had to earn his livelihood by **silk-**
weaving, and his conduct was nothing but that of an **insolent**
upstart."

After a wholesome course of training such as this, Gian
Luigi repaired to Genoa in his eighteenth year, to take **up**
the honours of his family, now greatly refreshed by a **long**
minority. No stimulus of poverty, therefore, had he to **incite**
him to rebellion ; for he had thirty-three castles of his **own**
outside Genoa, and revenues sufficient for a prince **accumu-**
lated for him in the Bank of St. George. But the seeds **of**
his policy had been sown in his youth, and carefully **pruned**
and perfected by subtle advisers and the run of circumstances.

Report tells us that the enmity between the young **D'Oria**
and the young Fieschi was heightened by a love **affair ;**
that Gian Luigi was about to wed the daughter of **Adamo**
Centurione, a wealthy noble ; but deeming the heir of **Prince**
D'Oria a more suitable match for his daughter, **Centurione**
handed her over with her rich dower to Gianettino. **And**
evil report goes further, for it says that, not **contented**
with this prize, Gianettino was too fond of the wife **Gian**
Luigi eventually took to himself, the lovely Leonora **Cybo,**
daughter of the lord of Massa. But report says much **about**
this lady, and its testimony is conflicting.

Suffice it for our purpose that Gian Luigi bitterly **hated**
the D'Oria, that Gianettino was haughty and **unpopular,**
and that Gian Luigi was possessed of every quality that **could**
charm the world and gain for him popular applause. **He**

would with his well-filled purse smooth over the difficulties of any one in distress; he had a kind word for every one who came to his house, and he won the hearts of all the mothers in Genoa, not only by his handsome face and winning manner, but also by dandling their babes on his knee. In short, if female suffrage had been in vogue in Genoa, Gian Luigi's majority would have been overwhelming.

No less successful was he in winning the hearts of his enemies. On the very day of the conspiracy Gian Luigi, by his tender kindness to old Prince Andrea, won from the admiral a triumphant smile as he turned to the Spanish ambassador, Figuerroa, and said, " Could so open-hearted a man be guilty of any treachery?" for the astute Spaniard had scented the subtle air of treason, and tried in vain to arouse the suspicions of the old prince.

Also with Gianettino D'Oria, Gian Luigi kept outwardly on the best of terms. On this very day of the conspiracy, too, at the D'Oria's palace, he would have Gianettino believe that all former disagreements were hushed, and that nothing but love reigned in their breasts; and on this last day of both their lives the two greatest enemies in Genoa walked and talked together as the dearest friends.

So much for Gian Luigi Fieschi, his character and his plans. Let us glance at some of his aiders and abettors in the scheme of rebellion against Andrea's power. There is substantial proof that he had an understanding with Barnabo Adorno, son of the last doge Antoniotto, but it all came to nothing, and Prince Andrea himself professed not to believe a word of the accusation against his ward, the son of his old friend Sinibaldo.

To win over his young mind by means of gentle measures, the emperor appointed Gian Luigi to a post from which he should receive a pension of two thousand scudi; but through some oversight, none of this was ever paid him, and thereby contributed towards further fanning the discontented flame

which burnt in his breast.   But whatever his earlier plots may
have been, it is certain that in 1544 he occupied a position free
of suspicion, and that it was from outside Genoa that the first
tempting whisper came, which hurried him on to his fatal end.

Paul III. it was who, from the Vatican, set afloat the first
seeds of this conspiracy.   He hated Andrea D'Oria and the
emperor both with a bitter hatred : the former, because he
was a serious obstacle to his temporal aggrandizement, and the
latter, because he had got all out of him he could.   With
Prince D'Oria the Pope quarrelled over an inheritance in
Naples, which had been left to Andrea by an old bishop
Imperiale, but which Paul saw fit to appropriate for himself.
The pontiff drove all Genoese merchants out of his states,
and made overtures to the king of France, who readily
assented, and together they proposed to make Gian Luigi
Fieschi their tool.

Unfortunately for the veracity of the contracts between
these conspirators, there are no documentary proofs ; none, in
fact, but the confession of one of Gian Luigi's men when
put to the torture, which was written down by a bystander.
Gian Luigi, said this man, went to Piacenza, where he had
dealings with the Farnese duke, nephew of Paul III., and
thence to Rome, where the pontiff received him with great
state, spoke of the pleasant days he had spent in his father's
palace at Carignano, whilst still a cardinal, and finally proposed to make him admiral of his galleys.   Some say he sold
them to him, but the probability, however, is that the galleys
were to be employed against the D'Oria with the aid of French
gold : and from the archives of Simancas we gather that the
duke Farnese agreed to provide Fieschi with fourteen thousand
infantry, and that the sale of the galleys was a mere feint to
blind the suspicions of Andrea.   When handing over these
galleys to Gian Luigi, the Pope warned him with a sinister
smile to take heed lest they should fall into the hands of the
Gianettino D'Oria.

On his return to Genoa, Gian Luigi communicated his plan to his most intimate associates, one of whom, Giovanni Battista Verrina, lived close by his palace of Vialata on Carignano. He was a fierce, uncompromising man ; a hater of the old nobility, himself a member of the new. He is the man who comes forward throughout the whole conspiracy as the chief mover and designer. He could wind himself into the confidence of the people, and could well pave the way, and act as an *avant courier*, for the affable Gian Luigi. For instance, on one occasion, he became aware that the silk weavers were in low circumstances, that their trade was impoverished by the D'Oria's importations from Spain. He forthwith took the consul of the silk weavers to the palace on Carignano, where Gian Luigi readily alleviated their woes, distributed corn amongst them, adding that it was the custom of his house to assuage the sorrows of others.

But to Verrina, the plan of carrying out the conspiracy with French aid was highly displeasing. Gian Luigi was strong enough, he said, to strike the blow, and make himself master of Genoa without foreign aid. Such was Verrina, a wild, daring, subtle man, whose influence on the volatile Gian Luigi was unbounded. Second in command was Rafaelle Sacco, from Savona, who had held the position of judge in some of the Fieschi's territories. He was a weak, vacillating man, a man drawn into a vortex against his will, probably through the traditional hatred of his native town for Genoa, and the vague hope of a change.

Vincenzo Calcagno was another accomplice. He had been a page in the household of Sinibaldo Fieschi ; but few memorials of him are left, and what there are point to his having been a faithful servant of the Fieschi's, ready to live or die in their service. These were the principal actors. Girolamo Fieschi, a brother of Gian Luigi, likewise took an active part, but he was young, and inexperienced, and consequently entirely subordinate.

Whilst urging a single-handed insurrection, **Verrina** likewise urged a sudden and treacherous one. Nevertheless, through his fiendish plots there shines forth something noble ; a vague something one cannot help admiring. " The doge, or lord of Genoa," he said, " shall be without any higher domination over him, and without the protection of any foreign government. If we make ourselves the vile instrument of France, we shall act like the D'Oria are doing now with Spain, and instead of the favour and esteem of our fellow-citizens, we shall incur their hatred and malediction." Judging him by the age in which he lived, which looked on nothing but failure as a disgrace, were the means used sacrilegious, were they the height of cunning, falsehood, and deception, we cannot but say that he acted as any other politician of his day would have acted ; and he had the plea of patriotism, which was absent in most cases.

For the success of the scheme, ·Verrina asserted that Andrea D'Oria, his adopted son, Adamo Centurione, and most of the old nobility must be assassinated ; and at the same time, he admitted the difficulty of so doing at one swoop. At the church of S. Andrea, a young noble priest was to officiate for the first time at a mass, and there all the nobility were to be assembled ; what easier than to massacre the requisite victims before the altar. What was there so terrible, asked Verrina, in this ? Had not Lorenzo de Medici's brother fallen before the horns of the altar ? Had not the Duke Giovanni Maria Sforza but two years before been stabbed in the church of S. Stefano at Milan ? But Gian Luigi drew back from so sacrilegious a plan, though there are those who affirm that Prince Andrea's infirmities rendered this hazardous, and hence it was abandoned ; yet Gian Luigi is entitled to the benefit of the doubt.

It was then thought expedient to invite all the intended victims to a grand banquet at Carignano, to celebrate the marriage of Gian Luigi's brother-in-law, and then to

massacre them around the festal board ; but on the day fixed
for the festival, Gianettino D'Oria, for some cause or other,
had settled to leave Genoa, and thus this plan had likewise to
be abandoned.

At length, after much deliberation, a general rising was
determined upon on the night of the 2nd of January, 1547.
The town was to be carried by force of arms ; and accordingly
were their plans concerted. Beyond the facts as they themselves
happened but little can now be verified, with such secrecy did
they conceal their schemes ; and it is only from such writers
as Bonfadio, Casoni, etc., who wrote when the D'Oria were
omnipotent, and wrote from hearsay, that the preparatory
movements of this conspiracy can be culled.

Delay at all events was now impossible for them, since the
Spanish ambassador began to scent something in the wind,
and warned Andrea that a young brother of Gian Luigi's was
suspiciously popular at the court of France,[1] that the Duke of
Piacenza was evidently preparing for war, but so silent had
been his operations that he was unable to discover the object
of it.

At length arrived from Civita Vecchia the four galleys
which Gian Luigi professed to have bought from, or to have
been given by, the Pope, under pretence of an armed expedition against the Turks in the Archipelago. Such was the
pretext he gave to lull the suspicions of the D'Oria when they
saw these galleys full of armed men enter the harbour.

Under one excuse or another the palace of Vialata was
filled with soldiers ; they came in from the country dressed
as peasants or workmen, and thus entered the palace unsus-
pected ; they were brought in as galley slaves in chains ; they
came in secretly by the underground passages, until in one
way or another a perfect garrison was lodged under the
Fieschi's roof, awaiting the bidding of their host.

Poor old Paolo Panza was there too, Gian Luigi's old

[1] " Archives of Simancas."

tutor, a man of deep study, who had passed his days in literary pursuits. He was alarmed at the constant din of arms : a suspicion of awful dread haunted him ; but with bland words and caresses Gian Luigi lulled his anxiety, and with Leonora Fieschi, Gian Luigi's ill-fated wife, Panza passed those awful days of bustle and preparation in the realms of poetry and study, whilst all around reigned the restless, troubled air of a coming tempest.

The state of oblivion in which Prince Andrea allowed himself to remain during this time is most remarkable ; he turned a deaf ear to the admonitions of the Spanish ambassador, and when Gian Luigi appeared at his palace on the day of the conspiracy, he received him well. Gianettino, too, seemed equally influenced by the soothing words of his enemy ; and when Gian Luigi gaily told him that his meditated expedition against the Turks was to start that evening, and asked him to be so good as to leave the port open for their exit, and not to be alarmed if he heard stray shots in the night, as it would only betoken the departure of his ships, Gianettino assented with the greatest good grace. But this fact in itself is sufficient to prove the extent of the D'Orian power in Genoa, when a ship had to obtain their consent before issuing out of the harbour ; and the fact that thus they had full control over the going to and fro of men of such rank and influence as the Fieschi must have been especially galling to the mind of a man who at least was an equal if not a superior to the young D'Oria. No further proof than this is required of the chains with which Prince Andrea had enslaved Genoa, and no further extenuation is wanted for a conspiracy against him.

After leaving the D'Orian palace with every mark of friendship, Gian Luigi dashed through the city on horseback, paid friendly visits to his accomplices and foes alike, and towards evening repaired to his palace, there to await the time appointed for his plans.

Verrina, meanwhile, had laid the train of sedition well through the city, and appointed to each man his task, with such admirable tact and precision that not a word reached the ears of the D'Oria, who retired peacefully to their beds, little dreaming of the storm which was gathering round them.

That evening there arrived at Gian Luigi's palace numerous nobles, who had been bidden to a banquet, hoping that they would be induced to join in the conspiracy in this the eleventh hour, when confronted with the perpetrators of it ; at all events Verrina thought that if they refused to join they could at least be kept conveniently out of the way, as appeared best. Orders were given to the porter to admit any one who came, but to allow none to go out. And thus at length all the invited guests were assembled, and, to their surprise, were ushered into a large room with two candles burning on a bare table, whilst all around they heard the din of arms, which increased their alarm.

At length Gian Luigi entered the room with pallid face and resolute step, dressed in armour from head to foot, and taking up his position by the fitful, flickering light, he thus addressed his awe-stricken guests : " Young men and brave, to a novel, but priceless supper I have now invited you, to the liberation of your country, oppressed as it is by a few, threatened with imminent tyranny by one ; this is the supper, and these are the viands, which I have prepared for you." He then proceeded to speak of the chains woven for them by the D'Oria and by Charles V., and explained the plans he had prepared for breaking the same, and implored their assistance in his enterprise.

At first they hesitated ; Gian Luigi, thereupon, with theatrical address affirmed that unless they consented he would plunge his dagger into his own breast ; and with this, all swore the oath on bended knee, in that solemn half-lighted room, to compass the D'Oria's death, or to meet their own in the attempt. Two only resolutely refused, and two noble spirits must have been Giovanni Battista Cattaneo Bava and Giovanni Battista Giustiniani, who could thus hold out in the very jaws of death ; but they were mercifully treated, and only locked up in the palace to await the result of the conspiracy before their fate was decided upon.

But what of Leonora Fieschi and Panza during this time ? Throughout the whole of that day they had heard the clash of arms without knowing the reason why. Full of vague dread, they awaited the arrival of Gian Luigi, who towards evening entered the room, clad in full armour, and ready for action. In vain did they implore him to desist whilst there was yet time ; in vain did the heart-broken wife clutch his knees, and entreat him not to leave her. " To-morrow," said he, " thou shalt be either the most miserable or the proudest woman in Genoa."

About the after fortunes of this noble lady hangs much romance. Schiller would have us believe that she wandered throughout the city during this dreadful night, and finding the red mantle which the murdered Gianettino had worn, clothed herself therein by way of disguise, and that Gian Luigi meeting her, and ignorant who she was, plunged his dagger into her breast ; but Schiller, who moulded the doings of Genoa principally to suit his plot, who could make Andrea D'Oria a doge, and otherwise maltreat the story, cannot be much relied on for the authenticity of this story.

Another writer, Tebaldi Fores, paints her as sitting pallid, and maddened by grief on the shore of the Mediterranean, when the first grey of the dawn shone forth on her widowhood. It is somewhat painful, however, to have excellent proof against these touching stories,[1] for Leonora soon consoled herself after Gian Luigi's death by marrying the Marquis of Cetona, a soldier in Duke Cosmo De' Medici's service, a man celebrated for his exceeding corpulence, and whose thigh, they say, was broader than his wife's waist. This tremendous obesity pre-

---

[1] "Alberi Genealogici of Genoese families."

vented him latterly from walking, and hence he was always carried into battle on a litter. In 1575, at the siege of a fortress in Flanders, some Spaniards, enraged at having to carry so much Italian flesh, let him drop, and he was killed.

Thus was Leonora again a widow. She spent her latter days chiefly in Florence, and passed much time in the realms of poetry, with which to solace her woes. Two years after Gian Luigi's death we find her name entered in the books of the Bank of St. George for a goodly sum of money, worthy of a princess's dower.

To return to the conspirators. Many stories are told of the evil omens which forewarned Gian Luigi of the doom which was awaiting him. How crows careered round his head as he rode through the town; how his favourite dog broke from its chains as he passed to go forth, and held him with a grip so firm that it could only be loosened by a fatal blow from his master's dagger. But lo! as he left his house, Gian Luigi slipped—worse portent of all—which many before him and after him have done on those steep, slippery streets leading down from Carignano, the statistics of whose fate we have not.

After leaving his wife, Gian Luigi returned to his guests, who were partaking of a meagre, hasty repast, far otherwise than that they came prepared for. Verrina was sent out to see if the town was still, and on his bringing back a reply in the affirmative and that every train was well laid for the success of the attempt, the huge portal of Vialata opened its doors, and out into the dim night poured the conspirators, their soldiery, and their guests, whilst the strictest orders were given that whoever left this phalanx should forthwith be shot dead.

Whoever knows the labyrinth of Genoa as it now exists, its tortuous by-paths, and its narrow alleys, will recognize the ease with which an armed force, with a well-organized plan, could glide hither and thither about the town, causing nothing but wonder and dismay to those ignorant of their movements. As it was, they found every street defenceless and deserted ; men were too accustomed to revolutions in Genoa to think of disturbing themselves in their beds at the sound of the passing of a few soldiers. Thus a perfect stillness as of death pervaded everything, broken by the clattering of the little bands of conspirators as they hurried hither and thither to secure some point of vantage which was allotted to their care.

Thus one band under Cornelio Fieschi easily occupied the Porta dell' Arco ; Gian Luigi and his men scoured the centre of the town ; whilst Verrina mounted the four galleys to take the d'arsena. Girolamo and Ottobuono Fieschi possessed themselves of the Porta S. Tommaso nearest to the D'Oria's palace, and thus nearly the whole city fell into the conspirators' hands.

The evil portents, however, which had haunted Gian Luigi throughout the day, were soon to be fulfilled. Having executed his appointed task, he proceeded to join Verrina with the galleys ; but Verrina's galleys had struck on a sandbank, and only after superhuman efforts could they be removed. So Gian Luigi proceeded with his followers to attack the D'Orian galleys, all ready as they were for sailing on the break of day. Then burst forth wild noises and confusion throughout the harbour. The galley-slaves, Turkish and Christian, burst their bonds, and rushed to liberty and to plunder. All the precious goods on board Prince Andrea's ships fell into their hands ; they sacked the houses of the wealthy merchants down by the quay ; and some Turkish prisoners, taking this opportunity to make good their liberty and their plunder, hied them in hot haste to the coast of Africa with Prince Andrea's best galley, and reached their destination before pursuers could overtake them.

In this wild confusion and dismay on all sides, Gian Luigi hurried from ship to ship until he had left none of the D'Oria's galleys unoccupied. The crowning point of his success was almost within his grasp, and at all points was his attack successful. And the Fieschi "cat" purred pleasantly through the city, as their family cry and family badge were fast gathering round them the forces which ever congregate to success, and the life blood of the D'Orian eagle was fast being sapped away, when one false step dashed away for ever the hopes of the conspirators, and hurried their leader to an untimely grave.

Whilst passing from one galley to another, Gian Luigi lost his footing, and, heavily armed as he was, fell into the sea. Although the water was not deep, he was unable to arise ; and thus sank the hope of the conspirators—the hope of any resistance to the power of Prince Andrea. Verrina came up shortly afterwards, and sought high and low for him. He went from galley to galley, and along the quay, but sought in vain, for in his watery grave lay his leader and the hope of his party. It was in vain, too, that Verrina strove to conceal this untoward death. It was in vain that Girolamo, the younger brother, tried to assume the leadership of the insurgents ; fortune had declared herself on the side of the D'Oria, and with their usual fickleness men followed in her train.

But what of the D'Oria during this eventful night ? The Princess Peretta, the aged admiral's aged wife, was disturbed in her slumbers. She heard an unusual noise from the harbour. She arose, looked forth from her balcony, and beheld the port alive with some unknown disturbance. Hastily she awoke Gianettino, who likewise scented something unusual in the wind. He sent a servant to the town to make inquiries, and bade him return with all dispatch. At length, however, when the messenger did not return, Gianettino determined to go in person. Never suspecting more than a mutiny amongst the sailors, he donned a rough sea suit, and with one attendant proceeded to the Porto S. Tommaso, and demanded admittance, which was readily accorded him by the enemy, now in possession of the gate. No sooner did young D'Oria step inside than he was fallen upon and massacred by a host of men. And thus fell the two rivals—the young D'Oria and the young Fieschi—about whose supremacy in Genoa the chill night air was rent with cries of sedition, and the streets made to run with blood.

Old Prince Andrea, meanwhile, suffering acutely from gout, weighed down as he was by the weight of years, and his eye, which had never flinched before a foe, now grown dim, was seized with a vague terror of coming woe. Unable to learn how things were going in the city, and intent on preserving in himself at least the hope of his party, determined on a hasty flight. He placed his wife, his daughter-in-law, and her children in neighbouring convents, and rode off hurriedly to Voltri, where he first learnt of the death of his adopted son, for whom he had toiled so hard, and whom he had looked to as the one to carry on all the princely honours he had gained.

From Voltri Andrea fled along a rugged mountain path to the castle of Masone, which belonged to Adamo Centurione, and there awaited the issue of events, himself unable to raise a finger in his own defence. Many have blamed the octogenarian for thus hurriedly abandoning his cause, and abandoning the children of Gianettino, whom now he had to look to as his successors. But the plea of years alone is sufficient to give as his excuse; and from the turn events took, the policy he pursued proved that he was wise; for if Gian Luigi had been successful his presence in the city could have in no way checked the course of events; and if Gian Luigi fell, he felt sure of his influence with the senate to secure his rapid return.

Meanwhile in the city the wildest confusion raged; the din of voices, the rushing to and fro of the conspirators, now without a head to guide them, was all enhanced by the dimness of the night. A dull, dark night it was, with angry rolling clouds, scarce allowing the feeble rays of a pale moon to look down and behold the scenes of horror below, and fitfully to increase men's terror by faintly and weirdly exposing the blood-stained streets to view.

But not all Genoa's patricians were cowardly at this moment, when courage was required. A large portion of them betook themselves to the council hall. One Paolo Lavagna, a friend of the Fieschi, repaired there too, hoping by his presence to influence the senate in favour of his party, and to make them pass a decree which would free Genoa from the D'Oria-Spanish yoke. None of the senators knew yet of Gian Luigi's death, and, torn as they were by conflicting emotions, they received a deputation from Girolamo Fieschi, who had now assumed the command of the party, whilst Verrina held the galleys in the port, ready to open a way of escape on the side of France for his fellow conspirators in case of failure with the senate.

At length, when they learnt about Gian Luigi's death, the senate took up a more decided course. Hitherto rather inclined to waver towards the side of the Fieschi, they now took courage and determined to oppose to the best of their ability the force with which Girolamo hoped to gain for himself the ends his brother had so nearly achieved. But his soldiers had lost both heart and will and were driven backwards towards the Porta dell' Arco, and finding his influence insufficient to keep in check his already vacillating followers Girolamo finally determined to abandon all.

• Paolo Panza, the old tutor of his family, now came forwards as a peacemaker. He was sent as a deputy to the senate to demand terms for the insurgents, and the senate generously granted Girolamo a free and unconditional pardon if he would lay down his arms. These terms he readily accepted, and retired to his inland fortress of Montobbio, whilst the other conspirators forthwith set sail for Marseilles.

Thus did this mighty storm sweep over Genoa. The dawn

of day brought with it the still calm, as after a fierce hurricane, which had left behind it but the traces of its fury. The senators could return to their houses in perfect peace and tranquillity to eat their well-earned midday meal on the third day of January, having previously despatched a messenger to fetch old Prince Andrea from his mountain retreat.

Not a murmur passed the lips of the old warrior as he set foot in his palace, not twenty-four hours after he had left it in such hot haste ; he professed himself content that he had been able to serve his country with the loss of a few galleys and with an irrevocable wound in his heart ; in fact, the very excitement of this conspiracy seemed as if it had infused new life-blood into his aged veins, it verily seemed as if he refused to succumb to the hand of death before he had lived to see vengeance wreaked on his enemies, and before young Giovandrea, the son of the murdered Gianettino, was old enough to take from him the reins of government, and keep the name of D'Oria all-powerful and supreme in Genoa.

The conduct of the old prince after the conspiracy has met with universal blame. To revoke the pardon granted by the senate, to raze the palace of the Fieschi to the ground, to deny the body of Gian Luigi Christian burial, all prove the rancour of hatred which burnt in his aged brain under the cloak of humility and contentment. This, indeed, is a fitting sequel to his policy of cruelty, which in his younger days made Corsica a desert. Men extenuate him by saying that he did all this at the bidding of his imperial master ; but surely a man who could resist the importunities of Charles V. to build a fortress in Genoa,[1] a man whom Charles valued as the very mainstay of his power in Italy, could have acted leniently towards his foes if leniency had been his wish.

No sooner did Prince Andrea, accompanied by the Spanish ambassador, Figuerroa, set foot in the senate house than he at once urged the revocation of the pardon granted to the con-

[1] *Vide* ch. xiv.

spirators; he maintained that a pardon extorted by the force of circumstances was not binding; until at length, under this double D'Oria-Spanish pressure, the senate gave way, and Giro_lamo Fieschi, all his family, and all his accomplices, were declared traitors, their property was confiscated, and their houses razed to the ground.

Thus fell the glorious Fieschi palace on Carignano. Its countless treasures of art were sold by public auction, its walls and lovely frescoes were blown up with gunpowder; all to gratify the hatred of old Prince Andrea. Only one stone was left to mark its site, and that was a stone of infamy, which handed down to posterity the name of Gian Luigi as a traitor, and was not removed until the days of Louis XIV. of France, when the Fieschi honours were restored to them.

The mortal remains of the unfortunate hero of this drama were found the day after the conspiracy by a fisherman in the dockyard. Andrea D'Oria wished to have them hung up aloft in the city as a warning to all traitors; but prudent advisers, who feared a rising owing to the popularity that Gian Luigi had enjoyed, counselled otherwise; so Andrea, in a fit of rage, ordered the body to be taken and sunk in deep water, saying that "since he had chosen such a tomb it was only right that he should have it."

Of the old prince's resentful passion a quaint story is told, probably not true, but proving by its existence the spirit which men attributed to him. It is affirmed that for the remainder of his days the prince always kept a cat near him, to remind him of the fallen Fieschi's badge, and that when a fit of rage came on him he would mercilessly beat this cat with his stick, by way of symbolizing the punishment he would visit on his foes. There is an old picture in his palace of Fazzuolo, still hanging in his own private room, representing old Andrea in his ninety-third year. A meagre, worn-out old man he is, with scarce a gleam of fire in his sunken eye; by his side sits a well-favoured cat. Whether this was the unfortunate animal or not which acted the part of scape-goat report says not.

Numerous letters of congratulation poured in from all sides to felicitate Prince Andrea on his escape, and to condole with him for the loss of his adopted son ; amongst them came one from Pope Paul III., the principal instigator in the conspiracy, couched in the most fulsome strains of pity, and of apostolic benediction. Andrea consigned it to his desk, saying that he would answer it when occasion required ; and he had not long to wait, for on the assassination of the Duke of Piacenza, the old Pope's nephew, for whom he had exercised all the force of his pontifical arm to acquire a firm temporal kingdom, Andrea went to his desk, and drew forth Paul's unanswered letter of condolence, altered the names and what was necessary therein, and addressed it to his Holiness at the Vatican.

Meanwhile, in Genoa the spirit of insurrection arose at the news that the pardon which the senate had granted the insurgents had been cancelled, and Girolamo Fieschi, in his mountain fastness of Montobbio, was the centre of it.

There was a public bill of confiscation published, sentence of death was passed on the members of the Fieschi family, and an unseemly scramble took place amongst the neighbouring potentates for all their many castles and dependencies scattered along the confines of Liguria.

But Girolamo Fieschi, meanwhile, gathered around himself all the leaders of the conspiracy, Verrina, Calcagno, Cangialancia, and others, whose sole hope now lay in maintaining their position in the fortress of Montobbio, until chance, or French aid, might restore them to their native town.

In vain did the senate again employ Paolo Panza as a mediator, fixing the price of a fresh pardon at confiscation of Montobbio, and a compensation of fifty thousand scudi. Girolamo Fieschi was not again going to trust himself to the tender mercies of his country's rulers. He gave out that he held the castle for the king of France ; he sent his brothers to Paris for help ; but France was then but a broken reed on which to trust, and the help never came. The Duke of Piacenza helped him with money, but not with men, as an open outbreak with the emperor and the D'Oria would hardly suit his plans just then.

The siege of Montobbio began in May, and a difficult undertaking it was. From its position it was almost impregnable, perched on the summit of a lofty eminence ; and the Republic had been sorely crippled of late years, whilst Prince Andrea D'Oria's strength lay on the sea, and his galleys, his treasures, and his slaves had been destroyed on the night of the conspiracy; so that had it not been for seasonable aid sent by the Duke of Tuscany the siege would have had to have been altogether abandoned.

Pressed now on all sides, the garrison of Montobbio began to waver, more especially when a free pardon was granted to all the soldiers therein who would retire to their homes, except Girolamo and his most determined colleagues. And thus, deserted by his friends, the young Fieschi was captured, and with him Verrina ; these two arch-conspirators, together with Calcagno and Cangialancia, were reserved for trial ; but one of the more insignificant of the ringleaders, whose rank demanded not a more protracted trial, was hung and quartered by Andrea's orders on the spot.

Great was the sympathy felt in Genoa for this unfortunate member of one of her most popular families. Petitions for mercy poured in from all sides, amongst them one from a pious nun, Caterina, the sister of Gian Luigi and Girolamo, begging the senate to remember their father, Sinibaldo, and how he had worked with Andrea D'Oria for the constitution of 1528. But this was all to no purpose ; the inexorable will of Prince Andrea, backed up by the emperor's authority, demanded Girolamo's death, and there was no power in Genoa strong enough to oppose this combined determination.

Nevertheless, Girolamo was saved from some of the

horrors of death with which Verrina and the others were
visited, for he was beheaded in private, to obviate a rising in
his favour, whilst the others were subjected to excruciating
torture to extort from them all the facts of the conspiracy;
and to their confession, carefully narrated by the Spanish
ambassador, Figuerroa, to his imperial master, and deposited
by him in the archives of Simancas, we are chiefly indebted
for the points of minor detail connected with the conspiracy.

After the torture Verrina was beheaded, a privilege to
which his rank, as one of the lesser nobles, entitled him;
whilst Calcagno and Cangialancia were hung, and some
others of smaller moment had their throats cut.

Thus did the curtain fall on the Fieschi drama, a drama
which, though enacted on the quiet stage of Liguria, sent a
thrill throughout Europe, and had an import on the future of
Italy which coming ages realized. Prince Andrea D'Oria's
influence was now unchallenged, and through his instrumentality the nature of Italy was changed from being the battle-
field between French and Austro-Spanish rivals, to being
entirely the slave of the latter. As a sequel to the failure of
Fieschi's attempt to establish again the balance of power in
the peninsula, Florence and Siena lost their liberty, and Naples
groaned under a foreign yoke drawn now even tighter around
her; whilst beyond the Alps the emperor was enabled now
with a free mind to pursue his wars in Saxony and crush the
Protestant elector with redoubled vigour, instead of being
called off to superintend his affairs in Italy.

A sentence of death was passed against Ottobuono, Cornelio, and Scipione Fieschi, the brothers of the conspirators,
and banishment against their descendants to the fifth generation. Montobbio was pulled down, and the rock blasted on
which it was built; and it was made a capital offence for any
to build thereon.

A perpetual thorn in the side of Genoa were the exiled
Fieschi at the court of France, ever urging the French

monarchs to recover for them their lost inheritance in Liguria. At the peace of Câteau Cambresis Scipione did recover some small amount; but not until the days of Louis XIV. were they successful in obtaining a substantial restoration of their own, so great was the D'Orian influence in the town. Many of the Fieschi became able generals in the service of France. Otto-buono fought on the side of France at the siege of Siena, and was taken prisoner by the imperialists, and, with other prisoners, was put on board Prince Andrea D'Oria's galleys to be consigned to a Ligurian prison.

Great was the delight of the old admiral to have another of this hated family in his power. On the voyage from Leghorn to Genoa Andrea had this unfortunate man sewn up in a sack, and plunged into the water from time to time, so that he might feel all the sensations of death before his hour had fully arrived. At length, after the prince had sufficiently gloated in the sufferings of his fallen foe, the poor Fieschi was relieved from his persecutions and put to death; and thus perished the third of the sons of his old friend and ally Sinibaldo, whose death might be laid to the charge of the D'Oria.

Before bidding adieu to the subject of the Fieschi, a short tribute of thanks must be paid to the Genoese historian, Jacopo Bonfadio, for one of the most trustworthy and elegant prose works of the sixteenth century. After perusing generations of annalists, who have preserved for us naught save the dry bones of history, it is refreshing to come across one who presents us with some vivid pictures of real life, all the more valuable from their scrupulous authenticity.

Bonfadio was of humble origin, his home was on the Ligurian Riviere. By what means we know not, he obtained an excellent education; he graduated at Padua, and shone in the salons of Rome as a wit, a poet, and a literary genius of no mean standard. His eulogists praise his letters and compare them with those of Cicero and Tasso; they praise his poems as life-stirring, but it is for his annals of Genoa from 1528 to 1550 that we feel ourselves more deeply beholden to him. And he came to write them in this wise.

In 1545 he was offered and accepted the chair of philosophy in Genoa He did his best to drum Aristotle and Plato into the heads of the Ligurian money-makers, and many are the complaints which pervade his letters of the want of literary tastes in the purse-proud city. Regretful of days of bliss in scholastic Rome, he writes to a friend there in mournful strain, stating that during the winter he had read an essay on Aristotle to an audience " more mercantile than scholastic." And again he says, " How much happier would my life be here if a taste for letters was as much appreciated as a taste for traffic on the sea." Here is the character of the mediæval cottonopolis plainly set before us, a characteristic which will be further exemplified in our chapter on Ligurian art.[1]

In 1549, Bonfadio was deputed by Andrea D'Oria to continue the annals of Foglietta, and to write with his vivid pen of the D'Orian supremacy and the fall of the Fieschi. All libraries and archives were thrown open to him, wherein Bonfadio found himself confronted with all the secret truths of his country's history ; and, unmindful of the risk he ran, he transcribed them faithfully to paper. He did not extol with sufficient zeal the triumphant D'Oria, he did not anathematize with sufficient ardour the fallen Fieschi, and for this crime, if so it can be called, Bonfadio found himself arrested, tried on some fictitious charge of immorality, and sentenced to be burnt alive. Eventually this sentence was changed for the milder one of decapitation, and in the cold grim courtyard of the Palazzo del Podestà, Jacopo Bonfadio suffered the extreme penalty of the law, a sacrifice to the despotic power of a D'Oria. And thus did Genoa and her ruler treat perhaps the greatest literary genius whose name has honoured Ligurian annals.

[1] *Vide* ch. xvii.

CHAPTER XIV.

ANDREA D'ORIA'S LATTER DAYS, AND THE OUTCOME OF HIS
POLICY.

BUT Prince Andrea D'Oria would not die as his friends and
enemies fondly hoped. He lived on to thwart his imperial
master in obtaining the coveted lordship of Genoa; he lived
on to thwart the revolutionists, who anxiously watched for his
death as a signal for throwing off the existing state of affairs.
He lived on thirteen long years after Gianettino's death, until
he saw the young heir to the D'Orian honours able to maintain
them for himself. Even to his last breath the veteran
prince kept the clearest head for politics in Europe, though
his bodily strength was gone, though his galleys were not
the dread of the Mediterranean as of yore. Yet he had
that still within him which was more than a match for the
cunning of Philip II. of Spain, and equal to all emergencies
at home; for when Andrea sank Gian Luigi in the waves,
and beheaded Girolamo, he had by no means done with his
difficulties.

Under pretext of securing Genoa from further conspiracies, the emperor Charles V. immediately expressed a
wish to build a fortress in the city, and to place a permanent
Spanish garrison therein, thinking that thereby his influence
in the Ligurian capital would be indisputable. And even
amongst the Genoese themselves there was not wanting a
party who favoured this scheme.

Secondly, there was a strong party who wished for a

U

French occupation, and a restoration of the Fieschi. This was a thoroughly popular party, and one amongst whom any revolutionist found a hearty welcome. Again, Andrea's mainstay and support, Adamo Centurione, the father of Gianettino's widow, was ever hoping by a dexterous manipulation of affairs that his own son might succeed to all the posts of honour in the Republic which Gianettino had held, to the exclusion of Gianettino's son.

These were amongst the obstacles which surrounded Prince Andrea's path—a goodly array indeed for an octogenarian to contend with ; but he was equal to them all. The more the emperor suggested the building of a fortress in Genoa, and the more Ferrante Gonzaga, the imperial governor in Milan, pressed him in the interests of his master, the more did Andrea refuse to recognize such an act of oppression, and argued that if the government of Genoa was placed in the hands of a few, of whom he could insure allegiance to the imperial cause, all things would go well. Stubborn old man that he was, his immutable will was that the country he had liberated from French yoke should be held in bondage by no one but himself ; and no power was strong enough to alter it.

Even within his own family Prince Andrea had numerous enemies. The descendants of the victors of Meloria and Curzola looked with jealousy on the elevation of a junior branch. The Cardinal Girolamo D'Oria was one of them. In his younger days he had been married, and had a son, Niccolò, who was married to a sister of Gian Luigi Fieschi's, hence they resented bitterly the treatment, little short of persecution, with which the luckless family of the conspirators was treated. Whilst the father conspired with Gonzaga to gain the point of the fortress, the son openly espoused the Fieschi cause, and was in correspondence with France, and was backed up by members of the Spinola family and others of the old nobility.

This conspiracy was discovered in its infancy, and Niccolò D'Oria went to swell the army of discontented Genoese at the court of France. Nevertheless, Prince Andrea would not hear a word about the emperor's fortress ; and the Spanish ambassador wrote to his master that it would be better for the present to accept Andrea's scheme of reform, and await his death for taking more decided measures.

Meanwhile another curious conspiracy broke out—a sort of faint re-echo of the Fieschi—and further complicated the web of Genoese politics. The Marquisate of Massa had passed into the family of Cybo by marriage, thus : Lorenzo Cybo, grandson of Pope Innocent VIII., had married Riccarda, the heiress of the old marquises, who had previously been the wife of Scipione Fieschi, uncle of the unfortunate Gian Luigi. But Lorenzo and Riccarda were by no means of one mind— each anxious for the honour of governing the little marquisate in their own right ; and their two sons, Giulio and Alberico, carried on the paternal feud, the elder being his father's favourite, and the younger his mother's darling.

On the death of his father, Giulio Cybo seized the marquisate, to the discomfort of his mother and his younger brother, who retired to Rome to await a more prosperous turn of events ; for as Andrea D'Oria and the Duke of Tuscany both favoured Giulio's claims, she recognized that for the present at least she had better remain quiet.

But Giulio Cybo was of a restless, dissatisfied spirit ; he had the handsome bearing and winning ways which made Gian Luigi Fieschi so great a favourite, and he had moreover the same insatiable ambition, which liked not to rest contented in the battle of life. Thus it was when the first rumour of the Fieschi conspiracy reached him at Massa ; and forthwith he set off with five hundred men to assist whichever party might be victorious, not without, so said report, and so thought Prince Andrea, a secret understanding with Gian Luigi. However, as it was, Giulio Cybo only reached Genoa in time to congratulate Prince Andrea on the turn events had taken.

With a bland smile the prince received him. He gave him, as he had promised some time previously, Gianettino's daughter in marriage, with a promise of a handsome dower; but in his own subtle mind destined him for vengeance at a more fitting time.

At last, however, the exiled Marchioness of Massa had recourse to the emperor Charles V. to plead her cause; and Charles graciously vouchsafed to seize the marquisate as an imperial fief, until such time as the quarrel could be adjusted. Thus was Giulio Cybo adrift on the world. He first repaired to the court of Florence for advice and assistance, but got neither. He next addressed himself to Andrea D'Oria, demanding his wife's promised dower, which the old prince had wisely been dilatory in paying; and now he flatly refused to advance anything, and going to his account-book he showed Giulio Cybo that it had cost him far more than the promised dower to establish him in Massa against his mother's claims, and that instead of owing him anything Giulio Cybo was in truth his debtor.

Thus was the young marquis ruined in his hopes, and enraged at the abject position in which Andrea D'Oria had left him. It wanted but little to persuade him to listen to the tempting allurements of the French ambassador in Rome, the Cardinal de Bellay; it wanted but little to make him at home in the salons of the exiled Fieschi. And thus was he drawn into the vortex of a fatal conspiracy—fatal always when aimed at the aged D'Oria.

They planned that Giulio Cybo, with two or three galleys, should proceed to Genoa on pretext of visiting his wife. He was there to arrange a plan of action with all the discontented, and owing to his relationship with the D'Oria he could easily seek a private interview with the old admiral, and assassinate him amongst his household gods.

Giulio arrived safely in Genoa. He talked with the discontented, but he talked a trifle too freely, and the imperial partisans were too wide awake after the Fieschi conspiracy to allow of its repetition. They discovered the plot, and seized Giulio Cybo at Pontremoli as he was returning to Genoa from an interview with his allies. In vain did he seek to arouse the former Fieschi vassals around him with the well-known cry of the "cat," in vain did he strive to rally his own followers around him, he was captured on the 18th of May, 1548, and sent to Genoa. There he was tortured, confessed, and finally sentenced to death; but before the execution of the sentence he wrote a penitent letter to his mother and a sonnet of decided merit, proving his literary attainments to have been of no low order.

Thus did this faint echo of discontent murmur through the streets of Genoa. For the rest of his days Prince Andrea had no more attempts from within to overthrow his power; but this second conspiracy made the emperor still more strenuous in urging the necessity of a fortress, and Prince D'Oria still more determined to carry out his projects of reform. To gain time, Andrea in a measure agreed to entertain the idea of small Spanish forts placed here and there about the city, but never for a moment gave way about the castle.

However, the emperor and Gonzaga were not satisfied with this. So Adamo Centurione was sent to Spain to talk the matter over with the emperor, to concede, if necessary, about the smaller forts, and to insist on the government being placed in the hands of a few. Adamo Centurione was a man of great weight with the emperor, celebrated not only for his wealth and position, but also for his naval acquirements; he came of an old family well known on the seas, the Uso-dimare. The De' Mari and the De' Marini had done for Genoa in the Middle Ages in commerce and discovery what the D'Oria had done in maintaining her supremacy by force of arms.

At the reform of 1528 they lost their honoured names, which in themselves spoke of their renown, and were merged in one "albergo" under the name of Centurione.

Paolo Centurione was celebrated a little later for discoveries eastwards,[1] and Adamo had gained himself a name at the siege of Goletta, and Tunis, and in the German wars. His wealth was enormous, and in Genoa he acted the part of Pompey to the D'Orian Cæsar.

But Centurione could get no concessions out of the emperor, who at this time was flushed with his victories in Germany, and looked to making his son Philip king of Italy by the stepping-stone of Genoa. The Duke of Alva, Gonzaga, and the Duke of Florence, all favoured the emperor's ambitious scheme, and all the answer Centurione brought back to Prince Andrea was that the question should be deferred until Philip should visit Genoa.

Before receiving his august visitor, Prince Andrea determined to accomplish his reforms, and they were as follows. The old nobles, the nobles of S. Luca as they were called, from their place of rendezvous in the neighbourhood of the church of that name, were greatly in the minority in those days as compared with the new nobles, or the nobles of the Portico of S. Pietro, as they were called from meeting in the arcades in the Piazza dei Banchi; and these two classes of nobility formed the inherent cause of all the dissensions in the State.

In this year of 1547, Andrea D'Oria determined to check the overpowering influence of the new nobility, and by thus changing the government from an aristocratic to an oligarchic form he laid up a fertile source of discontent for the ensuing century. He called these reforms the "garibetto," because he said that thereby he gave the finishing touch (garbo) to his reforms of 1528, and the substance of them was as follows : That the councillors of the greater and lesser council should

---

[1] *Vide* ch. x.

be elected by the agency of voting, and not by lot as hereto-
fore, hence at once throwing the scale of power into the
hands of the old nobility, with their immense wealth and unlimited influence; and thus were the nobles of the Portico of
S. Pietro almost entirely excluded from a hand in the government, and the liberator of his country, the celebrated defender
of the people's rights, quietly monopolized the entire management of affairs. " Before whom," says Ariosto,

> " All others, who their country would enslave must blush,
> Nor dare to raise their eyes,
> Where'er be heard the whisper of the name of D'Oria."
>> *Orlando Furioso, Cant.* xv.

We are not surprised, as a sequel to this policy, to find
Prince Andrea's galleys, under command of the youthful
Giovandrea, assisting the emperor Charles V. in the establishment of the dreaded Inquisition in Naples, where popular
feeling resented such tyranny ; and thus did Andrea, not content with enslaving men's bodies, drive one of the first and
most substantial nails into the cross on which the freedom of
Italian thought was to be crucified.

Meanwhile Prince Philip was preparing for his voyage to
Italy, and Prince Andrea, as was his wont on such occasions,
repaired to Spain to convey the young prince on his galleys
to Genoa. Ninety-eight galleys in all formed this escort,
forty of which were Andrea's exclusive property. As they left
the harbour of Las Rosas, as they coasted along the Riviera,
everything was done with a pomp and magnificence new to
Italian eyes.

The emperor wished his son to enter Italy surrounded by
oriental magnificence, and no panoply and display of an
eastern monarch could surpass that escort which conveyed
the heir of such vast wealth past the shores of Provence. In
a large volume written by one Estrella, a Spaniard, we have
a list of the flags, the damask, and luxurious trappings which
adorned these galleys, and which turned them into gigantic

sailing birds of paradise. On Philip's own ship was carried all the plate of the Spanish court, worth, they say, a million golden ducats, to assist at the regal banquets, and to prove beyond dispute the wealth of the lords of the Indies.

The astonishment with which the Italians beheld such display is illustrated by a quaint little story of a peasant, who seeing a man pass one day with a profusion of lace and crimson silk, and accompanied by four men-servants, bearing each a lighted torch of white wax, and thinking that it could be nothing less than the holy sacrament which was passing by, knelt him down and devoutly said his prayers. But lo! it was no priestly procession to which his orisons were addressed, it was a goodly dish of stew being conveyed in full state to the Duke of Alva's table by his grace's head cook.

The lavish presents which Philip distributed amongst his intended subjects were on a scale befitting the display of his procession. To the wife of the governor of Milan, he gave a diamond ring valuing five thousand ducats; to her daughter, a ruby necklace worth three thousand. But under this gorgeous apparel lurked great discontent; and Philip's visit to Genoa was anything but a satisfaction to himself or to his hosts. As the squadron coasted along the Riviera, Philip casually asked Andrea D'Oria where he was to be lodged in Genoa. The admiral replied, " In my house, your highness, where your august father always lodged."

To this Philip somewhat curtly replied that he should prefer being housed in the public palace, from which Andrea, with feigned sorrow, tried to dissuade him; but seeing the prince determined to carry his point, D'Oria, with the dignity and patronizing air of a father, added, " I cannot allow you this favour, since it is not in my power. When we reach Genoa you can yourself ask it of those who have the power to grant it, and if it be accorded to you, by all means avail yourself of it; yet I fear me greatly that those gentlemen who are now therein will not feel inclined to turn out of it."

Enraged at this haughty speech Philip spoke no more with Andrea, and would have proceeded on his way to Milan by the Savona route, instead of halting at Genoa, had not the Duke of Alva dissuaded him, representing how much it was for his future interests not to arouse the anger of the Ligurian Republic.

It was equally galling to Ferrante Gonzaga, the imperial governor of Milan, who had come to Genoa to meet prince Philip, when the senate refused him lodging and stabling within the city walls. He amused himself by letting off all the reservoirs of water on the hills around, and rather disconcerting the inhabitants, who at length allotted him a lodging at Sestri befitting his requirements. But all this shows how indignant were the Genoese at the near approach of their Spanish taskmasters, and that some sparks of liberty still smouldered in their breasts.

On entering the harbour of Genoa, one of the galleys struck on a rock and sank, to the dismay of the bystanders. Not a few objects of value went to the bottom, including all the vestments and ornaments for Philip's private chapel; the fact of this disaster as he stepped on Italian soil not a little added to the Prince's already embittered spirit.

It was but small solace to him to tread the carpeted floors and gilded halls of Andrea's mansion; to be surfeited with banners and statues, to see a gilded globe surmounted by an imperial crown, symbolical of his father's power, on which the sun never set, when the very ground on which he trod, he coveted, but could not possess.

The fifteen days of Philip's stay in Genoa must have been a period of mortification to his youthful pride. Instead of the regal diadem of Italy he here hoped to gain, he found obstinate and determined opposition to his plans of a fortress. His sailors had continued brawls with the Genoese, which nearly led to open warfare. It was in vain that the Duke of Alva held private audiences with Adamo Centurione. Prince

Andrea was obdurate; he would hear of nothing but reforms which would place his own authority out of all dispute within his native walls.

On pretext of consigning to safe custody a Spanish delinquent, one Don Antonio D'Arze, who, to rid himself of his offspring, had drowned them in the fountain of his garden, Philip ordered his men to conduct the prisoner to the tower of the public palace, where he had himself wished to lodge. But at this apparent infringement of their exclusive right the Genoese were up in arms at once; not a few of the Spaniards were killed, and the tumult was not hushed until Andrea D'Oria, carried in a chair through the city, managed to calm men's minds with his venerable presence. Andrea then hurried to the senate and lamented the accident with flowing words, and was eventually chosen as deputy to make peace with the royal guest.

It was not, however, at all displeasing to Andrea, that his fellow-countrymen should show such feelings of liberty at this juncture. It enabled him to tell his guest, with cunning obsequiousness, that if it were possible to place the keys of paradise in Philip's hands, he, Andrea D'Oria, would be the first to do so. But he much feared that the question of the fortress would prove an equal impossibility unless it could be built by magic in one single night, and garrisoned whilst the good citizens of Genoa were sleeping in their beds.

The morning after the disturbance, the senate sent a deputation to crave his forgiveness for the past, and to beg for the pleasure of a personal visit from his royal highness within the walls; for as yet prince Philip had not entered the town gates. And thus the result of all his schemes and projects of self-aggrandizement faded away in further displays of oriental magnificence through the streets of Genoa, a grand mass in the cathedral of S. Lorenzo, and hollow words of friendship. So, after caressing his host with affected good-will, and after showering a goodly amount of

jewelry amongst the ladies of the D'Oria family, prince
Philip continued his journey towards Milan, writing bitterly
to his father about his fruitless visit to Genoa, and adding
that no fortress would ever be erected in Genoa unless by
force of arms.

It is surprising yet again to see the old worn-out bones of
Prince Andrea clad in armour. When all his compeers were
sleeping their eternal sleep, he mounted once more his galleys
to check the depredations of his old foe, the corsair Dragut.
This scourge of the Mediterranean in these years descended
on the coasts of Liguria, and carried his ravages almost to
the very gates of Genoa. Rapallo was laid waste by him, and
night after night the beacon towers which lined the coast,
and which still exist as a quaint ornament to each town along
the Riviere, shone forth with their lurid lights to tell the
trembling inhabitants that the infidel was at hand, hovering
like a wolf around the fold.

The emperor Charles, unable any longer to tolerate this
marauder along the coasts of his vast dominions, employed
Giovanni della Vega and Andrea D'Oria to hunt him out of
his fastnesses. The wary pirate was driven from point to point
by the allied galleys of Spain and Genoa, until at length he
was shut in by Andrea into the harbour of the island of Gerbe.
The admiral applied in vain for the aid of the infidel lord of
this island, arguing that Dragut was a pirate, an enemy to
Saracen and Christian alike. He replied that Andrea must
await his enemy in the open sea, and deal with him as he best
could there.

Dragut's cunning, however, was more than a match for the
old admiral, for by the aid of engineers and workmen, he cut
a road through the island, placed his ships on wheels, and
one morning, Prince Andrea awoke to find his enemy and all
the hostile fleet escaped from his clutches. But Dragut's
power was broken by this hot pursuit. He ceased to trouble
the Ligurian coasts from this date forwards, and ten years

later, at the siege of Malta, Christendom was relieved to hear of the death of Dragut.

Not so successful were Andrea's arms against his Christian foes in these his latter days, when he fought to relieve Naples from a combination of French and Turks, which threatened destruction to the imperial power in Italy. At Ponza, celebrated for a Genoese victory over Alphonso of Aragon,[1] Prince Andrea met with a signal defeat. Report says that he was surprised by the allied fleet, and when asked what course he would wish pursued, he exclaimed that the galleys should rush to the attack, and use their oars and their sails, but that his feeble voice of command was only half heard, and a cry went forth that the ships were to use their oars and their sails in self preservation. When too late, Andrea found that his orders had been misunderstood, and that his fleet was making the best of its way home. Thus ended Prince Andrea's last naval exploit, but a sorry closing scene in the career of him . who had once been the dread of the Mediterranean.

At the age of eighty-four he once more, and for the last time, put on his armour, and undertook to superintend the war in Corsica, where Genoa's interests were at a very low ebb. Here the cruelty of his youth was re-enacted ; age and the prospect of the grave did but little to mitigate his blood-thirstiness against his foes. Before Andrea's victorious arms fled the rebel Sampiero, and the cry of the stricken Corsicans ascended with the smoke of their burning homesteads to call for a release from their tormentor. At length old Andrea felt his vigour was gone from him, and with unwilling heart he relinquished the command of his troops and his galleys to his heir, Giovandrea, now of an age to take his place ; and it must have been the bitterest pang to his declining years to see how little of the inheritance of naval fame had fallen to the lot of Gianettino's son.

It was reserved for Andrea to outlive his imperial master

---

[1] *Vide* ch. ix.

in whose service he had fought so long. Though but an infant compared to his patriarchal admiral, Charles was far more enfeebled both in mind and body at the age of fifty-six, when he gave up the reins of government to his son. The emperor wrote a letter to Andrea to inform him of his resignation, and expressing a wish once more to see him, if Andrea's age and infirmities would permit of his making a pilgrimage to Spain. But Andrea's age and infirmities were an insurmountable obstacle to their meeting again. From his seclusion at St. Juste, Charles kept up a lively correspondence with his old admiral, who sent a large sea-chart by way of a gift to the monarch recluse, which is said to have been one of his greatest diversions in his hermitage.

At the peace of Câteau Cambresis, Andrea D'Oria urged the Genoese interests in Corsica, and urged them with success; and as a further mark of respect to this aged D'Oria, Philip II. was pleased to elect Giovandrea as Andrea's lieutenant in command of the Mediterranean fleet; and in this the dream of Prince D'Oria's latter days was realized—he beheld his adopted son occupying the position he had won, even if the young man occupied it with but a faint reflection of the glory and talent of the veteran.

For his last remaining years Prince Andrea D'Oria lived at home in peace, beautifying the last resting place of the D'Orian heroes, the little church of S. Matteo, which was soon to hold his own time-honoured bones, whilst Giovandrea led the D'Orian galleys to battle against the infidel. Of this expedition there is little to be told, except disaster upon disaster. The galleys proved unseaworthy, men were wanting to man them; at length Giovandrea D'Oria and his Spanish ally, the Duke of Medina Cæli, were pursued almost to the death by the Turks. The former managed to save himself with the loss of all his galleys on the island of Gerbe. Nevertheless, the evil news soon spread that Giovandrea was himself no more; and to old Andrea it was reported that the pride and hope of his life, a life now fast verging towards the grave, had been defeated and perhaps slain. There was none to tell him that he was saved.

For three long weary days the old veteran D'Oria sat huddled in his arm-chair, with his withered face sunk on his breast, his eyes closed, and men scarce knew that life was still in him, save by a faint heaving of the chest, which told that the last spark had not quite fled. At length there arrived a messenger with the glad tidings of Giovandrea's escape, but none durst venture to arouse the dying admiral until his trusted admiral, Antonio Piscina, whispered in his ear, "A messenger." Prince Andrea then raised his hollow eyes and murmured, "What news?" "By the grace of God, good," was the reply, and therewith he placed the letter in the old man's hands; but his eyes could not now decipher the writing, so Piscina ventured to take it from him, break open the seal, and read aloud of Giovandrea's safety.

With a bound the old prince raised his tottering frame from his chair to the amazement of those who stood around, and shouted, "Thanks be to God!" and with this final effort of exhausted nature he sank back fainting into his chair. For three days he lingered on, unable to rise, unable to eat, and unable to say aught but an incoherent wish that he might be spared to embrace his beloved adopted son once more.

But feeling his strength fast ebbing away, Prince Andrea summoned his household around him to take farewell, and begged them to give his last message of exhortation to the young heir to all his honours, namely, to remain firm in his allegiance to his Catholic Majesty and Spain, and to serve his country in the best way he could.

These were his last words, and thus passed away the great Andrea D'Oria, like the last flickering light of a candle burnt down to the very socket, on the 25th of November, 1560, a few days before reaching his ninety-fourth year.

He had asked for a quiet, peaceful burial, but this his

country would not permit ; and on the return of Giovandrea a
magnificent funeral was decreed by order of the senate, and
the mortal remains of this great Genoese admiral were taken
to repose amongst the heroes of his family.

ANDREA D'ORIA'S PALACE IN THE PIAZZA DI S. MATTEO.

There is a sort of romance attached to the D'Oria even in
their graves.   Whilst Andrea and his hero kinsmen repose in
the time-hallowed vaults of S. Matteo, buried and lost in the
midst of the busy life which surrounds them, so that he who
who would visit it must thread a labyrinth of narrow by-

paths, other members of this family rest in the ancient monastery of S. Fruttuoso, buried and lost in their solitude under the beetling cliffs of the promontory of Portofino. He who would approach it must do so by water, or by a steep mountain path impracticable in winter; and here, in Gothic marble tombs, in a decaying Gothic cloister, he will see the resting place of generations of D'Oria mouldering and dank through the effect of the sea waves, which lap the little bay some few feet beneath.

Everything around this little sanctuary is in keeping with these reminiscences of the past. Here a few hardy fishermen inhabit a handful of cottages, which scramble amongst the rocks, and here the watch-tower of the D'Oria, with the well-known eagle emblazoned on its walls, serves as a school-house for the children born in this secluded hamlet. An old Roman sarcophagus serves as a drinking-trough for the few stray mules which find their way thither. All around lurks the atmosphere of the past, and imagination pictures the floating hearse all glittering with the gold and silver which bore the mediæval D'Oria to his last resting-place along the watery paths of the element on which his life was spent, and on which his laurels were gained. But a few years ago a photographer who went to photograph this weird spot was stoned by the superstitious inhabitants, who took him for some uncanny magician bent on poisoning their wells. His camera was spoilt, and his life endangered. So benighted are these fishermen who watch over the spot where repose the remains of Ansaldo D'Oria—the hero of the Pisan wars, who died in 1290—and numbers of his successors, each with an epitaph attached speaking of their prowess and their skill in council chamber.

Before leaving this weird, sea-beaten monastery, sacred to the name of D'Oria, it may be interesting to learn its legend. It is dedicated to a Spanish martyr from Saragossa, showing the early connection between Genoa and Spain, a connection which pervades her language and her customs. As if it were a chapter from heathen mythology we read the early legend of its foundation—how an angel told some monks, as they bore on their ship the treasured body of their martyr, to cast anchor near the first mountain they came to beyond Genoa; that there dwelt a savage dragon in a cave, the dread of sailors; but amid the roaring of the tempest the guardian angel promised to protect them, and hurl the monster into the abyss below. So the monks did the bidding of the angel, and beheld with Christian eyes the fable of Hercules and Lichas re-enacted literally word for word according to the old legend.

> "Corripit Alcides, et terque quaterque rotatum
> Mittit in Euboicas, tormento fortius, undas."
>
> OVID.

In more authentic days rich Benedictine monks held sway along this rugged promontory, obtaining largesses from the German emperors, and other donations, until the whole coast line was theirs from Camogli to Sestri di Levante, for the almost isolated castle of which latter place they paid an annual tribute of a pound of incense. So strong were they in their mountain and seagirt fastness, that even a Genoese consul, in 1161, as a penalty for hunting on their promontory without permission, was compelled to pay the angry monks four times the value of the animals he had slaughtered.

Around their lovely Gothic church, with the sea rippling even into its very crypt, grew up a perfect paradise of ease and luxury, whither noble Genoese retired with their piety and their gold to lead a life of dreamy delight. A few palm-trees are still left to mark where their gardens ran up the mountain slopes. In the course of years many of the D'Oria family here entered their vows, and when at length with D'Orian gold S. Matteo was built, as a town branch of the S. Fruttuoso monastery, this luxurious retreat became more and more a D'Orian monopoly.

X

Andrea D'Oria it was who thought fit in after years to restore this family vault of theirs by the sea, which had suffered grievously from the raids of corsairs. He obtained from Pope Paul II. a bull permitting him to erect the tower which to-day watches over the little hamlet like the guardian angel of old, for ever warning the dragon, whether it appears in the shape of a sea monster or modern Vandal, from desecrating these sacred precincts.

Buried, too, in the sepulchre of bygone glory is the very name of D'Oria. No more do we read of this family as ruling supreme in the Mediterranean. With Prince Andrea was buried the talisman with which he had kept kings and emperors in check. Naught now remains of the might and the deeds that they wrought save the fast decaying inscriptions on the walls of S. Matteo, and on the tombs of S. Fruttuoso, whilst

> "widowed Genoa wan,
> By moonlight spells ancestral epitaphs,
> Murmuring—where is D'Oria?"[1]

For ten years after Andrea D'Oria's death peace reigned within the walls of Genoa ; not, indeed, from any contentment in the existing order of affairs, but from the necessity of keeping up an active war in Corsica, which was an outlet for discontent. No sooner, however, was peace restored in her island possession than at home the Genoese amused themselves with a furious outburst of hostilities between the two Portici—the two orders of nobility—showing how hated was the reform instituted by Andrea D'Oria, and how unequal was his successor, Giovandrea, to cope with the difficulties.

Hating the supremacy of the old nobility, the members of the Portico di S. Pietro allied themselves with the people, and demanded reform. As was usual on such occasions, men were not wanting to arouse the popular discontent, and a base triumvirate of the lowest type sprang up to plunge the city once more into scenes of confusion, ruin, and death. Tom-

[1] Shelley.

maso Carbone, an eloquent stump-orator, first fanned this flame of discord in many a turbulent meeting ; but he was surpassed by one Bartolomeo Coronato, an unscrupulous demagogue, who struck at the very root of order and good government ; whilst Stefano Invrea wormed himself into the people's confidence, and ruled them with a species of terrorism, more dangerous even than the influence of the other two.

All the old nobility found it necessary to flee from the city, and took refuge under the sheltering wing of Philip II. of Spain ; and amongst them was Prince Giovandrea D'Oria, who, by a sort of tacit consent, was chosen as the leader of the nobles of S. Luca. He did not for a moment hesitate to accept from the Spanish monarch the assistance of a fleet under the command of Don John of Austria, and forthwith to lay siege to his native town. It was with difficulty he obtained from the ambitious Spaniards that the war should be carried on under the Genoese flag ; since even he felt some qualms of conscience at subduing his country under a foreign banner.

At length, in 1576, order was again restored. The laws of 1528 were to be remodelled ; family names, which had become merged in the "alberghi," were in a measure to be restored ; the members of the guilds of silk, wool, and cloth-weaving were to be made eligible to nobility ; and the old system of electing the lesser and greater council by lot was to be restored.

By this compromise Giovandrea D'Oria obtained the position he had lost in Genoa, but not the overweening influence he had hitherto enjoyed, and the mere shadow of the power his predecessor had had. In fact, it was but the force of Spanish influence in the background which enabled him to hold his own. It was in vain that the French urged on the people to make further claims, to demand that a "Portico" of the people should be made, with the rights and privileges that the other two possessed. In vain did Coronato continue to harangue them; the rule of the demagogue was at an end, and, like many of his precursors in sedition, he paid the penalty of his crimes on the scaffold, whilst Giovandrea had a fine colossal marble statue put up to his own memory, side by side with Andrea's; and whereas the latter was termed the "liberator of his country," Giovandrea was honoured with the title of "maintainer" of this liberty. The shattered remains of these two statues are still to be seen in the cloisters of S. Matteo. It is a curious fact in Genoese history that so few statues adorn her city; these to the two D'Oria are the first, and this fact evinces the jealous feeling which pervaded the Ligurian capital, and which forbade that one man should be so exalted above his fellows. Of the countless heroes of victories not one can boast more than a modest inscription; whilst in the peaceful republic of the Bank of St. George, where nothing occurred to disturb the even tenor of affairs, the whole building is overflowing with statues to worthy men.[1]

No period of Genoese history is so thoroughly uneventful as the close of this century and the beginning of the next. Tyranny and foreign influence kept the people in check, and no period is so marked as this for the growth of magnificent palaces and works of art. Feeling secure of their position, and having no outlet for their hoarded gains, the wealthy Genoese nobility lavished their money on the erection of stately houses. Old streets were levelled to the ground, and in their place grew up the two glorious streets of palaces, the Strada Nuova and the Strada Balbi, with their frescoed halls and galleries of art, which are the admiration of every visitor to modern Genoa.

Whilst thus reposing in lazy magnificence, Genoa scarce noticed the growth of a new foe amongst the Alps, the warrior dukes of Savoy, under whose sway the ancient Ligurian

[1] *Vide* ch. xi.

Republic was destined to enter upon a new existence two centuries later. Emmanuel Philibert of Savoy, the conqueror of St. Quentin, in 1557 had a Genoese councillor and intimate friend, one Negrone Di Negro, who superintended his financial affairs, so did Emmanuel I., after Napoleon's days, entrust his financial affairs into the hands of the Genoese, Gian Carlo Brignole. A position on the Mediterranean so advantageous as Genoa was much coveted by the dukes of Savoy in their advance towards arousing a new life in decrepit Italy, and scarce a revolution or a conspiracy in Genoa occurred for the remainder of her independent existence without some suspicion of complicity from the side of Savoy.

Charles Emmanuel I. of Savoy was in those days the sole upholder of Italian freedom against the despotism of Spain. As he had seized Geneva, so did he wish to possess himself of Genoa, the stronghold of Spanish interests on Italian soil. He managed to pick a quarrel with Genoa about the possession of the marquisate of Zuccarello, near Albenga, which territory the republicans claimed as theirs by right of purchase in 1588; but the duke wished for a seaport, and hence put in his claims. In fact, he was ever on the alert to pick a quarrel with the Ligurians, as a story illustrates about a mock fight between some children, half of whom chose the name of the Duke of Savoy as their watchword, whilst the other half cried for St. George and Genoa. The ducal party were defeated, and carried through the town of Genoa by their victorious playfellows, and the government saw fit to punish them all, as some little disturbance was the result of their game. It certainly seems hardly credible, but the fact is well substantiated, that the Duke of Savoy sent an ambassador to Genoa to remonstrate about the punishment of his youthful partisans.

With French aid the duke nearly made good his claims on Zuccarello. He took Gavi, Voltaggio, and the outlying forts of Genoa ; but dissension between the allies allowed succour to come from the Spanish governor of Milan, and in 1626 a peace was signed between the belligerents by which Genoa retained possession of the disputed seaport.

By this time Prince Giovandrea D'Oria was no more. But little of the renown members of his family acquired as if by inheritance fell to his lot. We hear of him as an obsequious ally of Spain ; we hear of him too as a pious upholder of the Church. He and his wife proposed to add the old ruined church of S. Benedetto to the D'Orian estate; but on her death, before the completion of the project, Giovandrea bought it and adorned it with works of art in memory of his departed consort. Giovandrea's dog, the faithful Roldano, for its many virtues received befitting burial, and a laudatory epitaph underneath the great Jove by Montorsoli, representing Andrea D'Oria in colossal form. A right royal guardian was Roldano of the Olympian threshold, and still he watches the silent watch of death amidst the brambles and thickets of this now almost disused garden, where once the D'Oria wandered amidst hanging gardens and fountains, where now a few peasants till a few straggling vines, and where now the visitor is surprised to read that Roldano was not Andrea D'Oria's dog, as his guide-book tells him, and was not given him by the Emperor Charles V., as the story runs, but died at the age of nine, in 1605, when Andrea had been in his grave nearly half a century.

In the year 1628 a conspiracy took place in Genoa, illustrating in two ways the spirit of the times : firstly, how completely the old class of revolution had been stamped out in Liguria—it was no longer the outcome of rivalry between leading noble families, but emanated from the dregs of the populace so to speak. And secondly, that the ever-watchful eye of the Duke of Savoy was ready to grasp any opportunity afforded him for extending his power over the Republic.

Giulio Cesare Vacchero was the originator of it. His father was a man of low extraction, who had put some money together by gambling and other underhand means, and was able to give his son an education, which resulted rather in a proficiency in vice than in any other accomplishment. Vacchero was handsome, even as a tempting demon ; dark long curls hung around a subtle vicious face, with keen dark eyes, compressed lips, and a winning smile. Such was Vacchero, the very impersonation of vengeful ambition and inhuman cruelty. He scorned the nobles, and fawned on the lowest of the populace, and urged them in every way to insult their superiors.

Mainly that he might become doge did Vacchero get up this conspiracy ; no motives of liberating his country, or dislike of the existing order of things, actuated him. His principal agents in Genoa were Giugliano Fornari, a wealthy silk merchant, Clemente Corti, and Francesco Bertora, all men of violent passion and low origin, ready with hand or word for any deed of audacity. Others too were in the secret, especially one, Giovanni Francesco Rodino, who had formerly been banished from the Republic for homicide, and had now returned, and was captain of a band of three hundred men.

During his exile Rodino had spent much time in the service of the Duke of Savoy, but on his return to Genoa appeared to have entirely espoused the cause of the Republic. Bertora had married his daughter, and by this means contrived to win over his father-in-law to join the conspiracy, and hence the conspirators obtained an easy means of communication with the Duke of Savoy. Nothing loath, the Duke despatched a messenger to Genoa secretly to ascertain the state of affairs, and to offer assistance to any scheme which might further his interests in the Ligurian capital.

With these encouragements Vacchero set off for Turin, had an audience with the duke, and returned to Genoa to make his arrangements for a general massacre of the doge and council on Good Friday, in the council hall, and then, having thrown them out of the window, he proposed to reorganize the State anew, with himself as doge, and the Duke of Savoy as his firm ally and coadjutor.

However, on the day before the conspiracy Rodino was struck with misgivings, went direct to the senate and revealed the plot, demanding only a free pardon for himself, his son-in-law, and his three hundred soldiers. Thus Vacchero and all his fellow-conspirators were easily taken, and forthwith subjected to the most excruciating tortures. In his condemned cell Vacchero behaved like a caged lion; he refused food, he had to be guarded by day and by night for fear of his committing suicide, and when he was informed of his condemnation to be hanged like a common felon his exasperation knew no bounds. So ambitious a spirit could not brook such an indignity, and he clamoured for the honour of being beheaded, rushing all the time to and fro in his cell, and dashing himself against its walls as if bereft of reason.

At length the privilege of dying by the axe was granted him, and when once he heard it he became calm. He related without hesitation the objects and ends of his conspiracy, he told of his intercourse with the Duke of Savoy, and for his few remaining hours he sat tranquilly, more like a triumphant monarch than a condemned criminal. So great was the dread he had of an ignominious death, that death itself, when indicative of rank, was nothing, as compared to ignominy.

In Vacchero's own family the greatest fortitude was shown under the torturer's irons; his wife bore in silence the wrenching of her limbs, her mouth was sealed both on the rack and before the judge's promises and blandishments. So also was it with a young Greek slave and confidante of Vacchero's, who, when exposed to the severest tortures, uttered not a word, and

died three days afterwards carrying his secrets with him to his
grave.

Thus ended Vacchero's conspiracy. His house was razed to
the ground, and a stone of infamy was put up in its stead,
where now we can read that it was erected " to the infamous
memory of the most lost man, Giulio Cesare Vacchero, who, for
conspiring against the Republic, had his head cut off for the
public weal, his house pulled down, his goods confiscated, and
his sons banished."

The following account given of Vacchero's early life by the
annalist Carbone, though perhaps tinged with horrors to suit
the feelings of his countrymen, at all events must give some
true glimpses at his earlier career.   " When quite young
Vacchero was exiled from Genoa for homicide. No sooner did
he reach Nice than he treacherously slew a knight of Malta,
and fled thence to Florence. Whilst there he killed a Bentivoglio,
and was sentenced to perpetual imprisonment ; but owing to
the patronage of Antonio del Nero, and to his own wealth, he
succeeded in obtaining his freedom, which he used to terrify
the Florentines with unheard-of crimes and immorality.   The
inhabitants at length succeeded in having him removed to
Genoa, from whence he was exiled again and went to Corsica.
On his arrival at Bastia he took the earliest opportunity of
seducing the wife of his landlord, who was a Genoese, Salata
by name, and then got her assistance to help him to seduce
her two unmarried sisters.   Desirous of adding cruelty to his
crime of immorality he slew one Giambattista Falconetti, upon
which he returned to Genoa with Salata and his family, and
celebrated his arrival in his native town by putting Salata out
of the way and then poisoning the three sisters."   Such was
the man to whom the Genoese most justly erected one of their
severest stones of infamy.

Rodino, the divulger of the conspiracy, was amply rewarded
by his fellow countrymen. But men said that Carlo Emmanuele,
Duke of Savoy, was not believed when he asserted his innocence

in the whole affair ; that the rest of Europe reviled him for his low associates, and that the Vacchero conspiracy was a blot on the otherwise brilliant career of this soldier prince, who did much for the advancement of his ancestral domains, thereby enabling his son, Vittorio Amadeo, to add Nice to the Savoyard dynasty, which acquisition was the first step towards the aggrandizement of his house.

CHAPTER XV.

THE GENOESE IN CORSICA.

PART I.

FROM their possession of the island of Corsica the Genoese laid claim to the right of a royal diadem, which same diadem, in 1636, they placed with superstitious respect on the head of their Madonna. A veritable and substantial crown of thorns was this of Corsica, both for the rulers and the ruled, as a sketch of the Genoese affairs in this island will exemplify.

From the earliest date down to the close of the last century Corsica was never wanting in heroes of curious spontaneous growth to deck her annals and cover her history with the halo of romance. Her inhabitants were by nature vindictive, rebellious, and passionately attached to the idea of liberty, and to any one they thought could lead them towards that goal. But, unfortunately for themselves, this vindictive spirit was not only directed against their foes, but found ample scope for development in Corsican homesteads, and became a sort of inalienable property in the family into which it once crept, of which the entail never could be cut off.

For the origin of oppression and violence in this island we must travel back to the earliest days, when Genoa and Pisa broke lances for its possession, and popes loved to arouse discord between the two Republics by cunningly granting benefices therein to each; for on the grounds of the Pepinian donation, which presented the pontiffs with all the islands of the world,

Corsica was problematically included in their **temporal** dominion.

Pope Innocent II., in 1133, invested Genoa with several of the richest Corsican benefices, whilst Pisa looked on with jealous eyes for an opportunity for bettering herself. The Genoese, however, were not satisfied with their acquirements ; they seized the town of Bonifazio, whilst the inhabitants were making merry at a wedding, and, in 1217, Onorius III. confirmed it to them. And thus were the Ligurians firmly established in the island.

The Pisans at length saw fit to entrust the care of their interests in the island to one Sinucello della Rocca, or " Il Giudice," as he was most commonly called, the first in the long procession of heroes who will pass before our view in the course of this chapter. Though the recognized friend of Pisa for some time, Il Giudice was content to live on terms of intimacy with Genoa, and for many years he and his brother Latro held feuds under the Ligurian Republic. But Giudice was a restless, ambitious man, who could not be content with peace ; he quarrelled with his fellow nobles, he tyrannized over his dependents, he haunted the coast like a pirate, and at length, unfortunately for themselves, the Genoese took the initiative in suppressing him.

Il Giudice forthwith fled into the ever open arms of Pisa, and thereby lit the train of events which ended in her war with Genoa, and her final overthrow at Meloria.[1] But it was after the defeat of the Pisans, and when he was left to his own resources entirely, that the real character of Il Giudice came out as a national hero and intrepid warrior. For several years, in his mountain fastnesses, and with his brave followers, he managed to keep the Genoese at bay against fearful odds, and upon his deeds of valour Corsican legends love to dwell, for he was a perfectly typical Corsican hero. He had his inveterate foe, one Giovanninello, who conspired against him,

---

[1] *Vide* ch. iv.

was driven into exile in Genoa, and eventually returned, under the Genoese banner, and founded Genoa's second colony of Calvi. Il Giudice had his six daughters all married to his adherents, and six sons ready to carry on his " vendetta." Moreover, tradition says he was deservedly called " the judge," and was renowned far and wide for his equity.

On one occasion when some Genoese fell into his hands, he promised liberty to the married ones if their wives would come and fetch them. In due time these ladies appeared, trusting in his word ; a kinsman of Il Giudice, however, insulted one of them, whereupon the general ordered his head to be cut off, and sent back the prisoners and their wives true to his word.

The end of this hero was a sad one. Amongst his six sons there was a Judas, Salnese by name, who betrayed his aged blind father into the hands of the Genoese. They took him to end his days in a Genoese prison, cursing his offspring with his last breath, and lamenting the woes of his country.

In her transactions with Corsica from first to last the Genoese Republic has met with unlimited blame; but the diffi·culties she encountered at the very outset of her career were almost enough to daunt the courage of a more powerful state. There were the Pisan adherents, to begin with, always ready to foment revolt, and the clergy who adhered to Rome ; the Aragonese had their claims, which they were ready at any moment to proffer ; whilst the Corsicans themselves were a wild relentless race, who resented any appearance of tyranny, and were always ably provided with leaders to promote this spirit.

The utter deprivation to which the Corsicans during this early period of their struggle were reduced, is illustrated by the appearance of a curious communistic sect among them, started by two brothers, Polo and Arrigo. Under their guidance men and women professed to believe that the golden age had come ; everything was proclaimed to be common property, wives and children included. The converts to this creed repaired in a body to the churches, where, after celebrating all sorts of heathen rites, they extinguished the lights and proceeded with their orgies in the dark. After much trouble the papal legate and the Genoese combined and succeeded in putting down this insurrection, and a period of tranquillity ensued during which the Genoese granted fair laws and liberal charters to the towns of Bonifazio and Calvi, and various seignioral fiefs, and, in 1347, delegates were sent over by the doge to regulate affairs in the island ; but as the Republic was essentially weak at home, and unable to keep her own internal affairs in any-thing like order, but little could be expected for her de-pendencies.

Almost identical with the promulgation of these more liberal arrangements and equitable government was the outbreak of another rebellion, and this time the leader was Arrigo della Rocca, son of Il Giudice, who took up the line of policy eventually so fatal to the cause of Corsican independence, namely, that of proclaiming a foreign protector. And the Aragonese, whom he chose to summon to his assistance, were ready enough to embrace the opportunity, for they had ob-tained concessions from the Vatican for extending their dominion in the island, and della Rocca's invitation formed an excellent pretext.

To meet this contingency the Genoese adopted a policy which served to aggravate the discontent, and to lay up for themselves a store of evil for the centuries to come. Societies were formed, called "*azionisti*," by which money was advanced on the principle of the Mahone loans ;[1] and in return for this large portions of the island were allotted to the capitalists by way of security or repayment, and these portions they ground down to the utmost to recover, and make a profit on the money they had advanced.

Arrigo della Rocca, after a long weary struggle with the new proprietors of the island, was secretly poisoned, and the

---

[1] *Vide* ch. v.

greater part of Corsica became a feudatory of a Genoese family, the Lomellini, who bought up the "*azionisti*," and exercised intolerable despotism over their possessions, until the whole island, with the exception of the faithful towns of Bonifazio and Calvi, were in open revolt under Vincentello d'Istria, another wild scion of the house of Il Giudice, a son of one of the six daughters.

It was at this time that French influence was first felt on Corsican soil; the marshal Boucicault,[1] who ruled in Genoa with unparalleled tyranny, backed up the Lomellini in all their acts of oppression. In the war which ensued, the siege of Bonifazio by the joint fleet of Alphonso of Aragon and the Corsican rebels is the theme of Genoese triumph—how priests, women, and children held out with one accord against fire, pestilence, and famine until succour from home arrived; and how, when it did arrive, all communication with the beleaguered city was cut off by the Aragonese fleet in the harbour, until a brave coral diver, Andrea Magrone by name, precipitated himself into the waves with a hatchet in his mouth, and by swimming under water contrived to reach the king's ship, cut the cable of this and several others, and, owing to the roughness of the sea, such confusion was wrought by this that the Genoese obtained an easy victory and the city was relieved.

Amongst the Corsicans, d'Istria was unable to get together anything like unity in his rebellion. Numerous barons remained faithful to Genoa, and after the destruction of his Aragonese contingent, he was unable to withstand the moneyed resources of the Genoese; and after the failure under the walls of Bonifazio his cause gradually grew weaker, until his own folly brought about his ultimate ruin, for by insulting a noble lady of Biguglia, the "vendetta" of her family pursued him, and he was surrendered to the Genoese, and paid the penalty of his rebellion, in 1434, by losing his head on a scaffold erected before the gates of the cathedral in Genoa.

[1] *Vide* ch. ix.

Affairs, however, in Corsica were by no means ameliorated by the quelling of this revolt. There were papal claims under Eugenius IV. and Nicolas V. ; there were Aragonese claims, Milanese claims, and the national party who elected their *Conte* and *Vicario* to rule over them ; and then there were the Genoese, more powerful than them all, yet still not powerful enough to overcome the other obstacles.

Hence, in 1453, they took the desperate step of making over the island to the directors of the Bank of St. George,[1] and, saving supreme senatorial rights, the protectors of this wonderful bank ruled in Corsica. Terrible were their exactions and unscrupulous was their policy. Murders, exorbitant taxes without end, exasperated the already much oppressed population ; and, as a natural result of this policy, another hero of the della Rocca family appeared on the scene, Rinuccio by name, who scoured Europe with a view to collecting a force sufficient to resist the army of the bank.

Niccolò D'Oria, however, offered effectual resistance to all his attempts, and, together with his wife and children, Rinuccio was carried prisoner to Genoa. In 1504, however, he managed to effect his escape, and got a small army together. As a counter irritant to Rinuccio's disturbances in Corsica, the Genoese proceeded to wreak their vengeance on his unfortunate family. They killed his eldest son, and threatened the same by his other children if he still continued in his rebellion. But Rinuccio had the stern blood of Il Giudice flowing in his veins, and proclaimed that as long as he had twenty followers behind him, he would never give in to the hated Republic. He was again taken prisoner, and again effected his escape, and lived like a wild beast in his mountain fastnesses, the terror of every Genoese adherent.

Andrea D'Oria it was who put the final stroke to the suppression of Rinuccio. In 1511, Andrea was in command in Corsica, and by craftily reducing the limit of Rinuccio's

[1] *Vide* ch. xi.

circle without hazarding an engagement, he eventually starved him out ; and one day, the last of this brave house, della Rocca, who carried on the war of vengeance against Genoa, was found dead in a rocky cavern. Andrea D'Oria's eulogists are silent about this part of his life, for in subduing the rebellious Corsicans there was not an inhumanity of which he was not guilty. He burnt every house that came within his reach, he put every one remorselessly to the sword, and ruled with a species of terrorism, the details of which for ever shake the opinions of those who are inclined to admire the so-called liberator of his country, the so-called greatest of the D'Oria.

After the death of Rinuccio the period of ill-organized revolts in the island was, for a short time, at an end ; and for a while the Bank of St. George ruled with a certain degree of prudence. If Rinuccio had effectuated nothing else, he had taught the Genoese a lesson which they continued to act upon for a time, and the islanders were saved from bloodshed and misery during a period which appears like a little oasis in their wilderness of centuries.

An annual governor was sent out by the bank, who resided at Bastia. He had a "*vicario*" under him, who superintended judicial and military affairs. There were lieutenants appointed to govern all the important posts, from whose courts there was an appeal to the governor ; and moreover, there were native syndics appointed, to whom any complaints against the acting magistrates might be brought, and conveyed thence to the supreme tribunal. Many of the old institutions were left *in statu quo*, and the Corsicans were admitted to a share in their own government.

But the Bank of St. George was an essentially mercenary foundation, and when the expensive luxury of an Andrea D'Oria, and continual internal troubles, brought Genoa to the brink of ruin, the protectors of the bank thought fit again to grind down the Corsicans, to whom cessation from warfare had now brought a measure of prosperity. Commissioners were sent to intimate to the inhabitants, that the bank wished for statistics of all their property and goods, and the simple-minded Corsicans, wishing to make a good appearance, entered all their useless land in the same category with the arable, and hence a heavy tax was imposed, not only on their cultivated fields, but on the mountains, with which Corsica was well stocked.

In addition to other acts of oppression, the governor for the bank in Corsica caused commissions to be given in the Genoese army to some of the most obnoxious leaders of revolt. They were invited to taste the clemency of the Republic, and to embark for Genoa. Those of them who were foolish enough to trust to the promises of their oppressors, found, on their arrival in Genoa, that the Ligurian clemency extended no further than the four walls of a prison.

These oppressions on the part of the bank gave rise to the genius of one of the most remarkable characters of the age, who, with Pasquale Paolo, is an object of Corsican veneration. Sampiero di Bastelica was a man of humble origin; in his youthful days he had been occupied in serving in the armed bands of which Italy was then full. He had served in the "Bande Nere," he had assisted the Medici against the Pazzi, and eventually became the leader of Francis I.'s Corsican band. Whilst fighting against Spain, Sampiero appears to have forgotten his country, until 1547, when he repaired to Corsica with the object of marrying, and obtained the hand of Vannina d'Ornano, the only daughter of one of the first Corsican nobles.

For some trifling offence, Sampiero was put in prison by the Genoese governor, who liked not his anti-Spanish politics, and he was only liberated by the combined exertions of his father-in-law and the French king. This was enough to make the enraged Corsican thirst for vengeance, and henceforth all other objects were forgotten, and he lived only to free his country from the hated Genoese.

After obtaining aid from Henry II. of France, who sent the Maréchal des Thermes with a considerable force to Corsica, Sampiero wandered through the island fanning a revolt. By this time the French had learnt the advantage of securing a footing in Corsica, and from henceforth, in every rebellion against Genoa may be traced the subtle hand of French diplomacy. Dragut, too, the Saracenic scourge of the Mediterranean, was not slow with his assistance, glad enough of an opportunity of striking a blow at Genoa. And soon the Genoese were deprived of all their possessions in the island, save the faithful towns of Calvi, Bonifazio, and Ajaccio.

At this, the second siege of Bonifazio, the Genoese had another opportunity of showing off their heroism. Priests, women, and children, again came forward. But this time they were not so successful ; an envoy was cut off on his road to Genoa, craving assistance for the besieged inhabitants ; false letters were sent back to the governor of Bonifazio, saying that all hope from Genoa must be abandoned, and the garrison surrendered unconditionally, but were immediately fallen on by the treacherous Turks, who would have butchered them had it not been for Sampiero's timely intervention.

Finally the Genoese discovered that nothing but a desperate effort would resuscitate their fallen fortunes in Corsica, and their effort was entrusted to the care of the patriarch, Andrea D'Oria, now in his eighty-fourth year. Through his instrumentality assistance was obtained from the emperor and Cosmo de' Medici ; and to the aged warrior, the Ligurian Republic gave her standard amidst a profusion of pomp and display before the altar of her cathedral.

With Andrea's arrival in Corsica the tide of events was changed. The Genoese arms were universally successful, and, as he had done in his youth, the aged warrior visited every prisoner who fell into his hands with remorseless cruelty. But it was not till the peace of Câteau Cambresis, in 1559, that Corsica was finally reduced and handed over to absolute Genoese rule. A wild cry of desperation went up throughout the island at this the wholesale desertion of her allies. Sampiero, the hero of their liberty, now came forth more prominently than ever with his indomitable spirit. He wandered from court to court in Europe seeking aid for his stricken country. He was well received by Barbarossa in Algiers, by the Sultan in Turkey, and by Catherine de' Medici in France, but beyond empty promises was not successful in obtaining aid.

During Sampiero's absence the Genoese tried the power of blandishments on his unfortunate wife Vannina, who with her children was residing at Marseilles. They promised her a restoration of her property of Ornano, and excellent terms for her husband, if she would but come to Genoa and place herself and family under the Republic's care. So accordingly the poor woman was induced to set sail; but a friend of Sampiero's kept her husband well informed of her movements, as he was at the court of Algiers; and thus no sooner had she left the port of Marseilles than a galley followed her in hot pursuit under the command of her husband's friend, who captured her and conducted her to Aix.

When Sampiero had concluded the business he was transacting, he hurried thither and conveyed his trembling wife back to Marseilles. Unconscious of her husband's intentions, but well aware of his revengeful, uncompromising spirit, she begged hard for mercy, for life to make amends, for another opportunity to prove her fidelity, but with the dogged determination so characteristic of the Corsican he would hear of none. He gave her three days to make her preparations, and then plunged his dagger into her breast, or as more unromantic authorities will have it, he strangled her with her garter. Such was the horror of anything like dishonour and disgrace in the mind of this wild, untutored man, whose hard creed permitted not a thought beyond the one narrow groove of emancipation from tyranny. He loved his wife tenderly, they say, but he loved his day dreams of Corsican liberty better, and to these the luckless Vannina fell a sacrifice.

After perpetrating this bloody deed Sampiero hied him on his way to Paris, in 1562, there to solicit the aid of Catherine de' Medici ; but the queen-mother and her court looked askance at the murderer and offered him no assistance. So Sampiero was constrained to return to Corsica with but forty-five men, determined to strike one more blow for his country's liberty ; for after the peace of Câteau Cambresis, the Genoese yoke was harder to bear than ever ; and matters were in no way ameliorated, when the Bank of St. George relinquished the well-squeezed sop of Corsica to the management of the Republic, when all that was profitable to them had been drained thereout.

After taking the castle of Istria, Sampiero, with a band of one hundred men, made rapid advances against the Genoese, until at length the town of Vescovato fell into his hands, and with this the cause of liberty grew apace, in spite of an army of four thousand strong, sent from Liguria under Stefano D'Oria, which, with the customary cruelty, burnt all that came into their hands, including Bastelica and Sampiero's own house and home. But for this the reckless general cared but little, and hurried to his mountain fastnesses, from whence he could defy the enemy and be free.

One of his followers, however, Campolasso by name, was more tender-hearted than his commander ; for when the Genoese threatened to put his aged mother to excruciating tortures if he did not surrender himself, Campolasso forthwith presented himself at the Genoese camp. But this goes far to prove the unscrupulous cruelty with which the Ligurians treated their rebellious subjects ; indeed Stefano D'Oria himself avowed it as his wish that every Corsican over fourteen should be put to death, and the island repeopled and re-organized with a more peaceful subordinate race. In this campaign one Napoleone di Santa Lucia gave celebrity for the first time to this glorious Corsican name, fighting under the standard of Sampiero, whose descendant in after years proudly dictated terms to Genoa and Italy.

In their assistance during this campaign the French were exceeding lukewarm. A small sum of money and thirteen flags with "*pugna pro patriâ*" emblazoned thereon, were all their contributions, and thus the war dragged out a weary existence, with varied fluctuations on either side, until, in 1567, Sampiero was decoyed by a monk with a false message into an ambush, and fell fighting desperately to the last. Though sixty-nine years of age, Sampiero was hale and strong, and knew not what fatigue was. He was certainly one of Corsica's most remarkable heroes ; his grateful countrymen would have made him a king, but he spurned a diadem. He always wore the loose cloak of his country, always slept on the ground. In another country, and with a life directed in another groove, he would have been a remarkable man, very much after the fashion of the first Napoleon, and with many points in common with him which form an interesting comparison between the two sons of this unfortunate island.

At Sampiero's funeral his son Alfonso, a youth of seventeen, took up the gauntlet against the Genoese; but he displayed none of his father's vigour, and his youth was against his success as a general. Worn out by continual warfare the Corsicans at length accepted a peace in 1569, and Giorgio D'Oria was sent out as governor, a man of much moderation, who during his life kept the Corsicans contented ; but after his death, and for the century which followed, Corsica was the most wretched country in Europe—famines, plagues, feuds, and corsairs, all devastating it in turn.

Alfonso d'Ornano, as the representative of Sampiero and the unfortunate Vannina d'Ornano, was allowed by Giorgio D'Oria to repair to France, where in another and more fertile soil he planted the fortunes of his family.

Charles IX. received Sampiero's son with great honours at

Paris, and with the permission of Genoa he made him colonel of a regiment of Corsicans, who did great service against the Swiss in 1587, and on the expiration of the Valois dynasty, Alphonso wisely espoused the cause of Henry of Navarre. In this reign Ornano was made a marshal, decorated with the order of the Holy Ghost, and held the office of Lieutenant-Governor of Guyenne. At Bordeaux his name is still honoured for his works, and a street is still called after him.

Thus did the descendants of the Corsican hero continue to reap laurels for themselves in the country of their adoption. Under both empires the Counts d'Ornano distinguished themselves in every campaign, and the present head of the family is to-day an esteemed citizen of the new Republic.

After Giorgio D'Oria's death an idea of entire extermination of their rebellious subjects was often mooted amongst the Genoese, so when a Greek colony, the Mainoti, from the Gulf of Kolokytia, tired of Turkish rule, threw themselves into the arms of Genoa, a portion of Corsica was allotted to them containing a few villages. Seven hundred and thirty Greeks in all landed on the island in 1676, but as Genoese *protégés* the inhabitants naturally hated them, and no amalgamation or understanding ever took place, till, after a century of discontent and misery, the Greeks with one accord took sail for Sardinia, hoping under another government to find a more hospitable resting-place.

Suppressed groans and dogged determination kept the Corsicans from entirely giving way to their oppressors, whose finances now were not so flourishing as to like the idea of a standing army always at work in their island dependency. In fact, it is difficult to give a period for the cessation of secret rebellion and the outbreak of open war. Certainly towards 1729 events culminated in undisguised hostilities, which continued for the remaining forty years that the Genoese flag had any pretensions to float over Corsican towers.

No abatement of taxes would be admitted. Pinelli, the

Genoese governor at this time, was severity itself. He hanged fifteen Corsican soldiers one day who had strayed almost unconsciously outside the precincts of the camp. The city of Valeria, which offered a slight remonstrance to his scheme of taxation, was seized, and every male within its walls put to the sword. Thus did the Genoese treat their refractory subjects; whilst the Corsicans, in their turn, would occasionally strip their tax-collectors naked, and whip them home with broom twigs. The Genoese garrison at Finale, on the Western Riviera, contained a few Corsican soldiers, one of whom for some slight misdemeanour was condemned to a delightfully refined instrument of torture, entitled the wooden horse, on the knife-like back of which he was made to ride with heavy weights attached to his feet. Such treatment as this could not be brooked by his comrades, who fired on the Genoese, and a regular rising occurred in Finale; however, the Corsicans were easily subdued, and their ringleaders shot.

In the island itself affairs were rapidly drawing towards open hostility; and under the joint generalship of two native heroes, Ceccaldi and Giafferi, and their successors, the Corsicans kept up the flag of revolt until their annexation with France. At the outbreak of this war the Austrians assisted the Genoese with troops, for which the Ligurian government paid the large sum of thirty thousand florins a month, and a compensation of one hundred florins for each man killed; hence, when a German fell, with a shout of delight the Corsicans would exclaim, "Another hundred florins for Genoa!"

A temporary cessation of hostilities occurred in 1732, which continued for three years; and in 1735 the Corsicans, in their national assembly, gave themselves a constitution which at that time could make the rest of Europe blush. Separation from Genoa was the basis of it, and government by a parlia_ ment of its own. A "giunta" of six was to be formed every three months out of this parliament as a supreme governing body, and a civil magistracy of four over finance, commerce, and justice, whilst the people in their own hands retained the right of electing members for this parliament.

But the lack of provisions and ammunition prevented the Corsicans from establishing this free constitution, and they were on the point of surrendering to their oppressors when two ships were seen on the horizon. These presently put into a Corsican harbour and disgorged themselves of a handsome supply of provisions and ammunition and boots. The captain refused all payment, and only asked for a glass of wine to drink to the success of the brave Corsicans.

The inhabitants looked upon this good piece of luck as something supernatural, and attributed it to the interposition of the Madonna. However, they eventually learnt that the gift was due to solid flesh and blood, and English to boot. Some British admirers of Corsican liberty had taken this means of testifying their regard for bravery.

But this assistance was only transitory, and so was their success. Again were the brave rebels reduced to the greatest distress. However, before sinking for ever out of the pale of history, Corsica was to be the theatre for the exploits of two remarkable men, the Baron Theodor von Neuhoff and Pasquale de Paoli, whose careers deserve separate notice as a sort of sequel to the Ligurian affairs in this island.

In this rapid sketch of Corsica's troubles, we are, perhaps, apt to visit Genoa with too much blame. Certain it is that her position was one of the greatest difficulty ; her hold was too uncertain to enable her to carry out the good laws, which in the inception she attempted, and which she continued to promulgate until the complications which arose after 1347. Then the island became the property of grasping individuals without any settled government. Nevertheless the cities of Bonifazio, Calvi, Bastia, and Ajaccio, where the Genoese system of government was carried out to a certain extent, always

remained faithful to the Republic. But Genoa was too weak
a power to keep all the island in obedience; outside the
walls of these towns all was a mass of robbery, feuds, and
confusion, resulting not so much from the inherent defects
of the government, as from the want of force to exercise it
properly.

PART II.

Early in March, in the year 1736, the almost despairing inhabitants of Corsica beheld a ship with the British flag approaching the harbour of Aleria. Many were their speculations as to its contents, and great was their surprise when there disembarked from the strange craft a still stranger apparition, dressed as a person of royal state, with a cockade and sceptre, and all the accoutrements of theatrical royalty. Moreover, his attendants, a motley crew indeed, consisting of eleven Italians, two Corsicans, two French, and three Moors, all treated him with the respect due to a crowned head. He paced about the shore with a majestic air ; he superintended the disembarkation of twelve cannon, four thousand arquebuses, three thousand pairs of shoes, seven hundred sacks of grain, and a fair amount of ammunition.

This extraordinary apparition was the Baron Thèodor von Neuhoff, in whose adventurous career this expedition to Corsica forms about the most eccentric episode.

To the exhausted Corsicans the sight of all this ammunition and panoply of war came as a straw before the vision of a drowning man; a mysterious glamour seemed to hang over this personage, a glamour they could not resist ; and as if fascinated by some spell which spread its infection from the would-be courtiers, the oldest and youngest, the wisest and the most infatuated amongst the bystanders were soon bowing to the stranger as to a king.

But who this strange person was, and what his former career had been, must needs be explained before we describe his dealings with Corsica, and how he set up his claim to the diadem of the island as against the rulers of Genoa.

His father was a Baron von Neuhoff, of Westphalia, who,
whilst at Liège, contracted a mésalliance with a tradesman's
daughter. His family cut him, and he lived in great penury
for some time in Lorraine, and died early, leaving his wife
with a son, Theodor, and a daughter.

Owing to influence at court the baroness was enabled to
get both her children into the service of the Duchess of
Orleans, the German Princess Palatine. Theodor early
developed extraordinary precocity, grew tired of being page
to the duchess, grew tired of an appointment he got in the
French army, and determined to carve out a career for himself amongst the pitfalls of European politics.

Neuhoff first directed his steps to Sweden, and served
under Charles XII. Eventually Baron Gortz recognized his
talent for diplomacy, and dispatched him on a secret mission
to England, there to foster one of the Swedish minister's wild
plans for the restoration of the Stuarts. It was in this plot
that he became known to Cardinal Alberoni, the Spanish
revivalist; and after the fall of Gortz, Theodor betook himself to the Spanish capital to be the tool of Alberoni.
Theodor had talents above those of an ordinary adventurer ;
he had a persuasive, winning manner, and a character far
from ungenerous. Though a plotter of the darkest nature,
and though he made money in many ways from his intimacy
with Law and the South Sea speculators, yet he always spent
it on some foolish freak of the moment.

When Alberoni fell, Theodor managed to worm himself
into the good graces of Ripperda, and lived a life of splendour
and plotting at Madrid. It was at this time he married a
lady of the name of Sarsfield, a lady-in-waiting to the Queen
of Spain, the daughter of that old Irish house which had been
influential since the days of Henry II., one of which, Sir
Dominick Sarsfield, was made premier Baronet of Ireland
and Viscount Kilmallock, and whose successor was deprived
of his lands for his catholic tendencies by Cromwell, after

which event this branch of the family retired abroad, lived at continental courts, and favoured the Jacobites.

Theodor did not live long with his wife. Ripperda was displeased with him for marrying; so one morning he disappeared from his palace, carrying off with him all that was valuable, including his wife's jewels.

In course of time Theodor found himself one day in Genoa. He was employed as usual on a secret commission, namely, that of discovering for the Austrian emperor the rights of the Corsican rebellion, and how far Austria was authorized in assisting Genoa to put it down. Here he met numerous Corsican exiles, and in the pursuit of his business he made himself thoroughly master of Corsican affairs. At length, thinking that nothing could be lost by a brilliant *coup de main*, and that much might be gained, he hatched the wild scheme of making himself king of Corsica.

At Leghorn he interviewed many Corsican discontents. He hurried from place to place to collect resources, and at length at Tunis he met with an English ship whose captain agreed to carry him and his goods to the island. Poor Captain Dicks for this escapade got into hot water at home; a manifesto was issued by the British government, at the instigation of the Genoese minister, forbidding any British subject to assist the Corsicans, reprimanding severely the consul at Tunis, and ordering Captain Dicks and his ship to be seized and brought home. The unfortunate captain learnt this news one day on his arrival at Smyrna, and forthwith shot himself.

Wherever he went, Theodor had made friends—in Paris, Holland and the East, especially amongst the Jews, from whom he frequently contracted large loans to aid him in his various schemes.

Such was the apparition that now arrived in Corsica. The islanders, as they were situated, had nothing much to lose, pressed on every side as they were by the Genoese, and without any hope from without; so the adventurer was received with open arms, more especially as his promises were specious, and he represented his resources as numerous, and that money would soon arrive from Holland and troops from the East, for Theodor had had his own private negotiations with Algiers, Tunis, and Tripoli. One of his plans even had been to hold Corsica as a fief of the Sultan of Turkey.

The Corsicans now promised Theodor a crown for himself and his heirs on the sole conditions that he would convene a council of twenty-four, and would take no steps without consulting it ; that all magistrates should be Corsicans and that legislation should be carried on by the nation and the parliament. At a general council of about two thousand Corsicans, held at the convent of Alesani, Theodor was publicly crowned with a diadem of brass (gold being out of the question) and with a wreath of laurel and oak.

He began his reign as Teodoro I., and took up his regal residence in the palace of the archbishop of Cervione. Pleased with this his incipient success, king Teodoro spent much valuable money on royal show. He appointed as his prime ministers Giaffori and Giacinto de' Paoli, and spontaneously created a goodly array of marquises, counts, and court officials. He coined money with T.R. under a crown on one side, and "*pro bono et libertate*" on the reverse ; he got a flag of green and yellow, with "*in te, Domine, speravi*" emblazoned thereon, and founded an order of chivalry, styled " of the Redemption," of which there were four hundred members, and out of which he raised a little money.

Meanwhile the Genoese looked on and laughed at this phantom monarch ; the game, they thought, lay entirely in their own hands, and for some time they did not deem it necessary to increase their forces in the island. They contented themselves with issuing a proclamation for his apprehension, with a large reward fixed on his head, and representing him as "a cheat, a vagabond, and a quack doctor." When the Corsicans read it they shouted all the more lustily,

"Long live King Teodoro," and when the monarch had a copy shown him, he jocosely remarked, "Since the Genoese have endeavoured to make me pass for a mountebank, I hope soon to demonstrate what conjurers we are, and to set up my stage in the middle of the city of Bastia."

At length the Republic realized to their cost that the novelty was working wonders in Corsica. By peremptory justice King Teodoro put down all private feuds and litigations, and for a while the august presence of a monarch kept in check the conflicting elements which had all along prevented success attending the Corsican revolts.

So the Genoese were constrained to send reinforcements to their army there, and by way of doing a dastardly act of injustice they let loose on the island fifteen hundred criminals and galley slaves, thereby increasing the confusion and misery in a wholesale fashion ; for these lawless bandits, whose freedom depended on the amount of damage they could do, haunted the mountains, and swooped down on any luckless Corsican who came within their reach.

After the lapse of some months the Corsicans themselves began to look askance at their new king. His promised fleet and reinforcements never arrived, and a revolutionary party arose, who styled themselves the "*indifferenti*," and King Teodoro perceived his influence to be rapidly on the wane. However, if depart he must, he determined to do so with good grace. He summoned the people in council and thus addressed them :—

"My children, when you raised me to this envied greatness you gave me a power over yourselves, but invested me with no authority over the winds or those accidents which lie out of the reach of human forethought.

"Your safety depends upon yourselves. Be but unanimous, and you may be safe, free and happy ; but if you fall again into your old dissertations, the quickest supplies will come too late, and the greatest succour do you no good.

" As to the promises I have made, I engage they shall be fulfilled by the end of next month, or I will renounce that dignity which, though burdensome to me, has been beneficial to you ; and for this I pledge you the faith of a gentleman and the word of a prince."

Teodoro sent messengers to Holland, France, England, and the East, but all was in vain ; so he announced to the Corsican assembly that he must go himself to fetch help.   He assured his subjects of his devotion to their cause, and left Giaffori and two brothers Ornano as his deputies during his absence.   On his voyage to France he narrowly escaped falling in with a Genoese ship, but eventually contrived to reach Amsterdam in safety, disguised as a priest.

Many were the doubts and fears experienced by the Corsicans. Their faith in their absent monarch was indeed small, but in whom else could they trust ? And Teodoro managed to keep awake their lukewarm allegiance by from time to time sending them what money he could scrape together.   Well for them was it that they knew not that their absent monarch was passing his time at the expense of the Dutch Republic, for on his arrival at Amsterdam, some Jewish creditors put him in prison for debt. Nevertheless his powers of intrigue were such that during his incarceration he continued to send his subjects small sums of money by secret channels.

Meanwhile the Corsicans fought on against overwhelming odds in their mountain fastnesses.   Even when the French sent a detachment under General Boissieux, in 1737, to assist the Genoese, they did not give in.   Each village had its squadron, and each man was armed, and thus they carried on their rebellion until the Austrian war drew off the French, in 1742, and the Genoese were in their turn reduced to the greatest straits, as we gather from the fact that a company was especially formed this year in the Ligurian capital for furthering the Corsican war, and whoever contributed thereto, or served therein, received a dispensation to eat meat in Lent.

At this juncture King Teodoro reappeared on the scene in Corsica, having by his persuasive eloquence induced the rich houses of Boom and Neuville in Amsterdam to advance him money and help him out of prison. But the joy of the Corsicans in again seeing their long lost monarch was of short duration, for a fresh influx of the French obliged the king again to re-embark. All further efforts to reinstate himself in his kingdom were futile. In vain did he send to England " a proposal of his person and his crown to Lady Lucy Stanhope," [1] hoping thereby to gain some monetary assistance, and, an exile once more, Teodoro repaired to London, where some of his creditors, instigated by the Genoese, put him into the King's Bench prison, and here he would have ended his days had not Horace Walpole chosen to interest himself in his behalf, and had not Garrick recited for him.

" I wrote to promote a subscription for King Theodore, who is in prison for debt. His majesty's character is so bad that it only raised fifty pounds, and though that was so much above his deserts, it was so much below his expectation, that he sent a solicitor to threaten the printer with a prosecution for having taken so much liberty with his name. Take notice, too, that he accepted the money." [2]

In short, enough was raised to release him from his prison, but not enough to keep him in comfort. " As soon as Theodore was at liberty, he took a chair and went to the Portuguese minister, but did not find him at home. Not having six-pence to pay, he prevailed on the chairman to carry him to a tailor he knew in Soho, whom he prevailed upon to harbour him ; but he fell sick the next day, and died in three days more." [3]

He was buried in St. Anne's, Westminster, Soho, where his

---

[1] H. Walpole's letter to Sir H. Mann.
[2] Ibid.   [3] Ibid.

patron, Horace Walpole, put up the following epitaph, which the curious may read to this day :—

"Near this place is interred Theodore, king of Corsica, who died in this parish December 11th, 1756, immediately after leaving the King's Bench prison by the benefit of the act of insolvency, in consequence of which he registered his kingdom of Corsica for the use of his creditors.

> The grave, great teacher, to a level brings
> Heroes and beggars, galley slaves and kings ;
> But Theodore the moral learnt ere dead.
> Fate poured its lesson on his living head—
> Bestow'd a kingdom, and denied him bread."

His son, Frederic von Neuhoff, followed his father to England in 1754. He wrote a useful book of statistics on Corsican resources, and a panegyric on his luckless father. But fate never smiled for long on the Neuhoff family ; he fell into abject penury and distress, and put an end to his own existence in 1797.

Corsica soon fell a prey to the combined forces of France and Genoa after the departure of their king. General Boissieux imposed a peace upon them, which was, however, but of short duration, for in 1745 a fresh insurrection broke out, aided and abetted by Carlo Emmanuele, king of Sardinia. The office of general was on this occasion filled by Giampietro Giaffore, another of Corsica's brave sons, who, at the siege of Corti, when he beheld the Genoese holding out his own son as a target for the besiegers, ordered unhesitatingly the siege to be continued ; and with that extraordinary patriotism which seemed to outweigh in the Corsican breast every other senti_ ment, he gave orders for an increased vigour in the assault. He was rewarded by the capture of the city, and by finding that his son had escaped unhurt.

The Genoese had again recourse to French aid, being utterly powerless of themselves to hold their own. And thus we see the gradual development of French interests in the island, superseding step by step the Ligurian element, and a much more serious obstacle to Corsican liberty and independence.

About this time the celebrated Corsican hero, Pasquale Paoli, came forward, the youngest of the five sons of Giacinto, King Teodoro's *ci-devant* prime minister. He had been educated at Naples in a good school of political economy, and early developed a remarkable aptitude for affairs of state. In 1755 his elder brother, Clemente, summoned him to assume the command of the Corsican insurgents. He landed at Aleria on the spot where Teodoro had first set foot on his ephemeral kingdom. He was a fine manly youth of twenty-nine, and as a native Corsican, was able to command far more respect than the German adventurer.

No life perhaps has been the subject of more romance than that of this Corsican. He has been extolled to the skies by Guerazzi and others as the hero without fault, the patriot and the unselfish; and perhaps as a natural consequence of so much eulogy, no life has been more grossly misunderstood.

Bitter uncompromising hatred of Genoa on the one hand, and great personal ambition on the other, are the two leading qualities to which he owed his reputation. From letters and papers which have recently come to light in the Genoese archives, these points are brought more particularly into notice, and the glory usually awarded to the Corsican hero has been much impaired thereby.

For some years after his arrival in Corsica, Paoli legislated well and commanded the inhabitants with great skill and precision; everywhere his arms were victorious over Genoa, and the laws he promulgated struck at the very root of the evils of his country. The "vendetta" was made punishable by law, a complete representative system was organized, and a wide scope was given to local government.

Paoli then set on foot a complete system of militia, every man from fifteen to sixty was made to serve in the army, education was promoted; and, in short, many of the reforms not introduced into England, America, and France, until some decades later, were introduced by him into the wild island of Corsica. In

1765 a university was opened at Corte, at which an eloquent
rhetorical address was given out of compliment to the occasion.
And Paoli's general organization was of so high a nature that
the Genoese were not only driven out of Corsica, but several
raids were made on the coast of Liguria, and the island of
Capraia was even taken from the Republic.

Then it was that Pasquale took his first false step, a step
which for ever dashed to the ground a hope of establishing
Corsica as an independent country. A Genoese embassy was
sent to negotiate with the rebels, and to offer terms of complete independence for the island, retaining possession only of
the faithful towns of Bonifazio and Calvi, which still held out
for Genoa, and which the Genoese could not hand over to
the rebels after adhering so long and so faithfully to their cause.

But Pasquale Paoli harangued the Corsican assembly
in bitter terms. They must not accept these concessions ;
nothing but entire abandonment of the whole island by the
Genoese would satisfy him. His motives in refusing these
terms cannot have been truly patriotic, for a man so well
versed in politics, as he was, could not have been ignorant that
the French were hovering around like birds of prey eager to
seize the island, and Paoli was himself on most intimate terms
at that time with the Duc de Choiseul, whose pet scheme
was this occupation of Corsica.

The fact was, Paoli was determined to drive the Genoese
entirely out of the island, and his country's well-being was
sacrificed to this point.

This determination of the Corsicans to hear no terms,
finally drove the Genoese to play their last card in their
dealings with the island, and to sell it to France; more
especially as the French king had withdrawn his auxiliary
troops from Corsica, fearing the contaminating influence the
Jesuits might have on his soldiers ; for when the disciples of
Ignatius Loyola were driven from Portugal, Spain, and
France, and when even the Pope refused to receive them

within his states, the unfortunate priests, in 1768, had recourse
to the Genoese, who assigned them posts in their two garrison
towns in Corsica.   It is a curious feature in Genoa's dealings
with her island dependency, that whenever an opportunity
occurred she presented it, from spiteful motives, with any
surplus population of a disagreeable nature which came to
her hands, whether errant Greeks, condemned bandits, or
outcast Jesuits.   As it was, this action only precipitated
events. Without French aid, and pressed by Pasquale, Genoa
could not long have held her two faithful towns, and so she
wisely decided to sell her claims to the French, the articles
for which sale were drawn up at Versailles, in 1768, between
the Duc de Choiseul, and the Genoese Domenico Sorba.

This wholesale traffic in nations has been severely blamed,
and the Genoese have come under especial obloquy for the
same.   Motives most sordid were attributed to them.   Report
says that to gain his country so lucrative a bargain Sorba did
not shrink from the most underhand means ; that he changed
bank notes on the French Canadian bank, which were then
entirely valueless, for those of the Genoese Bank of St. George,
in favour of a maid-servant who had the ear of the Duchesse
de Gramont, whose influence was great over the Duc de
Choiseul, who in his turn governed the king.

But in reality Genoa did not part with Corsica until all hope
was gone, until Pasquale Paoli had refused the best of terms,
until she was almost bankrupt, with Austria hovering over her
for possession, and even almost dependent on French aid to
maintain the only two strongholds in Corsica which remained
firm to their allegiance.   England was averse to her, and
would not assist her, as being too French, and at home she
had no force, no commerce, and nothing left save the shell of
her former greatness, which could be temporarily adjusted by
the small sum of money resulting from her proposed sale of
Corsica ; and thus was it that this island passed into the hands
of France.   For some little time Paoli held out against the

new owners, but his troops were thoroughly routed in 1769, at the battle of Porto Nuovo, and the Corsican general fled to England.

From the Genoese archives we obtain much information of Paoli's life in England.[1] Ageno, the Genoese ambassador at the court of London, kept his country carefully informed of the doings of the Corsican general.

Writing on the 29th of September, 1769, he speaks of the extraordinary delight with which the English received him, how the "milords" *fêted* a person who had resisted the arms of France, how the journals extolled him, and likened him to Fabius Maximus. "Pasquale Paoli," he says, "dined with the Duke of Grafton, head of the ministry; was presented to George III. as General Paoli, and his Majesty kept him in conversation for some time. Next day Pasquale was presented to the queen, accompanied by his aide-de-camp, Antonio Gentile. Paoli," adds Ageno, "goes about with an air of great reserve, as if plotting great things."

On the 6th of October, 1769, Ageno writes that Pasquale Paoli had had further conferences with the king, and stated that it was beyond doubt that Pasquale would be granted a pension, and sent to make a diversion in Corsica in case of war with France.

On the 3rd of December, 1769, in another letter to Genoa, he related that Pasquale's popularity continued, that he visited the universities and arsenals, that he had a pension of one hundred and fifty guineas a month, and that it was soon to be awarded to him for life; that he frequented the court with liveried servants, and was always accompanied by Gentile and the priest Barnaby. Paoli was ready, he continued, to receive everybody who would go to his apartment, nor was he in the least annoyed when a Quaker spoke to him with his hat on, having previously heard that Boswell, a firm friend of the Corsican hero's, had been the introducer.

---

[1] "Archivio di Stato," mazzi 19–21.

At these receptions, added Ageno, a curious ceremony was gone through. A servant, before introducing the visitors into Paoli's study, was accustomed to open a cupboard, to show a loose coat pierced with bullets, which he would tell the admiring guests was the one the general had worn in his last battle against the French, and for this sight a gratuity was expected to go towards a vague "Corsican fund."

On the 3rd of July in the following year, another letter from Ageno informs us that Pasquale Paoli's pension was increased, and that he now got at least two thousand pounds a year; that he had exchanged visits with the ambassadors of Moscow, Denmark, and Prussia, and that a few days before he had had a conversation with a man of the highest sphere, and said that he had not come to Great Britain as a "Pretender" to the crown of Corsica, and much less to solicit aid for carrying on war in that island. But still "if England wanted him he was always ready."

On the 4th of October, 1771, Ageno writes that "Paoli is busy exciting the English against the French by saying that with the possession of Corsica all the best ports and all the commerce of the Mediterranean will pass into the hands of France."

At length the desire of Paoli's heart was brought about in 1778, and England was at war with France; but far from regarding Corsican interests, the objects of England lay elsewhere, and, terribly chagrined, Pasquale Paoli was constrained to relinquish all hopes from the side of England.

Contrary to the treaty he had signed, Pasquale repaired to Corsica, and put himself under the French flag, on the 3rd of April, 1790. From here he shortly afterwards proceeded to Paris, and there was received, as he had been in England twenty years before. From the Genoese ambassador to the court of France,[1] we learn that the Corsican general courted the French king much as he had done George III., and was

[1] "Archivio di Stato," mazzo 86.

received with open arms by both the sovereign and his consort, being anxious to make use of him in quelling the disturbances in Corsica.

On the 12th of April, 1790, the king wrote to Pasquale expressing his wish to see him restored to his country, and asserting how great his confidence in him was. But Paoli got no pension in France, and at length, disgusted with empty promises, and seeing the clouds which were gathering round, he again crossed the channel, and repaired to London, where an opening at length occurred for action in his native country.

In 1793-4, Pasquale was again head of affairs in Corsica, for England had despatched Admiral Hood into the Mediterranean, to operate, in conjunction with the king of Sardinia, against the French. In Genoa, the English consul, Drake, backed up by the presence of the English fleet, tried to induce the Ligurians to join the allegiance.[1] Meanwhile, Corsica was occupied, and a constitutional monarchy arranged therein between Paoli and the English, by which the island recognized George III. as sovereign, Hood as admiral, Elliot as minister, and Pasquale Paoli as generalissimo, and, by these, war was declared against Genoa.

Then it was that Paoli's vindictive nature more than ever demonstrated itself. All Genoese prisoners were to be treated as slaves, and put to work in the fields ; all booty, and everything Genoese, was to be divided amongst the Corsicans. A reward of one hundred scudi was to be paid for each Genoese slave that was taken, and a zecchino for each Genoese head. And when the Corsicans did get a Genoese prisoner into their hands, they treated him even worse than a slave.

The remonstrances, however, of the Ligurian Republic were at length heard in London ; the siege of Genoa was raised, and the independence of Corsica was recognized under English protection, whilst the inhuman cruelty of Paoli against the

---

[1] *Vide* ch. xviii.

Genoese, in contravention of all laws of nations, was to be put a stop to, and the prisoners were restored to their liberty and their homes.

No eulogist of the Corsican hero can attempt to palliate this life-long grudge against Genoa, and his cruelty towards everything Ligurian, at a time when the Republic was in no way harming the Corsicans, and a quarter of a century after she had ceased to have any hand in Corsican affairs. It was well for the Corsicans that William Pitt kept this wild son of theirs quiet in England for so long a time by holding out hopes which he never intended to fulfil; far better were these islanders under the control of France than in the power of a man who scrupled not at any means by which he could arrive at the ends he desired. Well it was for romance that the glamour which hung over his name was not dispelled, that at home and abroad he was considered the Corsican Washington, and that his real colours did not show themselves until they were in a measure shrouded by the British flag, on which they brought but little honour.

It was to a Corsican general, the offspring of a brave old Corsican family, who had fought for their country's liberty for centuries, that Corsica owed her final annexation to France. Napoleon's name and fame in 1796 gathered all Corsican exiles around his standard, and, on the departure of the English from the island, Corsica was finally written on the map of France.

Before leaving the subject of Corsica, allusion must be made to the extraordinary history of one, Count Guiseppe Gorani, a Milanese by birth. A most eccentric character was this count; by turns a soldier, a politician, a sectarian, and an advocate of Roman Catholicism; he was an ardent freemason, and a member of most of the secret societies of which Europe was full.

But his one ruling passion, a passion which made him the laughing stock of Europe, was his wish to wear a crown. He came of a good Piedmontese family, and his mother, in his boyhood, told him stories of how an ancestor, in fabulous days, had once been king of Scotland, the consequence of which was that young Gorani sighed bitterly for a diadem. Amongst his friends he was regarded as almost a maniac, and was called the second Cagliostro ; but maniac or not, Gorani had read and heard of the ease with which Theodor von Neu-hoff had placed the brazen crown of Corsica on his head, and he determined to follow in his steps.

Perhaps Gorani's plans and schemes would have sunk into oblivion had he not carefully written his autobiography, and thereby made known his ambitious projects to the world. Gorani served in the Seven Years' War, and was offered the command of a regiment by Frederic of Prussia. He served under the Emperor of Russia, and was offered a brevet rank by him ; but he sighed for greater things, and on the 6th of March, 1764, he found himself at Genoa, ready to sail for Corsica and reconnoitre his future field of action.

Pasquale Paoli was then in command of the centre of the island, and to his good government and excellent legislation Gorani gives ample testimony in his autobiography ; but notwithstanding this, he wished to supplant him, and establish on the wretched island the Utopia of a maniac. By way of example we may state that he proposed to dress up twenty thousand women as Amazons, who should brandish torches, and give to a small handful of men the semblance of a vast host.

Having conquered and established himself in Corsica, he next proposed to conquer Genoa, and to remove the nobles and rich citizens to his island monarchy, after which Sardinia and Elba, together with other islands in the Mediterranean, were to be added to his insular dominions.

For such schemes, however, he wanted plenty of money and an army, so he betook himself to Constantinople, and laid his projects before the sultan, who was, however, too busy with his own affairs to think of establishing a dependency in Corsica and Genoa. He then planned a visit to Tunis, Angiers, and Morocco, but a Ligurian merchant offered him a gratuitous passage to Genoa, which he was constrained to accept, reduced as he was to great penury.

Bent still on ambitious fantasies, he visited Marseilles and Madrid, where he was detained for a while by love affairs, but eventually he buried himself in the wilds of Africa, vainly seeking to arouse a kindred ardour in the hearts of the Bey of Algiers and the Emperor of Morocco.

After fruitless wanderings and fruitless solicitations at barbarian courts, Gorani at length returned to Europe, and left the field of politics for that of literature—luckily for the Corsicans, for the first of a numerous list of works he published was entitled "The True Despotism,"[1] in which he propounded a plan for monarchical government, stating that the real object of a sovereign was to render himself a despot, and that reigning by will was infinitely superior to reigning in accordance with written laws.

[1] "Il vero despotismo," by Conte G. Gorani, Genève, 1770.

CHAPTER XVI.

THE BEGINNING OF THE END.

IT was a day of great rejoicing in Genoa—a day of flags, processions, and brilliant costumes—when the senate, in accordance with a solemn decree enacted a short time previously, handed over the Republic to the Madonna, and accepted her as the legitimate sovereign queen of Liguria. Finding the uselessness of appeal to all earthly monarchs, dukes of Milan and kings of France to boot, for warding off conspiracies, plagues, and famines, the somewhat superstitious lawgivers of Genoa hoped that by making of themselves a free gift to the Queen of Heaven, they would in return obtain immunity from the ills to which men, and Genoese in particular, were heirs.

On the 25th of March, 1636, over the tower of the public palace, and from the mainmast of the captain's galley, floated the flag of the Republic, and on it was depicted the Madonna, wearing a regal crown. Moreover, in the cathedral, which was hung with flowing tapestries, to the sound of lovely music, the Cardinal Giovanni Domenico Spinola celebrated a high mass before the assembled multitude. Then stepped forth the doge, Francesco Brignole, and in a golden basin presented the golden sceptre, the regal crown, the keys, and every symbol of full dominion, to his eminence, who placed them upon the altar, above which was suspended in mid-air a statue of the newly-elected queen, amidst a crown of angels. And thus was the gift solemnized, and the public chancellor proclaimed the fact aloud to the populace.

As the queen's vicegerent on earth the doge was to have a mantle of royal purple, and on state occasions was to wear a royal diadem. The Republic was to be termed henceforth "the most serene," and the public council hall was to be re-christened "the royal palace."

So much for the Genoese and their new *régime*. They enjoyed themselves immensely for a few days with *feux-de-joie*, illuminations and processions ; workmen were busily employed in casting iron crowns for the Madonnas, which were placed at every available point about the town ; women adopted a new form of dress which befitted the subjects of so saintly a queen—long thin veils of muslin, which floated behind them like cherubs' wings, a style of dress which even now is greatly in vogue amongst the Genoese, and is called the "pezzotto," and which the present Queen of Italy adopts when on a visit to Genoa, out of compliment to the national tastes.

But this self-assumption of royal state by a decrepit republic fast approaching its fall, was not pleasing to the German emperor and his vague seignioral rights. In vain the government sent Geronimo Rodino to represent that the change was only consistent with the dignity of those who ruled over Corsica, and had claims, though now long forgotten, over Cyprus, and numerous Eastern towns now in Turkish hands. The emperor was inexorable, and refused to recognize the royal state, he refused to speak of the Republic as most serene, and positively denied the doge's right to a royal mantle and a crown.

But the emperor Ferdinand III. was in difficulties ; the electors of the empire were troublesome ; and by a judicious advance of three hundred thousand florins, Rodino obtained leave for his country to play with their royal baubles ; and on the 2nd of September, 1641, at the Diet of Ratisbon, Ferdinand III. publicly declared the Republic to be most serene, and the doge was publicly crowned in the church of

S. Caterina ; and on the Genoese coins was placed a figure
of their queen surrounded by a starry halo.

The fact that the doge was crowned in S. Caterina instead
of the cathedral is but a fitting sequel to this royal farce ; for

CHIEF DOOR OF THE CATHEDRAL.

the archbishop had grown jealous of the doge and the
authority he had assumed as the queen's representative. So
he shut the cathedral doors against him ; the statue of the
Madonna was removed elsewhere, and for several years,
whenever a public procession was held, the doge and arch-

bishop respectively took different rounds, each deeming that his was the most acceptable and most orthodox homage to the phantom queen. It was not till 1652 that the difference was adjusted, when a new bronze statue was put up in the cathedral, at which ceremony the quarrel between Church and State was healed by the presence of both.

In warding off conspiracies the newly-elected queen was of little avail. Scarcely had the doge grown accustomed to his royal crown and mantle, than an outburst of a dangerous nature nearly placed the Republic in the hands of a more tangible monarch, in the shape of the king of France. Gian Paolo Balbi and Stefano Raggio hated the old nobility, and took advantage of the general dislike to the appointment of six state inquisitors, whom the senate had thought fit to elect to look into peoples' private affairs too closely after the Vacchero's conspiracy.[1]

These two conspirators had secret intercourse with Mazarin in France, and got together plenty of discontent at home. But, thanks to their vigilance, the senate discovered the plot. Raggio was captured and condemned to death, and his family was banished. By concealing a penknife in a favourite crucifix, Raggio's wife managed to convey to him the means of destroying himself, and hence of avoiding public ignominy. Balbi, on the other hand, managed to escape. But Balbi's relations had no idea of being punished for his delinquencies; so they offered twenty-four thousand francs for his head, and ten thousand to any one who would produce him alive. Thus the stone of infamy erected to the conspirator's memory was removed by order of the senate out of consideration for the feelings of his rich kinsmen. Raggio, however, still figures in Genoa on the base of the people's tower. Further, to evince their disgust at their relative's conspiracy, the family of Balbi contrived to execute a problem with which to puzzle the heads of future generations. There was, and is still, a fine picture of

---

[1] *Vide* ch. xiv.

the conspirator on horseback in the Palazzo Balbi, by Van-dyke. His relatives forthwith cut from out of it the head of the delinquent, and asked Velasquez, who then chanced to be in Genoa, to paint another in its place; so that the picture-lover of to-day marvels to see the head of Philip IV. of Spain gracefully reposing on the shoulders of a Vandyke figure.

The newly elected queen of Genoa was about as successful in warding off plagues and pestilences as she was in checking conspiracies, for in 1656-57, a terrible pestilence counted its victims by tens of thousands. Of ninety thousand souls in Genoa before the outbreak, but ten thousand remained when it ceased; and of those who had fled, but thirty thousand were found to return to their homes at the close of the year 1657.[1]

This terrible scourge, however, brought forth much that was brave in the Ligurian nature. Bands of men lived, as it were, buried amongst the putrid bodies of the dead and dying, healing and relieving the distressed. Amongst these heroes, stands forth conspicuously the senator, Raggio, who, firm to his post, underwent incredible fatigues. He took his food whilst walking, and hardly allowed himself any rest. He superintended the removal of corpses, he purified the infected air with perfumes, and checked as far as within him lay the grossness and ribaldry which follows in the train of pestilence. Through his influence the government made wise regulations, and on the whole a more healthy state of discipline reigned in Genoa than in other plague-stricken cities of this period, mainly through his instrumentality.

Worn out by fatigues and anxiety, he fell a sacrifice to the pestilence just as the worst was over and men were beginning to look towards a reprieve from their miseries. The name of Raggio, by the deeds of this brave citizen, deserved to be freed from the stone of infamy, by which Stefano Raggio, the conspirator, was known to posterity.

[1] " Accinelli compendio della storia di Genova."

But of these two Genoese cousins who appeared so near to one another on the pages of history, the patriot was forgotten and the villain's memory alone perpetuated.

Again does the history of Genoa prove the growing development and the growing ambition of the house of Savoy, each succeeding prince of which seemed to look upon it as a matter of duty that he should add fresh territory to his ancestral domain. Charles Emmanuel II. was for some years under the guidance of his mother, a French princess, and was ever ready to lend an ear to disaffected Genoese.

His reign was signalized by his cruel, relentless war against the Waldenses, and by an attack on Genoa, in 1673, which nearly made him master of the Ligurian capital. How far he was interested in the conspiracy of Balbi does not appear, but doubtless he had something to say to it. The acquisition of Nice, instead of satisfying, rather added to the cupidity of the dukes, and the fact of getting their objects of commerce straight from the Mediterranean, even though by difficult mountain roads, taught them how advantageous it would be if they could establish a more direct communication by some of the valleys which lead down from the plain of Lombardy to the Ligurian sea.

In those days, one Raffaelle della Torre, a Genoese of old and illustrious family, was the duke's counsellor and adviser. He was of an unquiet and restless disposition, he had committed a murder, he had lived an almost piratical life at sea, and was hence exiled from his country, which fact found him a ready asylum with the Duke of Savoy. Della Torre represented to the duke that his adherents within the city were not a few, that if an attack was made simultaneously from the side of Savona and the Bisagno valley, he could ensure a goodly array of followers, who would gladly open the gates to the Savoyards.

But Raffaelle della Torre counted without his host ; none but a band of ruffians could he get together outside the walls, and those to whom he communicated his designs within the city went straight to the senate, and told how the attack was to be made during the festival of St. John the Baptist, how the prisons were to be opened and the malefactors released, how the Bank of St. George was to be sacked, and how the city was to be turned upside down.

The senate were aghast, the people terrified, but all came bravely forward with plate and jewels ; monasteries and convents disgorged their wealth, and when Raffaelle della Torre arrived in the Val di Bisagno, he found no news of his supposed adherents, but instead an energetic and effective defence to oppose him. He forthwith took flight for Turin, and the duke, with ignominious haste, withdrew his forces from the Republic's territories.

Thus ended this attempt.· Side by side with Stefano Raggio's stone of infamy on the people's tower, we can now read how Raffaelle della Torre was voted a most abandoned reprobate, and here posted up for everlasting shame. However, in his exile he managed notwithstanding to enjoy life. Though banished from the state of Savoy, he found an asylum in Paris, where he spent his days trying to encompass Louis XIV., and urge him on to attack Genoa. From thence he went to Holland, where he amused the Dutch with a magnificence and display unknown to those phlegmatic merchants. He even had a hand in their government for a while, and all went well for him as long as his lavishness and his money lasted; but when this was over he was driven to lead a dissolute and wandering life, until, in 1681, he was killed at Venice by a priest in a masquerade. In Genoa, his immediate family were excluded from holding any public office, and his brother, Pasquale della Torre, died under the torturer's lash without revealing a word.

Very piteous are the ensuing pages of Genoa's history ; the story of the heartless attack made upon the weak Republic by the "grand monarque," Louis XIV. of France, is painfully illustrative of Genoa's weakness, of her departed glory, and of the unscrupulous conduct of the French king towards a weaker vessel. The seeds of this policy, sown for a long term of years, at length bore fruit in 1684. Years before this, King Louis had exclaimed that Genoa ought to be considered as the port of Italy, and that if he could possess himself of her, he would then have the keys and be the depository of peace and war in this fair country, and that it was the axiom which Philip II. of Spain had adhered to, who never ceased to blame his imperial father for not subjugating her when he could.

With views such as these revolving in the mind of a monarch, whose will was immutable, and whose ambition knew no bounds, it is hardly to be wondered that Genoa suffered, and well nigh lost her liberty. Along the Riviera and in the east Louis managed to pick various little quarrels with the Ligurians, his "dearest and good friends," as he would term them. If the Genoese sent an embassy to ask for some of the old commercial liberties they had enjoyed in the Turkish empire, the French ambassador was always ready to oppose them. If a Genoese ship neglected some salute to a French ship, which Louis was determined to exact, an embassy of remonstrance would be sent with insulting messages to Genoa. In 1679, the French monarch went so far as to order some bombs to be thrown into Sampierd'arena, close to Genoa, seized some Genoese ships at San Remo, and would hear of no reprisals.

At the same time the French minister in Liguria, M. de St. Olon, was busy totting up statistics in Genoa about défences, and occasionally whetting his master's appetite for conquest by trumped up stories of bad government and internal discord ; moreover, at the court of France were the ever insinuating Fieschi exiles, clamouring for a restoration of property and power, which Gian Luigi's conspiracy had forfeited.

Thus in the first place was Louis' ambition aroused, and

secondly, his *amour propre* was hurt by Genoa's firm adherence to the cause of Charles II. of Spain. At length, in 1683, an opportunity, if so it can be called, presented itself for an open rupture. Genoa had manned a fleet of four ships to go against the Algerine pirates. St. Olon wrote word to Louis that they were destined to assist the Spanish against the French, and accompanied the statement with a tempting programme for ruining the Republic's commerce, and for making objectionable demands, namely for a salt depôt at Savona, for disarming the aforesaid ships, and for restitution of the Fieschi property, and adding *par parenthése* that "Genoa and Marseilles under the sole standard of the lilies would give laws to Cadiz and the Dardanelles, would reduce Barbary to a compulsory respect, and would make even the Sultan tremble in his seraglio at Constantinople."

This was just one of the savoury morsels the grand monarch could not resist, so he forthwith sent an ambassador to Genoa with the following demands: (1) Genoa must abandon her Spanish allies, and join the side of France. (2) Genoese ships must salute the French standard according as Louis himself wished. (3) Magazines of salt must be established at Savona. (4) Entire restoration of the Fieschi property.

Such concessions as these Genoa felt would be tantamount to entire loss of liberty; and so the senate thought, and thus they bravely prepared themselves for a defence. But it was with woeful misgivings at their own impotence that they beheld the French fleet of one hundred and sixty sail, with 8000 soldiers on board, approaching their city to carry out the dictates of the French potentate.

After four days of heavy bombardment, during which the stately palaces of Genoa crumbled like sand hills before a winter's torrent, and during which the government was removed to the Albergo dei Poveri to be out of reach of the terrible scourge, the Marquis Seignelais, the French admiral, sent a herald to the stricken town, demanding in addition to the above claim, sixty thousand francs as a war indemnity, and four senators to be sent to Versailles to crave for pardon. But the senators bravely responded to this overpowering demand that they had done nothing to merit so terrible a treatment, and death amongst the ruins of their city would be sweeter to them than to submit.

The result of this refusal of the proffered terms was a perfect deluge of fire on the heads of the devoted Genoese; the scared inhabitants fled in all directions from the falling houses. On the 17th and 18th of May, 1684, Seignelais ceased not to pour his rain of fire upon them until every bomb was expended, and little else but ruin left in Genoa. Thirteen thousand three hundred bombs, they say, fell in those few days with their message of death into the city. Some of them, preserved as mementos of that awful time, are still kept in the church of S. Maria di Castello, and outside S. Silvestro, whilst a fresco representing the trembling monks imploring the Virgin's aid adorn the walls of the former temple.

It is not to be wondered at that the inhabitants thus belaboured from without fell into an excess of dread. It was rumoured amongst them that a huge infernal machine was in course of construction, which would destroy the town and its inhabitants at one blow; great chains and huge blocks of wood were thrown across the harbour to prevent its entry, and when the French fleet, having exhausted their ammunition, set sail, their fears were in no way allayed. They thought they had departed, merely to reach a place of safety before the awful explosion. And terrible was the scene which ensued in the streets and *piazze*. Hither and thither rushed wildly about men, women, and children in an agony of dread; they wrung their hands as if their last hour had come; they implored heaven to save their city from becoming a second Sodom.

But the outpourings of brimstone and fire, or whatever

their vivid imaginations conjured up, came not. Hour after hour passed away and fear gave place to fury, so that scarcely could the populace be restrained from massacring the French prisoners within their walls. For two raids made by the French on the coast had not been so effectual as the bombardment, and had been repulsed with loss, and many prisoners found their way into Genoese jails. At length, however, quiet was restored, and in the more sober atmosphere of the council hall the senators looked at their position with anything but an easy mind.

The French had gone ; only, however, to return with more exorbitant demands, and a large supply of bombs ; and in addition to this, it was rumoured that Louis was preparing an army to send by way of Turin ; so the senate wisely determined that surrender to the French demands would be preferable to entire annihilation, since in every direction the arms of the grand monarch were successful. Germany was busy fighting with the Turks in Hungary, no assistance could be hoped from England under the Sunderland and Arlington administration, and Spain was reduced to about the same pitch of helplessness as Genoa.

In this strait the senate determined to have recourse to Pope Innocent XI., by whose instrumentality a wretched pretence at a peace was patched up on the 2nd of February, 1685, by which the four ships were to be dismantled, the Spanish cause was to be abandoned, and one hundred thousand scudi were to be paid to Count Fieschi, besides a large war indemnity, and the doge was to proceed to Versailles to make his humble apology to the victorious monarch.

Thus was the Ligurian Republic humbled to the lowest depths ; yet if she were humbled, let her be proud that she checked the grand monarch in at least one of his ambitious schemes. By exhausting on Genoa the French bombs, Louis was prevented from carrying out his plan of seizing Milan, by which his projects of aggrandizement in Italy would have been complete. The League of Augsburg could not have taken place; and thus did Genoa earn for herself the credit of putting one spoke in the wheel of decadence which rolled the proud monarch from the summit of his overweening ambition.

The visit of the doge, Francesco Maria Lecaro, his attendant nobles, and his suite of one hundred persons to Versailles, is one of the most humiliating episodes in Genoese history, at the same time partaking strongly of the ludicrous and bringing out in a high degree Louis XIV.'s great delight in publicly trampling upon a fallen foe. No Roman emperor in his triumphal entry with fallen monarchs in his train, ever gloated more in ignominious exactions than Louis XIV.; and the poor doge, who thus uneasily wore his country's newly acquired crown, felt the full bitterness of the stinging, biting irony with which Louis received him and *fêted* him, whilst the courtiers looked on at the deputation of Genoese much as we now should contemplate the fallen hero of the Zulu war and his scantily clad followers.

To meet his guests Louis despatched his own carriages, whilst three of the doge's followed, richly adorned with the republican arms, and surmounted by that royal crown, the Madonna's own, thus brought captive to the feet of the French monarch. Eight grey horses conveyed the doge in his royal mantle to Versailles, followed by eighteen other carriages for his attendants, and thus did this *cortège* reach the entrance to the royal palace on the 15th of May, 1685, on the day appointed for the audience.

The marshal, Duc de Duras, dressed in black out of compliment to the Italian nobles and their customary garb, greeted the doge and led him into the reception-hall, where sat Louis on a silver throne, with all the princes of the kingdom around him. On seeing the doge approach, Louis left his throne hat in hand, and hurried forward to give him a royal embrace. They met and saluted, and then each re-

covered his head, and both stood together on the first step of
the throne, whilst the doge poured forth his story in fulsome
words of abject humility.

Louis then regretted that such a misfortune should have
befallen Genoa, begged the doge to reassure himself, and after
a little commonplace conversation whilst both remained standing, Louis ordered his master of the ceremonies to conduct the
doge to a splendid banquet, to drown his woes in the best
that the royal *chef* could offer him.   The doge and senators
all sat at one table, the former dressed in a violet-coloured
robe, whilst many ladies of the court came in to look at the
Genoese as they ate, bestowing all their wiles on the poor
old man, heaping up his plate with the most *recherché*
viands, until at length he had fain give way to these female
attacks on his internal economy, as his country had cowered
before the monarch's bombs.

During dinner Louis talked much to the doge, and was
pleased to express an opinion that the Genoese had the air
of being well conducted, and of great spirit ; moreover, that
he had the air and bearing of a prince, and was worthy of the
Republic which he represented.   After dinner the king took
him for a walk in the grounds, and had some wonderful
waterwork displays for his benefit in the royal gardens ; he
showed him his stables, his menagerie, and his park, and then
asked his guest what surprised him most of all he saw.   " To
see myself here," sighed the doge.   And on the following
day, laden with presents, he set off for his humbled bleeding
country, where his return was heralded with no display.   The
returned wanderers entered the city by night, and no man
spoke of the bitter humiliation which had befallen one of
Italy's proudest and richest towns.   In silence they mourned
the wreck of their temples and their palaces, and in silence
amidst the din of European wars did Genoa quietly recoup
her fallen fortunes.

Though her commercial enterprise was stagnant, though

she had been humbled at the feet of France, great wealth was still to be found in the coffers of the nobles and in the Bank of St. George. Colossal proofs of riches and private generosity about this period are still left in the city. The Albergo dei Poveri, a vast workhouse built on the slopes of Carbonara, was the offspring of this century, and is adorned with frescoes without and statues of the beneficent within, who founded and endowed it.

The gigantic edifice of the Carignano church was completed about this time by members of the Sauli family. The story runs that Bendinelli Sauli years before had a bitter quarrel with one of the Fieschi on this wise. Sauli had no church of his own, and was in the habit of attending mass at the Fieschi's church of Vialata. One day mass was held half an hour earlier than usual, and Sauli to his disgust arrived too late. To his remonstrances Fieschi replied that every gentleman should have a church of his own. So Bendinelli Sauli determined there and then to build himself the most magnificent basilica that the debased Renaissance art could invent, and future generations saw the completion of that colossal, lobster-like edifice, which to-day forms the most conspicuous object in Genoa.

To another member of this family, a descendant of Bendinelli's, the Genoese are indebted for the magnificent bridge which spans the valley between the hills of Sarzano and Carignano. Seeing the peasants with their heavy burdens toiling down the slopes of one hill and up the other towards his palace, Stefano Sauli, in a generous moment, determined to build them this bridge, which was concluded with immense expense and labour in 1724. Of all the many striking views in Genoa, perhaps none equals the one from this bridge. One looks down into the dim dark streets, all alive with the bustling to and fro of Genoa's busiest inhabitants, whilst the clear waters of the Mediterranean lead the glittering vision on to the distant snowy peaks of the Nice mountains, whilst all around nestle churches and towers beneath the slopes of Genoa's own especial fort-capped Apennines. Such a panorama as this few cities of the world can disgorge as it were from her very centre. So great has been the awe-inspiring qualities of this view, with its yawning abyss beneath, that it has been chosen by many Ligurian citizens weary of this life as a fitting place for suicide, and so numerous did these self-sought deaths become, that the Sauli family were constrained to add to their generosity by placing lofty railings all along, to check the avidity of those who would thus encompass their own end.

Manufacture in Genoa seems still to have been active, even though her colonies and her merchandize had in a great measure departed from her. Paper and velvet were the chief commodities in which she excelled, so much so that, in 1712, men were sent from Paris to gain information on the manufacture of the former, the French minister writing to know "if, in case of need, they could persuade some skilful workmen to come and work in France." And in 1742, a Frenchman, M. Vaucauson, was in Genoa, "to see the manufacture of damask and velvet, and above all, the irons for cutting velvet, of which we have not the secret in France."

Meanwhile, the course of events passed sluggishly on, and but little arose to disturb the Ligurian equanimity for some decades. Corsican troubles grew worse and worse, as the life blood of her mistress was fast ebbing away. But prior to the final overthrow of Genoa's independence, another sharp fierce struggle was to arouse the exhausted spirit of the Republic. As in the seventeenth century the outcome of all her intercourse with the outer world centres in the invasion of Louis XIV., so in the eighteenth century does the interest of her intercourse with European politics centre in the Austrian invasion of 1746.

It is one of those curious outbursts of stagnant liberty which we now have before us, which, by its fierce and successful resistance to apparently overwhelming odds, turned the channel of events in Europe, which were fast threatening to overthrow the balance of power established by the Peace of Utrecht; and this time it was from Austria that the danger came, and not from the side of France. The victorious arms of Maria Theresa had reduced Italy, and were, together with their Sardinian ally, threatening France from the side of Provence. Humbled, crushed Genoa, by a monstrous effort, suddenly checked this tide of victory and saved France, threatened as she was by the Huguenots from within, and by the Austrians from without.

At the battle of Piacenza, fought on the 16th of June, 1746, the French were defeated, and obliged to abandon the approaches to Genoa by Serravalle and Novi. It was in vain the Genoese implored not to be abandoned in this extremity· The French sailed away from the Ligurian coast, and no sooner were they gone than the Austrians occupied all the posts of strength around Genoa, and were in a position to dictate what terms they pleased to the Ligurian capital.

The vanguard of the Austrians, under General Braun, reached Sampierd'arena on the 14th of September, and established their quarters in the empty bed of the Polcevera river. Messages of anything but a peaceful nature passed between him and the senate. However, at night a fearful storm came on in the mountains, and the bed of the river from being but a trickling rivulet became a roaring torrent. Advised of their danger by an old woman, the Austrians hurried to the bank, but with the loss of one thousand men, who were carried out to sea and drowned, and with the loss of nearly all their tents, horses, and provisions. Thus did fortune smile on the Genoese from the very outset.

Next day the main body of the besieging army arrived in the neighbourhood of Genoa, under General Botta-Adorno. To him, as to a fellow-citizen, for his father had been Genoese, the senate sent a supplicating appeal, but he was inexorable;

he replied, that "he looked upon Genoa as an enemy, and intended to treat her as such; that the gates must be put into his hands, that the doge and six senators must go to Vienna to crave pardon for their sins," and that the Republic must disburse a sum of money, amounting to fifteen thousand pounds, besides contributing to the war—and twenty-four hours were given them for their answer.

Terrified and dismayed, the senate called a council of war; they deliberated that the city was unequal to the defence, that resistance would be a folly, and thus the fatal despatch was sent, accepting most humbly Botta's demands.

No sooner had he entered the gates than he announced that his imperial mistress, in her benign clemency, would be content with the moderate sum of eight hundred thousand pounds of our money, to be paid by three instalments, one in forty-eight hours, another in eight days, and the third in fifteen, intimating gently that in default of payment fire and sword would be the penalty. Indescribable was the terror and astonishment which this exorbitant demand created in Genoa; in vain did they protest that to disgorge so large a sum would ruin their bank, their town, and their credit. "You will have your eyes left to weep with," the Austrian general savagely replied; but, as the result will show, they had still hearts and arms left to them with which to burst asunder the iron chain in which the Republic was entangled.

Thus driven by necessity, the senate determined to attack the resources of the Bank of St. George, and towards the disbursement of the first instalment the bank came bravely to the fore, and with heavy hearts the Genoese beheld their golden florins borne away to the Austrian head-quarters, exasperated, moreover, to a pitch of frenzy by the heartless outrages of the soldiery, billeted amongst the houses, on all that was dear to them at home.

Meanwhile, the Duke of Savoy was pursuing his attack on Provence, but owing to the badness of the roads he was

unable to convey his artillery as fast as he could wish, so he
wrote to his German allies in Genoa, to send by sea all the
Genoese artillery they could lay hands on. And forthwith the
Austrians gave orders that the cannons and artillery from the
arsenal should be removed to the lighthouse, to be thence
embarked for Provence. At the same time the second instalment was demanded, amidst threats of fire and sword, and
amidst groans and lamentations as before.

In all these outbursts of exasperation it · was from the
people and artizan class that the greatest indignation arose, as
they stood sullenly by, whilst their wealth and their artillery
were being removed under their very eyes, to do service
in a hated cause ; and it wanted but a small spark to kindle
this flame of indignation into an open opposition, and this
was not long in being afforded them through the brutal
violence of the Austrian soldiery.

On the 5th of December, a large piece of ammunition
which was being dragged towards the lighthouse, stuck fast
by the way, and the Austrians, unable to move it by themselves, compelled some of the passers-by, with blows and hard
words, to assist them. This was the spark required, and soon
a wild shout of rage and revenge went up from amongst the
people. A youth, Gian Battista Berasco by name, who bore
the sobriquet of Balila, seventeen years of age, picked up a
huge stone, hurled it with fatal effect at a soldier who was
striking him, and turning to his comrades, exclaimed, " *O che
l'inse ?* " which in the powerful Genoese dialect meant, " Why
don't we begin?" At this exhortation a terrible scene took
place ; men, women, and children rushed with stones on the
Austrians, who, terrified at the unexpected onset, fled pre-
cipitately.

Thus did the stream of vengeance soon swell into a mighty
torrent. Thousands of brave citizens rushed wildly about the
town crying, " *Viva Maria, our Queen ! to arms ! to arms !* "
It was midnight when they reached the royal palace, where

the senators sat in great alarm ; they clamoured for arms to be distributed amongst them ; but this spirit of resistance did not infuse itself into the more coolly-judging rulers of Genoa. They trembled for the results of an attack on the Austrians ; they shut the doors of the palace, they redoubled the guards, and bid the people return peacefully to their homes.

On the morrow, at the break of day, a hundred Austrian grenadiers entered the gate of S. Tommaso with fixed bayonets, but they had not proceeded far when from the roofs and windows were showered down upon them such a volley of stones that they were obliged to retreat.   With courage renewed by their success, the people again flocked to the palace to demand arms, again to be refused ; they then rushed wildly through the streets, broke open any shops or houses where they thought arms and ammunition could be obtained, and thus equipped, they determined to resist the Austrian attack to the death.

Up one of the steepest of Genoa's steep alleys, un-assisted by anything but their own strength, men, women, and children, dragged enormous pieces of artillery to a spot commanding the gate of S. Tommaso, which was held by the Austrians, and from this vantage ground, from whence the most timid could never have anticipated an attack from heavy artillery, considering the approach to it was as sloping as the roof of a house, the Genoese showered down in right good earnest on their foes messages of hatred and of revenge.

Curious it must have been to see the people thus leading an attack on their own account, whilst the senators were on their side doing all they could to restrain their ardour, by opposing the robbery of arms, and by setting up gallows in the squares on which to suspend those who might disobey their orders.

It was in vain that Pope Benedict XIII., tried to pour oil on the troubled waters, that Prince D'Oria, trembling for his city, and perhaps more so for his own property around which the war was raging, tried to induce Botta to come to more reasonable terms ; but to the entreaties even of his own brother for their paternal country the Austrian general turned a deaf ear, and thus for the insurgents the only hope of life was to proceed as they had begun.

On the eighth day after the rising, Botta at length had collected all his forces together for a general assault on the city on all sides. The inhabitants of the Bisagno, in this emergency came to the assistance of their fellow countrymen, and from the height above the valley, a fire was poured down on the approaching Austrians. A band of fifty of the enemy were assembled in an inn, which the Genoese determined to attack ; during the deliberation, a boy of eleven, Pittamuli by name, came forward, seized a pistol and a lighted torch, shouting "Leave it to me." He advanced boldly, shot dead the first Austrian who opposed him, and set fire to the building. In this manner did the Genoese on the Bisagno side receive their foes, and in this manner did they conquer, and return home with prisoners, amidst great applause and rejoicing in the city.

Meanwhile, on the S. Tommaso side the attack was resisted with equal vigour, and when the regular Genoese soldiers were forced or persuaded to join the side of their fellow citizens, the resistance to Austria was effectually carried on. On the old church of the Hospitallers of St. John, where the Austrian stronghold was, the Genoese artillery showered down volley after volley, until within an hour they were forced to leave the building, which was falling around them on all sides. Then arose a cry, " To the gate of S. Tommaso," and with a fierce rush, heated by their success, the Genoese populace, soldiers and all, rushed pell-mell upon the Austrians and drove them inch by inch outside the city walls, until thoroughly disorganized and terrified the Austrians cried, " For the love of heaven no more fire, we are all Christians," and hurried in headlong flight to their fortress behind the lighthouse.

The fall of this place soon followed; Botta was forced to remove his quarters to Sampierd'arena, and the townsfolk were relieved from any immediate anxiety.

The "White Cross" was in those days a well-known inn in Genoa, and Giovanni Carlone was a well-known waiter therein, a leading spirit among the dregs of the population. He had taken an active part in the repulse of the Austrians, so he considered himself fully authorized to seize the keys of the gate of S. Tommaso, and with gory face and bare arms he hastened to the doge and council, and addressed the august rulers of Genoa in the following words:—" My lords, these are the keys that your serene lordships gave to our enemies; take better care of them for the future, since we with our life-blood have won them back for you."

To add to the universal rejoicing, it was discovered that only twelve Genoese were missing, whilst the Austrians had left behind them one thousand dead, and four thousand prisoners; and Botta, fearing a rising amongst the villages of the Polcevera valley, withdrew from the neighbourhood of Genoa into Lombardy.

But after this glorious and unexpected success, affairs within the city walls did not run so easily as could be wished, since there were two conflicting parties—the senate, abashed and ashamed of their pusillanimity, and the populace, who spared no pains to cast the same in their teeth. And now that all danger from without was removed, these two conflicting elements did not find it easy to amalgamate. The more affairs looked like a reconciliation, the more did the scum of the populace, urged on by their demagogues, become up-roarious. A policeman, a fishmonger, and a butcher formed the aristocratic triumvirate, whose sole aim was to subvert the existing order of things for their own ends. Possessed of ammunition, and followers who had just tasted blood, and who thirsted for more, they gave out that the time had come for chastising the nobles, to whose door must be laid the folly of ever admitting the Austrians, and giving them two of the demanded instalments of money.

Carrying with them artillery, they raised the cry, " To the palace! to the palace," where the senators sat in timid conclave as to what should be done. When all seemed lost to them, when it wanted but the word of command amongst the rebels to destroy the building and the assembled council, a noble Genoese patrician, Giacomo Lomellini by name, stepped forth before the people. He had been one of the few nobles who had assisted them against the Austrians, consequently his influence with them was great. Many were moved to pity at the sight of him, others said that it was but a ruse on the part of the nobles to gain time, and their leader gave orders that at once the cannon should be discharged at him, and thus clear from his path so dangerous an opponent.

With consummate courage and presence of mind, Lomellini stepped forward and stood before the cannon's mouth, exclaiming, "Be it far from you to damage this august building ; less heinous a crime would it be to lacerate these poor limbs of mine than to destroy the very bulwark of your country, and gladly shall I die that I may not witness so foul a crime." Hushed and awestruck by such noble presence the people gave way; their leaders cowered before this bravery; and by Lomellini's prompt and able conduct, the senators were saved, order was again restored, and the old *régime* continued.

In the following spring the Austrians advanced up the Polcevera valley almost to the gates of Genoa to try and avenge their disgrace ; but by this time the French had been able to take sufficient precautions that Genoa should not again fall into Austrian hands. On the 1st of May the Duc de Boufflers reached Genoa, and the succour that he brought was dispersed through the city ; but the Austrians advanced and nearly made good their position, as in the previous year ; and had not the Duke of Savoy seen fit to quarrel with his

2 B

German allies, Genoa would again have fallen under the Austrian yoke.

When the Austrians had taken their departure, the Duc de Boufflers was all powerful in Liguria, and as a saviour and deliverer, was idolized by the Genoese. Great was their grief when he shortly afterwards died of the small-pox. His funeral was a scene of national mourning, and so despondent were the people at his loss that the government saw fit to appoint certain persons to go round and harangue the people, and publicly console them by giving them hopes, that there were other equally great and good men in the world, who would help them in their emergencies. A fine tomb was erected to his memory in the French chapel of St. Louis in the Church of the Annunziata, and as a mark of special honour his descendants were allowed to quarter the Republic's arms.

The Duc de Richelieu succeeded him in command, who by frequent sallies at the head of his troops finally dislodged the Austrians from every post they had held in the confines of the Republic, and at the Peace of Aix-la-Chapelle everything was restored to Genoa which she had possessed before the war. Festivals were ordained, and processions of thanksgiving to the Queen of Heaven, who had vouchsafed thus bravely to assist her terrestrial subjects in Genoa.

To the young man Balila who had cast the first stone against the Austrians, some small remuneration was made. He was by trade a painter, and to compensate him for his bravery he was set up in a shop at the public expense, and died, in 1781, if not an opulent, at least a highly honoured citizen. To his memory was erected a statue in front of the Pamatone hospital, and a commemorative tablet inserted near the spot where he had cast his historical stone, and thereby encouraged his countrymen to free themselves from their oppressors.

Thus ended the terrible days of the Austrian invasion. It was indeed the beginning of the end for Genoa. During another half century the old constitution dragged on a weary shattered existence, like some tottering old man waiting but one more stroke entirely to paralyze his feeble frame. Her bank, the mainstay of the Republic, was fast losing its credit; the fearful drain of the two instalments paid to Austria, the enormous effort required to shake off the foreign yoke, all tended to impoverish her strength, which entirely succumbed to the devastating torrent of the French Revolution.

CHAPTER XVII.

ART AND ARTISTS IN LIGURIA.

OF the Ligurian school of art but little notice has been taken by the moths who for ever flutter around the brilliancy of Raphael and the more finished Italian schools. Perhaps it is because little originality blossomed forth in Genoa, and most of her artistic productions are but reflections of the greater artists ; yet it is from studying these bypaths of art that we arrive at a better knowledge of the unlimited benefit and of the wide extended influence which the great masters of the higher schools exercised over the tastes of the world at large.

As Raphael, through the person of his pupil Pierino del Vaga, worked a revolution in the almost extinct artistic feeling of Liguria, so did Rubens and Vandyke work the same revival in later years amongst a chaos of degenerate followers of the Roman school.

Moreover, in studying the works of her native painters we get an insight into the character of this mercantile Republic, and on the countless canvases of Ligurian artists, which still adorn her churches and her palaces, we see faithfully delineated characteristics for which Genoa is singled out and set apart from the rest of Italy.

It is characteristic of the Republic, who got her architectural designs from all quarters of the globe, who brought home from every seaport where her ships traded some relic of foreign art, that she should have a school of painters who

preferred following in the steps of others to originating anything for themselves.

It is characteristic of Genoa, that her rich mercantile
nobility, when they turned their attention to art, and to the
beautifying of their palaces and their monuments, should

DETAILS OF ARCHITECTURE IN THE CLOISTER OF S. ANDREA.

offer the contents of their long purses to artists of the first
order from Rome and Florence, since at home the profession
of art in all its branches was neglected and set aside for the
more profitable pursuits of commerce. In fact, Genoa was the
Manchester and Liverpool of Italy, and the taste for art in
this mediæval cottonopolis was correspondingly grand and

pompous; their fresco painters were paid by the yard rather than by merit. For example, Luca Cambiaso, the Genoese Raphael as he has been termed, gained for himself the credit of being one of the fastest painters then in existence; he wielded a brush in each hand at the same time with equal ease, and could execute in one hour what took others twelve.

This love of huge frescoes and great canvases displayed by the unappreciative *parvenus* of Genoa was the ruin of their school. Brilliant genius—for talent was not wanting—was spoilt by this rapidity of execution and consequent deficiency in colouring and want of careful arrangement of the subject.

Again, in Genoa painting was looked upon too much as a business. A father artist would bring up all his sons as artists, whether the talent existed or not; hence painting became a sort of monopoly in certain families, outside the precincts of which any lurking genius was sure to be wasted. A parent would vehemently oppose any taste for painting developed by a son as a waste of time, and thus many an incipient artist was checked in his career, and sent to earn a more substantial livelihood in his father's office.

Thus we have the Piola, De'Ferrari, and Castiglione families in Genoa, whose business was to execute frescoes and paintings to order; and to their studios a wealthy merchant sent as the recognized decorators of his palace. Hence the two great evils with which Genoese artists had to contend were, firstly, the temptation to execute an order too rapidly for an unappreciative employer, and secondly, the exclusive nature of the craft, which strove to confine a talent within the narrow limits of a guild.

It is to the earliest days of Genoese history that we have to look for the origin of this disastrous system of making painting more of a trade than of an accomplishment. For her earlier crusading wars, shields were painted, standards and ships were decorated; and thus, hand in hand with the ship-wrights, and with the makers of shields and bucklers, did the art of painting progress, and we find the art or guild of the painters early constituted into a body, with their own statutes and their own internal organization.

There is a rude specimen of early Genoese productions left to us on the title page of the manuscript of Caffaro, the old crusading annalist, dating from 1164. It is still to be seen in the library of the Paris university, and, as an example of any early Ligurian art, is almost unique; for their civil wars, which raged throughout their mediæval history, destroyed their palaces and their churches, and destroyed, too, the precious contents of incipient art.

Perhaps the first tangible artist who can be fixed upon as having originated in some degree a Ligurian school, is Ludovico Brea, of Nice, who painted along the Riviera about 1480. A good specimen of his work still adorns the church of S. Maria di Castello in Genoa. It is a picture representing the Calling of the Just, and is one vast conglomeration of well studied heads and neatly pencilled robes, rich both in colour and in design. Brea, and a certain Fazolo of Pavia, another wandering artist who found a home in Genoa about this period, fix the date of the first development of anything like native genius. Before this, many foreign artists had worked in the Ligurian capital from Siena, Pisa, and Germany; but Brea and Fazolo appear to have been the first to have led the Genoese to understand that they were capable of competing with their neighbours in works of art.

Fazolo, moreover, is a good instance of the parental artist who wished his cloak to descend on his offspring. He had a son, Bernardino, and two daughters, each married to young men whom Fazolo introduced into his studio. Thus did the father, his son, and two sons-in-law, work hard together in the same cause. Antonio da Semino, one of the sons-in-law, was, perhaps, the most brilliant executor of the quartette, and the one destined to hand down to posterity old Fazolo's heritage of art. He had two sons, Ottaviano and

Andrea, who were trained to handle the brush from infancy, and both, when old enough, were sent to Rome to profit by the divine works of Raphael ; and Ottaviano da Semino proved himself no mean disciple of this great master. For on his return to Genoa he painted a frieze in one of the D'Orian palaces, representing the Rape of the Sabines, with such success, that a great art critic on seeing it expressed his surprise that so wonderful a work of Raphael's existed in Genoa without his knowledge. Great was his amazement when his mistake was explained to him.

Ottaviano da Semino, though exceeding cunning with his brush, has left a name for untidiness and dirt scarce equalled in the annals of the *beaux arts.* Never was he known to wear anything save the most ragged and tattered garments. In fact, the possession of a good suit of clothes was a pain and grief to him. If he saw a hole in his stocking, he sought to mend the same by applying a dab of the necessary coloured paint to his leg, in preference to undergoing the agony of putting on a clean pair. This painter was the last scion of the house of Fazolo, and died in 1604.

This, however, has anticipated the great revival in art which was wrought in Genoa when Andrea D'Oria summoned Pierino del Vaga, the pupil of Raphael, and Montorsoli, the pupil of Michael Angelo, to beautify his palaces, and arrange his festive receptions on the most extravagant and artistic scale. This, in fact, is one of the great landmarks in the history of Ligurian art which raised the school from the depths of ignorance to being one of the best representative schools in Italy.

The calamities which threatened Rome after the sack of the eternal city by Cardinal de Bourbon, and the wealth which filled the pockets of the Genoese merchants, attracted many of the minor lights to the Ligurian capital ; and the impetus thus given to painting and the adornment of palaces, gave birth to all that Genoa could herself produce of native talent.

Of these Ligurian artists, Luca Cambiaso shone forth with the greatest brilliance; indeed, Cambiaso was a great artist, and endowed with great power of design. His faults were weakness and want of grace in colouring, engendered, perhaps, by the rapidity with which he executed. He was the son of a peasant, Giovanni Cambiaso, of the Polcevera valley, who was of an ingenious turn of mind, and is said to have invented the method of drawing the human figure by means of cubes.[1] He kept young Luca hard at work studying models in his workshop; and so ardent was he in furthering his son's education, that he hid his clothes to prevent him escaping from his work, and obliged him to pursue his studies in a state of nature.

Great was the enthusiasm and admiration inspired in the mind of this peasant by the works of Beccafumi, Pierino del Vaga, and others, which he saw in Prince D'Oria's palace, and the result of all this was the lesson of art he instilled into the mind of his son. The better to train the youth in the ways of art, he took him to a retired spot on the Riviera, and set before him the models and designs of great masters. Some of Luca Cambiaso's earlier efforts were exceeding strong in design, emulating Michael Angelo in boldness of limb and fierceness of expression. But of these but few are left to us; an altar-piece in the church of S. Giorgio in Genoa, and the Adoration of the Magi in the Lercari chapel in the cathedral, being perhaps the only extant representations of this his most successful period.

Cooped up in his father's workshop from morning till night, Luca grew up a sorry specimen of humanity, puny and dwarfed. At seventeen he looked more like a boy of twelve, but with an ardent fire burning in his eye which told of glowing passion and a determined will; and this proved to be the bane of his life. After the loss of his wife, Luca fell violently in love with his sister-in-law, who lived with him, and

[1] Soprani, "Vita dei pittori Ligustici."

looked after his children. This hopeless attachment preyed upon his mind and ruined the vigour of his style, except when by some mighty effort of artistic skill he hoped to gain his end. With this object in view he went to Rome, and painted some of his best pictures for the Pope ; but his Holiness was inexorable, and sternly forbade the banns.

For long after this his pencil lost its vivacity. His tints were pale, and the arrangement of his figures careless, testifying to the mental grief under which he laboured. At length, however, as age grew on, and his love passion remained unabated, Cambiaso determined to make one final effort by an appeal to Philip II. of Spain. So accordingly he repaired to Madrid, where the monarch employed him in decorating the ceiling of the Escurial chapel with a fresco, representing the Coronation of the Virgin.

At this mighty work Luca laboured assiduously, and employed in the execution of it all the vigour of his youth, buoyed up with hopes that if successful the monarch would favour his suit at the Vatican ; but alas ! he was again doomed to disappointment. When, after fifteen months, the work was finished, and Philip was contemplating it with one of those few smiles which ever illumined the face of the stern and melancholy monarch, Cambiaso thought the opportunity a fitting one for proffering his suit. But the religious Philip soon turned his smile into his accustomed frown, and withered the little painter with a scornful, contemptuous refusal.

Poor Luca was carried fainting from the scene of his labours to a bed of sickness, from which he never arose. It was in vain that Philip, wishful to save the life of so valuable an artist, sent him four thousand ducats more than the stipulated sum ; it was in vain that the best physicians of the Spanish court used all their nostrums and all the resources of their art to aid his recovery. Luca Cambiaso passed away some few days after this last blow to his hopes of happiness.

In Spain Luca was held in high esteem. Ximenes alludes

to his painting in the Escurial with great praise, but also blames his colouring as too faint. Perhaps one of his best productions is in the refectory of S. Bartolomeo degl' Armeni, in Genoa, representing a last supper. It came into the hands of the brotherhood in this wise. Luca was one day playing some game of chance with some of the monks, a supper was decreed to be the stake for which they played. Luca Cambiaso chanced to lose, and as his fulfilment of the debt of honour, he handed them over this picture, one of the figures therein being a portrait of himself.

Lazaro Tavarone was Cambiaso's pupil, and a faithful attendant of his in his Spanish tour. He it was who carried him to his bed, and closed his eyes after his failure with Philip of Spain ; and after his master's death he remained nine years in Madrid, where he put together much money and returned to Genoa in 1594. Tavarone, like his master, was of obscure origin. He was put into Cambiaso's workshop when quite a boy, and together, master and pupil studied and worked in a small studio, now long neglected and forgotten, in the Piazza dei Tessitori in Genoa. After his return from Madrid, Tavarone worked with a vigour and rapidity worthy of his master ; and one is surprised to learn that he suffered throughout his life from a grievous malady, which confined him much to his bed and sorely trespassed on his working hours, for Genoa is full of his frescoes and his canvases. He adorned the Bank of St. George with a gigantic fresco of their patron saint. Scarcely a palace exists which has not some ceiling or wall adorned by his brush. He died at a ripe old age, in 1641, and but few Ligurian artists left more behind them to testify to an active well-spent life.

Around Luca Cambiaso scintillates a numerous following of lesser stars, all of whom were the outcome of the Raphaelesque revival in Genoa. Prominent amongst them were the Castello family, of whom Bernardo was a hot-headed, pedantic man. He married when eighteen, and travelled through Italy for a great part of his life, partly from a love of art, and partly from a desire to get rid of his wife. He took up the study of art in all its branches. He was an intimate friend of Tasso's, and when the poet was about to publish his "Jerusalem Liberated," Bernardo gave him a present of the illustrations of the principal scenes, and from subjects in "Jerusalem Reconquered," he adorned the ceiling of one of the Spinola palaces in Genoa. Tasso had the illustrations engraved on copper for an edition which came out in 1590, and addressed to Bernardo Castello a letter of thanks, and wrote a sonnet in his honour. .

His brother, Gian Battista Castello, was a celebrated miniature painter, much honoured and esteemed in his native Republic, so much so that the doge appointed him artist-laureate in Genoa, and gave him large immunities as a citizen. His eldest son acquired a fief in Sicily, whither he invited his father to pay him a visit; but Gian Battista preferred to remain in his humble house in Genoa, with his objects of art around him, and died at the green old age of one hundred and five, leaving his second son to carry on, though after a feeble fashion, the name and occupation of artist.

Ludovico Calvi is another curious specimen of the Ligurian artist, who combined the qualities of art with those of the intrepid mariner and zealous captain against the Turks. Extremely jealous that Andrea D'Oria should pass over his merits, and choose Luca Cambiaso to execute some designs in S. Matteo, Calvi forthwith left his workshop in disgust, and took to the seas, where his prowess was rewarded by permission from the Republic to quarter the head of a Moor in his arms. He always went about clad in armour under his coat, and was ofttimes engaged in the brawls for which Genoa in those days was famous.

For twenty years he continued this wandering warlike life, and then came back to his paint-brush and his easel, with a hand which had not lost its cunning by disuse, and continued to paint vigorously and fiercely till his death, which did not occur for many a good year after ; for at the age of eighty-five he would climb about his scaffolding and execute his frescoes with the agility of youth.

Giovanni Domenico Cappellino marks the decay of this revival ; he was but a feeble successor of these greater masters. He was an exceedingly handsome man, but excessively eccentric. Dirt and dust were his pet aversions, and to so great an extent did he carry this antipathy, that he forbade any one in his room to take off his cloak or move a chair for fear of disturbing his enemy. His mother once had the misfortune to fall in the mud ; he refused to go to her assistance, and would not go near her for some time afterwards, affirming that she smelt of it. His over-cleanliness often betrayed him into the greatest filth, for he would refuse admittance to any one who offered to sweep out his bedroom, or to change his sheets, which office he would perform himself when the direst necessity obliged him—and it was but seldom in his lifetime said his gossiping neighbours.

His pictures are principally sacred subjects, insipid, and the conception of a diseased mind, and pointing to the decline of all feeling for real art in Liguria. But, before degenerating below the state which Pierino del Vaga found, the Ligurian school was to produce another bright follower in the steps of Cambiaso, who adorned her palaces and churches with some excellent workmanship.

Bernardo Strozzi, in his youthful aspirations to become an artist, met with vehement opposition from his father ; but on the death of this parent he obtained leave from his mother to take a few lessons. Strozzi, however, developed a taste for piety which overcame his love of art ; and at the age of eighteen he assumed the garb of a Capuchin, and entered a convent. He busied himself while there in the production of saints on canvas without end. And in this obscurity his talents would have been squandered on saintly lore had they not been recognized by a certain Rivera, who managed to get leave for him to leave his cell during the lifetime of his mother and his sister's maidenhood. His mother lived, and his sister remained unmarried, long enough to allow Bernardo time to drink sufficiently of the sweets of the outer world and the delights of success to make him loath to return to his seclusion when the time of his liberty had expired. So enraged were the Capuchins at his tardy return to his cell, that they prevented him getting more than a six months' extension of the period from the Pope; and true to the day appointed for his return, he was summoned by the archbishop, and handed over to his angry brethren, who forthwith put him in prison, where he languished for three years.

Weary at length of this constraint, he assumed a feigned zeal for religion. He renewed his vows, he confessed, he fasted, and finally obtained pardon for his sins, and the Capuchins restored him once more to the comforts of a cell, though always under the strictest supervision. One day, however, he obtained leave to go and visit his sister, at whose house he changed his cowl for the garb of a priest, and thus disguised, hurried to the harbour and embarked for Venice, where, in the rival Republic, he received a welcome and a home.

At Venice we have the products of Strozzi's later works, and there we see his tomb in the church of S. Forca with the following epitaph—"Bernardo Strozzi, the glory of painters, and the honour of Liguria, lies here," which was no small praise for a man and a foreigner in the home of Titian and Tintoretto, and proves that his talents were highly esteemed out of his own country.

Throughout Italy he was known, and nicknamed "the Genoese priest;" and though his later productions are more valuable as works of art, nevertheless, in the days of his early liberty he did much work for the churches and palaces of Genoa. In the church of S. Domenico he painted a much esteemed "Paradise" by the light of a solitary lamp; and in the Brignole-Sale palace is a picture of St. Thomas, which ranks with a Guido Reni or a Guercino; and in the entrance hall of the Balbi palace we see a boldly designed, richly coloured picture, representing Joseph in prison holding converse with the chief butler. Strozzi far excelled all the Genoese artists of his day in boldness of design; there is the character in all his works which speaks of the man who would ill brook monkish tyranny, and that the history of his life was a remarkable one could be easily surmised simply from a study of his pictures.

Of the disciples of the Raphaelesque school, numbers bloomed and faded in Genoa, and continued to languish, prolific indeed in their works, but degenerate possessors of the Ligurian brush, until a new impetus was given to painting in Genoa by the residence of three distinguished Flemish artists amongst them. They were Vandyke, Rubens, and Vincent Malò, and the seventeenth century witnessed a corresponding revival to that ushered in by the followers of Raphael; and, with their aptitude for following in the train of others, Ligurian artists adopted the style of one or other of these foreign masters. And with this revival is ushered in the second great landmark in the history of Ligurian art.

Next, perhaps, to Antwerp and the galleries of the north, Genoa affords the lover of Vandyke the best opportunity of studying this Flemish master. In wandering through her famous streets of palaces, and their treasures of art, the traveller's attention is at once riveted by the numerous portraits by Vandyke with which their walls are alive. His guide-book points them all out to him one by one, and thus a whole army of Genoa's worthies passes before his gaze. But should he wander down a bypath leading into a maze of the vilest squalor, he may chance to visit an old palace of the Cataneo family, where no less than nine portraits attributed to Vandyke, two of which at least are beyond all doubt, stare down in lonely grandeur upon a busy world of dirt, and adorn the panels of a dimly lighted room, which is approached through merchants' offices, and scenes of poverty worthy of the purlieus of St. Giles.

Of Rubens' most ardent followers, the Castiglione family perhaps occupies the highest place. This family presented Genoa with no less than three painters of a high order, of whom Giovanni Benedetto Castiglione was the chief. He had studied under Paggi, a master of the decayed school, but soon shook off the trammels of his youth, and blossomed forth as a new being under the tuition of Rubens. He travelled much, and added to his store of knowledge in Florence and in Rome ; but in Mantua he spent some of the best years of his life, where the marquis pressed him to stay and assist at the beautifying of his palaces.

Castiglione was the great portrait painter of his day in Genoa, and he was nicknamed " Il Grechetto " by his fellow-townsmen, or the second Rembrandt by his most ardent admirers. His success, however, lay principally in his landscapes and animals. In a bull-fight or the chase his touch was good, and much spirit and life was thrown into his subject ; nevertheless, a Holy Family, in the church of S. Luca, in Genoa, proves that he could likewise turn his attention to the sacred with success. In the French occupation, after the Revolution, Napoleon talked much about sending this picture to Paris, but the people rose up in arms to protect it, and it was saved its journey.

The two other brothers were but indifferently successful in establishing for themselves a name.

On the other hand, the De' Ferrari, another artistic family, were scrupulous disciples of Vandyke in portrait painting, and together with their kinsmen, the Piola, afford us an interesting picture of a Genoese artistic *côterie*. Some of them returned rather to the Italian school, under the guidance of the Carloni, another family whose frescoes adorn the church of

S. Ambrogio; and in this clique of artists we walk as in a confusing labyrinth in Genoa, and scarce a church or a palace we visit is without its score of productions from the De' Ferrari, the Carloni, and the Piola studios.

But of these three families the Piola merits our greatest attention, both from the "*chef d'œuvre* of Liguria," as it is termed, which the young and unfortunate Pellegro Piola executed for his country, and from the fact that we can to-day visit their house on the steep slopes of Carignano, the walls of which are still covered with paintings by the six members of this family, who distinguished themselves in the art.

In this little house we seem as if wafted two centuries back, as we examine each panel adorned by one of the family with some design, while their descendants, still living under the same roof, pride themselves in keeping everything as their distinguished ancestors left it. Here, too, we see all the presents they received from their brothers in art. A stone Madonna, for instance, over the lintel, was given to them by the sculptor Schiaffino, an intimate friend of one of the Piola. The ladies of this family were no less distinguished than their brothers, two of whom excelled in painting; and by the marriage of one of Pellegro Piola's sisters to Gregorio de' Ferrari, the union of these artistic families was firmly cemented.

The tragic death of young Pellegro Piola, who executed that shrine in the goldsmith's street, has added a further interest to the picture, which in itself no way lacks the aid of tragedy to establish its claim to notoriety. It is a beautiful soft representation of the Virgin and Child, rivalling in the delicacy of its shading an Andrea del Sarto. S. Eloy, the patron saint of smiths, supports her, and from its position in the open street—the quaint, narrow, glittering street of the Genoese goldsmiths—with glass in front of it, it at once attracts the eye of the passer by.

2 C

This picture was executed on this wise : In 1641, the gold-smiths of Genoa wished to put up a picture to the honour of the Madonna, and their patron saint, which should superin-tend their daily work. Pellegro Piola, a youth of two and twenty, and of great promise, was entrusted with the task ; and on the 25th of November, in that year, it was put up in the place which it still occupies.

Great was the praise heaped upon Pellegro as he stood and contemplated his work. A friend passed by and con-gratulated him on the vigour of his style, "a credit," he said, "to the Ligurian school, that must silence the jealous dogs who bark around." Piola modestly replied, that he hoped heaven would grant him life to continue his work ; but that very evening was to be his last.

Everything was joy and gladness that day in the house on the slopes of Carignano. The De' Ferrari were invited to join at a festive family gathering, and to drink to the success of the young artist. Pellegro spent the afternoon with his relatives and his wife, whom he had married some few months before ; and towards evening, some friends called for him to go out with them for a stroll. They got no further than the Piazza Sarzano before they came to angry words, and from words to blows, and a fatal dagger entered Piola's breast. The dead body of their hope and pride was carried back to the mourning family, and the shouts of revelry and joy, which had that day gladdened their homestead, were turned into deep lamentation and woe.

A mysterious story long hung over this assassination. Men said that his master, Carlone, jealous of his pupil's success, had been the murderer, and then to avoid justice had fled to the church of S. Ambrogio, during which time he executed the frescoes there. But the legal process lately come to light clears up this mystery, and tells us that the assassin was one Bianco, a pupil of no account in Carlone's studio ; that he did it in a sudden fit of rage, and from no motives of jealousy ; that

he sought and obtained the forgiveness of the bereaved relatives, and that by way of punishment he got five years at the
galleys and two of banishment.

Thus died young Pellegro, the brightest star of the
Ligurian school. His younger brother, Domenico, was twelve
years old at the time of the murder, and in him boiled the
blood of an artist, anxious to achieve the success from which
his brother had been thus mercilessly torn. And Domenico
Piola's name in Genoa is a well known one ; his pictures adorn
many of the churches, his frescoes have a grace and elegance
which recall Correggio, in the style which he learnt from his
master, Carlone ; but his gracefully entwined cherubs usher
in the ornate and fantastic era of Italian art, an era in which
all the beauty of nature and firmness of touch is sacrificed to
an attempt at labyrinthine wonders and ethereal grandeur.

Paolo Gerolamo Piola, Domenico's son, trespassed more on
this dangerous ground, and with less brilliancy of design, than
his father. Thus did the decay of art set in in Genoa. Her
school never had been of such transcendent merit as those in
the neighbouring Italian cities ; yet, placed anywhere else
than on Italian soil, it would have shone forth nobly and well.
But as it was, Ligurian painters, with but few exceptions, were
eclipsed by their more accomplished neighbours.

In the sister art of sculpture, the entire absence of
originality in Genoa is perhaps even more striking than in
that of painting. When Niccolò da Pisa came to Genoa, in
1313, to raise a monument therein to the defunct empress,
wife of Henry VII. of Luxembourg, in the convent of St.
Francis, he may be said to have inaugurated the art in Genoa,
which in Pisa, and in other mediæval Italian towns, had by
this time reached a high pitch of excellence. As in painting
so in sculpture, the Genoese were servile imitators of the men
their wealthy merchants paid to adorn their palaces, and to
the designs of foreign artists we owe most that is beautiful in
this city.

Thus Antonio della Porta fashioned most of the statues in the Bank of St. George; and to his taste is due the many carved portals of Genoa, which in the dark slate-marble of Lavagna form such conspicuous objects even now in the town.   And thus if a Genoese wished to accomplish anything really grand he invariably summoned an artist of high repute from abroad.   As an instance of their distrust in home productions, let us quote the case of the chapel built to contain the ashes of St. John the Baptist.   To erect a fitting superstructure, Matteo Civitali was summoned from Florence, and on his death before accomplishing the task, so diffident were they about native talent that Andrea Sansovino was entrusted with the completion of the task.

Again, Andrea D'Oria's magnificence summoned to Genoa a goodly array of sculptors, and amongst them Andrea da Fiesole and Montorsoli, to adorn his palace and his church. Montorsoli gave a tone to the Ligurian school, which henceforth followed studiously in Michael Angelo's style.   A native artist, Filippo Parodi by name, gave a considerable impetus to the love of sculpture in his native city.   He was a cabinet-maker, whose talents the painter Domenico Piola recognized, and advised his going to study in Rome, which he accordingly did.   His statue of St. John the Baptist, outside the Carignano church, is a nobly conceived figure, and some of his groups are graceful.

At Venice he distinguished himself not a little, and at Padua, where in the church of S. Guistina a deposition by him is perhaps his *chef-d'œuvre*.

The brothers Schiaffino followed in his footsteps, and adorned Genoa with many marble cherubs over the numerous fountains in the town, and many circular "pietà" over their doorways; but theirs was a debased style, and saints lost in long flowing robes testify that they recognized their own weakness in reproducing the human form, when they were constrained to disguise their figures in folds of unmeaning drapery.

In the most ancient days, the Genoese were most skilful engineers. However incredulous we may be about their
earlier achievements in the taking of cities, and the production
of wonderful stone-propelling instruments, nevertheless the
frequent repetition of the same story proves that there must
have been much truth in their claim to engineering skill.
Jerusalem, Aleria in Spain, and Damietta in Egypt, were all
captured, they say, by the ingenuity of the Ligurian contingent
under their walls. And at home there are ample proofs of
their mediæval skill as engineers and in building.

Marino Boccanegra, brother of the first captain of the
Republic, was a clever architect. To him is due the mighty
aqueduct which supplied Genoa with water from the side of
Staglieno, and is still a conspicuous object along the Bisagno
valley, as the traveller is driven to visit the modern cemetery
reckoned amongst the chief "lions" of Genoa. Marino, too,
is said to have constructed that long line of arcades down
near the port, with its aqueduct and walk above, and redolent
with all the odours of commerce, and resounding with the din
of vivacious Italians. He also constructed the first pier for
the protection of the harbour from sudden storms ; and under
his supervision the building of the Bank of St. George, as it
stands to-day, was raised in accordance with the plans of one
Oliviero, in 1260.

As long as they adhered to the Lombardo-Gothic style,
the Genoese erected stately and glorious buildings. Their
cathedral,[1] the small black and white marble church of Porto
Venere, built in 1118, the gates of S. Andrea and dei
Vacca, are noble specimens we can contemplate to-day, and
learn that in architecture at least Genoa could compete with,
and perhaps excel, most towns in Italy.

But with the deluge of the Renaissance revival, all this
was swept away, and in Genoa the Renaissance had its fullest
scope for development. It occurred at a time when her nobles

---

[1] *Vide* ch. iii.

were at their richest, and seeking for some outlet for their hoarded wealth they lavished it on their palaces. Galeazzo Alessi, a disciple of Michael Angelo's, came from Perugia, at the invitation of the patricians, and this visit changed the whole aspect of the city. Palaces, churches, and public buildings arose ; all that was squalid, old, or deemed unsightly, was swept away to give place for regiments of palaces ; and as Pierino del Vaga and Montorsoli had inaugurated a new life in their departments of art, so did Alessi commence a new age of architecture on the ruin and decay of the old.

The combination of every age of art in Genoa, and of every species existing in every age, makes the city a perfect museum for the study of architecture. Upon pillars with Byzantine capitals, with intricate designs of animals and flowers, stand exquisite Gothic arches in the cloisters of the old church of S. Andrea, now used as a prison. Moorish and Arab tracery puzzle the eye on the walls of her cathedral, whilst nowhere was the Renaissance more lavish in her eccentricities ; and then from these relics of the past the visitor is hurried into one of the most realistic specimens of nineteenth century art in the monuments to the dead at Staglieno.

A Genoese sculptor of to-day is valued according to his lifelike representations in marble of human distress and agony, to be placed over the tomb of some departed relative. There stands a marble widow, mourning over her husband's marble deathbed ; a marble tear trickles down her marble cheek, and a marble pocket-handkerchief is outheld in constant readiness to receive the petrified token of grief. Thus does Genoa, bereft of life and vigour, now expend all that is left to her of genius and art in lavishly adorning the resting-place of her dead.

CHAPTER XVIII.

THE END.

OF the death-bed scenes of nations, but few offer incidents
of a more thrilling nature than that of the Ligurian Republic.
The tottering fabric, which had survived ages of revolutions
and ages of constitutional peril, fell a sacrifice at length to the
fever and delirium of the French Revolution. Here all the
scenes of horror which shook Paris to her basis were re-enacted
with equal fury, until Napoleon, with the scythe of death in
his hand, swept Genoa from the list of nations, and the
Congress of Vienna consigned the mortal remains of the once
"proud mistress of the seas" to the mausoleum in which the
Sardinian dynasty gathered together one by one the dry
bones of all Italy's many states, to mould thereout as best
they could a new being entitled "United Italy."

At the murmur of the revolution across the Alps, an
under current of agitation grew apace in Genoa, fostered as it
was by men sent for the purposes of promoting it from the
French national assembly, Simonville and Naillac. Whilst
the king of Sardinia, the Pope, and the king of Naples
united to check the torrent which threatened to overwhelm
them, Genoa and Venice remained prudently neutral; but this
neutrality, their only safeguard against annihilation, was not to
be tolerated by the enemies of France, and England, above
all, refused to recognize it.

Mr. Drake, the English consul in Genoa, insisted that the

Republic should dismiss the French minister, Tilly, as a promoter of discord and anarchy; that she should ally herself to England, and should admit into her harbour George III.'s ships; and that if she refused she should be treated as England's enemy. To back up Drake's demands, Admiral Hood was in the Mediterranean with a dozen vessels, and Admiral Hood was not always strictly orthodox in his observance of the laws of nations. In the Genoese neutral waters two English ships attacked and seized a French ship, the *Modesta*, some high words between the respective sailors being the origin of the quarrel.

Poor Genoese! the gathering storm around them had well nigh burst. If the English clamoured for their alliance and threatened a blockade, the French were no less imperative in demanding an indemnity for their loss; and the Ligurian rulers, in this their dire extremity, determined to pay the demands of the French out of their own pockets, as the last hope of maintaining their neutrality.

In the ensuing spring Drake was more vehement than ever in his demands of a declaration of allegiance from Genoa; and with the Spanish fleet in the port to back up his cause, he proceeded to the council hall and imperatively demanded the dismissal of all French agents from Genoa; and on receiving a quiet but firm refusal from the doge, Maria D'Oria, he forthwith declared Genoa to be at war with England, and set off with his credentials for Leghorn.

The French were now beginning to recover from their anarchy, and under the "Directoire" French armies were now marching south, and equally regardless of Genoa's neutrality, seized San Remo, Ventimiglia, and other towns in Liguria. The young general, Bonaparte, in 1796, at the head of these troops, was prepared to seize upon the faintest excuse for marching upon Genoa, and an opportunity was soon given him by the massacre of some Frenchmen within the Republic's territory; for the superstitious peasantry looked upon the

FRESCO BY PIERINO DEL VAGA IN THE D'ORIA PALACE REPRESENTING THE TRIUMPH OF SCIPIO.

name of France as impersonating every horror, subversion of religion, and subversion of all that they held sacred. Thus in the valley of the Polcevera, towards Novi, every Frenchman was massacred ; and Bonaparte, pretending to believe that it was by orders of the senate that this had been done, wrote demanding for himself the cession of the fortress of Gavi, and a further sum of money based on the *Modesta* claims. Thus with the victorious enemy at their very door, with the new French minister, Faypoult, using all his efforts to arouse the French interests amongst the inhabitants, the government could do nothing but despatch an envoy to make the best terms he could with the French.

So exorbitant, however, were Bonaparte's demands that the Republic were constrained to send to Paris for a mitigation of them, and with fair success. But it was another English outrage which put the finishing stroke to the union with France. For if Bonaparte was exorbitant by land, Nelson was no less unscrupulous by sea. On the 11th of September, 1796, the French were unlading a ship close to Genoa full of arms and implements of war ; Nelson, happening to be in the harbour of Genoa at the time, under the neutral flag, hearing how busy the French were close by, forthwith sailed from the harbour as if to put out to sea ; but no sooner had he proceeded on his course a mile or so than he turned sharply round, seized the French ship, and made off with it.

Faypoult, in Genoa, made the worst of this, and at length the Ligurian rulers, seeing no further chance of maintaining their neutrality, sent their agent, Vincenzo Spinola, to Paris, with instructions to make the best terms he could with the Directoire, and they were as follows :—The ports to be closed to the English, no succour to be given to any enemies of France, and if Great Britain should attack Genoa, France engaged to protect her ; and France, moreover, would respect the Ligurian territories ; and, as a proof of friendship, and as a further bond of union, Genoa should go to the coffers of her bank and hand over two millions of francs by way of indemnity for real or supposed misdemeanours, and a further sum of two millions was to be advanced by way of loan by her wealthy citizens. Thus was Genoa dragged against her will into a French alliance, and thus was she exposed to all the pernicious influences of French revolutionists, who, when the way was opened to them, hied them right gladly to the Ligurian capital, there to disseminate profusely seeds of discord and anarchy.

One of the first of these to arrive in Genoa was Morando, a druggist, whose education in all branches of villainy in Paris had produced in his Italian born mind a perfect storehouse of corrupt morality. Second to him alone was one Vitaliani, a Neapolitan, a man of the same stamp ; and together, these two found favour and support from the French minister, Faypoult, who employed them officially ; so it was in vain that the senate put Vitaliani in prison as a seditious spirit. Faypoult demanded his release as an official *employé* of France, and the senate reluctantly granted it.

Emboldened by this, Morando and Vitaliani worked harder, and with redoubled energy, in their plots for subverting in Genoa every form of government, and a young D'Oria, Filippo by name, joined them. Outside the city, the press and public opinion, under Napoleon's influence, wrote and spoke vehemently against the Genoese aristocracy, and within the city, the people lent a willing ear to this attack. The senate, in their weakness, appointed state inquisitors to look into men's private affairs ; but the imprisonment of any seditious ring-leader only added fresh contingents to the already overwhelming numbers of the discontents. And thus were the senate powerless and almost prostrate, and thus were the Jacobine principles of the French revolution firmly established in the kindly atmosphere of Italian soil.

Headed by the above-named triumvirate, a crowd singing

the *Marseillaise* gathered in the streets, and in its onward progress towards the royal palace grew into a mighty, seething, and excited mob, demanding the immediate delivery of the prisoners the senate had made. Shops were shut ; the quietly-disposed fled ; the senate, with a strong guard, tried to appease their wrath by saying that they would shortly explain their purpose, and the crowd, unable to force an entry into the council hall, betook themselves for comfort and exhortation to Faypoult, who promised to use his influence with the senate to obtain their demands.

Elated with these promises, the crowd dispersed throughout the city, got them to the wine-shops and the taverns, and gave themselves up to scenes of drunkenness and debauchery. Most in Genoa passed this night awake. In every square, in every alley, arose the excited yells of the stump orators and their drunken audience, which, with the wine fumes and the glare of torches, gave Genoa the appearance of a city of demons.

The dawn of the 22nd of May, 1796, burst forth most mournfully over the excited city. Out from their lairs streamed forth the insurgents, with reddened eyes and maddening yells ; to their standard flocked countless adherents ; from the side of Lombardy poured in colleagues on the watch for such a disturbance, and of these many were French. As a standard of rebellion they placed in their caps the tricoloured tassel, and went forth to the shouts of " *Viva la libertà ! Viva il popolo !* " They visited Faypoult, who gave them a welcome and a cheer. They visited the prisons, and dragged from thence all the malefactors, and adorned them with their tricoloured badge. They did the same by the galley slaves in the dockyard, and having these armed robbers and murderers as their fitting allies, they proceeded to overthrow one of the most venerable governments of Europe.

The senate remained petrified, as it were, by this sudden calamity in the council hall. They stirred not a finger in their own defence, when it was still in their power to crush the rising, as events afterwards proved ; unaccountably stolid they awaited their fate.

Morando and his motley crew meanwhile paraded the city crying that Genoa was free, that the aristocracy was abolished, that tribute and taxes were to be heard of no more. Gate after gate, fort after fort, fell into their hands. They talked of appointing new magistrates from amongst themselves, whilst the senators in their abject distress sent in vain to Faypoult to use his influence to check the evil he had helped to arouse. In vain did they promise reforms. Faypoult went to them in person, exhorted them to give way to the times, and let the democracy have its own way ; and so, as a last resort, they settled to send a deputation of four to make terms with the populace, but the rabble would hear of none. "Liberty," and "Death to the Aristocracy," were the cries which rent the air ; and had not the palace been well guarded, not a senator would have escaped a terrible death at the hands of the triumphant adherents of Morando.

But if the senators were demoralized and panic-stricken, not so were some of the steady-going Genoese citizens, who looked with horror on the subversion of everything that was dear to them, government and religion alike. A large number of them assembled — these likewise were of the lowest of the people, artizans, porters, and coal-heavers— they shouted in their turn for arms, and rendered the victory of the Morandists, before almost a matter of certainty, now doubtful. " *Viva Maria ! Viva religione,*" "Death to the Jacobines," were amongst the cries of those upholders of the old *régime*, and for their badge they tied to their caps a small image of the Madonna ; and for this they incurred Napoleon's sneer, who called them " Genoese priests ; " but be they priests or porters, they stood the senators in good stead, and by seizing the arsenal, they came forth to meet their antago-nists better armed, better equipped, and with the support of most of the regular soldiery.

Unhappy Genoa! Again was she torn in twain by conflicting factions, again father fought against son, brother
against brother. Throughout the whole of this day the battle
raged; every corner of Genoa flowed with the blood of her
own citizens. As the tide fluctuated from side to side in the
intensity of animosity, the death struggle became more acute;
but at length the upholders of the old *régime* gained the upper
hand. Filippo D'Oria was slain fighting bravely at his post.
Morando and his men, seeing the day was lost, abandoned the
city, and their adherents fled hither and thither, and tried to
conceal their complicity in the events in the inmost recesses
of their houses, whilst D'Oria's corpse was kicked about the
town, and held up to public scorn by his insatiate conquerors.
A poor Turkish slave, who had been liberated from the galleys
on condition that he would cry " *Viva il popolo*," wandered
through the city proclaiming this parrot-learnt phrase, the
price of his liberty, when suddenly he fell in with a band of
the opposite faction, who beat him, and only allowed him to
escape with life on condition that for the future he would cry
" *Viva Maria.*" This he willingly did until he fell across
another band of revolutionists, who silenced his lusty lungs
with many a hard blow, until the poor man lay stricken and
almost lifeless on the pavement. Unable to account for such
rough treatment, he groaned aloud—" The Christians must be
mad."

Be this story true or not, the conclusion arrived at by the
poor Turk was a fact indisputable.

Imperious before in his tone of addressing Genoa,
Napoleon was doubly imperious now. He complained of the
loss of life which French subjects had sustained during the
late rebellion, slurring over the fact that it was in sedition
that they had died; he complained that the porter-priests, with
their Madonna badge, had been employed by the government
to assassinate the French. Of a truth the victors after the
insurrection were slightly indiscriminate on whom they

wreaked their vengeance; not only was Morando's house spoiled and plundered, but also those of innocent citizens. Bonaparte demanded, through his mouthpiece Faypoult, the surrender of all prisoners, French, Lombards, Genoese alike; and hence the senators were obliged tó let loose on the world again all those who had subverted Genoa, and were compelled to persuade their adherents to disarm; and then, and not till then, would Faypoult grant a pardon to the senators, leaving the same element of disturbance and disorder still abroad in Genoa.

Intent on establishing his influence above all dispute in Liguria, Napoleon advanced towards the Polcevera valley; and thus, constrained by turmoils from within, and dangers from without, the senate determined at length to admit without further trouble whatever scheme of reform Napoleon might dictate. To his head-quarters at Montebello a deputation was sent, and the result was anxiously awaited at home. It was as follows: That the French Government should return the sovereignty conceded to them by the Genoese, but that this sovereignty should be placed in the hands of a doge and council representing the whole class of citizens; that all the privileges of the nobles should be abolished, and that in consideration of another large indemnity, the French would pardon the Genoese Republic and recognize its independence.

On the 14th of June, 1796, the new reforms dictated by Napoleon were proclaimed throughout Genoa; shouts of joy echoed throughout the town of "Long live Napoleon," "France, and Liberty" and "Death to the Aristocrats" was the burden of their song. Not a piazza, not an alley was there without its flag of liberty, whilst women distributed to eager recipients tricolour caps of liberty, which had been secretly woven the day before. Morando was in ecstasies. Vitaliani preached sermons of democratic zeal, the nobles hid themselves, whilst Napoleon smiled grimly at Montebello, and called the Genoese " foolish idiots."

A servile imitation of the French revolution was the result. The mob rushed to the royal palace, brought forth "the book of gold," in which all the names of the nobility were entered, and carried it to the Piazza d'Aquaverde, where a fire was lighted ; and around the burning embers of the letters patent of Genoa's noble sons danced a maddened, joyous crowd of demagogues, stirring with their bayonets the leaves of the hated volume, and fondly dreaming that with this they were destroying for ever the hated name of rank. Ballot boxes, ducal chairs, coats of arms, and other symbols of a patrician order were cast into this bonfire, and deafening sounds of music, stump oratory, and applause chimed in with a would-be pæan to the burning effigies of rank. The statues of Prince Andrea D'Oria and his successors were dashed to the ground, and their trunkless heads kicked opprobriously through the town.

"O sublime and majestic spectacle of an entire people, which has traversed centuries of slavery and humiliation under a yoke of iron, rising to its feet and casting off the heavy weight of its rusty chains, and throwing them in the face of its dethroned tyrants." Thus they spoke, and thus they cheered their orators. Could the bones of old Andrea slumbering in the vaults of S. Matteo rest in their coffin? Could the hero of ninety years brook such indignities even in death?

As before, the criminals and the malefactors were released to swell the discordant scenes of the hour, and a message of thanks and adoration was despatched to Napoleon, praising his benevolence and the privileges he had vouchsafed to them. On the day of the declaration of this new *régime* a priest, Cuneo by name, thus addressed an excited audience—"O Brutus! O my beloved Brutus! lend me for a moment thy dagger, dripping still with the blood of the tyrant, with which to write on the walls of this hall, under the eyes of the provisionary government, the sacred name of liberty and equality."

Following in the footsteps of the French, the newly appointed government, of which Gian Carlo Serra was appointed generalissimo, proceeded to attack religious institutions, and this element, hitherto absent, entered the ranks of the revolutionists.

The archbishop was commanded to act in no way without authority from the government, religious orders were to be abolished, and men declared themselves weary of priestcraft and their mockeries. Every one unwilling to drop the cowl and the cassock was ordered to leave the republican territories ; and to take their place, the president, Serra, appointed men who should celebrate services in the churches, and afterwards preach to the people democracy and independence. These apostles wore around their necks a white and red ribbon with a small crucifix attached thereto, but men did not care much about them. The Genoese, as Napoleon had affirmed, had too much of priestcraft about them, and in inculcating equality they did not see fit to oblige their Madonna-Queen to leave her throne. And this spirit of religious discontent the nobles carefully fanned, as a stepping-stone by which they hoped soon to return to power.

It was a secret dislike of the movers in these innovations which at length began to work a counter revolution in Genoa. They disliked to see their golden florins being transferred to French coffers; they were jealous of two French generals, who were sent to reorganize the Ligurian troops—thinking that this showed a want of trust in the native capabilities; and at length the echo of the discontented voices was heard from the neighbouring valleys, where the inhabitants, suspicious of anything that struck at their religion, began to complain. In the Bisagno valley they rang their bells, they recalled their priests, and in the country villas of the nobles secret conclaves were held. Those who were willing to act were armed with whatever came to hand, and, after celebrating a high mass, the crowd of peasants marched towards the capital. But these zealous upholders of their faith found that it required more than prayer-books, and priestcraft, to carry their point against the well-trained and well-armed French soldiery under General Duphot, and were beaten back with great loss near Albaro.

No sooner was this insurrection quelled than another outburst arose in the Polcevera valley. Many of the vanquished inhabitants of the Bisagno crossed over the mountain ridges to assist their friends. Fierce was the struggle around the heights of S. Benigno, but again Duphot was victorious, and, after a few hours' fight, old soldiers and good discipline again prevailed, and peace was restored by terror, but not by love; for throughout the length and breadth of the Riviera burnt a fierce hatred against the French, and against those Genoese who had subverted everything, and had accepted a foreign yoke without a blow. The appointment of a military council to judge, hang, or condemn to the galleys the ringleaders of these risings served to keep alive this hatred and thirst for vengeance.

At this moment Bonaparte arrived in Liguria, and again took the ordering of Genoa's government into his own hands, and with the characteristic levity of the Genoese disposition, their tyrant's arrival was heralded by ringing of bells, and sounds of joy throughout the town. Though full three thousand French soldiers occupied the gates and strongholds of the city, still they ceased not to cry " Liberty ; " and every fresh step which Napoleon took towards absolute government in their city was ushered in by fresh outbursts of· joy and delight.

During Bonaparte's absence in Egypt, however, affairs did not go on so smoothly for him in Italy. The emperors of Russia and Austria, acting in conjunction with their English ally, brought disasters on the French arms in Lombardy and Piedmont. Napoleon hurried back to Paris ; he chased away the directorate at the point of the bayonet, and established two consuls, of whom he was the first ; and having thus settled affairs in France he offered peace to his enemies, which was accepted by Russia and Prussia, but steadfastly refused by England and Austria; and against these powers war was forthwith declared, and into this the Genoese were drawn, and therewith entered upon one of the most disastrous episodes of her history.

In the spring of 1800, Massena, Soult, and Suchet were Napoleon's generals in Liguria; and the Austrian army, under Melas, and an English fleet acting in unison contested every point along the coast and inland with the French, until the superior force of the allies obliged the French to shut themselves up within the walls of Genoa; hence the Ligurian capital experienced all the horrors of a protracted siege, and once more famine, pestilence, and the sword were let loose upon the wretched Genoese, whose yearning had been for neutrality, but whose fate was to be driven by the force of circumstances into the vortex of foreign quarrels.

Each castle along the coast was the object of a fierce struggle between the belligerents. Of the taking of one of them by the allied forces an amusing story is told. It was Casteluccio, which now stands boldly into the waves between Pegli and Voltri, and was once a fortress of the Lomellini family, around which their galleys were collected, and to which they brought the products of their rich coral fisheries from their island dependency of Tabarca.[1]   —

In this castle, a small garrison of French soldiers were besieged by land and sea, and when driven to the last extremity, and at the point of surrender, they made use of the following stratagem to effect their escape. At nightfall they tied a lighted lantern round the neck of a donkey, so that the enemy might not suspect their departure, and stealing away quietly they left the donkey in sole charge of the fortress, free to meander about where he wished, and by the continued motion of the light the besiegers never for a moment dreamt

[1] *Vide* ch. v.

of the deception that was being practised upon them. Next morning the artifice was discovered, and the donkey found alone in its glory. This victory, says the facetious Genoese annalist, was the cause of great rejoicing in London and Vienna.

Horrible were the privations the Genoese experienced during this siege. Provisions soon fell short, and then they began to adulterate them. Happy was he who could get the flesh of horse, cat, mouse, bat, or worms for his supper. All the windmills around the town were in the possession of the Austrians, and curious was the effect produced in the streets by each house setting up some novelty in the shape of windmill. But soon all grain was exhausted, and seeds of flax and millet took their place; but up to this period of the siege a genius in the way of a cook could manage to make out a very decent bill of fare.

But at length there came a time when the flax, and the bats, and horses began to grow scarce, and only luxuries for the tables of the rich, whilst bran and beans formed the meagre diet of the poor, and happy he who died before the final death struggle set in. Solid fears by day and vague phantasies by night, constant weary fatigue in search of food, all contributed to convert the well-to-do Genoese into haggard careworn ghosts wandering about the streets. Over the hills within the walls they would wander too, wherever grew a green blade or a sorrel leaf to be gathered with a view to sustaining yet a little longer the tender thread of life. Noble matrons and noble maids were seen wandering side by side with the withered hags, wrinkled by half a century of toil, over the green slopes behind the town, with baskets in their hands, eagerly digging up some few roots and herbs.

In elegant baskets, adorned by lovely flowers, some hideous stew of corrupt and abominable food would be sold for a fabulous sum to a hungry Crœsus, perhaps a dish of rats in the morning, and a few lumps of sugar in the evening, but all adorned with a lavishness of beauty contrasting piteously with the worn, eager faces of the buyer and seller, and perchance mixed with plaster instead of meal, so base and sordid did men become, with death staring them in the face, that they cared not if they sold messages of death, provided they could secure money enough to purchase themselves one more meal.

Amidst groans of the dead and dying might be seen men and women tearing out their hunger-gnawed vitals, thus preferring to add to the number of the corpses, which lay piled in the streets around them, to continuing their agonized existence. None heeded their cry for pity—each man was for himself, and continued scenes of horror made even the most merciful callous to the sufferings of their fellow-creatures. Children abandoned by their parents, and aged parents by their children, might cry for help to their last breath, and none came to help them ; and whilst groping in the gutters and drains of the city to seek for some vestige of food, many a child, and many a grey-haired old man, would lay them down and die.

Thus it was with the citizens, and thus it was with the French garrison, of whom many, unable any longer to carry their arms, threw them away and stole off to the English and Austrian camps, where food, even though in prison, was preferable to dying of hunger in the beleaguered city. But perhaps the most piteous scene of all was that of the German and English prisoners of war, who were kept in some old barges down in the port. When necessity prevented their jailers from giving them any more food, they ate their shoes and the skins of their knapsacks. At length, when their guards left them, they tried to fall upon each other, but were too weak ; they then tried to sink the ships, preferring drowning to starvation, but were unable, and thus did they perish to a man.

It was almost with thankfulness that men learnt how the

plague had broken out in the famished city. By this new scourge numbers were added to the heaps of bodies which lay around unburied, and under the same roof would death sweep away a whole family, one of hunger, another of virulent fever, another from sheer exhaustion, and a fourth with the livid plague spot beneath his arm, all to be heaped together in a seething, putrid pile of unburied corpses, the decaying odour of which added fuel to the pestilential fire which swept through the city.

No agony, in her long career, had Genoa endured more keen than this. Better far were the bombs showered on her by Louis XIV.; better far the insolent extortion of the Austrians. Alone amongst all this misery, Massena, the French commander, remained firm. He kept his mind steadfastly fixed on this cause, and on his reputation as an invincible warrior; but at length he had to succumb, and a convention (as his surrender, out of compliment to his dignity, was called) took place by way of capitulation. It was drawn up on the 4th of June, 1800. Massena, his officers, and his eight thousand men were permitted to go free to France by way of land, and those who could not travel thus the English engaged to transport to Antibes by sea.

On this day, at two in the afternoon, Genoa was handed over to the combined forces of Austria and England, and the most ardent democrats departed with the French; and again the bells were rung, and hymns of praise were sung, whilst bread, meat, and food of all descriptions was lavishly distributed amongst the needy, and not a few fell a sacrifice to the frenzied joy of eating food once more—more fatal to their emaciated forms than the abstinence they had gone through.

A regency was appointed by the allies, containing the names of some of the most honoured citizens, whereupon the aristocrats and their adherents now raised the cry of "Long live the Emperor!" whilst France and liberty were things of the past. Not a spark of patriotism was there in all this and not a word was said about restoring the government on its ancient basis ; the Genoese were content to be tossed to and fro as an apple of discord between the contending armies of Europe, by way of by-play to their more extended field of action.

The Anglo-Austrian occupation of Genoa was exceeding short-lived. Ten days afterwards they heard of the victory of Marengo, and that the Austrians were flying through the plains of Lombardy before the conquering hosts. Hohen-zollern, the German governor of Genoa, rapidly evacuated the late conquests, and on the 24th of June, the French, under Suchet, re-entered the Ligurian capital. Over the town, Napoleon placed a temporary governing body under his own special protection, and when, after the peace of Luxembourg, in 1801, the Austrian emperor gave up all that he held in Italy, Napoleon forthwith set to work to map out the country into Republics and representative governments, which were eventually destined as principalities for his deserving relatives and generals.

Genoa thus found herself merged in the unmeaning term of a Cisalpine Republic, and found herself called upon to send representatives to Lyons in 1802. There were no means of opposing Napoleon's arbitrary demands, so the Genoese sent, and supplicated their conqueror to deign to give them a con-stitution worthy of their ancient liberty and religion ; and this he vouchsafed to do ; and with this gracious concession the final stroke was given to the liberties of Genoa. On the 29th of June, 1802, the new magistrates and the new doge entered into office, under the superintendence of the French plenipoten-tiary. Still Genoa rejoiced in the name of Republic, and alone, from the Alps to Calabria, with the exception of the little San Marino, did Genoa, under her ancient name, send am-bassadors to felicitate the French emperor at Milan, on his coronation with the iron crown of Lombardy as king of Italy.

Napoleon received this deputation well, with gracious

honeyed words, as was his wont; but underneath the surface he quietly determined to wipe off this blot from the face of his fair Italian kingdom. Amidst the splendour of the coronation, murmurs were spread abroad that humble, republican Genoa did not prosper in those days, that her commerce was fast dying away, that she could ill protect her seas from the African robber, and that if the tricoloured flag of France floated on her towers affairs would be otherwise ; and these reports, added to frequent seditions, had the effect the emperor desired.

It could be but little surprise to any one that the Ligurian Republic was thus ruined, after the fiery trials of the last ten years, and that when she was ordered to vote in her assembly on the subject of a union with France, there were but few dissentient voices, more especially as it was ordained that those who did not vote should be counted as assenting thereto. Consequently the majority was overwhelming in favour of the union, and Gerolamo Durazzo, the last of the long line of doges, was despatched to Milan, to beg that the emperor king would secure the happiness of his ancient country by incorporating it in his glorious empire.

It was a task fated by a curious destiny, that the last of Genoa's doges should have to kneel in humble supplication before a great Corsican general, and if feelings of country and ancestral pride influenced the minds of the conqueror and the conquered at this moment their respective triumph and humiliation must have been complete. The descendant of a family whose hands for generations had been against Genoa, and the representative of that haughty Republic, for whom cruelty in Corsica had been an heirloom, since the island in the dark ages of mediæval annals had first fallen under their sway, were here brought face to face under circumstances especially significant to each.

Pallid but dignified was the face of Durazzo as Napoleon raised him from his kneeling posture with bland and com-

forting words, promising to send Lebrun forthwith to eff
the union, and to visit Genoa in person ere long.

On the 11th of June, 1802, French banners floated o
the towers of Genoa ; their territory was divided into th
French departments, namely, those of Genoa proper, Mor
notte, and the Apennines, and the doge, Gerolamo Duraı
was further humbled by being made prefect of the Geno
department. The dawn of the 30th of this month bro
placidly over Genoa and her inhabitants. At the first ı
pearance of it the clanging of bells, the sound of artillery fr
fortress and from ship burst forth. In her most splendid dı
of victory never were signs of joy and gala more glorious.
right gaudy, merry funeral had the time-honoured Repul
of Genoa, when Napoleon came to read his funeral orat
over her fallen glories.

At the gate of S. Tommaso an eager, fluttering cro
stood waiting for Napoleon's arrival ; just such an eaş
fluttering crowd as had welcomed home a score of victorie
D'Orias from their many conquests. In the sumptuⲉ
palace where Andrea had breathed his last was Napolⲉ
lodged, and there he received the keys of the city and ı
adulation of his new subjects. Under the same walls ⲇ
Genoa and her great admiral draw their last breath, bⲉ
decrepit and worn out by the vicissitudes of glorious ɑ
eventful careers.

In the cathedral of S. Lorenzo, amidst the fumes ⲓ
incense, and to the music of an Ambrosian chant, did ᵗ
mouth of the archbishop utter the fatal oath of allegiance ᵗ
Napoleon ; the people here assembled praised heaven ᶠ
giving them so beneficent a ruler. And this ceremony cⲇ
cluded, the beneficent ruler hied him joyfully on his way ᵗ
Paris, leaving Lebrun, arch-treasurer of the empire, to arraı
the new form of government.

Certainly, from her union with France, Genoa receiveⲇ
temporary impetus to her commerce, such as had been ı

known under the later years of the dominion of the red cross ; and, until Napoleon's overthrow in 1814, Genoa plodded on her way peacefully, contented and obedient. But her identity was lost. She was no longer of greater weight in the scale of nations than any other well-to-do seafaring city.

Genoa's fortunes immediately after the downfall of Napoleon, pending her union with the house of Savoy, are interesting, most especially to England. The more youthful St. George [1] then took his aged, enslaved parent under his own wing, and for a time it was thought would re-establish the parental banner again on the walls of Genoa, but political interests required it to be otherwise ; and at the Congress of Vienna it was England who advocated most warmly her final union with the Sardinian dynasty.

It was with feelings of alarm that the Genoese saw an English fleet hovering outside the harbour in 1814. They still had an unpleasant recollection of the blockade which had taken place fourteen years before. They felt that the French general, Fresia, then within the walls, might act the part of Massena, and that once more they might be subjected to meagre diet. There existed, as usual, two parties within the walls, one who advocated an unconditional surrender, and the other for holding out to the last. These latter opinions were chiefly held in the freemasons' lodges, of which there were three in Genoa at that time ; and a wretched revolutionary set they were, with Morando for their grand master, and all the relics of the revolutionary days as his supporters. Morando, we are told, afterwards repented him of his errors, and, becoming eminently pious, passed his declining years in a convent.

Vincenzo Spinola, the city prefect, calmly awaited the turn events might take ; and when a large mob, headed by the opponents of blockades and starvation, presented itself before the council hall, he was willing enough to listen to them. They

---

[1] *Vide* ch. ii.

seized the French eagle and tore it down; and on the following day a crowd of men, women, and children paraded the strects, calling down imprecations on the French, and woe to any Frenchman who came across their path. One unfortunate individual in the Via Giulia was seized, insulted, and pelted, and on his trying to escape the women scratched him and the men pommelled him, and it was with difficulty he was extracted alive from the hands of his persecutors, so bitter was this sudden flame of wrath kindled against the French. Napoleon's statue was knocked down, and his head turned into a public foot-ball amidst imprecations on the fallen prisoner in Elba, so lately the idol of their hearts.

The discovery of some gunpowder placed about the town, and the suspicion that the French had done it, finally exasperated the people so much that it was impossible to hold out any longer, and the government admitted the English admiral, William Bentinck, amidst the same applause and the same festivities which had greeted Napoleon so short a time before.

On the 20th of April, the British fleet, under Vice-admiral Pellew, entered the port, and a commissary of marines, Giustiniani by name, presented himself to him, and thinking he was Admiral Bentinck, addressed him in courteous French. Forthwith Pellew indignantly responded in Italian, "Who are you? Are you another of those French devils?" "No," replied Giustiniani; "I am a Genoese noble." "Then," answered the British lion, "if you are Italian, why the devil don't you speak your own language." A rebuffed and wiser man, we may hope, the Genoese returned to his town.

When Bentinck entered Genoa he was received with loud acclamations of joy. He talked much about the establishment of the old *régime*, and in fact went so far as to appoint a provisionary government on the method of the old Republican government, pending the receipt of instructions from home.

For England and Austria, the welfare of Genoa, and the

future fortunes of the Ligurian capital, were to be one of the important subjects of discussion in the coming congress. The aggrandizement of the house of Savoy, as a counterpoise to French influence in Italy, had been a favourite scheme of William Pitt. Lord Castlereagh carried on the same project, and the Austrian prince, Metternich, was of the same mind ; hence the annexation of Genoa to the Sardinian dominions was with them a foregone conclusion, a plan conceived by the British ministry in London and matured by the congress of Vienna.

To Paris, the Genoese despatched one Pareto, to watch over their interests, and, if possible, to maintain for them their independence. To Vienna they sent Brignole for the same purpose, but without avail. Prince Metternich told a Genoese lady in Paris, that he considered few Genoese sincerely desired the re-establishment of the old republic, scarcely one in ten of the inhabitants ; whilst the emperor Francis told Brignole that " the republic is no longer of our days." And a gloomy foreboding that their day was over possessed the governors of Liguria.

Moreover, the inhabitants of the two Riviere, from Savona to Spezia, disliked Genoa. They had suffered, like Corsica, from centuries of oppression. If they had no distinguished leader like Corsica, no Sampiero, no Pasquale de Paoli, they had, at least, plenty of banditti and robbers who haunted their mountains—and formed nests for the discontented who disliked living peacefully under Genoa, and determined that none others should.

Hence a reconstruction of Genoa on her former basis was impossible. They talked much of making her a sort of Hanseatic town, with no territory outside her walls, dependent on Anglo-Austrian protection. They talked much of a principality on the same basis, but it soon became manifest that nothing short of absolute surrender of the city to the king of Sardinia would suit the policy of the allies. So, with mournful hearts, the Genoese learnt their fate. A sadness and gloom pervaded the city, which contrasted mournfully with their joyous reception of Bentinck, when the proclamation came ; and on the 27th of December, Dalrymple publicly notified to the Genoese the orders he had received from Vienna ; and thus was the once "proud mistress of those inland seas," the haughty Ligurian Republic, who had owned kings for her vassals, finally enrolled amongst the dominions of the house of Savoy as a duchy.

Now no city in Italy is more loyal, now no city in Italy gives a heartier welcome to the sovereign of the peninsula : and if this humiliation caused the doge, whom Bentinck had temporarily set up, to resign his post and kneel before Victor Emmanuel I., yet it took place before an Italian prince. It was no longer a Louis XIV., or a Napoleon, to whom an Italian did homage, but it was to the hope of the Italian future, to whom Genoa was to become the chief corner-stone.

Life and vitality were not extinct in the old Ligurian capital. Mazzini was born here. Mazzini was buried in her gorgeous cemetery. As the port of the Sardinian Government her commerce again flourished, and a new era opened before her. From Genoa, Garibaldi started on his world-famed expedition to Sicily ; and Genoa, in the advance and progress of united Italy, has acted no idle part. Far better thus than dragging on a weary existence as a factious, querulous republic, when this form of government was superannuated in Italy. All hope of restoring her past glory faded away when Christopher Columbus set foot on America. And better for her would it have been if the last three centuries could be blotted from her history, and that she had died whilst her honours lay thick around her.

As it is, we cannot separate her past from her latter history ; we look upon her rather in the light of one of those troublesome blots on the map of Europe which furnished occasions for war between conflicting monarchs, rather than

as the once flourishing Ligurian Republic, whose banner
floated over countless towers, from the Pillars of Hercules to
the remotest confines of the Black Sea.

> " Proud city, that by the Ligurian sea
>   Sittest as at a mirror, lofty and fair ;
>   And, towering from thy curving banks in air
> Scornest the mountains that attend on thee ;
> Why, with such structures to which Italy
>   Has nothing else, though glorious to compare,
>   Hast thou not souls with something like a share
> Of look, heart, spirit, and ingenuity ? "
>   LEIGH HUNT, *Ode to Genoa.*

APPENDIX.

ROMAN LIGURIA.

IT is a matter of speculation as to whether the name "Liguria" is of Celtic, Greek, or Roman origin ; some trace in it the name of a mystic hero called "Ligure," whilst others would derive it from "Legume," vegetables, from the fact, perhaps, that the barren Liguria was more wanting than other countries in this commodity. Most probably it is from the Latin word "ligurio," to lick, poetically illustrative of the way their whole territory is bathed by the Mediterranean.

In their origin the Ligurians were a wild Celtic race, who inhabited the rocky shores about Genoa, without a history until the Carthaginians warred against Rome: They threw in their lot with Carthage, and suffered for it accordingly. In the second Punic war Genoa alone of the towns of Liguria espoused the cause of Rome, and for this they were visited with condign punishment by Mago, Hannibal's brother ; the city was sacked, and the walls were razed, B.C. 205. Nevertheless, in the end Rome conquered, and Rome was not unmindful of her ally ; henceforth Genoa became the queen of Liguria, and her supremacy along this coast dates from the second Punic war.

A few years later Liguria threw in its lot with the cisalpine Gauls. They invaded Placentia and Cremona, but eventually the Ligurian valour and strength was overthrown by Paulus Emilius, near Albenga, and thenceforth this portion of Italy was incorporated with triumphant Rome.

But Liguria was a troublesome restless province ; again and again it rebelled, and again and again strong consular armies were sent against it.

"Adsuetumque malo Ligurem,"

says Virgil in his Georgics, and in these words he sums up the history of early Roman Liguria. Each insurrection was followed by a defeat, and each defeat brought with it attendant horrors. Nevertheless, Roman influence was the foundation of Genoa's prosperity. Recognizing the impossibility of establishing a firm influence in this part without adequate roadways, the Romans decided, with their usual skill, to open out a communication. From Tortona there branched off a road from the Aurelian, called the Via Postumia, through the mountain fastnesses to Acqui, and thence two branches diverged right and left, one leading into Gaul, and the other, after passing through Genoa, joined the Aurelian way at Luna. And thus was the first step established in the rise and development of Genoa.

Together with the advantages of direct communication with the Roman world, Liguria obtained the privileges of Roman civilization. Genoa was made a " municipium," and was inscribed in the tribe Galeria, which facts we gather from undisputable monuments—one at Tortona, which speaks of one Caius Marius Eliarus, as " Decurio et Flamen municipii Genuensis," and another, which was discovered at Rome in 1796, which bears testimony to Genoa's having been inscribed in the tribe Galeria.

Furthermore, we gather from a curious tablet found in the Polcevera valley in 1506, that in the year B.C. 118, on the occasion of a quarrel having arisen about territorial limits between the Genoese and the inhabitants of this valley, two Roman judges were sent to decide the dispute, and the disputants abided thereby. This tablet, which is of bronze, is still to be seen in the palace of the municipio at Genoa.

Without entering into the merits of a Roman " municipium," we may add that Genoa derived from these days of prosperity her later ideas of self-government and freedom—the right of the plebs to make itself heard in the affairs of the community ; and thus, whilst instilling order and tranquillity into the bosom of the Ligurian mountains, Rome acquired for herself the strong military assistance of these stalwart, seafaring mountaineers.

Thus, when Marius fought in Numidia against Jugurtha, it was a Ligurian soldier who discovered a hazardous path by which the capture of Capsa was effected, hitherto deemed impregnable, and where Jugurtha had concealed his treasures.

Great was the opposition raised by the Ligurians to the establishment of the empire in Rome. A fine monument at Torbia, between Monaco and Nice, was put up to testify to the triumphs of Augustus in subduing these refractory subjects ; and when Italy was divided by him into eleven districts, Liguria formed the ninth.

Turning herself now to the employments of peace, Genoa, as Strabo tells us, rapidly grew in commercial importance, and from her dependencies of Vado and Albenga went forth two low-born military rulers of the empire, namely, Pertinax, who for eighty days in A.D. 193, governed Rome, and Proculus, who, in A.D. 280, placed upon himself for a short time the imperial crown by an insurrection in Gaul.

The division of Augustus, and the rule of the empire continued unaltered in Liguria till the days of Constantine, when it became a consulate extending from the Po to the sea. At last came the downfall of the

Roman fabric, and the invasion of the Lombards, when Genoa, from her retired position on the sea away from the high roads of central Italy, became for years the residence of the Milanese bishops, and the spot where the institutions of Rome continued longest and most unadulterated, to blossom forth in succeeding centuries as the Genoese Republic.

II.

ON GENOESE COINS.

THE most ancient coin of the Genoese mint was the *danaro*, twelve of which went to a *soldo*, and two hundred and forty, or twenty *soldi*, to a *lira*. The *lira* and the *soldo* were, however, at that time not actually coined, but used only in reckoning.

Conrad III., when king of the Romans, gave permission to the Republic to coin their own money in December 1138, when the first *danaro* was struck. On the obverse is seen the *griffo* or castle of Genoa, with the three towers and the king's name, on the reverse is the cross, the banner of Genoa, and the inscription " *Janua.*"

This *danaro* was divided into halves and quarters, called respectively *medaglia* and *quartaro*. It was not long before a larger coin appeared, called the *grosso*, about 1172, as was the case in most other Italian mints. It was of silver, and is supposed to have been worth four *danari*, equal to about the value of the old Italian *danaro* of Otho I. And in contradistinction to this *grosso*, the ordinary *danaro* was called *piccolo* or *minuto*.

About a century later (1272) a new *grosso* came out, which, though bearing the name of the old coin, was double its value. But owing to the great debasement of coinage which is noticeable in all mints of this period, the new *grosso* could not be issued at the value of eight *danari* as it should have been, but was given out for twelve *danari*, and therefore was the first actual *soldo* in Genoa.

By this progressive law of debasement this double *grosso* passed by the end of the fourteenth century from the value of one to two *soldi*, and continued this apparent though fictitious increase in value down to our times. Under the doge Battista Fregoso (1478–83) this *grosso* was legally announced as worth five *soldi*.

Such was the condition of the chief silver coin of Genoa when, in 1488, G. G. Maria Sforza, duke of Milan, obtained the lordship over Genoa.[1] Desirous of pleasing the Republic he appointed Genoese

' *Vide* ch. ix.

2 E

governors, the first of whom was Pietro Campofregoso, the former doge, and a cardinal. He was succeeded by Agostino Adorno. Both these governors, as a mark of special favour, were permitted to put their name or arms with those of the duke on the coins.

The Avvocato Avignone has ably and intelligibly deciphered an inscription, which runs as follows—P : C : CA : DUCALIS : GUBER : IA, which is found around coins of the first of these above-named governors, to mean " Petrus Campofregosus Cardinalis Ducalis Gubernator Janua," instead of an unintelligible desire to introduce the word ducat, which I have seen in the explanation of it contained in eight or nine Dutch and French numismatical works.

Cardinal Campofregoso was governor from January to August, 1488, and after a short interval Agostino Adorno succeeded him, and his name is found in like manner on the coins, the reverse being the same in both cases, with S.A., the initials of the mint-master.

About this period, owing to the plentifulness of silver, all mints began to coin in that metal in hitherto unknown sizes. The Duke G. G. Maria Sforza was amongst the first to coin at Milan an actual silver *lira*, which, from having the duke's head on it, was called a *testone*. The monetary system of Genoa and Milan being somewhat different, the coin which in Milan was worth twenty *soldi*, was at Genoa only worth fourteen *soldi* eight *danari*. Hence the duke, wishing to have a Genoese coin similar to the *testone*, but conformable to the Genoese system, had a coin struck in Genoa worth fifteen Genoese *soldi*. Hence we find that G. G. Maria Sforza's coin struck at Genoa is rather heavier than his Milanese *testone*.

Soon after this the Genoese expressed a wish to have an actual *lira* of twenty Genoese *soldi*. We have documentary proof of the existence of the coin of fifteen *soldi* in 1490, and three years later of that of twenty *soldi*, and both of them are not unfrequent in collections. They were both denominated *grossoni* to distinguish them from the *grossi* of five *soldi* ; and although they had no head stamped upon them, nevertheless, out of imitation of Milan, the Genoese ordinarily spoke of them as *testoni*, a name which is even now in use there, slightly puzzling to the uninitiated.

The most ancient gold coin, except one or two which never obtained currency, was the *genovino d'oro*, afterwards called *fiorino* after the Florentine usage, and finally *ducato* after the fashion of the Venetians. It was about the same weight as the silver *grosso* of Fregoso.

Louis XII. of France, on his first arrival in Genoa in 1499, preserved the form of the ducat, but put on it his own name and French lilies ; but after the revolution in 1507,[1] when the type of the silver coins was changed, he introduced the gold *scudo* (*écu* of France), which, like its French proto-

---

[1] *Vide* ch. ix.

type, was called *del sole,* from the representation of the greater planet which appeared over the crown and shield of lilies.

After the recovery of her freedom, Genoa continued to coin *scudi,* and in 1541 the weight of this *scudo* was decided by a decree of the senate, and was called *delle cinque stampe* " of the five mints," from the fact that five or more Italian and foreign mints agreed to coin money of equal value, though with their own types. And this became the monetary basis of gold down to the fall of the Republic, varying but little in weight from the *scudi* struck in 1571, and is always referred to in the subsequent financial documents of the Republic, or, to speak more correctly, it is the *doppia delle cinque stampe,* being merely a double *scudo* of that weight.[1]

The earliest appearance of the gold coinage of Genoa was in the first half of the thirteenth century, and was valued at eight *soldi,* and called, as above mentioned, the *genovino d'oro.* It was subdivided into two smaller gold coins, namely, a *quartardo* of two *soldi* and an *ottavo* of one. This latter coin was very small, and but little used. There was also a *terzarolo,* or a third of a *genovino d'oro,* coined by some of the doges in gold, having only the inscription DUX IANUÆ, and no ordinal numbers.

The *genovino* of Genoa and the *fiorino* of Florence progressed by the beginning of the fourteenth century to the value of sixteen or seventeen *soldi;* and in 1309 in Genoa it became twenty *soldi* or the first actual gold *lira.* It continued thus to rise in value up to twenty-five *soldi* until the beginning of the fifteenth century, when its name was changed to *ducato,* probably because the *fiorino* of Florence had been debased. Nevertheless, the name of *fiorino* continued to be used in ordinary speech as a fixed equivalent for twenty-five *soldi* whilst the *ducato* continued to rise in value, and this has continued down to our own times.

In 1412 the *ducat* was worth approximately thirty soldi, or one-and-a-half *lira,* in 1434 two *lire,* in 1454 two-and-a-half *lire,* from 1484–89 three-and-a-half *lire.* It continued rising to sixty-two and sixty-four *soldi* until 1507, when Louis XII. substituted his *écu* of less value, which fixed it at three *lire.* After this no more ducats were coined, but continued long in circulation.

In like manner the *scudo* perpetually rose in value owing to the debasement of *soldi* and *danari,* and from the change in value of silver and gold. In 1541 it was worth sixty-eight *soldi,* and the *scudo delle cinque stampe* was legally established at that value. The governor of Genoa wished it to remain immutable, but this was impossible, and it remained a nominal *scudo* of sixty-eight *soldi,* just as the *fiorino* remained a nominal representative of twenty-five *soldi.*

---

[1] *Vide* Gandolfi della moneta antica di Genova.

But the real *scudo* continued its upward rise, and was called *d'oro in oro* to denote the genuineness of the metal of which it was made. In 1551 the *scudo* was of the value of three *lire* ten *soldi*, and in 1593 four *lire* eight *soldi*.

In this manner did the rulers of Genoa ineffectually strive to check the inconvenience arising from the increased value of gold ; and in 1593 a new silver coin was struck which bore the name of *scudo*. It is a well-known coin, and was called the *scudo coronato* from the fact that there appears a crown over the above-mentioned castle of Genoa, and also the *scudo d'argento* to distinguish it from its golden namesake. But as with the gold coin so it was with the silver, which kept rising in value until at the fusion of Genoa with the French Empire the Genoese silver *scudo* had a commercial value of nine *lire* sixteen *soldi*.

We have documentary evidence to prove that a silver *scudo* was issued·prior to 1593 without a crown, probably about 1563, of the value of four *lire*, and somewhat smaller than the *scudo coronato*, but there appear to be no specimens now in existence, and if such a coin did exist, its circulation must have been very limited, and was probably called in on the issue of the *scudi coronati*. For after the assumption of the title of "serenissimo" by the Republic, and its recognition by the emperor of Austria, an uncrowned coat-of-arms would be considered as a national indignity.

Subsequent to 1593 the silver *scudi* were multiplied in weight double, triple, and so forth, keeping the original type and basis until 1638, when the image of the Virgin was substituted for the castle.[1] In 1666 a coin was struck called *di San Giorgio*, or a piece of eight *reales*, showing the influence of the bank of St. George and of the Spaniards at this time over Genoese affairs. During the remainder of the Republic's natural life new pieces were issued for various amounts, two, three, four, or ten *scudi* in silver, and twelve, twenty-five, or fifty *scudi* in gold, all of which are plentiful in collections.

Apart from the Republic's coinage proper, there exist endless specimens of private mints, the Spinola, D'Oria, Grimaldi, and Fieschi, to dive into which would be an endless and unsatisfactory study.

[1] *Vide* ch. xvi.

PRINTED BY WILLIAM CLOWES AND SONS, LIMITED, LONDON AND BECCLES.

A LIST OF

C. KEGAN PAUL & CO.'S PUBLICATIONS.

3.81.

1 *Paternoster Square,*
London.

A LIST OF

C. KEGAN PAUL & CO.'S
PUBLICATIONS.

ADAMS (F. O.) F.R.G.S.—THE HISTORY OF JAPAN. From the Earliest Period to the Present Time. New Edition, revised. 2 volumes. With Maps and Plans. Demy 8vo. price 21*s*. each.

ADAMSON (H. T.) B.D.—THE TRUTH AS IT IS IN JESUS. Crown 8vo. cloth, price 8*s*. 6*d*.

THE THREE SEVENS. Crown 8vo. cloth, price 5*s*. 6*d*.

A. K. H. B.—FROM A QUIET PLACE. A New Volume of Sermons. Crown 8vo. cloth, price 5*s*.

ALBERT (Mary).—HOLLAND AND HER HEROES TO THE YEAR 1585. An Adaptation from ' Motley's Rise of the Dutch Republic.' Small crown 8vo. price 4*s*. 6*d*.

ALLEN (Rev. R.) M.A.—ABRAHAM ; HIS LIFE, TIMES, AND TRAVELS, 3,800 years ago. With Map. Second Edition. Post 8vo. price 6*s*.

ALLEN (Grant) B.A.—PHYSIOLOGICAL ÆSTHETICS. Large post 8vo. 9*s*.

ALLIES (T. W.) M.A.—PER CRUCEM AD LUCEM. The Result of a Life. 2 vols. Demy 8vo. cloth, price 25*s*.

A LIFE'S DECISION. Crown 8vo. cloth, price 7*s*. 6*d*.

ANDERSON (R. C.) C.E.—TABLES FOR FACILITATING THE CALCULATION OF EVERY DETAIL IN CONNECTION WITH EARTHEN AND MASONRY DAMS. Royal 8vo. price £2. 2*s*.

ARCHER (Thomas)—ABOUT MY FATHER'S BUSINESS. Work amidst the Sick, the Sad, and the Sorrowing. Cheaper Edition. Crown 8vo. price 2*s*. 6*d*.

ARNOLD (Arthur)—SOCIAL POLITICS. Demy 8vo. cloth, price 14*s*.

FREE LAND. Crown 8vo. cloth, price 6*s*.

BADGER (George Percy) D.C.L.—AN ENGLISH-ARABIC LEXICON. In which the equivalent for English Words and Idiomatic Sentences are rendered into literary and colloquial Arabic. Royal 4to. cloth, price £9. 9*s*.

BAGEHOT (Walter)—THE ENGLISH CONSTITUTION. A New Edition, Revised and Corrected, with an Introductory Dissertation on Recent Changes and Events. Crown 8vo. price 7*s*. 6*d*.

LOMBARD STREET. A Description of the Money Market. Seventh Edition. Crown 8vo. price 7*s*. 6*d*.

SOME ARTICLES ON THE DEPRECIATION OF SILVER, AND TOPICS CONNECTED WITH IT. Demy 8vo. price 5*s*.

BAGOT (Alan)—ACCIDENTS IN MINES : Their Causes and Prevention. Crown 8vo. price 6*s*.

BAKER (Sir Sherston, Bart.)—HALLECK'S INTERNATIONAL LAW ; or, Rules Regulating the Intercourse of States in Peace and War. A New Edition, revised, with Notes and Cases. 2 vols. Demy 8vo. price 38*s*.

THE LAWS RELATING TO QUARANTINE. Crown 8vo. cloth, price 12*s*. 6*d*.

BALDWIN (Capt. J. H.) F.Z.S. Bengal Staff Corps.—THE LARGE AND SMALL GAME OF BENGAL AND THE NORTH-WESTERN PROVINCES OF INDIA. 4to. With numerous Illustrations. Second Edition. Price 21*s*.

BARNES (William)—AN OUTLINE OF ENGLISH SPEECHCRAFT. Crown 8vo. price 4*s*.

OUTLINES OF REDECRAFT (LOGIC). With English Wording. Crown 8vo. cloth, price 3*s*.

BARTLEY (G. C. T.)—DOMESTIC ECONOMY : Thrift in Every-Day Life. Taught in Dialogues suitable for children of all ages. Small cr. 8vo. price 2*s*.

BAUR (Ferdinand) Dr. Ph., Professor in Maulbronn.—A PHILOLOGICAL INTRODUCTION TO GREEK AND LATIN FOR STUDENTS. Translated and adapted from the German. By C. KEGAN PAUL, M.A. Oxon., and the Rev. E. D. STONE, M.A., late Fellow of King's College, Cambridge, and Assistant Master at Eton. Crown 8vo. price 6*s*.

BAYNES (Rev. Canon R. H.)—AT THE COMMUNION TIME. A Manual for Holy Communion. With a preface by the Right Rev. the Lord Bishop of Derry and Raphoe. Cloth, price 1*s*. 6*d*.

BELLINGHAM (Henry) M.P., Barrister-at-Law—SOCIAL ASPECTS OF CATHOLICISM AND PROTESTANTISM IN THEIR CIVIL BEARING UPON NATIONS. Translated and adapted from the French of M. le Baron de Haulleville. With a preface by His Eminence Cardinal Manning. Second and Cheaper Edition. Crown 8vo. price 3*s*. 6*d*.

BENT (J. Theodore)—GENOA : How the Republic Rose and Fell. With 18 Illustrations. Demy 8vo. cloth, price 18*s*.

BONWICK (J.) F.R.G.S.—PYRAMID FACTS AND FANCIES. Crown 8vo. price 5*s*.

EGYPTIAN BELIEF AND MODERN THOUGHT. Large Post 8vo. cloth, price 10*s*. 6*d*.

BOWEN (H. C.) M.A., Head Master of the Grocers' Company's Middle Class School at Hackney.

STUDIES IN ENGLISH, for the use of Modern Schools. Small crown 8vo. price 1*s*. 6*d*.

ENGLISH GRAMMAR FOR BEGINNERS. Fcap. 8vo. cloth, price 1*s*.

BOWRING (Sir John).—AUTOBIOGRAPHICAL RECOLLECTIONS OF SIR JOHN BOWRING. With Memoir by LEWIN B. BOWRING. Demy 8vo. price 14*s*.

BRIDGETT (Rev. T. E.)— HISTORY OF THE HOLY EUCHARIST IN GREAT BRITAIN. 2 vols. demy 8vo. cloth, price 18*s*.

BRODRICK (the Hon. G. C.)—POLITICAL STUDIES. Demy 8vo. cloth, price 14*s*.

BROOKE (Rev. S. A.) M.A., Chaplain in Ordinary to Her Majesty the Queen, and Minister of Bedford Chapel, Bloomsbury.

LIFE AND LETTERS OF THE LATE REV. F. W. ROBERTSON, M.A., Edited by.

I. Uniform with the Sermons. 2 vols. With Steel Portrait. Price 7*s*. 6*d*.
II. Library Edition. 8vo. With Portrait. Price 12*s*.
III. A Popular Edition. In 1 vol. 8vo. price 6*s*.

BROOKE (*Rev. S. A.*) *M.A.*—cont.

THE FIGHT OF FAITH. Sermons preached on various occasions. Third Edition. Crown 8vo. price 7*s*. 6*d*.

THEOLOGY IN THE ENGLISH POETS.—Cowper, Coleridge, Wordsworth, and Burns. Fourth and Cheaper Edition. Post 8vo. price 5*s*.

CHRIST IN MODERN LIFE. Fourteenth and Cheaper Edition. Crown 8vo. price 5*s*.

SERMONS. First Series. Eleventh Edition. Crown 8vo. price 6*s*.

SERMONS. Second Series. Third Edition. Crown 8vo. price 7*s*.

FREDERICK DENISON MAURICE: The Life and Work of. A Memorial Sermon. Crown 8vo. sewed, price 1*s*.

BROOKE (*W. G.*) *M.A.*—THE PUBLIC WORSHIP REGULATION ACT. With a Classified Statement of its Provisions, Notes, and Index. Third Edition, revised and corrected. Crown 8vo. price 3*s*. 6*d*.

SIX PRIVY COUNCIL JUDGMENTS—1850–72. Annotated by. Third Edition. Crown 8vo. price 9*s*.

BROUN (*J. A.*)—MAGNETIC OBSERVATIONS AT TREVANDRUM AND AUGUSTIA MALLEY. Vol. 1. 4to. price 63*s*.

The Report from above, separately, sewed, price 21*s*.

BROWN (*Rev. J. Baldwin*) *B.A.*—THE HIGHER LIFE. Its Reality, Experience, and Destiny. Fifth Edition. Crown 8vo. price 5*s*.

DOCTRINE OF ANNIHILATION IN THE LIGHT OF THE GOSPEL OF LOVE. Five Discourses. Third Edition. Crown 8vo. price 2*s*. 6*d*.

THE CHRISTIAN POLICY OF LIFE. A Book for Young Men of Business. New and Cheaper Edition. Crown 8vo. cloth, price, 3*s*. 6*d*.

BROWN (*J. Croumbie*) *LL.D.*—REBOISEMENT IN FRANCE; or, Records of the Replanting of the Alps, the Cevennes, and the Pyrenees with Trees, Herbage, and Bush. Demy 8vo. price 12*s*. 6*d*.

THE HYDROLOGY OF SOUTHERN AFRICA. Demy 8vo. price 10*s*. 6*d*.

BROWNE (*W. R.*)—THE INSPIRATION OF THE NEW TESTAMENT. With a Preface by the Rev. J. P. NORRIS, D.D. Fcp. 8vo. cloth, 2*s*. 6*d*.

BURCKHARDT (*Jacob*)—THE CIVILIZATION OF THE PERIOD OF THE RENAISSANCE IN ITALY. Authorised translation, by S. G. C. Middlemore. 2 vols. Demy 8vo. price 24*s*.

BURTON (*Mrs. Richard*)—THE INNER LIFE OF SYRIA, PALESTINE, AND THE HOLY LAND. With Maps, Photographs, and Coloured Plates. 2 vols. Second Edition. Demy 8vo. price 24*s*.

*** Also a Cheaper Edition in one volume. Large post 8vo. cloth, price 10*s*. 6*d*.

BURTON (*Capt. Richard F.*)—THE GOLD MINES OF MIDIAN AND THE RUINED MIDIANITE CITIES. A Fortnight's Tour in North Western Arabia. With numerous illustrations. Second Edition. Demy 8vo. price 18*s*.

THE LAND OF MIDIAN REVISITED. With numerous Illustrations on Wood and by Chromolithography. 2 vols. Demy 8vo. cloth, price 32*s*.

BUSBECQ (*Ogier Ghiselin de*)—HIS LIFE AND LETTERS. By CHARLES THORNTON FORSTER, M.A., and F. H. BLACKBURNE DANIELL, M.A. 2 vols. With Frontispieces. Demy 8vo. cloth, price 24*s*.

CANDLER (H.)—THE GROUNDWORK OF BELIEF. Crown 8vo. cloth, price 7s.

CARPENTER (Dr. Philip P.)—HIS LIFE AND WORK. Edited by his brother, Russell Lant Carpenter. With Portrait and Vignettes. Second Edition. Crown 8vo. cloth, price 7s. 6d.

CARPENTER (W. B.) LL.D., M.D., F.R.S., &c.—THE PRINCIPLES OF MENTAL PHYSIOLOGY. With their Applications to the Training and Discipline of the Mind, and the Study of its Morbid Conditions. Illustrated. Fifth Edition. 8vo. price 12s.

CERVANTES—THE INGENIOUS KNIGHT DON QUIXOTE DE LA MANCHA. A New Translation from the Originals of 1605 and 1608. By A. J. DUFFIELD. With Notes. 3 vols. Demy 8vo. price 42s.

CHEYNE (Rev. T. K.)—THE PROPHECIES OF ISAIAH. Translated with Critical Notes and Dissertations. 2 vols. Demy 8vo. cloth, price 25s.

CLAYDEN (P. W.)—ENGLAND UNDER LORD BEACONSFIELD. The Political History of the Last Six Years, from the end of 1873 to the beginning of 1880. Second Edition, with Index and continuation to March 1880. Demy 8vo. cloth, price 16s.

CLODD (Edward) F.R.A.S.—THE CHILDHOOD OF THE WORLD: a Simple Account of Man in Early Times. Sixth Edition. Crown 8vo. price 3s.
   A Special Edition for Schools. Price 1s.

THE CHILDHOOD OF RELIGIONS. Including a Simple Account of the Birth and Growth of Myths and Legends. Third Thousand. Crown 8vo. price 5s.
   A Special Edition for Schools. Price 1s. 6d.

JESUS OF NAZARETH. With a brief sketch of Jewish History to the Time of His Birth. Small crown 8vo. cloth, price 6s.

COGHLAN (J. Cole) D.D.—THE MODERN PHARISEE AND OTHER SERMONS. Edited by the Very Rev. H. H. DICKINSON, D.D., Dean of Chapel Royal, Dublin. New and Cheaper Edition. Crown 8vo. cloth, 7s. 6d.

COLERIDGE (Sara)—PHANTASMION. A Fairy Tale. With an Introductory Preface by the Right Hon. Lord Coleridge, of Ottery St. Mary. A New Edition. Illustrated. Crown 8vo. price 7s. 6d.

MEMOIR AND LETTERS OF SARA COLERIDGE. Edited by her Daughter. With Index. Cheap Edition. With one Portrait. Price 7s. 6d.

COLLINS (Mortimer)—THE SECRET OF LONG LIFE. Small crown 8vo. cloth, price 3s. 6d.

CONNELL (A. K.)—DISCONTENT AND DANGER IN INDIA. Small crown 8vo. cloth, price 3s. 6d.

COOKE (Prof. J. P.) of the Harvard University.—SCIENTIFIC CULTURE. Crown 8vo. price 1s.

COOPER (H. J.)—THE ART OF FURNISHING ON RATIONAL AND ÆSTHETIC PRINCIPLES. New and Cheaper Edition. Fcap. 8vo. cloth, price 1s. 6d.

CORFIELD (Professor) M.D.—HEALTH. Crown 8vo. cloth, price 6s.

CORY (William)—A GUIDE TO MODERN ENGLISH HISTORY. Part I.— MDCCCXV.–MDCCCXXX. Demy 8vo. cloth, price 9s.

COURTNEY (W. L.)—THE METAPHYSICS OF JOHN STUART MILL. Crown 8vo. cloth, price 5s. 6d.

COX (Rev. Sir George W.) M.A., Bart.—A History of Greece from the Earliest Period to the end of the Persian War. New Edition. 2 vols. Demy 8vo. price 36s.

The Mythology of the Aryan Nations. New Edition. 2 vols. Demy 8vo. price 28s.

A General History of Greece from the Earliest Period to the Death of Alexander the Great, with a sketch of the subsequent History to the present time. New Edition. Crown 8vo. price 7s. 6d.

Tales of Ancient Greece. New Edition. Small crown 8vo. price 6s.

School History of Greece. New Edition. With Maps. Fcp. 8vo. price 3s. 6d.

The Great Persian War from the History of Herodotus. New Edition. Fcp. 8vo. price 3s. 6d.

A Manual of Mythology in the form of Question and Answer. New Edition. Fcp. 8vo. price 3s.

COX (Rev. Sir G. W.) M.A., Bart., and JONES (Eustace Hinton)—Popular Romances of the Middle Ages. Second Edition, in 1 vol. Crown 8vo. cloth, price 6s.

COX (Rev. Samuel)—Salvator Mundi; or, Is Christ the Saviour of all Men? Sixth Edition. Crown 8vo. price 5s.

The Genesis of Evil, and other Sermons, mainly expository. Second Edition. Crown 8vo. cloth, price 6s.

A Commentary on the Book of Job. With a Translation. Demy 8vo. cloth, price 15s.

CRAUFURD (A. H.)—Seeking for Light: Sermons. Crown 8vo. cloth, price 5s.

CRAVEN (Mrs.)—A Year's Meditations. Crown 8vo. cloth, price 6s.

CRAWFURD (Oswald)—Portugal, Old and New. With Illustrations and Maps. Demy 8vo. cloth, price 16s.

CROMPTON (Henry) — Industrial Conciliation. Fcap. 8vo. price 2s. 6d.

CROZIER (John Beattie) M.B.—The Religion of the Future. Crown 8vo. cloth, price 6s.

DALTON (John Neale) M.A., R.N.—Sermons to Naval Cadets. Preached on board H.M.S. 'Britannia.' Second Edition. Small crown 8vo. cloth, price 3s. 6d.

DAVIDSON (Rev. Samuel) D.D., LL.D. — The New Testament, translated from the Latest Greek Text of Tischendorf. A New and thoroughly revised Edition. Post 8vo. price 10s. 6d.

Canon of the Bible: Its Formation, History, and Fluctuations. Third and revised Edition. Small crown 8vo. price 5s.

DAVIES (Rev. J. L.) M.A.—Theology and Morality. Essays on Questions of Belief and Practice. Crown 8vo. price 7s. 6d.

DAWSON (Geo.) M.A.—Prayers, with a Discourse on Prayer. Edited by his Wife. Fifth Edition. Crown 8vo. 6s.

Sermons on Disputed Points and Special Occasions. Edited by his Wife. Third Edition. Crown 8vo. price 6s.

Sermons on Daily Life and Duty. Edited by his Wife. Third Edition. Crown 8vo. price 6s.

DE REDCLIFFE (Viscount Stratford) P.C., K.G., G.C.B.—WHY AM'I A CHRISTIAN? Fifth Edition. Crown 8vo. price 3s.

DESPREZ (Philip S.) B.D.—DANIEL AND JOHN; or, the Apocalypse of the Old and that of the New Testament. Demy 8vo. cloth, price 12s.

DE TOCQUEVILLE (A.)—CORRESPONDENCE AND CONVERSATIONS OF, WITH NASSAU WILLIAM SENIOR, from 1834 to 1859. Edited by M. C. M. SIMPSON. 2 vols. post 8vo. price 21s.

DOWDEN (Edward) LL.D.—SHAKSPERE: a Critical Study of his Mind and Art. Fifth Edition. Post 8vo. price 12s.

STUDIES IN LITERATURE, 1789-1877. Large Post 8vo. price 12s.

DREWRY (G. O.) M.D.—THE COMMON-SENSE MANAGEMENT OF THE STOMACH. Fifth Edition. Fcp. 8vo. price 2s. 6d.

DREWRY (G. O.) M.D., and BARTLETT (H. C.) Ph.D., F.C.S. CUP AND PLATTER: or, Notes on Food and its Effects. New and Cheaper Edition. Small 8vo. price 1s. 6d.

DU MONCEL (Count)—THE TELEPHONE, THE MICROPHONE, AND THE PHONOGRAPH. With 74 Illustrations. Small crown 8vo. cloth, price 5s.

EDEN (Frederick)—THE NILE WITHOUT A DRAGOMAN. Second Edition. Crown 8vo. price 7s. 6d.

EDGEWORTH (F. Y.).—MATHEMATICAL PSYCHICS. An Essay on the Application of Mathematics to Social Science. Demy 8vo. cloth 7s. 6d.

EDIS (Robert W.) F.S.A. &c.—DECORATION AND FURNITURE OF TOWN HOUSES: a Series of Cantor Lectures, delivered before the Society of Arts, 1880. Second Edition, Amplified and Enlarged. With 29 Full-page Illustrations and numerous Sketches. Square 8vo. cloth, price 12s. 6d.

EDUCATIONAL CODE OF THE PRUSSIAN NATION, IN ITS PRESENT FORM. In accordance with the Decisions of the Common Provincial Law, and with those of Recent Legislation. Crown 8vo. cloth, price 2s. 6d.

ELSDALE (Henry)—STUDIES IN TENNYSON'S IDYLLS. Crown 8vo. price 5s.

ELYOT (Sir Thomas)—THE BOKE NAMED THE GOUERNOUR. Edited from the First Edition of 1531 by HENRY HERBERT STEPHEN CROFT, M.A., Barrister-at-Law. With Portraits of Sir Thomas and Lady Elyot, copied by permission of her Majesty from Holbein's Original Drawings at Windsor Castle. 2 vols. fcp. 4to. cloth, price 50s.

EVANS (Mark)—THE STORY OF OUR FATHER'S LOVE, told to Children. Fifth and Cheaper Edition. With Four Illustrations. Fcp. 8vo. price 1s. 6d.

A BOOK OF COMMON PRAYER AND WORSHIP FOR HOUSEHOLD USE, compiled exclusively from the Holy Scriptures. Fcp. 8vo. price 1s.

THE GOSPEL OF HOME LIFE. Crown 8vo. cloth, price 4s. 6d.

THE KING'S STORY-BOOK. In Three Parts. Fcap. 8vo. cloth, price 1s. 6d. each.

** Parts I. and II. with Eight Illustrations and Two Picture Maps, now ready.

EX-CIVILIAN.—LIFE IN THE MOFUSSIL: or Civilian Life in Lower Bengal. 2 vols. Large post 8vo. price 14s.

FIELD (Horace) B.A. Lond.—THE ULTIMATE TRIUMPH OF CHRISTIANITY. Small crown 8vo. cloth, price 3s. 6d

FINN (The late James) M.R.A.S.—STIRRING TIMES ; or, Records from Jerusalem Consular Chronicles of 1853 to 1856. Edited and Compiled by his Widow ; with a Preface by the Viscountess STRANGFORD. 2 vols. Demy 8vo. price 30s.

FOLKESTONE RITUAL CASE : the Arguments, Proceedings, Judgment, and Report. Demy 8vo. price 25s.

FORMBY (Rev. Henry)—ANCIENT ROME AND ITS CONNECTION WITH THE CHRISTIAN RELIGION : An Outline of the History of the City from its First Foundation down to the Erection of the Chair of St. Peter, A.D. 42–47. With numerous Illustrations of Ancient Monuments, Sculpture, and Coinage, and of the Antiquities of the Christian Catacombs. Royal 'ᵒ cloth extra, £2. 10s ; roxburgh half-morocco, £2. 12s. 6d.

FOWLE (Rev. T. W.) M.A.—THE RECONCILIATION OF RELIGION AND SCIENCE. Being Essays on Immortality, Inspiration, Miracles, and the Being of Christ. Demy 8vo. price 10s. 6d.

THE DIVINE LEGATION OF CHRIST. Crown 8vo. cloth, price 7s.

FRASER (Donald)—EXCHANGE TABLES OF STERLING AND INDIAN RUPEE CURRENCY, upon a new and extended system, embracing Values from One Farthing to One Hundred Thousand Pounds, and at rates progressing, in Sixteenths of a Penny, from 1s. 9d. to 2s. 3d. per Rupee. Royal 8vo. price 10s. 6d.

FRISWELL (J. Hain)—THE BETTER SELF. Essays for Home Life. Crown 8vo. price 6s.

GARDNER (J.) M.D.—LONGEVITY : THE MEANS OF PROLONGING LIFE AFTER MIDDLE AGE. Fourth Edition, revised and enlarged. Small crown 8vo. price 4s.

GEBLER (Karl Von)—GALILEO GALILEI AND THE ROMAN CURIA, from Authentic Sources. Translated with the sanction of the Author, by Mrs. GEORGE STURGE. Demy 8vo. cloth, price 12s.

GEDDES (James)—HISTORY OF THE ADMINISTRATION OF JOHN DE WITT, Grand Pensionary of Holland. Vol. I. 1623—1654. With Portrait. Demy 8vo. cloth, price 15s.

GEORGE (Henry)—PROGRESS AND POVERTY : an Inquiry into the Causes of Industrial Depressions, and of Increase of Want with Increase of Wealth. The Remedy. Post 8vo. cloth, price 7s. 6d.

GILBERT (Mrs.)—AUTOBIOGRAPHY AND OTHER MEMORIALS. Edited by Josiah Gilbert. Third and Cheaper Edition. With Steel Portrait and several Wood Engravings. Crown 8vo. price 7s. 6d.

GILL (Rev. W. W.) B.A.—MYTHS AND SONGS FROM THE SOUTH PACIFIC. With a Preface by F. Max Müller, M.A., Professor of Comparative Philology at Oxford. Post 8vo. price 9s.

GLOVER (F.) M.A.—EXEMPLA LATINA. A First Construing Book with Short Notes, Lexicon, and an Introduction to the Analysis of Sentences. Fcp. 8vo. cloth, price 2s.

GODWIN (William)—WILLIAM GODWIN: HIS FRIENDS AND CONTEM-PORARIES. With Portraits and Facsimiles of the Handwriting of Godwin and his Wife. By C. KEGAN PAUL. 2 vols. Large post 8vo. price 28*s.*

THE GENIUS OF CHRISTIANITY UNVEILED. Being Essays never before published. Edited, with a Preface, by C. Kegan Paul. Crown 8vo. price 7*s.* 6*d.*

GOLDSMID (Sir Francis Henry) Bart., Q.C., M.P.—MEMOIR OF. With Portrait. Crown 8vo. cloth, price 5*s.*

GOODENOUGH (Commodore J. G.) R.N., C.B., C.M.G.—MEMOIR OF, with Extracts from his Letters and Journals. Edited by his Widow. With Steel Engraved Portrait. Square 8vo. cloth, 5*s.*

*** Also a Library Edition with Maps, Woodcuts, and Steel Engraved Portrait. Square post 8vo. price 14*s.*

GOSSE (Edmund W.)—STUDIES IN THE LITERATURE OF NORTHERN EUROPE. With a Frontispiece designed and etched by Alma Tadema. Large post 8vo. cloth, price 12*s.*

GOULD (Rev. S. Baring) M.A.—THE VICAR OF MORWENSTOW: a Memoir of the Rev. R. S. Hawker. With Portrait. Third Edition, revised. Square post 8vo. 10*s.* 6d.

GERMANY, PRESENT AND PAST. 2 vols. Large crown 8vo. cloth, price 21*s.*

GRIFFITH (Thomas) A.M.—THE GOSPEL OF THE DIVINE LIFE: a Study of the Fourth Evangelist. Demy 8vo. cloth, price 14*s.*

GRIMLEY (Rev. H. N.) M.A.—TREMADOC SERMONS, CHIEFLY ON THE SPIRITUAL BODY, THE UNSEEN WORLD, AND THE DIVINE HUMANITY. Second Edition. Crown 8vo. price 6*s.*

GRÜNER (M. L.)—STUDIES OF BLAST FURNACE PHENOMENA. Trans-lated by L. D. B. GORDON, F.R.S.E., F.G.S. Demy 8vo. price 7*s.* 6*d.*

GURNEY (Rev. Archer)—WORDS OF FAITH AND CHEER. A Mission of Instruction and Suggestion. Crown 8vo. price 6*s.*

HAECKEL (Prof. Ernst)—THE HISTORY OF CREATION. Translation revised by Professor E. RAY LANKESTER, M.A., F.R.S. With Coloured Plates and Genealogical Trees of the various groups of both plants and animals. 2 vols. Second Edition. Post 8vo. cloth, price 32*s.*

THE HISTORY OF THE EVOLUTION OF MAN. With numerous Illustra-tions. 2 vols. Post 8vo. price 32*s.*

FREEDOM IN SCIENCE AND TEACHING. With a Prefatory Note by T. H. HUXLEY, F.R.S. Crown 8vo. cloth, price 5*s.*

HAKE (A. Egmont)—PARIS ORIGINALS, with Twenty Etchings, by LÉON RICHETON. Large post 8vo. price 14*s.*

HALLECK'S INTERNATIONAL LAW; or, Rules Regulating the Inter-course of States in Peace and War. A New Edition, revised, with Notes and Cases, by Sir SHERSTON BAKER, Bart. 2 vols. Demy 8vo. price 38*s.*

HARTINGTON (The Right Hon. the Marquis of) M.P.—ELECTION SPEECHES IN 1879 AND 1880. With Address to the Electors of North East Lancashire. Crown 8vo. cloth, price 3*s*. 6*d*.

HAWEIS (Rev. H. R.) M.A.—CURRENT COIN. Materialism—The Devil — Crime — Drunkenness — Pauperism — Emotion — Recreation — The Sabbath. Third Edition. Crown 8vo. price 6*s*.

SPEECH IN SEASON. Fourth Edition. Crown 8vo. price 9*s*.

THOUGHTS FOR THE TIMES. Eleventh Edition. Crown 8vo. price 7*s*. 6*d*.

UNSECTARIAN FAMILY PRAYERS. New and Cheaper Edition. Fcp. 8vo. price 1*s*. 6*d*.

ARROWS IN THE AIR. Second Edition. Crown 8vo. cloth, price 6*s*.

HAWKINS (Edwards Comerford) — SPIRIT AND FORM. Sermons preached in the Parish Church of Leatherhead. Crown 8vo. cloth, price 6*s*.

HAYES (A. H.), Junr.—NEW COLORADO AND THE SANTA FÉ TRAIL. With Map and 60 Illustrations. Crown 8vo. cloth, price 9*s*.

HEIDENHAIN (Rudolf) M.D.—ANIMAL MAGNETISM : PHYSIOLOGICAL OBSERVATIONS. Translated from the Fourth German Edition by L. C. WOOLDRIDGE, with a Preface by G. R. ROMANES, F.R.S. Crown 8vo. price 2*s*. 6*d*.

HELLWALD (Baron F. Von)—THE RUSSIANS IN CENTRAL ASIA. A Critical Examination, down to the Present Time, of the Geography and History of Central Asia. Translated by Lieut.-Col. THEODORE WIRGMAN, LL.B. With Map. Large post 8vo. price 12*s*.

HINTON (J.)—THE PLACE OF THE PHYSICIAN. To which is added ESSAYS ON THE LAW OF HUMAN LIFE, AND ON THE RELATIONS BETWEEN ORGANIC AND INORGANIC WORLDS. Second Edition. Crown 8vo. price 3*s*. 6*d*.

PHYSIOLOGY FOR PRACTICAL USE. By Various Writers. With 50 Illustrations. Third and Cheaper Edition. Crown 8vo. price 5*s*.

AN ATLAS OF DISEASES OF THE MEMBRANA TYMPANI. With Descriptive Text. Post 8vo. price £6. 6*s*.

THE QUESTIONS OF AURAL SURGERY. With Illustrations. 2 vols. Post 8vo. price 12*s*. 6*d*.

CHAPTERS ON THE ART OF THINKING, AND OTHER ESSAYS. With an Introduction by SHADWORTH HODGSON. Edited by C. H. HINTON. Crown 8vo. cloth, price 8*s*. 6*d*.

THE MYSTERY OF PAIN. New Edition. Fcap. 8vo. cloth limp, 1*s*.

LIFE AND LETTERS. Edited by ELLICE HOPKINS, with an Introduction by Sir W. W. GULL, Bart., and Portrait engraved on Steel by C. H. JEENS. Third Edition. Crown 8vo. price 8*s*. 6*d*.

HOOPER (Mary)—LITTLE DINNERS : HOW TO SERVE THEM WITH ELEGANCE AND ECONOMY. Thirteenth Edition. Crown 8vo. price 5*s*.

COOKERY FOR INVALIDS, PERSONS OF DELICATE DIGESTION, AND CHILDREN. Crown 8vo. price 3*s*. 6*d*.

EVERY-DAY MEALS. Being Economical and Wholesome Recipes for Breakfast, Luncheon, and Supper. Second Edition. Crown 8vo. cloth, price 5*s*.

HOPKINS (Ellice)—LIFE AND LETTERS OF JAMES HINTON, with an Introduction by Sir W. W. GULL, Bart., and Portrait engraved on Steel by C. H. JEENS. Third Edition. Crown 8vo. price 8*s.* 6*d.*

HORNER (The Misses)—WALKS IN FLORENCE. A New and thoroughly Revised Edition. 2 vols. Crown 8vo. Cloth limp. With Illustrations.

> VOL. I.—Churches, Streets, and Palaces. Price 10*s.* 6*d.*
> VOL. II.—Public Galleries and Museums. Price 5*s.*

HULL (Edmund C. P.)—THE EUROPEAN IN INDIA. With a Medical Guide for Anglo-Indians. By R. S. MAIR, M.D., F.R.C.S.E. Third Edition, Revised and Corrected. Post 8vo. price 6*s.*

HUTTON (Arthur) M.A.—THE ANGLICAN MINISTRY: its Nature and Value in relation to the Catholic Priesthood. With a Preface by His Eminence Cardinal Newman. Demy 8vo. cloth, price 14*s.*

JENKINS (E.) and RAYMOND (J.)—THE ARCHITECT'S LEGAL HANDBOOK. Third Edition, Revised. Crown 8vo. price 6*s.*

JENKINS (Rev. R. C.) M.A.—THE PRIVILEGE OF PETER and the Claims of the Roman Church confronted with the Scriptures, the Councils, and the Testimony of the Popes themselves. Fcap. 8vo. price 3*s.* 6*d.*

JENNINGS (Mrs. Vaughan)—RAHEL: HER LIFE AND LETTERS. With a Portrait from the Painting by Daffinger. Square post 8vo. price 7*s.* 6*d.*

JOEL (L.)—A CONSUL'S MANUAL AND SHIPOWNER'S AND SHIPMASTER'S PRACTICAL GUIDE IN THEIR TRANSACTIONS ABROAD. With Definitions of Nautical, Mercantile, and Legal Terms; a Glossary of Mercantile Terms in English, French, German, Italian, and Spanish; Tables of the Money, Weights, and Measures of the Principal Commercial Nations and their Equivalents in British Standards; and Forms of Consular and Notarial Acts. Demy 8vo. cloth, price 12*s.*

JOHNSTONE (C. F.) M.A.—HISTORICAL ABSTRACTS: being Outlines of the History of some of the less known States of Europe. Crown 8vo. cloth, price 7*s.* 6*d.*

JONES (Lucy)— PUDDINGS AND SWEETS; being Three Hundred and Sixty-five Receipts approved by experience. Crown 8vo. price 2*s.* 6*d.*

JOYCE (P. W.) LL.D. &c.—OLD CELTIC ROMANCES. Translated from the Gaelic. Crown 8vo. cloth, price 7*s.* 6*d.*

KAUFMANN (Rev. M.) B.A.—SOCIALISM: Its Nature, its Dangers, and its Remedies considered. Crown 8vo. price 7*s.* 6*d.*

UTOPIAS; or, Schemes of Social Improvement, from Sir Thomas More to Karl Marx. Crown 8vo. cloth, price 5*s.*

KAY (Joseph) M.A., Q.C.—FREE TRADE IN LAND. Edited by his Widow. With Preface by the Right Hon. JOHN BRIGHT, M.P. Sixth Edition. Crown 8vo. cloth, price 5*s.*.

KEMPIS (Thomas À)—OF THE IMITATION OF CHRIST. A revised Translation, choicely printed on hand-made paper, with a Miniature Frontispiece on India paper from a design by W. B. RICHMOND. Limp parchment, antique, price 6*s.*; vellum, 7*s.* 6*d.*

KENT (C.)—Corona Catholica ad Petri successoris Pedes Oblata. De Summi Pontificis Leonis XIII. Assumptione Epigramma. In Quinquaginta Linguis. Fcp. 4to. cloth, price 15s.

KERNER (Dr. A.) Professor of Botany in the University of Innsbruck.—Flowers and their Unbidden Guests. Translation edited by W. Ogle, M.A., M.D. With Illustrations. Square 8vo. cloth, price 9s.

KIDD (Joseph) M.D.—The Laws of Therapeutics ; or, the Science and Art of Medicine. Second Edition. Crown 8vo. price 6s.

KINAHAN (G. Henry) M.R.I.A., of H.M.'s Geological Survey.—The Geology of Ireland, with numerous Illustrations and a Geological Map of Ireland. Square 8vo. cloth.

KINGSLEY (Charles) M.A.—Letters and Memories of his Life. Edited by his Wife. With Two Steel Engraved Portraits, and Illustrations on Wood, and a Facsimile of his Handwriting. Thirteenth Edition. 2 vols. Demy 8vo. price 36s.
  ** Also the Ninth Cabinet Edition, in 2 vols. Crown 8vo. cloth, price 12s.

All Saints' Day, and other Sermons. Edited by the Rev. W. Harrison. Third Edition. Crown 8vo. price 7s. 6d.

True Words for Brave Men. A Book for Soldiers' and Sailors' Libraries. Eighth Edition. Crown 8vo. price 2s. 6d.

KNIGHT (Professor W.)—Studies in Philosophy and Literature. Large post 8vo. cloth, price 7s. 6d.

KNOX (Alexander A.)—The New Playground ; or, Wanderings in Algeria. Large crown 8vo. cloth, price 10s. 6d.

LACORDAIRE (Rev. Père)—Life : Conferences delivered at Toulouse. A New and Cheaper Edition. Crown 8vo. price 3s. 6d.

LEE (Rev. F. G.) D.C.L.—The Other World; or, Glimpses of the Supernatural. 2 vols. A New Edition. Crown 8vo. price 15s.

LEWIS (Edward Dillon)—A Draft Code of Criminal Law and Procedure. Demy 8vo. cloth, price 21s.

Life in the Mofussil ; or, Civilian Life in Lower Bengal. By an Ex-Civilian. Large post 8vo. price 14s.

LINDSAY (W. Lauder) M.D., F.R.S.E., &c.—Mind in the Lower Animals in Health and Disease. 2 vols. Demy 8vo. cloth, price 32s. Vol. I.—Mind in Health. Vol. II.—Mind in Disease.

LLOYD (Francis), and TEBBITT (Charles)—Extension of Empire, Weakness? Deficits, Ruin? With a Practical Scheme for the Reconstruction of Asiatic Turkey. Small crown 8vo. cloth, price 3s. 6d.

LONSDALE (Margaret)—Sister Dora: a Biography. With Portrait, engraved on Steel by C. H. Jeens, and one Illustration. Nineteenth Edition. Crown 8vo. cloth, price 2s. 6d.

LORIMER (Peter) D.D.—John Knox and the Church of England. His Work in her Pulpit, and his Influence upon her Liturgy, Articles, and Parties. Demy 8vo. price 12s.

John Wiclif and his English Precursors. By Gerhard Victor Lechler. Translated from the German, with additional Notes. 2 vols. Demy 8vo. price 21s.

MACLACHLAN (Mrs.)—Notes and Extracts on Everlasting Punishment and Eternal Life, according to Literal Interpretation. Small crown 8vo. cloth, price 3s. 6d.

MACNAUGHT (Rev. John)—Cœna Domini : An Essay on the Lord's Supper, its Primitive Institution, Apostolic Uses, and Subsequent History. Demy 8vo. price 14s.

MAGNUS (Mrs.)—About the Jews since Bible Times. From the Babylonian Exile till the English Exodus. Small crown 8vo. cloth, price 5s.

MAIR (R. S.) M.D., F.R.C.S.E.—The Medical Guide for Anglo-Indians. Being a Compendium of Advice to Europeans in India, relating to the Preservation and Regulation of Health. With a Supplement on the Management of Children in India. Second Edition. Crown 8vo. limp cloth, price 3s. 6d.

MANNING (His Eminence Cardinal)—The True Story of the Vatican Council. Crown 8vo. price 5s.

MARKHAM (Capt. Albert Hastings) R.N.—The Great Frozen Sea : A Personal Narrative of the Voyage of the *Alert* during the Arctic Expedition of 1875-6. With Six Full-page Illustrations, Two Maps, and Twenty-seven Woodcuts. Fourth and Cheaper Edition. Crown 8vo. cloth, price 6s.

A Polar Reconnaissance : being the Voyage of the 'Isbjörn' to Novaya Zemlya in 1879. With 10 Illustrations. Demy 8vo. cloth, price 16s.

McGRATH (Terence)—Pictures from Ireland. New and Cheaper Edition. Crown 8vo. cloth, price 2s.

MERRITT (Henry)—Art-Criticism and Romance. With Recollections and Twenty-three Illustrations in *eau-forte*, by Anna Lea Merritt. Two vols. Large post 8vo. cloth, price 25s.

MILLER (Edward)—The History and Doctrines of Irvingism ; or, the so-called Catholic and Apostolic Church. 2 vols. Large post 8vo. price 25s.

The Church in Relation to the State. Large crown 8vo. cloth, price 7s. 6d.

MILNE (James)—Tables of Exchange for the Conversion of Sterling Money into Indian and Ceylon Currency, at Rates from 1s. 8d. to 2s. 3d. per Rupee. Second Edition. Demy 8vo. Cloth, price £2. 2s.

MINCHIN (J. G.)—Bulgaria since the War : Notes of a Tour in the Autumn of 1879. Small crown 8vo. cloth, price 3s. 6d.

MOCKLER (E.)—A Grammar of the Baloochee Language, as it is spoken in Makran (Ancient Gedrosia), in the Persia-Arabic and Roman characters. Fcap. 8vo. price 5s.

MOFFAT (R. S.)—Economy of Consumption : a Study in Political Economy. Demy 8vo. price 18s.

The Principles of a Time Policy : being an Exposition of a Method of Settling Disputes between Employers and Employed in regard to Time and Wages, by a simple Process of Mercantile Barter, without recourse to Strikes or Locks-out. Reprinted from 'The Economy of Consumption,' with a Preface and Appendix containing Observations on some Reviews of that book, and a Re-criticism of the Theories of Ricardo and J. S. Mill on Rent, Value, and Cost of Production. Demy 8vo. price 3s. 6d.

MOLTKE (Field-Marshal Von)—LETTERS FROM RUSSIA. Translated by ROBINA NAPIER. Crown 8vo. price 6s.

NOTES OF TRAVEL. Being Extracts from the Journals of. Crown 8vo. cloth, price 6s.

MORELL (J. R.)—EUCLID SIMPLIFIED IN METHOD AND LANGUAGE. Being a Manual of Geometry. Compiled from the most important French Works, approved by the University of Paris and the Minister of Public Instruction. Fcap. 8vo.' price 2s. 6d.

MORSE (E. S.) Ph.D.—FIRST BOOK OF ZOOLOGY. With numerous Illustrations. New and Cheaper Edition. Crown 8vo. price 2s. 6d.

NEWMAN (J. H.) D.D.—CHARACTERISTICS FROM THE WRITINGS OF. Being Selections from his various Works. Arranged with the Author's personal Approval. Third Edition. With Portrait. Crown 8vo. price 6s.

⁎⁎ A Portrait of the Rev. Dr. J. H. Newman, mounted for framing, can be had price 2s. 6d.

NEW WERTHER. By LOKI. Small crown 8vo. cloth, 2s. 6d.

NICHOLAS (T.)—THE PEDIGREE OF THE ENGLISH PEOPLE. Fifth Edition. Demy 8vo. price 16s.

NICHOLSON (Edward Byron)—THE GOSPEL ACCORDING TO THE HEBREWS. Its Fragments Translated and Annotated with a Critical Analysis of the External and Internal Evidence relating to it. Demy 8vo. cloth, price 9s. 6d.

THE RIGHTS OF AN ANIMAL. Crown 8vo. cloth, price 3s. 6d.

NICOLS (Arthur) F.G.S., F.R.G.S.—CHAPTERS FROM THE PHYSICAL HISTORY OF THE EARTH: an Introduction to Geology and Palæontology. With numerous Illustrations. Crown 8vo. cloth, price 5s.

NORMAN PEOPLE (THE), and their Existing Descendants in the British Dominions and the United States of America. Demy 8vo. price 21s.

NUCES: EXERCISES ON THE SYNTAX OF THE PUBLIC SCHOOL LATIN PRIMER. New Edition in Three Parts. Crown 8vo. each 1s.

⁎⁎ The Three Parts can also be had bound together in cloth, price 3s.

O'MEARA (Kathleen)—FREDERIC OZANAM, Professor of the Sorbonne: His Life and Work. Second Edition. Crown 8vo. cloth, price 7s. 6d.

OUR PUBLIC SCHOOLS—ETON, HARROW, WINCHESTER, RUGBY, WESTMINSTER, MARLBOROUGH, THE CHARTERHOUSE. Crown 8vo. cloth, price 6s.

OWEN (F. M.)—JOHN KEATS: a Study. Crown 8vo. cloth, price 6s.

OWEN (Rev. Robert) B.D.—SANCTORALE CATHOLICUM; or, Book of Saints. With Notes, Critical, Exegetical, and Historical. Demy 8vo. cloth, price 18s.

AN ESSAY ON THE COMMUNION OF SAINTS. Including an Examination of the Cultus Sanctorum. Price 2s.

PARKER (Joseph) D.D.—THE PARACLETE: An Essay on the Personality and Ministry of the Holy Ghost, with some reference to current discussions. Second Edition. Demy 8vo. price 12s.

PARR (Capt. H. Hallam, C. M. G.)—A SKETCH OF THE KAFIR AND ZULU WARS: Guadana to Isandhlwana. With Maps. Small Crown 8vo. cloth, price 5s.

PARSLOE (Joseph) — OUR RAILWAYS. Sketches, Historical and Descriptive. With Practical Information as to Fares and Rates, &c., and a Chapter on Railway Reform. Crown 8vo. price 6s.

PATTISON (Mrs. Mark)—THE RENAISSANCE OF ART IN FRANCE. With Nineteen Steel Engravings. 2 vols. demy 8vo. cloth, price 32*s.*

PAUL (C. Kegan)—WILLIAM GODWIN: HIS FRIENDS AND CONTEMPORARIES. With Portraits and Facsimiles of the Handwriting of Godwin and his Wife. 2 vols. Square post 8vo. price 28*s.*

THE GENIUS OF CHRISTIANITY UNVEILED. Being Essays by William Godwin never before published. Edited, with a Preface, by C. Kegan Paul. Crown 8vo. price 7*s. 6d.*

MARY WOLLSTONECRAFT. Letters to Imlay. New Edition with Prefatory Memoir by. Two Portraits in *eau-forte* by ANNA LEA MERRITT. Crown 8vo. cloth, 6*s.*

PAYNE (Prof. J. F.)—LECTURES ON EDUCATION. Price 6*d.* each.
II.   Fröbel and the Kindergarten System. Second Edition.

A VISIT TO GERMAN SCHOOLS: ELEMENTARY SCHOOLS IN GERMANY. Notes of a Professional Tour to inspect some of the Kindergartens, Primary Schools, Public Girls' Schools, and Schools for Technical Instruction in Hamburgh, Berlin, Dresden, Weimar, Gotha, Eisenach, in the autumn of 1874. With Critical Discussions of the General Principles and Practice of Kindergartens and other Schemes of Elementary Education. Crown 8vo. price 4*s. 6d.*

PENRICE (Maj. J.) B.A.—A DICTIONARY AND GLOSSARY OF THE KO-RAN. With Copious Grammatical References and Explanations of the Text. 4to. price 21*s.*

PESCHEL (Dr. Oscar)—THE RACES OF MAN AND THEIR GEOGRAPHICAL DISTRIBUTION. Large crown 8vo. price 9*s.*

PINCHES (Thomas) M.A.—SAMUEL WILBERFORCE: FAITH—SERVICE—RECOMPENSE. Three Sermons. With a Portrait of Bishop Wilberforce (after a Portrait by Charles Watkins). Crown 8vo. cloth, price 4*s. 6d.*

PLAYFAIR (Lieut-Col.) Her Britannic Majesty's Consul-General in Algiers.

TRAVELS IN THE FOOTSTEPS OF BRUCE IN ALGERIA AND TUNIS. Illustrated by facsimiles of Bruce's original Drawings, Photographs, Maps, &c. Royal 4to. cloth, bevelled boards, gilt leaves, price £3. 3*s.*

POLLOCK (Frederick)—SPINOZA, HIS LIFE AND PHILOSOPHY. Demy 8vo. cloth, price 16*s.*

POLLOCK (W. H.)—LECTURES ON FRENCH POETS. Delivered at the Royal Institution. Small crown 8vo. cloth, price 5*s.*

POOR (Laura E.)—SANSKRIT AND ITS KINDRED LITERATURES. Studies in Comparative Mythology. Small crown 8vo. cloth, 5*s.*

POUSHKIN (A. S.)—RUSSIAN ROMANCE. Translated from the Tales of Belkin, &c. By Mrs. J. Buchan Telfer (*née* Mouravieff). New and Cheaper Edition. Crown 8vo. price 3*s. 6d.*

PRESBYTER—UNFOLDINGS OF CHRISTIAN HOPE. An Essay shewing that the Doctrine contained in the Damnatory Clauses of the Creed commonly called Athanasian is Unscriptural. Small crown 8vo. price 4*s. 6d.*

PRICE (Prof. Bonamy)—CURRENCY AND BANKING. Crown 8vo. Price 6*s.*

CHAPTERS ON PRACTICAL POLITICAL ECONOMY. Being the Substance of Lectures delivered before the University of Oxford. Large post 8vo. price 12*s.*

PROTEUS AND AMADEUS. A Correspondence. Edited by AUBREY DE VER
Crown 8vo. price 5s.

PULPIT COMMENTARY (THE). Edited by the Rev. J. S. EXELL and the
Rev. Canon H. D. M. SPENCE.

EZRA, NEHEMIAH, AND ESTHER. By Rev. Canon G. RAWLINSON,
M.A.; with Homilies by Rev. Prof. J. R. THOMSON, M.A., Rev. Prof. R. A.
REDFORD, LL.B., M.A., Rev. W. S. LEWIS, M.A., Rev. J. A. MACDONALD,
Rev. A. MACKENNAL, B.A., Rev. W. CLARKSON, B.A., Rev. F. HASTINGS,
Rev. W. DINWIDDIE, LL.B., Rev. Prof. ROWLANDS, B.A., Rev. G. WOOD,
B.A., Rev. Prof. P. C. BARKER, LL.B., M.A., and Rev. J. S. EXELL. Third
Edition. One vol. price 12s. 6d.

I SAMUEL. By the Very Rev. R. P. SMITH, D.D.; with Homilies
by Rev. DONALD FRASER, D.D., Rev. Prof. CHAPMAN, and Rev. B. DALE.
Third Edition. Price 15s.

GENESIS. By Rev. T. WHITELAW, M.A.; with Homilies by the Very
Rev. J. F. MONTGOMERY, D.D., Rev. Prof. R. A. REDFORD, M.A., LL.B.,
Rev. F. HASTINGS, Rev. W. ROBERTS, M.A. An Introduction to the Study
of the Old Testament by the Rev. Canon FARRAR, D.D., F.R.S.; and Intro-
ductions to the Pentateuch by the Right Rev. H. COTTERILL, D.D., and Rev.
T. WHITELAW, M.A. Third Edition. One vol. price 15s.

JUDGES AND RUTH. By the Right Rev. Lord A. C. HERVEY, D.D.,
and Rev. J. MORRISON, D.D.; with Homilies by Rev. A. F. MUIR, M.A.,
Rev. W. F. ADENEY, M.A., Rev. W. M. STATHAM, and Rev. Professor
J. THOMSON, M.A. Super-royal 8vo. cloth, price 10s. 6d.

JOSHUA. By Rev. J. J. LIAS, M.A.; with Homilies by Rev. S. R.
ALDRIDGE, LL.B., Rev. R. GLOVER, Rev. E. DE PRESSENSÉ, D.D.,
Rev. J. WAITE, B.A., Rev. F. W. ADENEY, M.A.; and an Introduction by
the Rev. A. PLUMMER, M.A. Price 12s. 6d.

PUNJAUB (THE) AND NORTH-WESTERN FRONTIER OF INDIA. By an
Old Punjaubee. Crown 8vo. price 5s.

RABBI JESHUA. An Eastern Story. Crown 8vo. cloth, price 3s. 6d.

RAVENSHAW (John Henry) B.C.S.—GAUR: ITS RUINS AND INSCRIP-
TIONS. Edited by his Widow. With 44 Photographic Illustrations, and 25
facsimiles of Inscriptions. Royal 4to. cloth, price £3. 13s. 6d.

READ (Carveth)—ON THE THEORY OF LOGIC: An Essay. Crown 8vo
price 6s.

REALITIES OF THE FUTURE LIFE. Small crown 8vo. cloth, price 1s. 6d.

RENDELL (J. M.)—CONCISE HANDBOOK OF THE ISLAND OF MADEIRA.
With Plan of Funchal and Map of the Island. Fcp. 8vo. cloth, 1s. 6d.

REYNOLDS (Rev. J. W.)—THE SUPERNATURAL IN NATURE. A
Verification by Free Use of Science. Second Edition, revised and enlarged.
Demy 8vo. cloth, price 14s.

THE MYSTERY OF MIRACLES. By the Author of 'The Supernatural
in Nature.' Crown 8vo. cloth, price 6s.

RIBOT (Prof. Th.)—ENGLISH PSYCHOLOGY. Second Edition. A
Revised and Corrected Translation from the latest French Edition. Large post
8vo. price 9s.

HEREDITY: A Psychological Study on its Phenomena, its Laws,
its Causes, and its Consequences. Large crown 8vo. price 9s.

INK (Chevalier Dr. Henry)—GREENLAND: ITS PEOPLE AND ITS PRO-
DUCTS. By the Chevalier Dr. HENRY RINK, President of the Greenland
Board of Trade. With sixteen Illustrations, drawn by the Eskimo, and a Map.
Edited by Dr. Robert Brown. Crown 8vo. price 10s. 6d.

OBERTSON (The late Rev. F. W.) M.A., of Brighton.—LIFE AND
LETTERS OF. Edited by the Rev. Stopford Brooke, M.A., Chaplain in Ordinary
to the Queen.

    I. Two vols., uniform with the Sermons. With Steel Portrait. Crown
        8vo. price 7s. 6d.

    II. Library Edition, in Demy 8vo. with Portrait. Price 12s.

    III. A Popular Edition, in 1 vol. Crown 8vo. price 6s.

SERMONS. Four Series. Small crown 8vo. price 3s. 6d. each.

THE HUMAN RACE, and other Sermons. Preached at Cheltenham,
Oxford, and Brighton. Large post 8vo. cloth, price 7s. 6d.

NOTES ON GENESIS. New and Cheaper Edition. Crown 8vo. price
3s. 6d.

EXPOSITORY LECTURES ON ST. PAUL'S EPISTLES TO THE CORINTHIANS.
A New Edition. Small crown 8vo. price 5s.

LECTURES AND ADDRESSES, with other Literary Remains. A New
Edition. Crown 8vo. price 5s.

AN ANALYSIS OF MR. TENNYSON'S ' IN MEMORIAM.' (Dedicated by
Permission to the Poet-Laureate.) Fcp. 8vo. price 2s.

THE EDUCATION OF THE HUMAN RACE. Translated from the German
of Gotthold Ephraim Lessing. Fcp. 8vo. price 2s. 6d.

    The above Works can also be had, bound in half-morocco.

    *** A Portrait of the late Rev. F. W. Robertson, mounted for framing, can
    be had, price 2s. 6d.

ODWELL (G. F.) F.R.A.S., F.C.S.—ETNA: A HISTORY OF THE
MOUNTAIN AND ITS ERUPTIONS. With Maps and Illustrations. Square 8vo.
cloth, price 9s.

OSS (Alexander) D.D.—MEMOIR OF ALEXANDER EWING, Bishop of
Argyll and the Isles. Second and Cheaper Edition. Demy 8vo. cloth, price
10s. 6d.

ALTS (Rev. Alfred) LL.D.—GODPARENTS AT CONFIRMATION. With a
Preface by the Bishop of Manchester. Small crown 8vo. cloth limp, price 2s.

AMUEL (Sydney M.)—JEWISH LIFE IN THE EAST. Small crown 8vo.
cloth, price 3s. 6d.

AYCE (Rev. Archibald Henry)—INTRODUCTION TO THE SCIENCE OF
LANGUAGE. 2 vols. Large post 8vo. cloth, price 25s.

IENTIFIC LAYMAN. The New Truth and the Old Faith: are they
Incompatible? Demy 8vo. cloth, price 10s. 6d.

OONES (W. Baptiste)—FOUR CENTURIES OF ENGLISH LETTERS:
A Selection of 350 Letters by 150 Writers, from the Period of the Paston
Letters to the Present Time. Second Edition. Large crown 8vo. cloth,
price 9s.

OTT (Robert H.)—WEATHER CHARTS AND STORM WARNINGS. Second
Edition. Illustrated. Crown 8vo. price 3s. 6d.

SCOTT (Leader)—A Nook in the Apennines : A Summer beneath the Chestnuts. With Frontispiece, and Twenty-seven Illustrations in the Text, chiefly from Original Sketches. Crown 8vo. cloth, price 7s. 6d.

SENIOR (N. W.)—Alexis De Tocqueville. Correspondence and Conversations with Nassau W. Senior, from 1833 to 1859. Edited by M. C. M Simpson. 2 vols. Large post 8vo. price 21s.

SHAKSPEARE (Charles)—Saint Paul at Athens. Spiritual Christianity in relation to some aspects of Modern Thought. Five Sermons preached at St. Stephen's Church, Westbourne Park. With a Preface by the Rev. Canon Farrar.

SHELLEY (Lady)—Shelley Memorials from Authentic Sources. With (now first printed) an Essay on Christianity by Percy Bysshe Shelley. With Portrait. Third Edition. Crown 8vo. price 5s.

SHILLITO (Rev. Joseph)—Womanhood : its Duties, Temptations, and Privileges. A Book for Young Women. Third Edition. Crown 8vo. price 3s. 6d.

SHIPLEY (Rev. Orby) M.A.—Church Tracts: or, Studies in Modern Problems. By various Writers. 2 vols. Crown 8vo. price 5s. each.

Principles of the Faith in Relation to Sin. Topics for Thought in Times of Retreat. Eleven Addresses delivered during a Retreat of Three Days to Persons living in the World. Demy 8vo. cloth, price 12s.

Sister Augustine, Superior of the Sisters of Charity at the St. Johannis Hospital at Bonn. Authorised Translation by Hans Tharau, from the German 'Memorials of Amalie von Lasaulx.' Second Edition. Large crown 8vo. cloth, price 7s. 6d.

SMITH (Edward) M.D., LL.B., F.R.S.—Health and Disease, as Influenced by the Daily, Seasonal, and other Cyclical Changes in the Human System. A New Edition. Post 8vo. price 7s. 6d.

Practical Dietary for Families, Schools, and the Labouring Classes. A New Edition. Post 8vo. price 3s. 6d.

Tubercular Consumption in its Early and Remediable Stages. Second Edition. Crown 8vo. price 6s.

SPEDDING (James)—Reviews and Discussions, Literary, Political, and Historical not relating to Bacon. Demy 8vo. cloth, price 12s. 6d.

STAPFER (Paul)—Shakspeare and Classical Antiquity : Greek and Latin Antiquity as presented in Shakspeare's Plays. Translated by Emily J. Carey. Large post 8vo. cloth, price 12s.

St. Bernard. A Little Book on the Love of God. Translated by Marianne Caroline and Coventry Patmore. Cloth extra, gilt tops, 4s. 6d.

STEPHENS (Archibald John) LL.D.—The Folkestone Ritual Case. The Substance of the Argument delivered before the Judicial Committee of the Privy Council on behalf of the Respondents. Demy 8vo. cloth, price 6s.

STEVENSON (Rev. W. F.)—Hymns for the Church and Home. Selected and Edited by the Rev. W. Fleming Stevenson.

The most complete Hymn Book published.
The Hymn Book consists of Three Parts :—I. For Public Worship.—II. For Family and Private Worship.—III. For Children.
*** Published in various forms and prices, the latter ranging from 8d. to 6s. Lists and full particulars will be furnished on application to the Publishers.

STEVENSON (Robert Louis)—AN INLAND VOYAGE. With Frontispiece by Walter Crane. Crown 8vo. price 7s. 6d.

TRAVELS WITH A DONKEY IN THE CEVENNES. With Frontispiece by Walter Crane. Crown 8vo. cloth, price 7s. 6d.

VIRGINIBUS PUERISQUE, and other Papers. Crown 8vo. cloth 6s.

SULLY (James) M.A. — SENSATION AND INTUITION. Demy 8vo. price 10s. 6d.

PESSIMISM : a History and a Criticism. Second Edition. Demy 8vo. price 14s.

SYME (David)—OUTLINES OF AN INDUSTRIAL SCIENCE. Second Edition. Crown 8vo. price 6s.

TAYLOR (Algernon)—GUIENNE. Notes of an Autumn Tour. Crown 8vo cloth, price 4s. 6d.

THOMSON (J. Turnbull)—SOCIAL PROBLEMS ; OR, AN INQUIRY INTO THE LAWS OF INFLUENCE. With Diagrams. Demy 8vo. cloth, price 10s. 6d.

TODHUNTER (Dr. J.)—A STUDY OF SHELLEY. Crown 8vo. cloth, price 7s.

TWINING (Louisa)—WORKHOUSE VISITING AND MANAGEMENT DURING TWENTY-FIVE YEARS. Small crown 8vo. cloth, price 3s. 6d.

VAUGHAN (H. Halford)—NEW READINGS AND RENDERINGS OF SHAKESPEARE'S TRAGEDIES. 2 vols. demy 8vo. cloth, price 25s.

VILLARI (Professor)—NICCOLO MACHIAVELLI AND HIS TIMES. Translated by Linda Villari. 2 vols. Large post 8vo. price 24s.

VYNER (Lady Mary)—EVERY DAY A PORTION. Adapted from the Bible and the Prayer Book, for the Private Devotions of those living in Widowhood. Collected and Edited by Lady Mary Vyner. Square crown 8vo. extra, price 5s.

WALDSTEIN (Charles) Ph.D.—THE BALANCE OF EMOTION AND INTELLECT ; an Introductory Essay to the Study of Philosophy. Crown 8vo. cloth, price 6s.

WALLER (Rev. C. B.)—THE APOCALYPSE, reviewed under the Light of the Doctrine of the Unfolding Ages, and the Relation of All Things. Demy 8vo. price 12s.

WATSON (Sir Thomas) Bart., M.D.—THE ABOLITION OF ZYMOTIC DISEASES, and of other similar Enemies of Mankind. Small crown 8vo. cloth, price 3s. 6d.

WEDMORE (Frederick)—THE MASTERS OF GENRE PAINTING. With Sixteen Illustrations. Crown 8vo. cloth, price 7s. 6d.

WELLS (Capt. John C.) R.N.—SPITZBERGEN—THE GATEWAY TO THE POLYNIA ; or, a Voyage to Spitzbergen. With numerous Illustrations by Whymper and others, and Map. New and Cheaper Edition. Demy 8vo. price 6s.

WETMORE (W. S.)—COMMERCIAL TELEGRAPHIC CODE. Second Edition. Post 4to. boards, price 42s.

WHITE (A. D.) LL.D.—WARFARE OF SCIENCE. With Prefatory Note by Professor Tyndall. Second Edition. Crown 8vo. price 3s. 6d.

WHITNEY (Prof. William Dwight)—ESSENTIALS OF ENGLISH GRAMMAR, for the Use of Schools. Crown 8vo. price 3s. 6d.

WICKSTEED (*P. H.*)—DANTE: Six Sermons. Crown 8vo. cloth, price 5*s*.

WILLIAMS (*Rowland*) *D.D.*—LIFE AND LETTERS OF; with Extracts from his Note-Books. Edited by Mrs. Rowland Williams. With a Photographic Portrait. 2 vols. large post 8vo. price 24*s*.

PSALMS, LITANIES, COUNSELS, AND COLLECTS FOR DEVOUT PERSONS. Edited by his Widow. New and Popular Edition. Crown 8vo. price 3*s*. 6*d*.

STRAY THOUGHTS COLLECTED FROM THE WRITINGS OF THE LATE ROWLAND WILLIAMS, D.D. Edited by his Widow. Crown 8vo. cloth, price 3*s*. 6*d*.

WILLIS (*R.*) *M.D.*—SERVETUS AND CALVIN : a Study of an Important Epoch in the Early History of the Reformation. 8vo. price 16*s*.

WILLIAM HARVEY. A History of the Discovery of the Circulation of the Blood : with a Portrait of Harvey after Faithorne. Demy 8vo. cloth, price 14*s*. Portrait separate.

WILSON (*H. Schütz*)—THE TOWER AND SCAFFOLD. A Miniature Monograph. Large fcap. 8vo. price 1*s*.

WOLLSTONECRAFT (*Mary*)—LETTERS TO IMLAY. New Edition with Prefatory Memoir by C. KEGAN PAUL, author of 'William Godwin : His Friends and Contemporaries,' &c. Two Portraits in *eau-forte* by Anna Lea Merritt. Crown 8vo. cloth, price 6*s*.

WOLTMANN (*Dr. Alfred*), *and* *WOERMANN* (*Dr. Karl*)— HISTORY OF PAINTING. Edited by Sidney Colvin. Vol. I. Painting in Antiquity and the Middle Ages. With numerous Illustrations. Medium 8vo. cloth, price 28*s*. ; bevelled boards, gilt leaves, price 30*s*.

WOOD (*Major-General J. Creighton*)—DOUBLING THE CONSONANT. Small crown 8vo. cloth, price 1*s*. 6*d*.

WORD WAS MADE FLESH. Short Family Readings on the Epistles for each Sunday of the Christian Year. Demy 8vo. cloth, price 10*s*. 6*d*.

WRIGHT (*Rev. David*) *M.A.*—WAITING FOR THE LIGHT, AND OTHER SERMONS. Crown 8vo. price 6*s*.

YOUMANS (*Eliza A.*)—AN ESSAY ON THE CULTURE OF THE OBSERVING POWERS OF CHILDREN, especially in connection with the Study of Botany. Edited, with Notes and a Supplement, by Joseph Payne, F.C.P., Author of 'Lectures on the Science and Art of Education,' &c. Crown 8vo. price 2*s*. 6*d*.

FIRST BOOK OF BOTANY. Designed to Cultivate the Observing Powers of Children. With 300 Engravings. New and Cheaper Edition. Crown 8vo. price 2*s*. 6*d*.

YOUMANS (*Edward L.*) *M.D.*—A CLASS BOOK OF CHEMISTRY, on the Basis of the New System. With 200 Illustrations. Crown 8vo. price 5*s*.

THE INTERNATIONAL SCIENTIFIC SERIES.

I. FORMS OF WATER : a Familiar Exposition of the Origin and Phenomena of Glaciers. By J. Tyndall, LL.D., F.R.S. With 25 Illustrations. Seventh Edition. Crown 8vo. price 5*s*.

II. PHYSICS AND POLITICS; or, Thoughts on the Application of the Principles of 'Natural Selection' and 'Inheritance' to Political Society. By Walter Bagehot. Fifth Edition. Crown 8vo. price 4*s*.

III. Foods. By Edward Smith, M.D., LL.B., F.R.S. With numerous Illustrations. Seventh Edition. Crown 8vo. price 5s.

IV. Mind and Body: the Theories of their Relation. By Alexander Bain, LL.D. With Four Illustrations. Seventh Edition. Crown 8vo. price 4s.

V. The Study of Sociology. By Herbert Spencer. Tenth Edition. Crown 8vo. price 5s.

VI. On the Conservation of Energy. By Balfour Stewart, M.A., LL.D., F.R.S. With 14 Illustrations. Fifth Edition. Crown 8vo. price 5s.

VII. Animal Locomotion; or, Walking, Swimming, and Flying. By J. B. Pettigrew, M.D., F.R.S., &c. With 130 Illustrations. Second Edition. Crown 8vo. price 5s.

VIII. Responsibility in Mental Disease. By Henry Maudsley, M.D. Third Edition. Crown 8vo. price 5s.

IX. The New Chemistry. By Professor J. P. Cooke, of the Harvard University. With 31 Illustrations. Fifth Edition. Crown 8vo. price 5s.

X. The Science of Law. By Professor Sheldon Amos. Fourth Edition. Crown 8vo. price 5s.

XI. Animal Mechanism: a Treatise on Terrestrial and Aerial Locomotion. By Professor E. J. Marey. With 117 Illustrations. Second Edition. Crown 8vo. price 5s.

XII. The Doctrine of Descent and Darwinism. By Professor Oscar Schmidt (Strasburg University). With 26 Illustrations. Fourth Edit. Crown 8vo. price 5s.

XIII. The History of the Conflict between Religion and Science. By J. W. Draper, M.D., LL.D. Fourteenth Edition. Crown 8vo. price 5s.

XIV. Fungi: their Nature, Influences, Uses, &c. By M. C. Cooke, M.D., LL.D. Edited by the Rev. M. J. Berkeley, M.A., F.L.S. With numerous Illustrations. Second Edition. Crown 8vo. price 5s.

XV. The Chemical Effects of Light and Photography. By Dr. Hermann Vogel (Polytechnic Academy of Berlin). Translation thoroughly revised. With 100 Illustrations. Third Edition. Crown 8vo. price 5s.

XVI. The Life and Growth of Language. By William Dwight Whitney, Professor of Sanscrit and Comparative Philology in Yale College, Newhaven. Second Edition. Crown 8vo. price 5s.

XVII. Money and the Mechanism of Exchange. By W. Stanley Jevons, M.A., F.R.S. Fourth Edition. Crown 8vo. price 5s.

XVIII. The Nature of Light. With a General Account of Physical Optics. By Dr. Eugene Lommel, Professor of Physics in the University of Erlangen. With 188 Illustrations and a Table of Spectra in Chromo-lithography. Third Edition. Crown 8vo. price 5s.

XIX. Animal Parasites and Messmates. By Monsieur Van Beneden, Professor of the University of Louvain, Correspondent of the Institute of France. With 83 Illustrations. Second Edition. Crown 8vo. price 5s.

XX. Fermentation. By Professor Schützenberger, Director of the Chemical Laboratory at the Sorbonne. With 28 Illustrations. Third Edition. Crown 8vo. price 5s.

XXI. The Five Senses of Man. By Professor Bernstein, of the University of Halle. With 91 Illustrations. Second Edition. Crown 8vo. price 5s.

XXII. The Theory of Sound in its Relation to Music. By Professor Pietro Blaserna, of the Royal University of Rome. With numerous Illustrations. Second Edition. Crown 8vo. price 5s.

XXIII. Studies in Spectrum Analysis. By J. Norman Lockyer. F.R.S. With six photographic Illustrations of Spectra, and numerous engravings on Wood. Crown 8vo. Second Edition. Price 6s. 6d.

XXIV. A History of the Growth of the Steam Engine. By Professor R. H. Thurston. With numerous Illustrations. Second Edition. Crown 8vo. cloth, price 6s. 6d.

XXV. Education as a Science. By Alexander Bain, LL.D. Third Edition. Crown 8vo. cloth, price 5s.

XXVI. The Human Species. By Prof. A. de Quatrefages. Third Edition. Crown 8vo. cloth, price 5s.

XXVII. MODERN CHROMATICS. With Applications to Art and Industry. By Ogden N. Rood. With 130 original Illustrations. Second Edition. Crown 8vo. cloth, price 5s.

XXVIII. THE CRAYFISH : an Introduction to the Study of Zoology. By Professor T. H. Huxley. With 82 Illustrations. Second Edition. Crown 8vo. cloth, price 5s.

XXIX. THE BRAIN AS AN ORGAN OF MIND. By H. Charlton Bastian, M.D. With numerous Illustrations. Second Edition. Crown 8vo. cloth, price 5s.

XXX. THE ATOMIC THEORY. By l Wurtz. Translated by G. Cle shaw, F.C.S. Second Edition. Cr 8vo. cloth, price 5s.

XXXI. THE NATURAL CONDITIONS EXISTENCE AS THEY AFFECT ANI LIFE. By Karl Semper. With 2 M and 106 Woodcuts. Second Edit Crown 8vo. cloth, price 5s.

XXXII. GENERAL PHYSIOLOGY MUSCLES AND NERVES. By Pro Rosenthal. Second Edition. V Illustrations. Crown 8vo. cloth, 5s.

MILITARY WORKS.

ANDERSON (Col. R. P.)—VICTORIES AND DEFEATS : an Attempt to explain the Causes which have led to them. An Officer's Manual. Demy 8vo. price 14s.

ARMY OF THE NORTH GERMAN CONFEDERATION : a Brief Description of its Organisation, of the Different Branches of the Service and their *rôle* in War, of its Mode of Fighting, &c. Translated from the Corrected Edition, by permission of the Author, by Colonel Edward Newdigate. Demy 8vo. price 5s.

BLUME (Maj. W.)—THE OPERATIONS OF THE GERMAN ARMIES IN FRANCE, from Sedan to the end of the War of 1870–71. With Map. From the Journals of the Head-quarters Staff. Translated by the late E. M. Jones, Maj. 20th Foot, Prof. of Mil. Hist., Sandhurst. Demy 8vo. price 9s.

BOGUSLAWSKI (Capt. A. von)—TACTICAL DEDUCTIONS FROM THE WAR OF 1870-1. Translated by Colonel Sir Lumley Graham, Bart., late 18th (Royal Irish) Regiment. Third Edition, Revised and Corrected. Demy 8vo. price 7s.

BRACKENBURY (Lieut.-Col.) C.B., R.A., A.A.G. MILITARY HANDBOOKS FOR REGIMENTAL OFFICERS. I. Military Sketching and Reconnaissance, by Lieut.-Col. F. J. Hutchison, and Capt. H. G. MacGregor. Second Edition. With 15 Plates. Small 8vo. cloth, price 6s. II. The Elements of Modern Tactics Practically applied to English Formations, by Major Wilkinson Shaw. Second and Cheaper Edition. With 25 Plates and Maps. Small cr. 8vo. cloth, price 9s.

BRIALMONT (Col. A.)—HASTY TRENCHMENTS. Translated by Li Charles A. Empson, R.A. V Nine Plates. Demy 8vo. price 6s

CLERY (C.) Lieut.-Col.—MINOR T TICS. With 26 Maps and Pl Fifth and revised Edition. D 8vo. cloth, price 16s.

DU VERNOIS (Col. von Verd STUDIES IN LEADING TROOPS. authorised and accurate Translatio Lieutenant H. J. T. Hildyard, Foot. Parts I. and II. Demy price 7s.

GOETZE (Capt. A. von)—OPERATI OF THE GERMAN ENGINEERS C ING THE WAR OF 1870-1. Publi by Authority, and in accordance Official Documents. Translated 1 the German by Colonel G. Grat V.C., C.B., R.E. With 6 l Maps. Demy 8vo. price 21s.

HARRISON (Lieut.-Col. R.) — ' OFFICER'S MEMORANDUM BOOK PEACE AND WAR. Third Edit Oblong 32mo. roan, with pencil, 3s. 6d.

HELVIG (Capt. H.)—THE OPERATI OF THE BAVARIAN ARMY Co Translated by Captain G. S. Schw With Five large Maps. In 2 v Demy 8vo. price 24s.

TACTICAL EXAMPLES : Vol. I. Battalion, price 15s. Vol. II. Regiment and Brigade, price 10s. Translated from the German by Sir Lumley Graham. With ne 300 Diagrams. Demy 8vo. cloth.

HOFFBAUER (*Capt.*)—THE GERMAN ARTILLERY IN THE BATTLES NEAR METZ. Based on the Official Reports of the German Artillery. Translated by Captain E. O. Hollist. With Map and Plans. Demy 8vo. price 21*s.*

LAYMANN (*Capt.*) — THE FRONTAL ATTACK OF INFANTRY. Translated by Colonel Edward Newdigate. Crown 8vo. price 2*s.* 6*d.*

NOTES ON CAVALRY TACTICS, ORGANISATION, &c. By a Cavalry Officer. With Diagrams. Demy 8vo. cloth, price 12*s.*

PARR (*Capt H. Hallam*) *C.M.G.*—THE DRESS, HORSES, AND EQUIPMENT OF INFANTRY AND STAFF OFFICERS. Crown 8vo. cloth, price 1*s.*

SCHELL (*Maj. von*)—THE OPERATIONS OF THE FIRST ARMY UNDER GEN. VON GOEBEN. Translated by Col. C. H. von Wright. Four Maps. demy 8vo. price 9*s.*

THE OPERATIONS OF THE FIRST ARMY UNDER GEN. ' VON STEINMETZ. Translated by Captain E. O. Hollist. Demy 8vo. price 10*s.* 6*d.*

SCHELLENDORF (*Major-Gen. B. von*) THE DUTIES OF THE GENERAL STAFF. Translated from the German by Lieutenant Hare. Vol. I. Demy 8vo. cloth, 10*s.* 6*d.*

SCHERFF (*Maj. W. von*)—STUDIES IN THE NEW INFANTRY TACTICS. Parts I. and II. Translated from the German by Colonel Lumley Graham. Demy 8vo. price 7*s.* 6*d.*

SHADWELL (*Maj.-Gen.*) *C.B.*—MOUNTAIN WARFARE. Illustrated by the Campaign of 1799 in Switzerland. Being a Translation of the Swiss Narrative compiled from the Works of the Archduke Charles, Jomini, and others. Also on the Campaign by General H. Dufour on the Campaign of the Valtelline in 1635. With Appendix, Maps, and Introductory Remarks. Demy 8vo. price 16*s.*

SHERMAN (*Gen. W. T.*)—MEMOIRS OF GENERAL W. T. SHERMAN, Commander of the Federal Forces in the American Civil War. By Himself. 2 vols. With Map. Demy 8vo. price 24*s. Copyright English Edition.*

STUBBS (*Lieut.-Col. F. W.*) — THE REGIMENT OF BENGAL ARTILLERY. The History of its Organisation, Equipment, and War Services. Compiled from Published Works, Official Records, and various Private Sources. With numerous Maps and Illustrations. 2 vols. demy 8vo. price 32*s.*

STUMM (*Lieut. Hugo*), *German Military Attaché to the Khivan Expedition.*—RUSSIA'S ADVANCE EASTWARD Based on the Official Reports of. Translated by Capt. C. E. H. VINCENT, With Map. Crown 8vo. price 6*s.*

VINCENT (*Capt. C. E. H.*)—ELEMENTARY MILITARY GEOGRAPHY, RECONNOITRING, AND SKETCHING. Compiled for Non-commissioned Officers and Soldiers of all Arms. Square crown 8vo. price 2*s.* 6*d.*

VOLUNTEER, THE MILITIAMAN, AND THE REGULAR SOLDIER, by a Public Schoolboy. Crown 8vo. cloth, price 5*s.*

WARTENSLEBEN (*Count H. von.*)—THE OPERATIONS OF THE SOUTH ARMY IN JANUARY AND FEBRUARY, 1871. Compiled from the Official War Documents of the Head-quarters of the Southern Army. Translated by Colonel C. H. von Wright. With Maps. Demy 8vo. price 6*s.*

THE OPERATIONS OF THE FIRST ARMY UNDER GEN. VON MANTEUFFEL. Translated by Colonel C. H. von Wright. Uniform with the above. Demy 8vo. price 9*s.*

WICKHAM (*Capt. E. H., R.A.*)—INFLUENCE OF FIREARMS UPON TACTICS : Historical and Critical Investigations. By an OFFICER OF SUPERIOR RANK (in the German Army). Translated by Captain E. H. Wickham, R.A. Demy 8vo. price 7*s.* 6*d.*

WOINOVITS (*Capt. I.*) — AUSTRIAN CAVALRY EXERCISE. Translated by Captain W. S. Cooke. Crown 8vo. price 7*s.*

POETRY.

ADAMS (W. D. — LYRICS OF LOVE, from Shakespeare to Tennyson. Selected and arranged by. Fcp. 8vo. cloth extra, gilt edges, price 3s. 6d.
Also, a Cheaper Edition. Fcp. 8vo. cloth, 2s. 6d.

AMATEUR—A FEW LYRICS. Small crown 8vo. cloth, price 2s.

ANTILOPE : a Tragedy. Large crown 8vo. cloth, price 6s.

AUBERTIN (J. J.)—CAMOENS' LUSIADS. Portuguese Text, with Translation by. Map and Portraits. 2 vols. Demy 8vo. price 30s.

SEVENTY SONNETS OF CAMOENS. Portuguese Text and Translation, with some original Poems. Dedicated to Capt. Richard F. Burton. Printed on hand made paper, cloth, bevelled boards, gilt tops, price 7s. 6d.

AVIA—THE ODYSSEY OF HOMER. Done into English Verse by. Fcp. 4to. cloth, price 15s.

BANKS (Mrs. G. L.)—RIPPLES AND BREAKERS : Poems. Square 8vo. cloth, price 5s.

BARNES (William)—POEMS OF RURAL LIFE, IN THE DORSET DIALECT. New Edition, complete in one vol. Crown 8vo. cloth, price 8s. 6d.

BAYNES (Rev. Canon R. H.) M.A.—HOME SONGS FOR QUIET HOURS. Fourth Edition. Fcp. 8vo. price 2s. 6d.
This may also be had handsomely bound in morocco with gilt edges.

BENNETT (Dr. W. C.)—NARRATIVE POEMS AND BALLADS. Fcp. 8vo. sewed, in Coloured Wrapper, price 1s.

SONGS FOR SAILORS. Dedicated by Special Request to H.R.H. the Duke of Edinburgh. With Steel Portrait and Illustrations. Crown 8vo. price 3s. 6d.
An Edition in Illustrated Paper Covers, price 1s.

SONGS OF A SONG WRITER. Crown 8vo. price 6s.

BEVINGTON (L. S.)—KEY NOTES. Small crown 8vo. cloth, price 5s.

BOWEN (H. C.) M.A.—SIMPLE ENGLISH POEMS. English Literature for Junior Classes. In Four Parts. Parts I. II. and III. price 6d. each, and Part IV. price 1s.

BRYANT (W. C.)—POEMS. Red-line Edition. With 24 Illustrations and Portrait of the Author. Crown 8vo. cloth extra, price 7s. 6d.
A Cheap Edition, with Frontispiece. Small crown 8vo. price 3s. 6d.

BUTLER (Alfred J.)—AMARANTH AND ASPHODEL. Songs from the Greek Anthology. Small crown 8vo. cloth, price 2s.

CALDERON'S DRAMAS : the Wonder-Working Magician—Life is a Dream —the Purgatory of St. Patrick. Translated by Denis Florence MacCarthy. Post 8vo. price 10s.

COLOMB (Colonel) — THE CARDINAL ARCHBISHOP : a Spanish Legend. In 29 Cancions. Small Crown 8vo. cloth, price 5s.

CONWAY (Hugh)—A LIFE'S IDYLLS. Small crown 8vo. cloth, price 3s. 6d.

COPPÉE (Francois)—L'EXILÉE. Done into English Verse, with the sanction of the Author, by I. O. L. Crown 8vo. vellum, price 5s.

COWAN (Rev. William)—POEMS : chiefly Sacred, including Translations from some Ancient Latin Hymns. [Fcp. 8vo. cloth, price 5s.

CRESSWELL (Mrs. G.)—THE KING'S BANNER : Drama in Four Acts. Five Illustrations. 4to. price 10s. 6d.

DAVIES (T. Hart.)—CATULLUS. Translated into English Verse. Crown 8vo. cloth, price 6s.

DENNIS (J.)—ENGLISH SONNETS. Collected and Arranged. Elegantly bound. New and Cheaper Edition. Fcp. 8vo. price 2s. 6d.

DE VERE (Aubrey)—ALEXANDER THE GREAT : a Dramatic Poem. Small crown 8vo. price 5s.

DE VERE (Aubrey)—con.

THE INFANT BRIDAL, and other Poems. A New and Enlarged Edition. Fcp. 8vo. price 7s. 6d.

LEGENDS OF THE SAXON SAINTS Small crown 8vo. cloth, price 6s.

THE LEGENDS OF ST. PATRICK, and other Poems. Small cr. 8vo. price 5s.

ST. THOMAS OF CANTERBURY : a Dramatic Poem. Large fcp. 8vo. price 5s.

ANTAR AND ZARA: an Eastern Romance. INISFAIL, and other Poems, Meditative and Lyrical. Fcp. 8vo. price 6s.

THE FALL OF RORA, THE SEARCH AFTER PROSERPINE, and other Poems, Meditative and Lyrical. Fcp. 8vo. 6s.

DOBELL (Mrs. Horace)—ETHELSTONE, EVELINE, and other Poems. Crown 8vo. cloth, 6s.

DOBSON (Austin) — VIGNETTES IN RHYME, and Vers de Société. Third Edition. Fcp. 8vo. price 5s.

PROVERBS IN PORCELAIN. By the Author of 'Vignettes in Rhyme.' Second Edition. Crown 8vo. price 6s.

DOLORES : a Theme with Variations. In Three Parts. Small crown 8vo. cloth, price 5s.

DOROTHY : a Country Story in Elegiac Verse. With Preface. Demy 8vo. cloth, price 5s.

DOWDEN (Edward) LL.D.—POEMS. Second Edition. Fcp. 8vo. price 5s.

DOWNTON (Rev. H.) M.A.—HYMNS AND VERSES. Original and Translated. Small crown 8vo. cloth, price 3s. 6d.

DUTT (Toru)—A SHEAF GLEANED IN FRENCH FIELDS. New Edition, with Portrait. Demy 8vo. cloth, 10s. 6d.

EDWARDS (Rev. Basil) — MINOR CHORDS; or, Songs for the Suffering : a Volume of Verse. Fcp. 8vo. cloth, price 3s. 6d.; paper, price 2s. 6d.

ELLIOT (Lady Charlotte)—MEDUSA and other Poems. Crown 8vo. cloth, price 6s.

ELLIOTT (Ebenezer), The Corn Law Rhymer.—POEMS. Edited by his son, the Rev. Edwin Elliott, of St. John's, Antigua. 2 vols. crown 8vo. price 18s.

ENGLISH ODES. Selected, with a Critical Introduction by EDMUND W. GOSSE, and a miniature frontispiece by Hamo Thornycroft, A.R.A. Elzevir 8vo. limp parchment antique, price 6s. ; vellum, 7s. 6d.

EPIC OF HADES (THE). By the Author of 'Songs of Two Worlds.' Twelfth Edition. Fcp. 8vo. price 7s. 6d.

⁎⁎ Also an Illustrated Edition, with seventeen full-page designs in photomezzotint by George R. Chapman. 4to. cloth, extra gilt leaves, price 25s.; and a Large Paper Edition with Portrait, price 10s. 6d.

EVANS (Anne)— POEMS AND MUSIC. With Memorial Preface by ANN THACKERAY RITCHIE. Large crown 8vo. cloth, price 7s.

G. H. T.—VERSES, mostly written in India. Crown 8vo, cloth, price 6s.

GINEVRA AND THE DUKE of GUISE : Two Tragedies. Crown 8vo. cloth, price 6s.

GOSSE (Edmund W.)—NEW POEMS. Crown 8vo. cloth, price 7s. 6d.

GREENOUGH (Mrs. Richard)—MARY MAGDALENE : a Poem. Large post 8vo. parchment antique, bevelled boards, price 6s.

GWEN : a Drama in Monologue. By the Author of the 'Epic of Hades.' Third Edition. Fcp. 8vo. cloth, price 5s.

HAWKER (Robt. Stephen)—THE POETICAL WORKS OF. Now first collected and arranged. With a Prefatory Notice by J. G. Godwin. With Portrait. Crown 8vo. cloth, price 12s.

HAWTREY (Edward M.)—CORYDALIS : a Story of the Sicilian Expedition. Small crown 8vo. cloth, price 3s. 6d.

HOLMES (E. G. A.)—POEMS. First and Second Series. Fcp. 8vo. price 5s. each.

INCHBOLD (J. W.)—ANNUS AMORIS : Sonnets. Fcp. 8vo. price 4s. 6d.

JENKINS (Rev. Canon)—THE GIRDLE LEGEND OF PRATO. Small crown 8vo. cloth, price 2s.

JEROVEAM'S WIFE, and other Poems. Fcp. 8vo. cloth, price 3s. 6d.

KING (Edward)—ECHOES FROM THE ORIENT. With Miscellaneous Poems. Small crown 8vo. cloth, price 3s. 6d.

KING (Mrs. Hamilton)—THE DISCIPLES. Fourth Edition, with Portrait and Notes. Crown 8vo. price 7s. 6d.

ASPROMONTE, and other Poems. Second Edition. Fcp. 8vo. price 4s. 6d.

LAIRD-CLOWES (W.)—LOVE'S REBELLION : a Poem. Fcp. 8vo. cloth, price 3s. 6d.

LANG (A.)—XXII BALLADES IN BLUE CHINA. Elzevir 8vo. parchment. price 3s. 6d.

LEIGHTON (Robert)—RECORDS AND OTHER POEMS. With Portrait. Small crown 8vo. cloth, price 7s. 6d.

LOCKER (F.)—LONDON LYRICS. A New and Revised Edition, with Additions and a Portrait of the Author. Crown 8vo. cloth elegant, price 6s.
Also, an Edition for the People. Fcp. 8vo. price 2s. 6d.

LOKI.—THE NEW WERTHER. Small crown 8vo. cloth, price 3s. 6d.

LOVE'S GAMUT and other Poems Small crown 8vo. cloth, price 3s. 6d.

LOVE SONNETS OF PROTEUS. With Frontispiece by the Author. Elzevir 8vo. cloth, price 5s.

LOWNDES (Henry) — POEMS AND TRANSLATIONS. Crown 8vo. cloth, price 6s.

LUMSDEN (Lieut.-Col. H. W.)—BEOWULF : an Old English Poem. Translated into Modern Rhymes. Small crown 8vo. cloth, price 5s.

MACLEAN (Charles Donald)—LATIN AND GREEK VERSE TRANSLATIONS. Small crown 8vo. cloth, 2s.

MAGNUSSON (Eirikr) M.A., and PALMER (E. H.) M.A.—JOHAN LUDVIG RUNEBERG'S LYRICAL SONGS, IDYLLS, AND EPIGRAMS. Fcp. 8vo. cloth, price 5s.

MARIE ANTIONETTE : a Drama. Small crown 8vo. cloth, price 5s.

MIDDLETON (The Lady)—BALLADS. Square 16mo. cloth, price 3s. 6d.

MONMOUTH : a Drama, of which the outline is Historical. (Dedicated, by permission, to Mr. Henry Irving.) Small crown 8vo. cloth, price 5s.

MOORE (Mrs. Bloomfield)—GONDALINE'S LESSON : The Warden's Tale, Stories for Children, and other Poems. Crown 8vo. cloth, price 5s.

MORICE (Rev. F. D.) M.A. — THE OLYMPIAN AND PYTHIAN ODES OF PINDAR. A New Translation in English Verse. Crown 8vo. price 7s. 6d.

MORSHEAD (E. D. A.)—THE AGAMEMNON OF ÆSCHYLUS. Translated into English Verse. With an Introductory Essay. Crown 8vo. cloth, price 5s.

MORTERRA (Felix)—THE LEGEND OF ALLANDALE, and other Poems. Small crown 8vo. cloth, price 6s.

MY OLD PORTFOLIO. A Volume of Poems. Crown 8vo. cloth, price 4s. 6d.

NICHOLSON (Edward B.) Librarian of the London Institution—THE CHRIST CHILD, and other Poems. Crown 8vo. cloth, price 4s. 6d.

NOAKE (Major R. Compton) — THE BIVOUAC ; or, Martial Lyrist. With an Appendix : Advice to the Soldier. Fcp. 8vo. price 5s. 6d.

NOEL (The Hon Roden)—A LITTLE CHILD'S MONUMENT. Small crown 8vo. cloth, 3s. 6d.

NORRIS (Rev. Alfred) — THE INNER AND OUTER LIFE POEMS. Fcp. 8vo. cloth, price 6s.

ODE OF LIFE (THE). By the Author of 'The Epic of Hades' &c. Third Edition. Crown 8vo. cloth, price 5s.

O'HAGAN (John) — THE SONG OF ROLAND. Translated into English Verse. Large post 8vo. parchment antique, price 10s. 6d.

PALACE AND PRISON AND FAIR GERALDINE : two Tragedies. By the Author of 'Ginevra' and the 'Duke of Guise.' Crown 8vo. cloth, price 6s.

PALMER (Charles Walter)—THE WEED: a Poem. Small crown 8vo. cloth, price 3s.

PAUL (C. Kegan)—GOETHE'S FAUST. A New Translation in Rhyme. Crown 8vo. price 6s.

PAYNE (John)—SONGS OF LIFE AND DEATH. Crown 8vo. cloth, price 5s.

PENNELL (H. Cholmondeley)—PEGASUS RESADDLED. By the Author of 'Puck on Pegasus,' &c. &c. With Ten Full-page Illustrations by George Du Maurier. Second Edition. Fcp. 4to. cloth elegant, 12s. 6d.

PFEIFFER (*Emily*)—GLAN ALARCH: His Silence and Song: a Poem. Second Edition. Crown 8vo. price 6*s*.

GERARD'S MONUMENT and other Poems. Second Edition. Crown 8vo. cloth, price 6*s*.

QUARTERMAN'S GRACE, and other Poems. Crown 8vo. cloth, price 5*s*.

POEMS. Second Edition. Crown 8vo. cloth, price 6*s*.

SONNETS AND SONGS. New Edition. 16mo. handsomely printed and bound in cloth, gilt edges, price 4*s*.

RHOADES (*James*).—THE GEORGICS OF VIRGIL. Translated into English Verse. Small crown 8vo. cloth, price 5*s*.

ROBINSON (*A. Mary F.*)—A HANDFUL OF HONEYSUCKLE. Fcp. 8vo. cloth, price 3*s*. 6*d*.

SAPPHO. A Dream, by the Author of 'Palace and Prison' &c. Crown 8vo. cloth, 3*s*. 6*d*.

SHELLEY (*Percy Bysshe*) — POEMS SELECTED FROM. Dedicated to Lady Shelley. With Preface by Richard Garnett. Printed on hand-made paper, with miniature frontispiece, elzevir 8vo. limp parchment antique, price 6*s*.; vellum, 7*s*. 6*d*.

SKINNER (*James*)—CŒLESTIA. The Manual of St. Augustine. The Latin Text side by side with an English Interpretation in Thirty-six Odes with Notes, *and* a plea *for the* study *of* Mystical Theology. Large crown 8vo. cloth, 6*s*.

SONGS OF TWO WORLDS. By the Author of 'The Epic of Hades.' Fifth Edition. Complete in one Volume, with Portrait. Fcp. 8vo. cloth, 7*s*. 6.

SONGS FOR MUSIC. By Four Friends. Containing Songs by Reginald A. Gatty, Stephen H. Gatty, Greville J. Chester, and Juliana Ewing. Square crown 8vo. price 5*s*.

STEDMAN (*Edmund Clarence*)—LYRICS AND IDYLLS, with other Poems. Crown 8vo. cloth, price 7*s*. 6*d*.

STEVENS (*William*)—THE TRUCE OF GOD, and other Poems. Small crown 8vo. cloth, price 3*s*. 6*d*.

SWEET SILVERY SAYINGS OF SHAKE-SPEARE. Crown 8vo. cloth gilt, 7*s*. 6*d*.

TAYLOR (*Sir H.*)—Works Complete in Five Volumes. Crown 8vo. cloth, price 30*s*.

TENNYSON (*Alfred*) — Works Complete:—

THE IMPERIAL LIBRARY EDITION. Complete in 7 vols. demy 8vo. price 10*s*. 6*d*. each; in Roxburgh binding, 12*s*. 6*d*.

AUTHOR'S EDITION. In Six Volumes. Post 8vo. cloth gilt ; or half-morocco. Roxburgh style.

CABINET EDITION. 12 Volumes. Each with Frontispiece. Fcp. 8vo. price 2*s*. 6*d*. each.

CABINET EDITION. 12 vols. Complete in handsome Ornamental Case.

POCKET VOLUME EDITION. 13 vols. in neat case, price 36*s*. Ditto, ditto. Extra cloth gilt, in case, price 42*s*.

THE ROYAL EDITION. In 1 vol. With 25 Illustrations and Portrait. Cloth extra, bevelled boards, gilt leaves, price 21*s*.

THE GUINEA EDITION. Complete in 12 vols. neatly bound and enclosed in box. Cloth, price 21*s*.; French morocco, price 31*s*. 6*d*.

SHILLING EDITION. In 12 vols. pocket size, 1*s*. each, sewed.

THE CROWN EDITION. Complete in 1 vol. strongly bound in cloth, price 6*s*. ; cloth, extra gilt leaves, price 7*s*. 6*d*. ; Roxburgh, half-morocco, price 8*s*. 6*d*.

*** Can also be had in a variety of other bindings.

IN MEMORIAM. Choicely printed on hand-made paper, with a miniature portrait in *eau-forte* by Le Rat, after a photograph by the late Mrs. Cameron. Bound in limp parchment, antique, price 6*s*. ; vellum, 7*s*. 6*d*.

THE PRINCESS: A Medley. Choicely printed on hand-made paper, with a miniature frontispiece by H. M. Paget and a tail-piece in outline by Gordon Browne. Limp parchment, antique, price 6*s*. ; vellum, price 7*s*.

TENNYSON (Alfred)—cont.

TENNYSON'S SONGS SET TO MUSIC by various Composers. Edited by W. J. Cusins. Dedicated, by express permission, to Her Majesty the Queen. Royal 4to. cloth extra, gilt leaves, price 21s.; or in half-morocco, price 25s.

Original Editions :—

BALLADS, and other Poems. Fcp. 8vo. cloth, price 5s.

POEMS. Small 8vo. price 6s.

MAUD, and other Poems. Small 8vo. price 3s. 6d.

THE PRINCESS. Small 8vo. price 3s. 6d.

IDYLLS OF THE KING. Small 8vo. price 5s.

IDYLLS OF THE KING. Complete. Small 8vo. price 6s.

THE HOLY GRAIL, and other Poems. Small 8vo. price 4s. 6d.

GARETH AND LYNETTE. Small 8vo. price 3s.

ENOCH ARDEN, &c. Small 8vo. price 3s. 6d.

IN MEMORIAM. Small 8vo. price 4s.

HAROLD : a Drama. New Edition. Crown 8vo. price 6s.

QUEEN MARY : a Drama. New Edition. Crown 8vo. price 6s.

THE LOVER'S TALE. Fcap. 8vo. cloth, 3s. 6d.

SELECTIONS FROM THE ABOVE WORKS. Super royal 16mo. price 3s. 6d. ; cloth gilt extra, price 4s.

SONGS FROM THE ABOVE WORKS. 16mo. cloth, price 2s. 6d.; cloth extra, 3s. 6d.

IDYLLS OF THE KING, and other Poems. Illustrated by Julia Margaret Cameron. 2 vols. folio, half-bound morocco, cloth sides, price £6. 6s. each.

TENNYSON FOR THE YOUNG AND FOR RECITATION. Specially arranged. Fcp. 8vo. 1s. 6d.

THE TENNYSON BIRTHDAY BOOK. Edited by Emily Shakespear. 32mo. cloth limp, 2s. ; cloth extra, 3s.

*** A superior Edition, printed in red and black, on antique paper, specially prepared. Small crown 8vo cloth, extra gilt leaves, price 5s.; and in various calf and morocco bindings.

THOMPSON (Alice C.)—PRELUDES : a Volume of Poems. Illustrated by Elizabeth Thompson (Painter of ' The Roll Call '). 8vo. price 7s. 6d.

THRING (Rev. Godfrey), B.As.—HYMNS AND SACRED LYRICS. Fcp. 8vo. price 3s. 6d.

TODHUNTER (Dr. J.) — LAURELLA, and other Poems. Crown 8vo. 6s. 6d.

ALCESTIS : a Dramatic Poem. Extra fcp. 8vo. cloth, 5s.

A STUDY OF SHELLEY. Crown 8vo. cloth, price 7s.

TOLINGSBY (Frere) — ELNORA : an Indian Mythological Poem. Fcp. 8vo. cloth, price 6s.

TRANSLATIONS FROM DANTE, PETRARCH, MICHAEL ANGELO, AND VITTORIA COLONNA. Fcp. 8vo. cloth, price 7s. 6d.

TURNER (Rev. C. Tennyson)—SONNETS, LYRICS, AND TRANSLATIONS. Crown 8vo. cloth, price 4s. 6d.

COLLECTED SONNETS, Old and New. With Preface by ALFRED TENNYSON; also some Marginal Notes by S. T. COLERIDGE, and a Critical Essay by JAMES SPEDDING. Fcp. 8vo cloth, price 7s. 6d.

WALTERS (Sophia Lydia)—THE BROOK : a Poem. Small crown 8vo. cloth, price 3s. 6d.

A DREAMER'S SKETCH BOOK. With 21 Illustrations by Percival Skelton, R. P. Leitch, W. H. J. BOOT, and T. R. PRITCHETT. Engraved by J. D. Cooper. Fcp. 4to. cloth, price 12s. 6d.

WATERFIELD (W.) — HYMNS FOR HOLY DAYS AND SEASONS. 32mo. cloth, price 1s. 6d.

WATSON (William)—THE PRINCE'S QUEST, and other Poems. Crown 8vo. cloth, price 5s.

WAY (A.) M.A.—THE ODES OF HORACE LITERALLY TRANSLATED IN METRE. Fcp. 8vo. price 2s.

WEBSTER (Augusta) — DISGUISES : a Drama. Small crown 8vo. cloth, price 5s.

WET DAYS. By a Farmer. Small crown 8vo. cloth, price 6s.

WILLOUGHBY (*The Hon. Mrs.*)—ON THE NORTH WIND—THISTLEDOWN : a Volume of Poems. Elegantly bound, small crown 8vo. price 7s. 6d.

WOODS (*James Chapman*)—A CHILD OF THE PEOPLE, and other Poems. Small crown 8vo. cloth, price 5s.

YOUNG (*Wm.*)—GOTTLOB, ETCETERA. Small crown 8vo. cloth, price 3s. 6d.

WORKS OF FICTION IN ONE VOLUME.

BANKS (*Mrs. G. L.*)—GOD'S PROVIDENCE HOUSE. New Edition. Crown 8vo. cloth, price 3s. 6d.

BETHAM-EDWARDS (*Miss M.*) KITTY. With a Frontispiece. Crown 8vo. price 6s.

BLUE ROSES; or, Helen Malinofska's Marriage. By the Author of ' Véra.' New and Cheaper Edition. With Frontispiece. Crown 8vo. cloth, price 6s.

FRISWELL (*J. Hain*)—ONE OF TWO ; or, The Left-Handed Bride. Crown 8vo. cloth, price 3s. 6d.

GARRETT (*E.*)—BY STILL WATERS : a Story for Quiet Hours. With Seven Illustrations. Crown 8vo. price 6s.

HARDY (*Thomas*)—A PAIR OF BLUE EYES. Author of ' Far from the Madding Crowd.' New Edition. Crown 8vo. price 6s.

THE RETURN OF THE NATIVE. New Edition. With Frontispiece. Crown 8vo. cloth, price 6s.

HOOPER (*Mrs. G.*)—THE HOUSE OF RABY. Crown 8vo. cloth, price 3s. 6d.

INGELOW (*Jean*)—OFF THE SKELLIGS: a Novel. With Frontispiece. Second Edition. Crown 8vo. cloth, price 6s.

MACDONALD (*G.*)—MALCOLM. With Portrait of the Author engraved on Steel. Fourth Edition. Crown 8vo. price 6s.

THE MARQUIS OF LOSSIE. Second Edition. With Frontispiece. Crown 8vo. cloth, price 6s.

ST. GEORGE AND ST. MICHAEL. Second Edition. With Frontispiece. Crown 8vo. cloth, 6s.

MASTERMAN (*J.*)—HALF-A-DOZEN DAUGHTERS. Crown 8vo. cloth, price 3s. 6d.

MEREDITH (*George*) — ORDEAL OF RICHARD FEVEREL. New Edition. Crown 8vo. cloth, price 6s.

MEREDITH (*George*)—cont.

THE EGOIST : A Comedy in Narrative. New and Cheaper Edition, with Frontispiece. Crown 8vo. cloth, price 6s.

PALGRAVE (*W. Gifford*)—HERMANN AGHA : an Eastern Narrative. Third Edition. Crown 8vo. cloth, price 6s.

PANDURANG HARI ; or, Memoirs of a Hindoo. With an Introductory Preface by Sir H. Bartle E. Frere, G.C.S.I., C.B. Crown 8vo. price 6s.

PAUL (*Margaret Agnes*)—GENTLE AND SIMPLE : A Story. New and Cheaper Edition, with Frontispiece. Crown 8vo. price 6s.

SAUNDERS (*John*) — ISRAEL MORT, OVERMAN : a Story of the Mine. Crown 8vo. price 6s.

ABEL DRAKE'S WIFE. Crown 8vo. cloth, price 3s. 6d.

HIRELL. Crown 8vo. cloth, price 3s. 6d.

SHAW (*Flora L.*)—CASTLE BLAIR ; a Story of Youthful Lives. New and Cheaper Edition, with Frontispiece. Crown 8vo. price 6s.

STRETTON (*Hesba*) — THROUGH A NEEDLE'S EYE : a Story. New and Cheaper Edition, with Frontispiece. Crown 8vo. cloth, price 6s.

TAYLOR (*Col. Meadows*) C.S.I., M.R.I.A. SEETA : a Novel. New and Cheaper Edition. With Frontispiece. Crown 8vo cloth, price 6s.

TIPPOO SULTAUN : a Tale of the Mysore War. New Edition, with Frontispiece. Crown 8vo. cloth, price 6s.

RALPH DARNELL. New and Cheaper Edition. With Frontispiece. Crown 8vo. cloth, price 6s.

A NOBLE QUEEN. New and Cheaper Edition. With Frontispiece. Crown 8vo. cloth, price 6s.

TAYLOR (Col. Meadows)—cont.

THE CONFESSIONS OF A THUG. Crown 8vo. price 6s.

TARA: a Mahratta Tale. Crown 8vo. price 6s.

THOMAS (Moy)—A FIGHT FOR LIFE. Crown 8vo. cloth, price 3s. 6d.

WITHIN SOUND OF THE SEA. New and Cheaper Edition, with Frontispiece. Crown 8vo. cloth, price 6s.

BOOKS FOR THE YOUNG.

AUNT MARY'S BRAN PIE. By the Author of 'St. Olave's.' Illustrated. Price 3s. 6d.

BARLEE (Ellen)—LOCKED OUT: a Tale of the Strike. With a Frontispiece. Royal 16mo. price 1s. 6d.

BONWICK (J.) F.R.G.S.—THE TASMANIAN LILY. With Frontispiece. Crown 8vo. price 5s.

MIKE HOWE, the Bushranger of Van Diemen's Land. New and Cheaper Edition. With Frontispiece. Crown 8vo. price 3s. 6d.

BRAVE MEN'S FOOTSTEPS. By the Editor of 'Men who have Risen.' A Book of Example and Anecdote for Young People. With Four Illustrations by C. Doyle. Sixth Edition. Crown 8vo. price 3s. 6d.

CHILDREN'S TOYS, and some Elementary Lessons in General Knowledge which they teach. Illustrated. Crown 8vo. cloth, price 5s.

COLERIDGE (Sara)—PRETTY LESSONS IN VERSE FOR GOOD CHILDREN, with some Lessons in Latin, in Easy Rhyme. A New Edition. Illustrated. Fcp. 8vo. cloth, price 3s. 6d.

D'ANVERS (N. R.)—LITTLE MINNIE'S TROUBLES : an Every-day Chronicle. With 4 Illustrations by W. H. Hughes. Fcp. cloth, price 3s. 6d.

PARTED : a Tale of Clouds and Sunshine. With 4 Illustrations. Extra fcp. 8vo. cloth, price 3s. 6d.

PIXIE'S ADVENTURES ; or, the Tale of a Terrier. With 21 Illustrations. 16mo. cloth, price 4s. 6d.

NANNY'S ADVENTURES : or, the Tale of a Goat. With 12 Illustrations. 16mo. loth, price 4s. 6d.

DAVIES (G. Christopher) — RAMBLES AND ADVENTURES OF OUR SCHOOL FIELD CLUB. With Four Illustrations. Crown 8vo. price 5s.

DRUMMOND (Miss)—TRIPP'S BUILDINGS. A Study from Life, with Frontispiece. Small crown 8vo. price 3s. 6d.

EDMONDS (Herbert) — WELL SPENT LIVES : a Series of Modern Biographies. Crown 8vo. price 5s.

EVANS (Mark)—THE STORY OF OUR FATHER'S LOVE, told to Children ; Fourth and Cheaper Edition of Theology for Children. With Four Illustrations. Fcap. 8vo. price 1s. 6d.

FARQUHARSON (M.)

I. ELSIE DINSMORE. Crown 8vo. price 3s. 6d.

II. ELSIE'S GIRLHOOD. Crown 8vo. price 3s. 6d.

III. ELSIE'S HOLIDAYS AT ROSELANDS. Crown 8vo. price 3s. 6d.

HERFORD (Brooke)—THE STORY OF RELIGION IN ENGLAND : a Book for Young Folk. Cr. 8vo. cloth, price 5s.

INGELOW (Jean) — THE LITTLE WONDER-HORN. With Fifteen Illustrations. Small 8vo. price 2s. 6d.

JOHNSON (Virginia W.)—THE CATSKILL FAIRIES. Illustrated by ALFRED FREDERICKS. Cloth, price 5s.

KER (David) — THE BOY SLAVE IN BOKHARA : a Tale of Central Asia. With Illustrations. New and Cheaper Edition. Crown 8vo. price 3s. 6d.

THE WILD HORSEMAN OF THE PAMPAS. Illustrated. New and Cheaper Edition. Crown 8vo. price 3s. 6d.

LAMONT (Martha MacDonald)—THE GLADIATOR : a Life under the Roman Empire in the beginning of the Third Century. With 4 Illustrations by H. M. Paget. Extra fcp. 8vo. cloth, price 3s. 6d.

LEANDER (*Richard*) — FANTASTIC STORIES. Translated from the German by Paulina B. Granville. With Eight Full-page Illustrations by M. E. Fraser-Tytler. Crown 8vo. price 5*s.*

LEE (*Holme*)—HER TITLE OF HONOUR. A Book for Girls. New Edition. With a Frontispiece. Crown 8vo. price 5*s.*

LEWIS (*Mary A.*)—A RAT WITH THREE TALES. New and Cheaper Edition. With Four Illustrations by Catherine F. Frere. Price 3*s.* 6*d.*

MC CLINTOCK (*L.*)—SIR SPANGLE AND THE DINGY HEN. Illustrated. Square crown 8vo. price 2*s.* 6*d.*

MAC KENNA (*S. J.*)—PLUCKY FEL- LOWS. A Book for Boys. With Six Illustrations. Fourth Edition. Crown 8vo. price 3*s.* 6*d.*

AT SCHOOL WITH AN OLD DRAGOON. With Six Illustrations. Third Edition. Crown 8vo. price 5*s.*

MALDEN (*H. E.*)—PRINCES AND PRIN- CESSES : Two Fairy Tales. Illustrated Small crown 8vo. price 2*s.* 6*d.*

MASTER BOBBY. By the Author of 'Christina North.' With Six Illus- trations. Fcp. 8vo. cloth, price 3*s.* 6*d.*

NAAKE (*J. T.*) — SLAVONIC FAIRY TALES. From Russian, Servian, Polish, and Bohemian Sources. With Four Illustrations. Crown 8vo. price 5*s.*

PELLETAN (*E.*)—THE DESERT PASTOR. JEAN JAROUSSEAU. Translated from the French. By Colonel E. P. De L'Hoste. With a Frontispiece. New Edition. Fcap. 8vo. price 3*s.* 6*d.*

REANEY (*Mrs. G. S.*)—WAKING AND WORKING ; or, From Girlhood to Womanhood. New and Cheaper Edition. With a Frontispiece. Cr. 8vo. price 3*s.* 6*d.*

BLESSING AND BLESSED : a Sketch of Girl Life. New and Cheaper Edition. Crown 8vo. cloth, price 3*s.* 6*d.*

ROSE GURNEY'S DISCOVERY. A Book for Girls. Dedicated to their Mothers. Crown 8vo. cloth, price 3*s.* 6*d.*

ENGLISH GIRLS: Their Place and Power. With Preface by the Rev. R. W. Dale. Third Edition. Fcap. 8vo. cloth, price 2*s.* 6*d.*

REANEY (*Mrs. G. S.*)—cont.

JUST ANYONE, and other Stories. Three Illustrations. Royal 16mo. cloth, price 1*s.* 6*d.*

SUNBEAM WILLIE, and other Stories. Three Illustrations. Royal 16mo. price 1*s.* 6*d.*

SUNSHINE JENNY and other Stories. 3 Illustrations. Royal 16mo. cloth, price 1*s.* 6*d.*

ROSS (*Mrs. E.*), ('Nelsie Brook') — DADDY'S PET. A Sketch from Humble Life. With Six Illustrations. Royal 16mo. price 1*s.*

SADLER (*S. W.*) *R.N.*—THE AFRICAN CRUISER: a Midshipman's Adventures on the West Coast. With Three Illustrations. New and Cheaper Edi- tion. Crown 8vo. price 2*s.* 6*d.*

SEEKING HIS FORTUNE, and other Stories. With Four Illustrations. New and Cheaper Edition. Crown 8vo. 2*s.* 6*d.*

SEVEN AUTUMN LEAVES FROM FAIRY LAND. Illustrated with Nine Etchings. Square crown 8vo. price 3*s.* 6*d.*

STOCKTON (*Frank R.*)—A JOLLY FEL- LOWSHIP. With 20 Illustrations. Crown 8vo. cloth, price 5*s.*

STORR (*Francis*) *and TURNER* (*Hawes*). —CANTERBURY CHIMES ; or, Chaucer Tales retold to Children. With Six Illustrations from the Ellesmere MS. Fcap. 8vo. cloth, price 3*s.* 6*d.*

STRETTON (*Hesba*)—DAVID LLOYD'S LAST WILL. With Four Illustra- tions. Royal 16 mo. price 2*s.* 6*d.*

THE WONDERFUL LIFE. Thirteenth Thousand. Fcap. 8vo. cloth, price 2*s.* 6*d.*

SUNNYLAND STORIES. By the Author of 'Aunt Mary's Bran Pie.' Illustrated. Small 8vo. price 3*s.* 6*d.*

TALES FROM ARIOSTO RE-TOLD FOR CHILDREN. By a Lady. With 3 Illus- trations. Crown 8vo. cloth, price 4*s.* 6*d.*

WHITAKER (*Florence*)—CHRISTY'S IN- HERITANCE. A London Story. Illus- trated. Royal 16mo. price 1*s.* 6*d.*

ZIMMERN (*H.*)—STORIES IN PRECIOUS STONES. With Six Illustrations. Third Edition. Crown 8vo. price 5*s.*